The Many Faces of Populism

Studies in Critical Social Sciences Book Series

Haymarket Books is proud to be working with Brill Academic Publishers (www.brill.nl) to republish the *Studies in Critical Social Sciences* book series in paperback editions. This peer-reviewed book series offers insights into our current reality by exploring the content and consequences of power relationships under capitalism, and by considering the spaces of opposition and resistance to these changes that have been defining our new age. Our full catalog of *SCSS* volumes can be viewed at https://www.haymarketbooks.org/series_collections/4-studies-in-critical-social-sciences.

Series Editor
David Fasenfest (York University, Canada)

Editorial Board
Eduardo Bonilla-Silva (Duke University)
Chris Chase-Dunn (University of California–Riverside)
William Carroll (University of Victoria)
Raewyn Connell (University of Sydney)
Kimberlé W. Crenshaw (University of California–LA and Columbia University)
Raju Das (York University, Canada)
Heidi Gottfried (Wayne State University)
Alfredo Saad-Filho (Queen's University Belfast)
Chizuko Ueno (University of Tokyo)
Sylvia Walby (Royal Holloway, University of London)

The Many Faces of Populism

Perspectives from Critical Theory and Beyond

Edited by
Mlado Ivanovic
Dustin J. Byrd
Jeremiah Morelock

Haymarket Books
Chicago, IL

First published in 2024 by Brill Academic Publishers, The Netherlands
© 2024 Koninklijke Brill NV, Leiden, The Netherlands

Published in paperback in 2025 by
Haymarket Books
P.O. Box 180165
Chicago, IL 60618
773-583-7884
www.haymarketbooks.org

ISBN: 979-8-88890-568-5

Distributed to the trade in the US through Consortium Book Sales and Distribution (www.cbsd.com) and internationally through Ingram Publisher Services International (www.ingramcontent.com).

This book was published with the generous support of Lannan Foundation, Wallace Action Fund, and the Marguerite Casey Foundation.

Special discounts are available for bulk purchases by organizations and institutions. Please call 773-583-7884 or email info@haymarketbooks.org for more information.

Cover design by Jamie Kerry and Ragina Johnson.

Printed in the United States.

Library of Congress Cataloging-in-Publication data is available.

Dedicated to the victims of authoritarian populism

Contents

Notes on Contributors IX

Introduction 1
    Mlado Ivanovic, Dustin J. Byrd and Jeremiah Morelock

1   "In This Land, You Could Live, and Not Only Die": Understanding Populism in Hungary through Popular Music 11
    Emília Barna and Ágnes Patakfalvi-Czirják

2   The Plague of Bannonism 42
    Ronald Beiner

3   The Populist Persona: a Jungian Approach to the Populism of Donald Trump 61
    Dustin J. Byrd

4   Algorithmic Populism 85
    Samir Gandesha

5   "Kultur ist ein Palast der aus Hundescheisse gebaut ist": Right-Wing Populism, Social Media and the Failure of Eurocentric Humanism 115
    Mlado Ivanovic

6   Who Is Afraid of the People? The Entanglement of Democracy, Populism and Stupidity 139
    Yonathan Listik

7   Left-Wing Populism in Power in Argentina and Greece 169
    Grigoris Markou

8   A Dialectical Constellation of Authoritarian Populism in the United States and Brazil 192
    Jeremiah Morelock and Felipe Ziotti Narita

9   Authoritarianism in Brazil: Interpretations from Theodor W. Adorno 218
    Maria Cristina Dancham Simões and Carlos Antonio Giovinazzo Júnior

10 Reimagining Saudi Arabia: Authoritarian Populism, State Power and Nationalism   244
    Hassan Zaheer

Index   277

Notes on Contributors

Emília Barna
is Associate Professor at the Department of Sociology and Communication, Budapest University of Technology and Economics. She is a sociologist and popular music scholar, her main research areas include the music industries and digitisation, popular music and gender, cultural labour, and popular music and politics. She has co-edited the books *Made in Hungary: Studies in Popular Music* (Routledge, 2017), *Popular Music, Technology, and the Changing Media Ecosystem: From Cassettes to Stream* (Palgrave, 2020), and *Populáris kultúra és politika* (Popular Culture and Politics) (Typotex, 2024), and published articles in *First Monday*, *Popular Music & Society*, and *Popular Music*. She is a member of IASPM and the Working Group for Public Sociology "Helyzet."

Ronald Beiner
is Professor Emeritus of Political Science at the University of Toronto and a Fellow of the Royal Society of Canada. His books include *Political Judgment* (Routledge, 1983), *What's the Matter with Liberalism?* (University of California Press, 1992), *Philosophy in a Time of Lost Spirit* (University of Toronto Press, 1997), *Liberalism, Nationalism, Citizenship* (University of British Columbia Press, 2003), *Civil Religion: A Dialogue in the History of Political Philosophy* (Cambridge University Press, 2011), *Political Philosophy: What It Is and Why It Matters* (Cambridge University Press, 2014), and *Dangerous Minds: Nietzsche, Heidegger, and the Return of the Far Right* (University of Pennsylvania Press, 2018). He is also the editor of Hannah Arendt's *Lectures on Kant's Political Philosophy* (University of Chicago Press, 1982), which has been published in many foreign-language editions, and has edited or co-edited six other books, including *Theorizing Citizenship* (State University of New York Press, 1995) and *Theorizing Nationalism* (State University of New York Press, 1999). His current project is a study of the diversity of appropriations of the Moses story in the Hebrew Bible through the course of the Western theory canon.

Dustin J. Byrd
is a Professor of Philosophy and Religion at The University of Olivet (formerly Olivet College). He is a specialist in the Critical Theory of the Frankfurt School, Psychoanalytical Political Theory, as well as contemporary Islamic and Russian thought. He earned his Ph.D. in Social and Political Philosophy at Michigan State University (2017). He is the Founder and Editor-in-Chief of Ekpyrosis Press, founded in 2019. He is also the Founder and Co-Director of the Institute

for Critical Social Theory, an international consortium of scholars working the fields of philosophy, sociology, anthropology, psychoanalysis, etc. Byrd also serves as the Editor-in-Chief of the journal *Critical Perspectives* (formerly *Islamic Perspective*). His recent publications include *The Dark Charisma of Donald Trump: Political Psychology and the MAGA Movement* (Ekpyrosis Press, 2023), *Syed Hussein and Critical Social Theory: Decolonizing the Captive Mind*, co-edited with Seyed Javad Miri (Brill, 2023), and *The Frankfurt School and the Dialectics of Religion: Translating Critical Faith into Critical Theory* (Ekpyrosis Press, 2020). He has also co-edited books on Malcolm X, Ali Shariati, and Frantz Fanon. www.dustinjbyrd.org

Samir Gandesha

is Professor of Global Humanities and the Director of the Institute for the Humanities at Simon Fraser University in Vancouver, Canada. He is co-editor with Johan Hartle of *Spell of Capital: Reification and Spectacle* (Amsterdam University Press, 2017) and *Aesthetic Marx* (Bloomsbury, 2017) both of which have been translated into Italian, co-editor of *The "Aging" of Adorno's Aesthetic Theory: Fifty Years Later* (Mimesis International, 2021), with Johan Hartle and Stefano Marino as well as *Adorno and Popular Music: A Constellation of Perspectives* (Mimesis International, 2019) with Colin Campbell and Stefano Marino. He is also editor of *Spectres of Fascism: Historical, Theoretical and International Perspectives* (Pluto Press, 2020), which has also been translated into Spanish. He is co-editor of the *Journal of Adorno Studies*. Gandesha has delivered over 100 talks at universities across the globe.

Carlos Antônio Giovinazzo Júnior

is Professor at the Pontifícia Universidade Católica de São Paulo (PUC-SP), Brazil, in the area of Education. A graduate of History, he has a Ph.D. in Education from the same University. He carries out investigations on the following themes: education, adolescents and young people; school, political education and consciousness; school organization, teaching and pedagogical practice; education and communication. In April 2024, he published the article "Political Education, Violence, Resistance: The Formation of Conscience and the Fight against Authoritarianism and Aggressiveness" (*Revista Brasileira de Educação*). In 2023, he co-authored the article "The Economy of Barbarism, Origin of the Socio-Environmental Crisis, and Climate Change: The Role of Environmental Education in the Paradox between Economic Progress and the Production of Catastrophe" (*Revista Eletrônica do Mestrado em Educação Ambiental*). Also in 2019, he co-authored the article "Cultural Industry and Semi-Formation: Democracy and Education under attack in Ibero-American

Countries in the Light of Critical Theory" (*RIAEE Magazine – Revista Ibero-Americana de Estudos em Educação*). Other publications include: "Poetry to Exist and Resist: The Experience of Soirees in Basic Education in the city of São Paulo Possible Contributions to the Construction of the Students' Ethnic and Racial Identities" (*PragMATIZES – Revista Latino-Americana de Estudos em Cultura*, 2022); "Educação, formação do indivíduo e experiência escola," in the book *Fundamentos dos processos educativos e formação humana* (2020); "A identidade docente e o movimento escola sem partido" (co-authored in the book *Identidades profissionais de professores: construções em curso* (2019).

Mlado Ivanovic
is Associate Professor in the Department of Philosophy at Northern Michigan University. His research interests are situated within the intellectual tradition of the Frankfurt School and Poststructuralism, primarily the works of Theodor W. Adorno, Walter Benjamin, and Michel Foucault. His academic focus is currently on moral, political, and environmental challenges tied with the forceful displacement and migration of people, particularly by examining both the socio-historical and political contexts of human vulnerability and exclusion. Ivanovic was awarded his Ph.D. from the Department of Philosophy at Michigan State University. He has published on humanitarianism, refugees, social and global justice, and human right and the media. He is currently working on a manuscript dealing with the epistemic, moral, and political underpinnings of forceful displacement and humanitarian management of displaced peoples, and their inclusion in Western societies. In addition to his academic commitments, Ivanovic is also engaged with humanitarian non-profit and non-governmental communities in Serbia, Greece, and Turkey, and serves as an advisor for various student organizations in Michigan that deal with humanitarianism and social justice. He is one of the directors of the Michigan based NGO, Refugee Outreach Collective.

Yonathan Listik
is a lecturer at Leiden University, teaching courses on cultural analysis, decolonial theory and critical political theory. His current field of research is philosophy, more specifically, exploring contemporary political ontology in the continental tradition. He is also interested in the connections between Jewish philosophy, decolonial theory and aesthetics. His main interest is the possible articulations of ideas such barbarism and stupidity. He explores those questions in his latest article "Barbaric Jewishness: Resistance to anti-Semitism and Judeo-Christianity" in *Horizontes Decoloniales / Decolonial Horizons*.

Grigoris Markou
is a postdoctoral researcher in the Department of Balkan, Slavic and Oriental Studies at the University of Macedonia (Thessaloniki, Greece), where he explores conspiracism through discourse analysis. In recent years, he has been working as a philologist in secondary education. He holds a Ph.D. in Political Sciences from the Aristotle University of Thessaloniki. His Ph.D. thesis focuses on left-wing populism in power in Europe and Latin America and specifically on SYRIZA (Greece) and Kirchnerism (Argentina). He completed a postdoctoral research in the same school about populism, anti-populism and minorities in Greece (2015–2023). He has received a BA in History and Ethnology from the Democritus University of Thrace and an MA in Political Analysis from the Aristotle University of Thessaloniki. He was an external associate in the research program "DEPRESPOP" at the University of Crete (2022–24), where he examined the academic discourse on the Prespa Agreement. His research interests include: Argentinian politics, Greek politics, discourse analysis, populism, anti-populism, conspiracism and radical parties. He has published articles and chapters in international academic journals, collective volumes and global media platforms.

Jeremiah Morelock
is an instructor of Sociology at Woods College of Advancing Studies, Boston College, and a psychotherapist in private practice, He is editor of *Critical Theory and Authoritarian Populism* (UWP, 2018), *How to Critique Authoritarian Populism: Methodologies of the Frankfurt School* (Brill, 2021), and *Feminism and the Early Frankfurt School* (Brill, 2024). He is also author of *Pandemics, Authoritarian Populism, and Science Fiction: Medicine, Military, and Morality in American Film* (Routledge, 2021), and *The Society of the Selfie: Social Media and the Crisis of Liberal Democracy* (UWP, 2021).

Felipe Ziotti Narita
received a postdoctoral training in the social sciences at the University of São Paulo (USP) and Federal University of São Carlos (UFSCar) and all four of his degrees from the São Paulo State University (UNESP). He is currently a pro-rector of graduate studies and research at Baron of Mauá University and lecturer in public policy at UNESP. He was commended with the Medal of the Order of Books of the National Library of Brazil. He is the author of *The Society of the Selfie: Social Media and the Crisis of Liberal Democracy* (University of Westminster Press, 2021) and his recent articles appeared in *Critical Sociology* and the *Journal of Contemporary Central and Eastern Europe*.

Ágnes Patakfalvi-Czirják

is a sociologist-anthropologist. Until recently, she was a Postdoctoral Researcher in the European project "Popular Music and the Rise of Populism in Europe" (https://musicandpopulism.eu), and now she is an Assistant Professor at the Department of Sociology and Communication at the Budapest University of Technology and Economics. Her main research areas include the everyday nationalism in CEE, popular music and national and ethnic identity, and popular music and politics. Her book *A székely zászló a politikától a hétköznapokig* (The Szekler Flag from Politics to Everyday Life) was published in 2021 by Napvilág, and awarded the Karl Polányi prize in 2022. She has co-edited the volume *Populáris kultúra és politika* (Popular Culture and Politics) (Typotex, 2024).

Maria Cristina Dancham Simões

is a psychologist with a master's degree and Doctorate in Education, both received at Pontifícia Universidade Católica de São Paulo (PUC-SP), Brazil. Recently, Simões assumed a post-graduation Professor position at the Programa de Pós-Graduação em Educação: História, Política, Sociedade in PUC-SP. She teaches Research Methodology in Psychology, Educational Psychology and School Psychology, from a Latin American critical perspective, at PUC-SP. She also supervises School Psychology trainees at Universidade Paulista (UNIP), Campus Marquês, São Paulo, Brazil. Member of ABRAPSO (Associação Brasileira de Psicologia Social), one of the biggest scientific associations in Brazilian Psychology, and ABRAPEE (Associação Brasileira de Psicologia Escolar e Educacional), she actively participates in both, in direction and coordination positions. Simões studies education, Brazilian education, teacher's training and topics on Critical Theory of Society. Her latest publications include articles in psychology and education journals; book chapters on Critical Social Psychology and Critical Theory of Society; books organizer over the last seven years, including *Aportes para uma teoria crítica da sociedade I: escritos sobre mundo administrado*, the first of a collection on Critical Theory in Brazilian Portuguese.

Hassan Zaheer

is a non-resident research associate at the Centre for Strategic and Contemporary Research (CSCR), Islamabad, where he researches nationalism, autocratic regimes, authoritarian politics, and security and international affairs. He is a Ph.D. candidate in Sociology at the University of Karachi where his research is centered on authoritarian legalism and Dual State in Pakistan, and specializes in Sociology of Law, Political Sociology, and Sociology of the

State. He regularly publishes commentary on power elite, state power, nationalist politics, and international and social affairs, and has published research on Hindu nationalism, Pakistani statecraft, military urbanism, populism, and authoritarian legalism. He also works as a teaching assistant at the Department of Sociology, University of Karachi.

Introduction

Mlado Ivanovic, Dustin J. Byrd and Jeremiah Morelock

Today, more than ever, it is easy to understand how *populism* has become such a contested concept in contemporary politics. Despite its relatively short history (i.e., the term dates to the late 19th century and the arrival of the populist *People's Party* in the United States), the term follows a rather volatile trajectory in terms of its historical development and presence as a political practice. When we look at its political and moral impact, one can see that despite its oftenstrict national commitments and narratives, populism is rather a global political phenomenon. As embodiment of anti-establishment narratives, polarizing attitudes, and emancipatory appeal, we can follow its occurrence from Central and Eastern Europe (i.e., in the form of nationalist strong figures such as Victor Orbán, Vladimir Putin, or the Law and Justice party in Poland), Latin America (i.e., the left-wing economic populists like Hugo Chávez and Nicolás Maduro), the USA and UK (i.e., in the form of white supremacist Donald Trump and nationalism of Brexit supporters), the Middle East (i.e., religious conservativism and nationalism spearheaded with the figure of Recep Tayyip Erdoğan in Turkey), all the way to China and India (i.e., the increasing authoritarianism of Xi Jinping and the Hindu nationalism of Narendra Modi).

The problem is that the term "populism" has become overly broad in its conceptualization, and that undifferentiated character and its proliferation in media leaves us with conflicting meanings, accompanied by a rather strong sense of crisis on which this phenomenon ultimately thrives. Today, a populist may be an individual who is either on the right or the left side of the political spectrum, nationalist and/or nativist, xenophobe, Fascist, conservative, liberal, a person with anti-globalization sentiments or a justified revolt in the face of inequalities. Although the versatile nature of populism makes it a relevant designator for the parties and leaders across the political spectrum, most of the time the general public and media see it as an inherently far-right phenomenon, which can be applied only to parties and leaders who fit the typical nationalist-xenophobic mold. For the most part, this is a consequence of the electoral success that far right populist establishments have gained in recent years (i.e., Donald Trump in the USA, Marine Le Pen in France, Alternativ für Deutschland (AfD) in Germany, Viktor Orbán's ruling Fidesz in Hungary, etc.). Relatively few populist parties on the left can claim the same kind of momentum or media attention (e.g., Podemos in Spain and Syriza in Greece). Of course, geographically and ideologically, right-wing populism in Europe and the United States is not a uniform development with clearly defined characteristics; it takes different forms depending on specific factors such as historical tradition, institutions, overall general appeal, the nature of social crisis, and, of course, culture.

In this edited volume, which is an attempt to help fill a gap in the existing literature on Critical Theory and populism, we focus on the multiple dimensions of *historical and contemporary contexts* for today's rising populist movements (e.g., political, moral, economic, ecological, cultural, identity, etc.), and their often – but not necessarily – hostile relations towards cosmopolitanism, globalization, environmentalism, and general notions of inclusion, and justice. By engaging with the multifaceted dimensions of populism – political, moral, economic, ecological, cultural, and identity-related – our work seeks to unpack the complex tapestry of factors that fuel the rise of populist ideologies and movements across the globe. This exploration is especially relevant today, as populism frequently presents itself as opposing global geostrategic phenomena, while simultaneously seeming to embrace ideas of justice and equity. Through a critical theory lens, this collection of essays endeavors to dissect the nuanced relationships between populist movements and these global forces, challenging and expanding the existing discourse.

The thematic focus of the volume invites a deep dive into the ideological underpinnings and strategies of contemporary populism, examining how these movements articulate grievances and aspirations within the political and social landscape. Critical theory, with its emphasis on power dynamics, social structures, and cultural narratives, provides a robust framework for analyzing how populist discourses construct notions of "the people" versus "the elite," and how they mobilize support through appeals to national sovereignty, economic justice, or cultural identity. This theoretical approach allows for a rich analysis of populism's impact on democracy, its interplay with technology and media, and its responses to global crises, such as climate change or pandemics, which transcend national boundaries. Furthermore, by situating populist movements within broader debates on globalization and cosmopolitan ethics, this volume aims to illuminate the tensions and contradictions at the heart of these ideologies. It explores how populist movements navigate the challenges of a globalized world, including economic inequality, migration, and environmental degradation, and how they position themselves in relation to universal values and human rights.

1   Historical Context of Populism

Tracing the historical roots of populism reveals its deeply ingrained presence in the fabric of political movements and discourses, stretching beyond its late 19th-century origins in the United States. The term "populism" was first used to encapsulate the ethos of the People's Party, which emerged as a formidable force advocating for the interests of farmers and laborers against the burgeoning industrial elites. This early manifestation of populism was characterized by a strong advocacy for agrarian rights, economic reform, and a direct challenge to the prevailing economic disparities and political oligarchies of the time. The People's Party, with its radical economic and political programs, such as the free coinage of silver and the establishment of a national public banking system, sought to restructure the economic foundations of the U.S. in favor of the working masses. This initial surge of populism was a response to the dramatic social and economic transformations of the era, underlining a recurrent theme in populist movements: the articulation of a collective struggle against perceived elites or establishments on behalf of the "common people."

As the 20th century progressed, the term "populism" evolved and expanded, capturing a diverse array of movements and ideologies across the globe, each adapting the populist ethos to their unique socio-political contexts. In Latin America, populism took on a distinctly different flavor, characterized by charismatic leaders like Juan Perón in Argentina, who mobilized the urban working class and the poor through policies aimed at social welfare and economic nationalism. These movements, while diverse in their policies and ideologies, shared the populist hallmark of forging a direct connection between a charismatic leader and the masses, bypassing traditional political institutions and party systems. This era underscored another pivotal aspect of populism: its chameleon-like ability to adapt and thrive within a variety of political systems and cultural settings, from democratic to authoritarian, underscored by its appeal to the masses over the elites or established order.

In the contemporary era, the resurgence of populism can be attributed to the growing disenchantment with globalization, economic inequalities, and a perceived erosion of national sovereignty. This modern wave of populism is marked by a sophisticated use of digital media to communicate, mobilize, and galvanize support, illustrating a significant shift in how populist messages are disseminated and how support is rallied. Moreover, today's populism is not confined to the economic and political disparities it once primarily contested but has expanded to include cultural and identity politics, reflecting deep societal divisions. The global proliferation of populist movements, from the Brexit referendum in the United Kingdom to the election of populist leaders in Brazil, Hungary, Serbia, and the Philippines, highlights a common thread: a potent response to feelings of marginalization and loss of control in the face of rapid economic, social, and technological change. This evolution of populism, from its agrarian-focused origins to its current manifestations, underscores its enduring relevance and adaptability as a political strategy that speaks to the foundational concerns of dignity, fairness, and autonomy.

By highlighting these historical trajectories, we are in a position to illuminate the resilience and malleability of this concept and phenomena as a moral, political, and social force. By examining its evolution, we can understand the enduring appeal of populism to various constituencies over time and its capacity to reshape political landscapes. The historical context of populism, with its rich tapestry of movements and ideologies, offers invaluable insights into the current populist wave, providing a nuanced lens through which to analyze its causes, its appeal, and its potential consequences for democratic governance and social cohesion.

2   Theoretical Frameworks

The evolution of populism from its historical roots to its contemporary manifestations presents a unique challenge for scholarly analysis, one that critical social theory in its broadest sense is particularly well-equipped to address. As populism has adapted and transformed across different periods and geographies, it has also intersected with various social, cultural, and economic issues that lie at the heart of critical theory. This approach, with its emphasis on critiquing and changing all spheres of society, provides a comprehensive toolkit for understanding the multifaceted nature of populism. By applying critical theory perspectives, scholars can explore the deeper implications of populism beyond its surface-level political strategies and rhetoric, revealing its impacts on societal structures, cultural norms, and economic systems that affect lives of people. Through a critical theory lens, populism can be seen not just as a political movement or ideology, but as a symptom of deeper societal fractures and contradictions. For instance, the rise of populist movements can be interpreted as a response to the disenchantment with neoliberal economic policies, growing inequalities, and the perceived erosion of national cultures and identities in the face of globalization.

Furthermore, critical theory offers valuable insights into the cultural and ideological mechanisms that enable populist leaders to resonate with their constituencies. Concepts like cultural hegemony, ideology, etc., allow for an examination of how populist movements construct narratives that appeal to common sense understandings and deeply held beliefs within specific cultural contexts. This perspective helps to unpack the ways in which populism capitalizes on cultural identities and grievances, framing itself as the true defender of national traditions and values against external threats or corrupt elites. Additionally, focus of social criticisms on discourse and communication provides a framework for analyzing the role of media and digital platforms in the spread and consolidation of populist sentiments. The critical analysis of media practices and the public sphere, sheds light on how populist messages are crafted and disseminated, influencing public opinion and shaping political discourse. This aspect is particularly relevant in the digital age, where social media and new communication technologies have become battlegrounds for political narratives, amplifying populist voices and facilitating the formation of echo chambers that further exploit and manipulate public opinions and sentiments.

Moreover, critical theory advocates for a comprehensive examination of the economic aspects of populism, challenging the capitalist frameworks that deepen the inequalities and dislocations that populist leaders often exploit. This approach delves into the economic foundations of populism, scrutinizing the interplay between economic policy, labor markets, and populist rhetoric. It illuminates how economic grievances and a sense of insecurity are potent drivers behind the surge of populist movements that further bleed into other aspects of social fabric such as solidarity, inclusion, etc. Embedding such critical perspectives within a broader narrative of social critique deepens our grasp of the far-reaching consequences of populism. This methodology prompts us to interrogate the extensive implications populism carries for democracy, societal unity, cultural identity, and even the emergence of violence. By examining the ways in which populism garners support through narratives of exclusion and community, critical theory peels back layers of populist discourse, revealing its complexities and the intricate ways it interacts with the fabric of contemporary society. Through this lens, the volume aims to enrich the dialogue around populism, moving beyond oversimplified analyses to underscore its multifaceted relations with key societal challenges.

3 Contemporary Issues and Populism: the Interplay between Global Perspectives and Local Realities

In our globalized present, the intersection of populism with contemporary global challenges reveals the adaptability and resilience of populist narratives in shaping public opinion and policy. The unprecedented challenges of our time, such as pandemics, climate change, violence, migration, and economic disparities, have not only tested the resilience of societies worldwide but have also offered fertile ground for populist leaders and movements to propagate their agendas. Populist narratives, which often emphasize national sovereignty, skepticism towards multiculturalism, and a dichotomy between the "ordinary" people and the "corrupt" elite, find resonance among populations feeling disenfranchised and anxious in the face of global crises. These narratives exploit existing fears and uncertainties, positioning populist movements as the defenders of the common people against the perceived failures of the international order and elite decision-making.

The COVID-19 pandemic serves as a poignant example of how populist leaders have capitalized on global crises to bolster their support, often by downplaying the severity of the situation, promoting nationalistic policies over international cooperation, or scapegoating minorities and foreign entities. This has not only influenced public health responses but also deepened societal divisions, demonstrating the profound impact of populist rhetoric on policy and social cohesion. Similarly, the climate crisis has been met with varying degrees of populist manipulation, ranging from outright denial of scientific consensus to framing environmental policies as elitist schemes that threaten jobs and national industries. These approaches underscore the populist strategy of exploiting complex global issues for political gain, often at the expense of nuanced debate and effective action. Moreover, the role of digital media in the proliferation of populist movements cannot be overstated. Social media platforms and digital communication tools have transformed the landscape of political discourse, enabling populist leaders and movements to reach wide audiences with unprecedented speed and efficiency. This digital dynamic plays a critical role in the adaptability of populism, allowing it to thrive even in the face of factual counterarguments and expert analysis. This capacity for populist narratives to be amplified in the digital age raises important questions about the responsibility of media platforms and the need for digital literacy among the public.

Understanding these dynamics is essential for comprehending the complex relationship between contemporary global challenges and the rise of populism. The ability of populist movements to adapt to and exploit these challenges highlights the need for robust public discourse, informed policymaking, and international cooperation. It also calls for critical engagement with the ways in which communication technologies shape our understanding of global crises and the political narratives that emerge in response. As the world grapples with ongoing and future challenges, the intersection of populism with these issues will undoubtedly continue to influence the course of global politics, requiring vigilant analysis and proactive engagement from scholars, policymakers, and the public alike. The interplay between global perspectives and local realities forms a complex backdrop against which contemporary populist movements operate. This dichotomy, characterized by the nationalist rhetoric of populist leaders on one hand and the undeniable interconnectedness brought about by globalization on the other, presents a fascinating paradox. Populist movements, while often championing a return to national sovereignty and the protection of local customs and economies against the perceived threats of global integration, simultaneously utilize the tools and networks that globalization provides. These dynamics underscore a nuanced relationship between globalizing forces and populist strategies that seek to affirm local identities and sovereignty in a global context.

Economic globalization has also played a significant role in the rise of populism, with global economic policies and agreements sometimes leading to local economic dislocations and discontent. Populist leaders capitalize on these grievances, framing themselves as defenders of the local economy against the forces of global capitalism. They argue that international trade agreements and economic policies benefit a global elite at the expense of the working class, and pledge to restore jobs and industries that have been outsourced abroad. This rhetoric resonates with those who feel left behind by globalization, driving support for populist policies that promise economic protectionism and a focus on local job creation. The ability of populist movements to link global economic trends with local economic challenges is a key aspect of their appeal, reflecting a deep understanding of the anxieties provoked by economic globalization. Moreover, the comparative analysis of populist movements across different regions provides valuable insights into how global forces are interpreted and acted upon within various national contexts. For instance, while right-wing populists in Europe and North America often focus on immigration and cultural identity as their main issues, populists in Latin America may emphasize economic inequality and the legacy of colonialism. These differing focuses highlight the local interpretations of global phenomena, demonstrating how populist movements adapt their strategies to the specific historical, cultural, and economic contexts of their countries. Such comparative analysis enriches our understanding of populism as a global phenomenon that is nonetheless deeply rooted in local realities.

This exploration of global perspectives versus local realities in the context of populism underscores the complexity of the phenomenon. It reveals how populist movements navigate the tensions between the global and the local, leveraging global tools to promote localized agendas. Understanding this dynamic is crucial for understanding the multifaceted nature of populism and the varied forms it takes across different contexts. This nuanced approach allows for a deeper comprehension of the challenges and opportunities presented by the global-local nexus in contemporary populist politics.

4 Future Directions

As we look towards the future, the trajectory of populism is poised to intersect with a myriad of global challenges and transformations. The ongoing technological revolution, environmental crises, and shifting social paradigms are likely to shape not only the form and substance of populist movements but also the responses of democratic institutions and international relations. The adaptability of populism to the digital age, with its capacity to leverage social media and other digital platforms for unprecedented outreach and influence, suggests that future populist movements may become even more sophisticated in their use of technology. This evolution could lead to more polarized public spheres, where the rapid dissemination of information, misinformation, and disinformation further entrenches divides. In response, critical theory must adapt and expand its analytical tools to decipher the complex interplay between technology, media, and populism, exploring new strategies for fostering informed and constructive public discourse.

Environmental challenges, particularly climate change, present another arena where the dynamics of populism are likely to evolve. As the impacts of climate change become increasingly tangible and urgent, populist responses may range from denialism and scapegoating to embracing environmentalist rhetoric in a bid to capture the growing public concern over ecological issues. This variability poses a challenge for global cooperation on environmental policy, potentially leading to fragmented responses to a universally shared problem. Critical theory can contribute to this discourse by examining the narratives employed by populist movements regarding environmental issues, identifying opportunities for integrating ecological concerns with broader social and economic justice movements to counteract simplistic populist solutions. Social changes, including shifting demographics, migration patterns, and evolving norms around identity and inclusion, will also influence the future of populism. As societies become more diverse, the reaction of populist movements – and the policies they advocate – will significantly impact social cohesion and the fabric of democratic life. Populist movements may either exploit these changes to exacerbate divisions or, conversely, could find their traditional narratives challenged by increasingly pluralistic societies. Critical theory's focus on power dynamics, identity, and discourse offers valuable insights into navigating these changes, proposing ways to reinforce democratic values and social solidarity in the face of populist divisiveness.

Moreover, the future of international relations in the context of rising populism will likely hinge on how states navigate the tension between nationalist impulses and the need for global cooperation. Populist movements' skepticism towards multilateral institutions and preference for bilateral dealings could reshape international politics, making responses to global challenges more cumbersome. Here, critical theory can provide a framework for understanding and critiquing the impact of populist foreign policies on global governance structures, suggesting pathways for reinvigorating international cooperation in a way that addresses the legitimate concerns of populations vulnerable to globalization's negative effects. In contemplating these future directions, it becomes evident that the relationship between populism, democracy, and global order is entering a critical phase. As populism continues to evolve, so too must the frameworks we use to understand and respond to it. Critical theory, with its capacity for nuanced critique and engagement with the complexities of power, identity, and resistance, is well-suited to guide this exploration. By continuously adapting to address new forms of populism and the changing landscapes they inhabit, critical theory can help navigate the challenges ahead, fostering a more inclusive, just, and resilient democratic order.

In the end, following chapters embark on an ambitious journey to dissect and understand the multifaceted phenomenon of populism through the lens of social criticism in general, encouraging submissions that span a wide array of interconnected themes. From conceptualizing populism alongside and within the framework of nationalism, authoritarianism, democracy, and socialism, to engaging in empirical critical analysis that respects the particularity of populist manifestations while applying general theoretical frameworks, our contributors are tasked with a complex intellectual endeavor. This volume seeks to challenge and expand the boundaries of critical theory, integrating it with decolonial, humanitarian, feminist, and broad poststructuralist paradigms to offer a diverse and rich understanding what populism is today. Through examining the nuances between "progressive" and "reactionary" populism, conducting comparative analyses of populist movements, and exploring populism's intersections with political ideologies, social psychology, national history, affect, identity politics, and media, this collection aims to uncover the intricate relations between populism and contemporary societal issues such as globalization, democracy, nationalism, and humanitarianism. By delving into these themes, we hope not only to contribute to the scholarly discourse on populism but also to offer insights into its contradictory nature, geographical specificities, and the challenges it poses to global and local understandings of democracy, identity, and justice.

CHAPTER 1

"In This Land, You Could Live, and Not Only Die": Understanding Populism in Hungary through Popular Music

Emília Barna and Ágnes Patakfalvi-Czirják

1   Introduction

The themes of political mobilization and the manipulation and affective control of the masses have been a definitive concern in Critical Theory approaches to popular culture, in particular of Frankfurt School theorists such as Theodor Adorno and Max Horkheimer.[1] In their theorizations of the social-political significance of the masses, the images of a homogenous quantity of people deprived of culture and those of organized power as a collective actor have been present in equal measure. In this system of relations, popular culture appears as a tool for organizing or integrating the masses and is capable of controlling their attention. In the analysis of Adorno and Horkheimer, mass-produced, industrialized popular culture ultimately appears as a means of producing social dispositions, feeling and behavior on a mass level, as a kind of psychotechnology, leading to the "withering of imagination and spontaneity in the consumer culture today [through products that] positively [debar] the spectator from thinking."[2] Contemporary public commentary on populism, which warns of its dangers, typically operates with similar representations of the masses. In this approach, the masses are "defenseless" against populism, "unable to resist" populist leaders, and are susceptible to political manipulation and conspiracy theories. Such fears have generated the growing academic interest that accompanies "the populist moment" in the western world.[3] Connecting Critical Theory and the addressing of contemporary populism is

---

1 Our chapter is based on research conducted for the Volkswagen Stiftung project "Popular Music and the Rise of Populism in Europe."
2 Theodor W. Adorno and Max Horkheimer, "The Culture Industry: Enlightenment as Mass Deception," in *The Cultural Studies Reader. Second Edition*, ed. Simon During (London and New York: Routledge, 1947/1999), 31–41, 100.
3 Roger Brubaker, "Why Populism?" *Theory and Society* 46, no. 5 (2017): 357–385.

the question of how masses – the "people" of populism – are being constructed through political, market, and cultural means.

In our chapter, we address the relationship between one particular segment of popular culture, namely popular music, and populism in Hungary after 2010 during the so-called "System of National Cooperation."[4] This period, which was introduced in 2010 by the second Viktor Orbán (Fidesz-KDNP Party Alliance) government and has continued so far through two subsequent government cycles, has been described as a new semi-peripheral regime of capital accumulation[5] or authoritarian capitalism.[6] In our research design, we attempted to revive critical approaches to popular culture, and popular music in particular, including Adorno's work as well as later popular music theorists, drawing on and partly critiquing Adorno, in order to connect aesthetic and formal-structural musical analysis with the political and social context of music.[7]

We combined the method of so-called *musicological group analysis* with anthropological fieldwork to analyze the ways in which popular songs create affordances for the mainstreaming of political ideas and discourses.[8] Our selected songs have all achieved broad and mainstream success in Hungary. They are partly connected to the Fidesz governments, both through direct political links and discursively through concepts of national unity and the logic of polarization. In addition, we look at songs produced and primarily consumed within the framework of the liberal opposition to the post-2010 governments. We ask what kind of affordances are created by these two groups of songs, and how these affordances are linked to populism in relation to the hegemony-building of Fidesz. This enquiry enables us a systemic view of the process of hegemony-building that integrates the cultural and the political.

---

4   The Fidesz government's politics was named as such by the party themselves in a declaration in 2010 as symbolic and ideological gesture.
5   Márk Éber, Ágnes Gagyi, Tamás Gerőcs, and Csaba Jelinek, "2008–2018: Válság és hegemónia Magyarországon," *Fordulat* 26 (2019): 28–75.
6   Gábor Scheiring, *The Retreat of Liberal Democracy. Authoritarian Capitalism and the Accumulative State in Hungary.* Cham: Palgrave Macmillan, 2020.
7   Richard Middleton, *Studying Popular Music* (Philadelphia: Open University Press, 1990); Antoine Hennion, "Music Lovers. Taste as Performance," *Theory, Culture and Society* 18, no. 5 (2001): 1–22; Tia DeNora, *Music in Everyday Life* (Cambridge: Cambridge University Press, 2000); Tia DeNora, *After Adorno: Rethinking Music Sociology* (Cambridge: Cambridge University Press, 2003).
8   André Doehring and Kai Ginkel, "Popular Music and the Rise of Populism in Europe," GfpM Conference "One Nation Under a Groove," Mainz, 1–3 November 2019; DeNora, *Music in Everyday Life*.

2 Critical Theory, Popular Music Analysis and Populism

The critique of mass culture and mass society by the group of German critical intellectuals known as the Frankfurt School was influenced by their historical and generational experience of Nazi totalitarianism on the one hand and by the experience of the mass industrial production of culture in the US as the new hegemonic center of global capitalism on the other, which scholars such as Adorno and Horkheimer encountered as a result of their forced emigration from Germany. According to Adorno, mass democracies such as the US first and foremost create needs among the masses, only to address these needs through their own framework. Contemporary critics of populism similarly argue that such politics are not aimed at community building and emancipation, but rather at producing a cycle of creating, maintaining, and ostensibly managing crises, which populist actors mediatize and convert into political capital.[9] Such interpretations can be compared to Adorno's description of the "fetish character in music,"[10] drawing on Marx's[11] theory of commodity fetishism as a form of reification, whereby social relations are perceived as relations between objects, and the market produces needs that have to be fulfilled through consumption. Mass-produced music, according to Adorno, is reduced to mere exchange value, and is appreciated through the act of recognition based on the perception of familiarity: "Mass listening habits today gravitate about recognition ... The basic principle behind it is that one need only repeat something until it is recognized in order to make it accepted."[12] Familiarity is ensured through standardized, assembly-line cultural production. The reception of culture thus degrades into an element of consumption, and content is replaced by spectacle and ready-made schemata.

Our goal in this chapter is not simply to honor the determining figures of Critical Theory, nor to provide a summary of the interrelations between popular culture and authoritarian systems. Rather, we aim to continue the methodological traditions of the Frankfurt School, in particular Adorno's analysis of popular music and the culture industry. We also consider its broader legacy

---

9   Benjamin Moffitt and Simon Tormey, "Rethinking Populism: Politics, Mediatisation and Political Style," *Political Studies* 62, no. 2 (2014): 381–397; Paul Taggart, *Populism* (Birmingham: Open University Press, 2000).
10 Theodor W. Adorno, "On the fetish character in music and the regression of listening." *The Culture Industry: Selected Essays on Mass Culture*, ed. Jay M. Bernstein (London: Routledge, 1938/1991): 29–60.
11 Karl Marx, *Capital: Volume One* (Mineola, NY: Dover Publications, 1867/2019).
12 Theodor W. Adorno, "On Popular Music. III. Theory about the Listener," https://ia800507.us.archive.org/26/items/ZeitschriftFrSozialforschung9.Jg/ZeitschriftFrSozialforschung91941.pdf.

in British cultural studies, notably the work of Stuart Hall, as well as popular music analysis through the work of Richard Middleton, Antoine Hennion and Tia DeNora. In our research design, we have employed the method of *musicological group analysis* combined with anthropological field work in order to connect the analysis of musical aesthetics and form with the studying of its political and social context. Along with the song texts, we consider the contexts of the production, distribution, and performance of songs which, in our particular case, combine the capitalist logic of the music industries with an authoritarian political system's practices of control.

"The connecting reaction [to music]" argues Adorno, "consists partly in the revelation to the listener that his apparently isolated, individual experience of a particular song is a collective experience."[13] While Adorno thinks of listeners as masses, highlighting one particular – mainstream, western – segment and mode of production of popular music and not paying attention to other examples, Middleton critiques this idea through drawing attention to the role of social relations such as class, gender, or geographical position in structuring the production as well as consumption of music. In agreement with this critique, we prefer to think of the ways in which music functions to construct *collectivities*. We argue that song lyrics, genre aesthetics, and compositional features help to construct particular audiences and affective spaces of reception, and to create affordances for particular meanings within these affective spaces. We rely on DeNora's utilization of the concept of *affordance* to make sense of "music's interpretive flexibility," which, however, by no means refers to arbitrary signification entirely dependent on context or the individual listener. Rather, music's affordances are constituted from within the social circumstances of use, which enables music to function as a resource for worldbuilding.[14] Similarly, Hennion shows how listening to music entails "more than the actualization of a taste 'already there', for they are redefined during the action, with a result that is partly uncertain", hence music is able to "both engage and form subjectivities."[15] DeNora formulates her theory in dialogue with Adorno, who derives his theoretical observations on listening (the reception of music) from the musical form, which in its formulaic style, bears a

---

13 Adorno, "On Popular Music."
14 DeNora *Music in Everyday Life*, 43–44. "In commodities as well as in the conventions of natural and aesthetic languages, desire is inscribed as an externalised and reified 'affordance'; it is what conventional and commodified forms 'afford' the subject in use" – writes Witkin, reformulating Adorno's theory. Robert W. Witkin, *Adorno on Music* (Abingdon and New York: Routledge, 1998), 56.
15 Hennion, "Music Lovers. Taste as Performance," 1.

structural relationship to its industrialized, standardized mode of production under capitalism.[16] Nevertheless, while Adorno connects production, form, and reception,[17] DeNora's starting point is an ethnography-based sociological account of listening as a complex and nuanced social practice – "a focus on particular, spatially, and temporally located instances of music's use and uptake ... the actual mechanisms through which doing music is simultaneously doing other things – thinking and remembering, feeling, moving/being, and co-operating, coordinating, and sometimes colluding with others."[18] Although she offers an instructive and empirically rich model for the sociological study of listening, DeNora also loses the system critique characterizing Adorno's work. In our own analysis, we focus on the relationship between song aesthetics and reception and the political processes taking place in Hungary at the time of the study.

In order to both analyze the musical aesthetics and model the process of reception, and ultimately to understand the relation between musical structure and the afforded social meanings and subjectivities, we used the method of *musicological group analysis* (MGA), developed by André Doehring.[19] Musicological group analysis is a method for understanding the relationship between the sonic and (where relevant) lyrical elements of a piece and the meanings listeners ascribe to it through a collective interpretative process. It combines a double perspective of music analysis and a collective reflection on our own listening, the latter in line with DeNora's approach. We organized one group analysis session for each of the songs, involving music experts (a musicologist as well as a professional musician) and also participated ourselves, in effect modelling the processes described by DeNora and Hennion. The group sessions were transcribed, coded, and analyzed according to our research questions of what kind of affordances are created by the songs, and how these affordances are linked to populism in relation to the hegemony-building of Fidesz. Middleton highlights the lack of attention Adorno paid in his analysis of popular music to the crucial aspect of performance.[20] In our research, we completed the group analyses with fieldwork conducted at festivals, village-days, and other events featuring the performers of the songs. In addition, we also reflected on aesthetic elements of performance during the group analysis sessions – for instance, by looking at video recordings of live

---

16   DeNora, *After Adorno*.
17   Middleton, *Studying*, 35–60.
18   DeNora, *After Adorno*, 155.
19   Doehring and Ginkel, *Popular Music*.
20   Middleton, *Studying*, 56.

performances of the songs in question – dissecting such elements as voice, gestures, communication among band members and with the audience. We completed this with an analysis of media content related to the songs and the artists, which informed us about politicization as well as the particularities of production and distribution.

The timeliness of researching the relationship between popular culture and populism is indicated by the recent spreading of populist discourses, along with scholarly reflections on those discourses – even if the majority of these reflections lack the attention to popular culture production, form, or reception that was paid by scholars of the Frankfurt School, especially Adorno. The decline of trust in prevailing institutional structures,[21] antagonism towards expert knowledge, the polarizing effects of populist discourses on society,[22] the emphasis on justified confrontation of the enemy[23] or the extremities of public discourse have all been identified as phenomena that simultaneously create and maintain[24] social crises. Along with Bice Maiguashca, however, we believe that there is a necessity to remain wary of "the populist hype" and insist on "thicker, historically and sociologically inflected, inductive forms of theorizing."[25] We argue that it is not sufficient to only view the spreading of populism in light of election results. Similarly, the fact that populist actors communicate in a convincing way on social media and make effective use of online publicity does not offer a satisfactory explanation or understanding of the phenomenon of populism, either. Our questions therefore do not concern the strict field of politics in a party politics sense, but rather the broader field of social relations into which populism is embedded. This is not only because, outside of politics, populism is driven by the goal of achieving cultural hegemony,[26] but also because the establishing and maintaining of cultural hegemony can be understood through the social contexts – the collectivities – of cultural production and consumption; in other words, through the process of meaning making.

---

21 Brubaker, *Why Populism*.
22 Emilia Palonen, "Political Polarisation and Populism in Contemporary Hungary," *Parliamentary Affairs* 62, no. 2 (2009): 318–334.
23 Taggart, *Populism*.
24 Ruth Wodak, *The Politics of Fear: What Right-Wing Populist Discourses Mean* (Los Angeles: Sage, 2015).
25 Bice Maiguashca, "Resisting the 'populist hype': a feminist critique of a globalising concept," *Review of International Studies* 45, no. 5 (2019): 17.
26 Ernesto Laclau and Chantal Mouffe, *Hegemony and Socialist Strategy* (London: Verso, 1985); Benjamin Moffitt, *The Global Rise of Populism: Performance, Political Style, and Representation* (Redwood City, CA: Stanford University Press, 2016).

Looking at the political and cultural relations of the capitalist state, Gramsci[27] points out that culture forms an organic part of community-building and the assertion of power. In order for those in possession of power to acquire a hegemonic position, they need to be able to control ideas about social order, and to establish a representation of the social consensus that legitimizes their power.[28] The struggles for hegemony, which involve establishing social norms and making them consensual, maintain a constantly changing system of relations between those in possession of power and the subaltern classes. It is therefore clear that the struggle for hegemony does not only take place on the level of political messaging or conflict, but it also promises the possibility of establishing a dominant culture. With the establishment of hegemony, however, those in power make their own worldviews and cultural practices valid for the subordinated classes as well.

According to Stuart Hall, popular culture is a unique territory of this hegemony-building, since it serves as an important context for the creation of collective identities and attachments, and for the association of different ideological and emotional elements.[29] This is possible because access to popular culture is uncomplicated, and the infrastructure of its distribution is widespread. Moreover – unlike Adorno – Hall views popular culture as something that is typically not controlled directly by the dominant power.[30] According to him, there is not necessarily a manifest relationship between hegemony-building and popular culture. In other words, cultural production – except for direct propaganda – is not usually an arena of conscious political manipulation.[31] At the same time, we argue that it is able to set the scene for the mainstreaming of populist ideas and create affordances that operate independent of political will. Moreover, in the process of hegemony-building, popular culture becomes politicized and instrumentalized, thus its relationship with political power is made explicit.

An important characteristic of populist discourse is that it incorporates the desired consensus, the cultural elements imagined as mainstream, and the messages intended for a wide audience. For the articulation of each of these,

---

27 Antonio Gramsci, *Selections from the Prison Notebooks* (New York: International Publishers, 1971).
28 Ibid.
29 Stuart Hall and Paddy Whannel, *The Popular Arts* (Durham, NC: Duke University Press, 2018); Stuart Hall, "Notes on Deconstructing 'The Popular,'" *People's History and Socialist Theory*, ed. by Raphael Samuel (London: Kegan Paul-Routledge, 1981): 231–239.
30 Stuart Hall, *Representation: Cultural Representations and Signifying Practices* (London: Sage Publications and The Open University, 1997), 1–12.
31 Hall, *Notes*.

they employ forms of expression perceived as familiar or easy to understand by an imagined "average" consumer.[32] For a more precise definition of populism that complements definitions centering on the dichotomy of "everyday people" versus the "corrupt elite," Pierre Ostiguy has established a socio-cultural conceptual framework.[33] He highlights such elements as informal discourse, directness, body language or gestures characterizing populist leaders, which express and perform belonging to a community. Benjamin Moffitt reached a similar conclusion, interpreting the phenomenon of populism as a political style, as "the repertoires of embodied, symbolically mediated performance made to audiences that are used to create and navigate the fields of power that comprise the political, stretching from the domain of government through to everyday life."[34] We argue, however, that these approaches lack an acknowledgment of the cultural and social embeddedness of the dichotomizing and polarizing discourses generated by populism.

3   The Case of Post-2010 Hungary

The structural transformations that have taken place in Hungary over the last decade provide the framework for our analysis. In relation to the establishment of the Orbán regime in 2010, Gábor Scheiring identifies three main factions of the new power block ensured by the new accumulative state, namely the political class, the national bourgeoisie, and transnational capital, within which the most powerful player is the German automotive industry.[35] To understand the politics of this new regime, he describes two important processes, specifically *institutional authoritarianism* and *authoritarian populism*. The first is used by Scheiring to point to the occupation and refeudalization of social institutions, including reforming the election system, the depletion of parliamentarianism, the controlling of mass media, as well as a "colonization" of the prosecution system and the courts.[36] He emphasizes that institutional authoritarianism "serves to limit the rise of a competitive civic and political

---

32   Pierre Ostiguy, *The High and the Low in Politics: A Two-Dimensional Political Space for Comparative Analysis and Electoral Studies*. Working Paper. Kellogg Institute, 2019. https://kellogg.nd.edu/sites/default/files/old_files/documents/360_0.pdf; Péter Csigó, *The Neopopular Bubble. Speculating on "the People" in Late Modern Democracy*. Budapest: CEU Press, 2016.
33   Cas Mudde, "The Populist Zeitgeist," *Government and Opposition* 39, no. 4 (2004): 541–563.
34   Moffitt, *The Global Rise*, 38.
35   Scheiring, *The Retreat*. See also Éber et al., *2008–2018*.
36   Scheiring, *The Retreat*, 295.

opposition by recourse to a kind of institutional bricolage, which preserves the façade of democratic institutions but tilts the political playing field to the advantage of the ruling party."[37] He describes authoritarian populism, on the other hand, as a strategy through which the governing power is able to control oppositional forces by manufacturing consent. Similarly to the observations of Stuart Hall, who first used this concept to describe the way in which Margaret Thatcher and the Conservatives gained support of their neoliberal politics in the United Kingdom, Scheiring shows how Fidesz "disaggregate[s] the opposition by addressing real contradictions in a way as to represent them within a logic of discourse which pulls them systematically in line with policies and class strategies of the new illiberal hegemony"[38] While Mary Taylor rightfully warns us that it "certainly is worth asking if Hall's quite deliberately contradictory term is useful in understanding what we are seeing with Trump or Orbán,"[39] we nevertheless aim to follow in the steps of Hall's analysis together with his insistence on taking popular culture seriously in understanding how hegemony is established and maintained.

The process of hegemony-building has involved presenting the strengthening of "their own camp" as a national interest. Within this, the connection of Hungarian communities outside the nation's borders and the centering of the issue of migration represented the political engagement of Viktor Orbán as the only guarantee of national unity and social security.[40] In relation to the transformation that has taken place in the financing of culture, education, and the systems of academic knowledge production and media, several critics identified the loss of autonomy these spheres suffered, along with their complete politicization.[41] Furthermore, in the field of popular music, "the post-2010 period can be characterized by increasing state control and incorporation"

---

[37] Scheiring, ibid., 296.

[38] Stuart Hall, "The Great Moving Right Show," *Marxism Today* 23, no. 1 (1979): 14–20. Quoted in Scheiring, *The Retreat*, 296.

[39] Ágnes Gagyi, "Populism or People's Movements? Interview with Mary Taylor," *LeftEast*, April 11. 2018. https://lefteast.org/populism-or-peoples-movements-interview-with-mary-taylor.

[40] Scheiring, *The Retreat*; Gábor Egry, "Beyond Electioneering. Minority Hungarians and the Vision of National Unification," *Brave New Hungary. Mapping the "System of National Cooperation,"* ed. János Mátyás Kovács and Balázs Trencsényi B. (Lanham, MD: Lexington Books, 2019).

[41] János Mátyás Kovács and Balázs Trencsényi, "Conclusion: Hungary: Brave and New? Dissecting a Realistic Dystopia," *Brave New Hungary. Mapping the "System of National Cooperation,"* ed. János Mátyás Kovács and Balázs Trencsényi (Lanham, MD: Lexington Books, 2019), 379–432.

through cultural policy and funding.[42] In 2014, the government introduced an extensive state program for the support of popular music through a grants system, through which artists and other music industry actors could apply for relatively small amounts awarded for composition, recording, touring or music videos. In addition, the government have also selectively supported certain artists by awarding one-off grants – typically much larger amounts – outside of this program, and state companies (such as the gambling service Szerencsejáték Zrt. and the power company MVM) are actively involved in the sponsorship of artists, as well as music venues and events such as festivals. A further question is how, besides structural transformation and political power relations, Fidesz' hegemony-building has been manifest in everyday situations and the consumption of culture. For this reason, we now turn to the analysis of popular songs.

4   Nation-Building and the "Fifteen Million"

Since 2010, the subsequent Orbán governments have introduced a series of measures for the institutionalization and strengthening of connections between the Hungarian state and ethnic Hungarians outside of the borders.[43] The process, termed "the reunification of the nation" by government-controlled media, incorporates a number of programs and forms of support belonging to "national policy" that bind to Budapest Hungarian communities that remained in neighboring countries after the 1920 Peace Treaty of Trianon. The most important element of this process in political as well as symbolic terms was the securing of a simplified dual citizenship for ethnic Hungarians in 2010. The measure, which was later extended to include the right to vote in Hungary, resulted in Hungary gaining 1.1 million new citizens by 2020, who predominantly continued to live in their homelands (mostly Romania, Serbia, and Ukraine). The discourse on the recreation of national unity has been ever present in the last decade in Hungary,[44] and the extending of the nation has reinforced, on an affective, political, as well as cultural level, the new national

---

42   Emília Barna, Kristóf Nagy, and Márton Szarvas. "COVID-19 Crisis in Hungarian Cultural Production – Vulnerability and deepening authoritarian control," *LeftEast*, February 12, 2019. https://lefteast.org/covid-19-crisis-in-hungarian-cultural-production-vulnerability-authoritarian-control.

43   Egry, "Beyond Electioneering."

44   Szabolcs Pogonyi, *Extra-Territorial Ethnic Politics, Discourses and Identities in Hungary* (Cham: Palgrave Macmillan, 2017); Egry, "Beyond Electioneering."

ideology of Fidesz, the sense of national togetherness, and the self-termed "System of National Cooperation." In the following we look at two pop-rock songs that have achieved mainstream popularity, with both addressing the issue of ethnic Hungarians living outside the borders of Hungary – an issue that has been thematized as part of the nation-building of the current hegemonic power.

5 "Nélküled"

In the period in question, the song "Nélküled" (Without you) became arguably the best-known and most popular national song in Hungary – a kind of unofficial national anthem to many. "Nélküled" is a rock ballad, recorded in its original version by the band Ismerős Arcok in 2007 with just a vocal track and a piano.[45] Formed in 1999, the band – playing music at the intersection of rock and rhythm and blues – was at that time regarded as belonging to the national rock scene, which in turn formed part of a radical right subcultural network.[46] When narrating their own biography, they attribute their "national turn" to a tour in Romania in the early 2000s, when the encounter with the Transylvanian ethnic Hungarian community had an elemental effect on singer and lyricist Attila Nyerges. From then on, according to him, he considered it his duty to pay attention to the situation of Hungarians outside the borders, the injustices they suffered, and to become involved in symbolic practices of national solidarity.[47] As we detail below, Transylvania and its representations associated with ethnic Hungarians, not only in Romania but outside of Hungary's borders in general, appear as crucial motifs in the song. In her account of the Hungarian *táncház* (dance house) folk dance and music movement, Taylor demonstrates that Transylvania has long functioned as a mythical place – "a familiar feature in Hungarian national mythology,"[48] as a "pure" source of knowledge, inspiration, and authenticity in folk revivals. The mythicized encounter with Transylvania in the band's narrative draws on the same

---

45   Ismerős Arcok, "Nélküled." *Éberálom* [LP]. Grund Records, 2007.
46   Margit Feischmidt and Gergő Pulay, "'Rocking the Nation': The Popular Culture of Neo-Nationalism," *Nations and Nationalism* 23, no. 2 (2017): 309–326.
47   Ferenc Sengel, "Szembesültünk a hazugságokkal," *Origo.hu*, November 25, 2018. https://www.origo.hu/kultura/20181120-nyerges-attila-interju.html.
48   Mary N. Taylor, *Movement of the People. Hungarian Populism, Folk Dance, and Citizenship* (Bloomington, IN: Indiana University Press, 2021), 2.

associations.⁴⁹ These experiences at the same time brought the band closer to the radical right, and later to the memory politics of Fidesz. Musically, the encounter meant that the band began integrating folk songs and elements into their repertoire.

The band's evolving status and the trajectory of the song can be understood by both being viewed in the context of the shifting political landscape. The second half of the 2000s witnessed the strengthening of national radicalism, which was demonstrated by the success of Jobbik, a dynamic and youthful right-wing party.⁵⁰ The two-thirds majority victory of Fidesz in 2010 resulted in a new setup where the governing Fidesz-KDNP parties competed and won against national radicals for the authentic and exclusive representation of the national interest.⁵¹ This has also influenced popular culture. Upon its release in 2007, neither the album *Éberálom*, nor the song "Nélküled" created much of a stir outside of the radical right-wing network. The band's songs were not played on public service or mainstream commercial radio stations, nor did they have much opportunity to perform outside of subcultural events. This changed radically after 2010. The song and the band were both gradually mainstreamed and legitimized by the hegemonic power.⁵² In 2014, "Nélküled" was selected to become the anthem of a Hungarian football team in Slovakia (FC DAC 1904). The support for football – for instance, through the building of stadiums around the country – became an important tool of Fidesz' nation-building. As part of this, Hungarian media began airing matches of ethnic Hungarian teams, which led to a popularization of "Nélküled" as a football anthem within the borders of Hungary as well. This further enhanced the popularity of the song, and with 49 million views on YouTube⁵³ and the lyrics consistently holding the number one position on the Hungarian lyrics database *Zeneszöveg.hu* (indicating the number of people searching for the song to sing along to), it can be considered among the best-known contemporary popular songs in Hungary. Before the COVID-19 pandemic, the band extensively performed at festivals and village days, as well as their own concerts around the country, typically in front of

---

49 The association is undoubtedly connected to the history of the territory, including its separate administration from the other lands during Habsburg domination. See Taylor, *Movement*, 31.
50 Feischmidt and Pulay, "Rocking the Nation"; Scheiring, *The Retreat*.
51 Scheiring, *The Retreat*.
52 Emília Barna and Ágnes Patakfalvi-Czirják, "'We are of one blood': Hungarian popular music, nationalism and the trajectory of the song "Nélküled" through radicalization, folklorization and consecration," *Journal of Contemporary Central and Eastern Europe* (2022).
53 "Ismerős Arcok – Nélküled." *YouTube*. January 3, 2010. https://www.youtube.com/watch?v=KmUMvShEq-E.

mainstream audiences in addition to fans. The song has also become a regular piece in wedding band repertoires and is frequently sung at school ceremonies, while also having inspired a huge variety of cover versions and fan videos uploaded to YouTube and other social media. Moreover, the band has received substantial support in the form of state grants, as well as sponsorship from companies close to the establishment. They have received multiple awards and have been personally endorsed by the Prime Minister – which gestures can be interpreted as a process of legitimation of the band.

In the rock tradition, piano-accompanied songs are often love songs. This standard formula is mobilized here, but in this case love of the country and Hungarian people are at the center, with a strong emphasis on a sense of loss. The words, rich with poetic images conjuring landscapes and natural phenomena, along with the melodic and harmonic structure, evoke a romantic aesthetic, sensibility, and emotionality. The male singing voice is raw, giving the impression of an untrained singer, which partly corresponds to a rock aesthetic and authenticity[54] linked to the early blues-rock credentials of the band. In addition, it can also be heard as a performance of the singer being "of the people," which corresponds to the strategy of "flaunting the low," which Ostiguy identifies as "a core feature of populism."[55] A kind of elective affinity is thus mobilized between the affordances of the rock aesthetic – the evoking of rock authenticity – and the "flaunting the low" of populism. Correspondingly, the tone of the piano is not smooth – rather, the somewhat dirty sound evokes the atmosphere of a small bar with a slightly off-key piano and a self-taught pianist.

Regarding the lyrics, the first verse begins with an abstract sense of imminent danger and the feeling of one grabbing their last chance: "There are so many things I still have to say [tell you] / If I don't do it [now], there might not be a chance."[56] This immediately creates an atmosphere of crisis. This part is followed by images of closeness, familiarity, and a reference to friends who understand one another without needing to speak: "Like good old friends, we speak as one, we think as one." The second verse begins in a markedly different and more personal tone from the first, (with an "I" speaking) – it is a list of poetic images of nature expressing loss and devastation, one after another: "Like the

---

54 Allan Moore, "Authenticity as Authentication," *Popular Music* 21, no. 2 (2002): 209–223.
55 Pierre Ostiguy, *The High and the Low in Politics: A Two-Dimensional Political Space for Comparative Analysis and Electoral Studies.* Working Paper (Kellogg Institute, 2019), 75. https://kellogg.nd.edu/sites/default/files/old_files/documents/360_0.pdf.
56 We present Hungarian lyrics in our own translations. This also applies to direct quotations from the MGA sessions and from Hungarian-language sources.

lonely pine tree struck by lightning / Like a stream that has lost its water, like a stone that has been kicked aside / Like the tired wanderer, who silently asks to eat / Who can no longer hope for a home, a house, a homeland" – with the last of these lines first referencing the homeland and thus mobilizing a new set of meanings. The chorus speaks in second person singular: "Although you cannot yet grasp the real meaning / Until you have lived through difficult times." While the reference is unclear upon first hearing, we soon reach the two most prominent lines, which start from the highest pitched note and follow a descending melody: "Whatever may happen / While we live and until we die / We are of one blood." While there is little variation in terms of dynamic in the track, the piano is played with more emphasis in this section, highlighting the theme of ethnic Hungarians in the lyrics. The change to "we" here signifies a community, and there is a strong reference to being bound "by blood." The words also echo the line "we be of one blood, ye and I" from "Kaa's Hunting" in Kipling's *The Jungle Book*, as was confirmed in an interview by the singer Nyerges.[57] This second part of the chorus is highlighted not only by the highest point in the melody, but also through a stress on the vocal ("whatever may happen"). It is a melodic line that is easy to sing – which is demonstrated by the crowds in football stadiums. The following line ("while we live and until we die") rephrases the poem "Szózat" by Mihály Vörösmarty, which was written in the context of 19th-century nation-building and is now an official second national anthem in Hungary. This phrase is often used in national-themed songs to represent national identity and a lifelong commitment to the homeland. The sparse instrumentation makes the words discernible and easy to remember – not only "evoking" the familiar standard rock ballad idiom, but also Romantic natural imagery that calls forth the myth of Transylvania, and the everyday national imagery conjured up by the words of "Szózat," or as Adorno put it, "the psychic processes of recognition, identification, and ownership."[58]

The song has thus provided a soundtrack to the topic of simplified dual citizenship through the expression and performance of the pain felt over the lost national territories, articulated from a populist, anti-elite position. The title "Without you" addresses Hungarians within Hungary's borders from the perspectives of those remaining outside, and clearly refers to the loss suffered after the Second World War. In addition to evoking national unity through the Romantic style of natural images, the lyrics are also in harmony with the

---

57 Sengel, "Szembesültünk." Nevertheless, operating with ambiguous references can be considered a frequent strategy by radical right-wing artists in order to be able to stave off accusations of racism.
58 Adorno, "On Popular Music."

political gestures of Fidesz' nation-building agenda. The line "like the five million Magyars unheard by the world" – which at live concerts is invariably accompanied by the ritual of the front singer and members of the audience raising their open palms to indicate the "five" million – refers to the lack of international solidarity with the Hungarian nation, and emphasizes the polarization of "us, oppressed Hungarians" and the neutral "world." In the discourse of Fidesz, there is only one political power that can effectively tackle both the lack of solidarity and the external enemy – which can be manifested in big capital (banks), "Brussels", (George) "Soros" or international migration – and lead a successful fight for freedom in order to unify the nation, and that is the governing party.[59]

6 "Tizenötmillióból egy"

The second song does not problematize the situation of Hungarian communities outside of Hungary's borders, and the performing band is also far removed from the radical right subculture. Rather, it utilizes the notion of the "fifteen million" as being self-evident. "Tizenötmillióból egy" (One of fifteen million) is a song recorded by the rock band Kowalsky meg a Vega in 2017.[60] Formed in 1999 – just like Ismerős Arcok – the band started out on the alternative rock scene, performing on the festival circuit, but are now reaching mainstream audiences and have enough popularity to fill the Budapest Aréna, the largest music venue in Hungary. Our field work confirmed that their audience and fan base include groups of young and middle-aged people, as well as occasional concertgoers and families on a night out. The eclecticism of the band's repertoire, and even of the song in question – with a stadium-rock-like chorus, spoken-singing style, light pop instrumentation, and varying registers in the lyrics (occasional "street" style mixed with more formal phrasing) – also strongly suggests that they are aiming to reach a mainstream audience. "For me it is really difficult to tell [who the intended audience are], precisely because with this monstrous eclectic, [the front singer and songwriter] wants to please so many people, as if he himself was unable to decide on the perspective or to pinpoint his own position" – as it was observed during the MGA session.[61]

The song was released with a music video that was produced in collaboration with the Hungarian Defense Forces, for whom it has served partly as

---

59 Scheiring, *The Retreat*, 296–297.
60 Kowalsky meg a Vega. "Tizenötmillióból egy," *Kilenc* [LP]. MFM Music, 2017.
61 MGA May 8, 2020.

a promotional tool, especially for the recruitment of voluntary reserves. The story narrated by the video highlights the self-sacrifice of a family man in the military, bringing individual acts of heroism, a sense of crisis – through military conflict – and the (nuclear) family to the fore as key values. The official video[62] includes a short behind-the-scenes clip at the end depicting members of the band in military training to demonstrate, through engaging their own bodies, their commitment to the Hungarian army and to defending the nation. The video has been viewed more than 12 million times, and countless comments on YouTube thank Hungarian soldiers and highlight their selfless efforts, along with the posters' own emotional engagement with the song as listeners and viewers. For instance:

> I'm only 13 but this really moved me. I'm thankful to those people that defend my life.

> I cried throughout your song, it is beautiful and moving. A million hugs to all Hungarian soldiers and police officers, and most importantly, respect, for they give and have given their lives for our beautiful country. They only deserve our respect and appreciation.

The comment section also includes posts by many current or former soldiers, expressing similarly their gratitude to the band for bringing attention to their work:

> As a Hungarian soldier, I'm really thankful to you for this wonderful song. I have always loved you and this will continue in the future!

The video is also used by the band during live performances. The song is characterized by its repetitive, loop-like musical structure. It has lengthy verses and a chorus that contains a contrasting melody line and a major sixth interval at "fifteen million", which serves to highlight the phrase and make it stand out. The track is accompanied by a drum sound that was identified as "military" during the musicological group analysis session, corresponding to the military context and the theme of the video. The fifteen million of the title is to be understood, similarly to "Nélküled," as a reference to a Hungarian nation that is inclusive of ethnic minority Hungarians outside of the borders. This symbolic

---

62 "Kowalsky meg a Vega – Tizenötmillióból egy (official klip + werk)," *YouTube*. November 21, 2017. https://www.youtube.com/watch?v=iApofrBykkA.

use of this number refers back to the 1989–1990 regime change. As Szemere observes:

> Following the Berlin Wall's fall, József Antall, head of the first postsocialist government, raised eyebrows by declaring himself leader of "15 million Hungarians," only about 10 million of whom lived within the borders. ... Orbán's regime took this ethnonationalist concept of citizenship further in 2011 when granting dual citizenship to all extraterritorial non-resident Hungarians in the name of national reunification beyond the borders.[63]

This line in the chorus – "You are a star of fifteen million" – with its unambiguous reference to the national community, however, seems to stand out from the rest of the lyrics, even though it is directly connected to the military theme of the video and the context of production. The chorus, moreover, is more in line with the conventions of rock music than the repetitive structure and loop-like piano accompaniment of the lengthy verses – in other words, it is the place where the song becomes most *familiar* in its sonic features. Throughout the rest of the song, the singing voice addresses its audience in second person singular through a spoken-singing style; a fairly soft voice accompanying the stereotypically tough appearance of a muscular, tattooed male body. The lyrics cover the theme of self-sacrifice: "Tell me, what does it mean to you that there is no greater love / Than you giving your life willingly for others." Through this, they connect to the theme of the video – together with images alluding to the crisis brought on by modern civilization ("Where people only talk to one another on the internet") and a sense of threat towards conservative values ("It is now debated what respect means"), including conservative gender roles ("Where the difference between man and woman / Is slowly fading, like the night behind the rising sun"). The voice and mode of address ("Where you think, now too, that I'm talking about others / You keep nodding, but I'm telling you about ourselves, about me, about you") creates affordances resembling a therapeutic situation – as it was observed during the song analysis session: "This guy just talks and talks, leading your thoughts while you relive or survive your traumas, deal with them."[64]

We identified the voice and corresponding persona as that of a guru, with a soft suggestive, even didactic tone that keeps the addressee locked into the conversation. The body of the performer in the meantime is the embodiment

---

63   Anna Szemere, "'But he has nothing on at all!' Underground videos targeting Viktor Orbán, Hungary's celebrity politician," *Celebrity Studies* 11, no. 3 (2020): 320–335, 12.
64   MGA May 8, 2020.

of a strict health regime – the front singer Gyula Balázs "Kowalsky" promotes his vegetarian lifestyle and used to work as a yoga instructor. Through his persona, the singing voice and the song's lyrical content, the theme of self-sacrifice is connected to neoliberal technologies of the self[65] – the individual's imperative to work on their body and soul – framed in moral terms, linked to conservative values, and directly connected to Hungarian national identity and the mythical "fifteen million." The individual focus appears alongside a representation of community: "the desire to recreate community by reassembling an atomized world that is falling apart."[66] When the voice sings, repeatedly, "We belong together, we belong together," at two-thirds of the way through the song, a bell rings in the background, endowing the notion of togetherness – and, ultimately, national unity – with a ceremonial, and even religious atmosphere (correspondingly, the line mentioned is preceded by "Before God, every human is the same"). Individual "sins" are listed, and people are asked to work on themselves, but they are also called on to realize that they are part of the fifteen million. The audience are thus addressed as responsible subjects of nation-building.

The song "Tizenötmillióból egy" is thus capable of setting the scene for the nation-uniting discourse of the Fidesz regime in a way that it references the issues of national solidarity and unity as defined by the hegemonic power in a routinized, matter-of-fact way. The huge popularity of the song enables this set of concepts and their associated moral values, operated within a political framework, to also become mainstream in everyday contexts. Pierre Nora[67] uses the concept of *realms of memory* to denote metaphorical and concrete places and things that reinforce and link identity to collective memory. In both songs, the "fifteen million" are constructed as a realm of memory through sound, genre aesthetics, and words, affording the reinforcement of corresponding feelings of intimacy and familiarity.

7   "Victims" of the New Hegemony: "Ne mondd (hogy nincs remény)"

As mentioned above, the populist discourse of Fidesz also relies on the production of its own representations of the enemy – those responsible for attacks on

---

65   Michel Foucault, "Technologies of the Self. Lectures at University of Vermont Oct. 1982," in *Technologies of the Self* (Amherst, MA: University of Massachusetts Press, 1988): 16–49.
66   MGA May 8, 2020.
67   Pierre Nora, *Realms of Memory. The Construction of the French Past, Volume 1* (New York: Columbia University Press, 1983/1996).

the system coming from outside and striving to dismantle the national unity.⁶⁸ The polarization characterizing the "System of National Cooperation" has enabled not only a symbolic victory over political opponents along with constant mobilization, but also, through the propagation of anti-elite discourses, more precisely the scapegoating of the self-identified pro-European, post-transition Hungarian intellectual elite. In the following, through the analysis of a song performed by Zsuzsa Koncz we intend to demonstrate that members of this intellectual elite are also active in positioning themselves in this dichotomy through assuming the same representational framework, self-defining and identifying as the victims of the new hegemony. Through this process, they also contribute to the reinforcing of the populist discourse, and, ultimately, the process of hegemony-building. As Barna, Madár, Nagy and Szarvas similarly observe:

> The [oppositional] critique of the excessive power of the state or the stigma of unprofessionalism fits into the dichotomies also used by the new hegemony (e.g., authentic Hungarian–European, liberal–national, etc.). These alternative and oppositional practices are, according to the description of Raymond Williams, merely counter-discourses since they are rooted in the categories of the dominant class and organize resistance according to the logic of the regime.⁶⁹

Zsuzsa Koncz is a well-known, iconic figure of the Hungarian popular music world, as well as being a member of the liberal elite at the time of the 1989–1990 regime change. The start of her career can be traced back to the 1960s, and she later performed with the most important beat music (rock and roll) bands of the time such as Illés, Metro and Omega. János Bródy, a former member of Illés, continued to act as her co-writer after the regime change, writing many of her songs and lyrics. As a celebrated star of the Hungarian beat music era, Koncz gained not only national recognition, but also the opportunity to reach international audiences, which secured a position for her that counted as privileged in the context of socialism. Throughout her career, she released almost one hundred solo albums in Hungary, and twenty-four abroad. The albums often include old songs recorded in new arrangements, which has

---

68 Scheiring, *The Retreat*, 297.
69 Raymond Williams, "Base and Superstructure in Marxist Cultural Theory," *New Left Review* 82 (1973): 3–16; cited in Emília Barna, Mária Madár, Kristóf Nagy, and Márton Szarvas. "Dinamikus hatalom. Kulturális termelés és politika Magyarországon 2010 után," *Fordulat* 26 (2019): 225–251, 247; our translation from Hungarian.

simultaneously helped her to maintain a sense of continuity and a structure of self-referentiality in her work.

In addition to performing, the career of Koncz has also been defined by her image as a public figure and her embeddedness into the bourgeois milieu of the capital city. Currently, in addition to her yearly show at the Budapest Arena, she performs in theaters and cultural community centers. Her work links her to the popular music field, yet thanks to the social prestige attached to her status, and according to the taste hierarchies solidifying in Hungarian society in the post-socialist period, she is clearly regarded as a (high) artist and intellectual. As a result of the young artists of the 1960s–70s Hungarian beat era integrating into the cultural elite after the regime change, and as the pop-rock music of that era had been elevated through their intermediation into symbols of resistance against the socialist system, both the era and the artists have been consecrated in a Bourdieusian sense.[70] The songs of Koncz are permeated by the coded language typically employed by artists before the regime change as a political strategy to avoid censorship and conflict with the governing power.[71] Metaphors, associations, word play, certain lyrical elements and sounds (see, for instance, the song "Sárga rózsa" [Yellow rose])[72] acquired a new purpose after 2010.

"Ne mondd (hogy nincs remény)" (Don't tell me [there is no hope]), a song released in 2016,[73] written by János Bródy and sung by Koncz, along with the accompanying video,[74] activates this ressentiment and the pre-'89 aesthetic language of resistance. The images and metaphors in the song follow are consistent with the stylistic tradition of her own oeuvre. At the same time, the instrumentation and production are markedly different from much of her repertoire. The particular use of guitar sounds, synthesizer, strings and drums – a metal sound and a female singing voice – evoke the styles of "fantasy metal," "gothic metal," or progressive rock – as observed in the song analysis sessions: "Even if not very modern, it certainly isn't the guitar sound that we can

---

70 Pierre Bourdieu, *The Field of Cultural Production* (New York: Columbia University Press, 1993).
71 Bence Csatári, "'Agyamban kopasz cenzor ül': A könnyűzenei élet politikai ellenőrzése a Kádár-korszakban," *Kommentár* 1 (2013): 55–70.
72 Anna Szemere, *Up from the Underground: The Culture of Rock Music in Postsocialist Hungary* (University Park, PA: Pennsylvania State University Press, 2001), 36.
73 Zsuzsa Koncz and János Bródy, "Ne mondd (hogy nincs remény)." *Vadvilág* [LP]. Hungaroton, 2016.
74 "Koncz Zsuzsa – Ne mondd (hogy nincs remény)." *YouTube*. June 18, 2019. https://www.youtube.com/watch?v=NTsU3qHTmlg.

link to her musical world established over the '80s. To me, this is much more '90s and 2000s."⁷⁵ Or:

> I was really surprised at the guitar entering with a bang at the beginning. It created an expectation of a hard sound, but then it was only the chorus that was more aggressive. There was a guitar pounding throughout, under the verses, it made [the song] quite agitated. The chorus sounded hard.⁷⁶

The participants of the session identified the song as work created by someone with a certain skill set attempting not only to create a certain atmosphere, but also to imitate or acquire a particular style for the purposes of the song.

The tension created by the military-style electric guitar riffs and the pounding drums is paralleled in the lyrics by a repetition of negative imperative sentences: "Don't tell me it hurts; don't tell me it is a shame / Don't tell me everything is in vain" (repeated twice every time). This tension and stifled anger is concretized in the lyrics when the singer, albeit in coded language, alludes to the dominant regime through the image of the Castle and the "new clothes of the *táltos*." As Szemere observes, the Prime Minister's relocation of his office to the (Royal) Castle in Buda can be interpreted as a symbolic gesture in line with his "regal aspirations,"⁷⁷ and it is this interpretation with which the lyrics engage. The "new clothes of the *táltos*" refer to the well-known folk tale of the emperor's new clothes, where the figure of the emperor is replaced by the Hungarian shaman-like mythological figure of the *táltos*.

In the song, realms of memory⁷⁸ are mobilized in two ways: they use an external referentiality and an internal referentiality, that is, one within the artist's own oeuvre. Firstly, the mentioned symbols of domination and their violent appropriation ("up in the castle somebody has lost the plot"; "The heroic past on the painted picture is fake"; "I'm not interested in the *táltos'* new clothes") are linked to the effect of anger. Secondly, she subtly refers to an older song, which has become a pop cultural reference to the Hungarian memory of the Holocaust. The song "Százéves pályaudvar" (A hundred-year-old railway station)⁷⁹ was written by Péter Gerendás and János Bródy, released in 1993, and was later performed at the Dohány Street Synagogue in Budapest as part of the

---

75   MGA February 20, 2020.
76   Ibid.
77   Szemere, "But he has nothing," 4.
78   Nora, *Realms of Memory*.
79   Zsuzsa Koncz, Péter Gerendás, and János Bródy, "Százéves pályaudvar," *Ne veszítsd el a fejed* [LP]. EMI-Quint, 1993.

2011 March of the Living Hungary event (as a duet with actor János Kulka). The song makes a direct reference to the victims of the Holocaust, recalling characteristic realms of memory through images such as the sign on the wall of the house, the railway station, the train tracks, and so on: "There are times when we need to go / When the sign appears on the wall of the house. ... Hate was marching down the streets / And the glow of the past appeared on the horizon / They felt that they now have to go." "Ne mondd." from 2016 revives the same social context of oppression and force: "Don't tell me you are ready for the journey if we need to go." However, instead of the melancholy and lyrical mode of the 1993 song, through the hard sound, the dynamism, the anger expressed in the lyrics, as well as the energetic gestures of the performer in the music video, it embodies resistance against this oppression.

The song manages to express both stifled anger and the gesture of fighting for freedom and equality: "There will be a new spring and a beautiful summer / We deserve the sweet sunshine"; "The world will be beautiful again, let's not give up / In this land, you could live, and not only die." The last of these lines similarly cites the poem "Szózat" – the second Hungarian national anthem – to "Nélküled" by Ismerős Arcok ("In the great world outside of here / There is no place for you / May fortune's hand bless or beat you / Here you must live and die" – in the translation of Watson Kirkconnell). The choice of genre, as well as the elitist positioning of the singer as the spokesperson of the oppressed, strengthens the interpretation that the songwriter and lyricist, as well as the performer, are attempting to conform to the imagined taste of the audience in order to reach a broader mass of people. Nevertheless, since it fails to work as a harmonic whole, it gives the impression of being an exercise in style that is condescending towards its audience, implying a classed positioning: "This is a classic attitude on the part of the intellectual elite, I [as the author] imagine [what I want to say] and I assume that I can only say this in this particular framework."[80]

In all, "Ne mondd." – with its direct and subtle referential framework – speaks and engages in a symbolic struggle on behalf of those that are excluded, oppressed, and deprived of their position, with authoritative force, while placing the aggression of the contemporary right-wing hegemony-building within the succession of traumas suffered during the 20th century by alluding the Hungarian victims of the Holocaust and socialism. The protest character of the song was also strengthened by media discourses around it: following its release, the oppositional press celebrated it as "throwing a punch" or "answering back",

---

80   MGA February 20, 2020.

that is, as symbolic resistance, and the high record sales (the album reached platinum status within weeks of its release), along with the sold-out shows was portrayed as a result of the mass-level need for an oppositional voice. In contrast, the government-friendly media referred to the song as disrespectful towards the Prime Minister and offensive. In part they attributed its tone to the artist's waning popularity and subsequent resentment, and in part labelled it as a money-making enterprise of the failed liberal party and the intellectual elite.

8   "Akit a hazája nem szeretett"

We looked at a second song with János Bródy as songwriter and lyricist, but this time he is also the performer. Besides Koncz, Bródy (as a former member of the bands Illés and Fonográf) is another of the best-known figures of the beat era. His solo career began towards the end of the 1970s, and throughout his career he has been involved in the production of around sixty LPs, has written around eight hundred song lyrics (some of which have appeared in edited poetry volumes), composed two hundred songs, and written librettos and lyrics for rock operas. His emblematic songs and lyrics have become important reference points as imprints of the socialist period, but to an extent remained a generational experience. In the period following the regime change, he received multiple awards for his work, through which – alongside opportunities for media publicity – the pre-2010 left-liberal governments legitimized his position as an artist and intellectual. After 2010, however, his songs no longer received airplay on public service broadcast media. On his part, he tied his symbolic silencing to the adverse governmental communication towards the left-liberal intellectual elite and assumed a victim position, evoking the representation of the "persecuted and censored" intellectual from the socialist period.[81]

The song "Akit a hazája nem szeretett" (The one who was not loved by their country) debuted in 2018 on YouTube and other digital platforms and was later released as a 7" single in 2019[82] and on the album *Gáz van babám!* (2020).[83] The form of the song can be characterized as a chanson, which simultaneously evokes the cultural representations of French political music traditions and socialist-era Russian bards (singer-songwriters such as Vladimir Vysotsky).

---

81   György Farkas, "Egy rádió mégis leadta Bródy János új dalát," *24.hu*, August 11, 2018. https://24.hu/kultura/2018/11/08/egy-radio-megis-leadta-brody-janos-uj-dalat/.
82   János Bródy, *Akit a hazája nem szeretett/ Magyarok közt európai* [7" single]. Grund Records, 2019.
83   János Bródy, "Akit a hazája nem szeretett," *Gáz van babám!* [LP]. Grund Records, 2020.

The representation of Bródy in recent years corresponds to the latter: on concert posters, album covers as well as on stage, he tends to stand alone with his acoustic guitar and a microphone, or at least separate from the rest of the band, as an intellectual leader of the masses. In the case of the official music video for "Akit a hazája nem szeretett," however, a guitar strap depicting the colors of the French national flag is added to this representation, turning the singer into the embodiment of the revolution.

At the same time, the MGA suggested that the revolutionary emphasis in the lyrics was mitigated by the lack of emphasis on the voice in the production and the complexity of the music, especially the rhythm. Nevertheless, since YouTube is an important medium for listening to this song, where the lyrics are included in the description, we may assume that many people also read along while listening. In addition, the songs and performance style of Bródy, in line with the singer-songwriter tradition, have consistently been lyric-centric, which has also contributed to his mentioned position as an intellectual and have served as a vehicle for the involvement of the audience. "The sound of Bródy's voice" moreover, "is recognized by everyone when it enters, in a Hungarian context."[84]

Written in third person singular, the lyrics center upon the relation towards the masses intolerant of dissenting opinions, who are exclusionary and oppressive, but at the same time easy to manipulate: "They had to learn while sitting at the back of the classroom / That truth would make one free, but they cannot be right"; "And they raised their voice in vain: hey, people, we are heading towards the abyss / The response was: those who do not follow us are traitors"; "And it is a traitor that imagines the bright future differently / And anyone that dares to doubt becomes an enemy." What is depicted by these words is the tension between the oppressed and the oppressive mob manipulated by the ruling power. Similarly, to the song performed by Koncz, the image of the citizen becoming an enemy of the state and of society is linked to tragic Hungarian historical references and creates a historical embeddedness for the victim narrative.

Beyond historical embeddedness, the words also suggest a kind of "distanciation"; an outside focus and position corresponding to the elite status of the intellectual. In the song, this outsider status is used to signify the inertia of the speaker–observer, his lack of tools against the oppression of the hegemonic power. Instead of assuming responsibility as a member of the intellectual elite, the speaker lays blame at the feet of those in power.

---

84   MGA May 14, 2021.

> Participant 1: An air of resignation and bitterness permeates these lyrics. It is not a combatant resolution, more like, "I told you it was going to be like this."
> Participant 2: [quoting from the lyrics] "They laugh bitterly"[85]

Or: "And the lyrics are full of pathos, big words, 'traitor,' 'enemy,' 'idol.' There is absolutely no self-irony, he really takes himself seriously, it's this position of the intellectual, 'I'm telling you how it is.'"[86]

Thus, the form of the song – chanson – as well as the lyrics create affordances that enable an identification with a position opposing the oppressive hegemony-building of the Orbán regime, and facilitate a generalization of this position as agency in opposition to authoritarian regimes. It is a stance assumed not only against the prevailing hegemony, but also in defense of the speaker's own hegemonic position as a (liberal) intellectual. At the same time, the speaker assumes the same populist discourse through the images used in the lyrics ("traitor," "among sinners I can be neither complicit nor silent," "enemy," "idol," "at the edge of the abyss") and through a representation of a majority oppressed by the dominant power.

Bródy actively uses online platforms for the involvement of his audience and to reinforce their commitment. After the release of the song, he started an online poll on his own social media profile, thematizing the difference between aligning with the hegemony in progress, the government, and nationalism on the one hand, and patriotism on the other: "Can one love their country and not love its government?"[87] This online poll mobilized more than 12 thousand users. The demographic of the majority of those mobilized corresponds to Bródy's audience, the generation above 40–50 years, a typically urban, bourgeois milieu. This resonates with the nostalgia for the pre-regime change opposition, the slogans of "freedom" and "civic democracy," and the rejection of ethnicist values associated with nationalism.

Bródy's fans view his songs as the top of the taste hierarchy of Hungarian popular music, as poetry and a kind of cultural-political compass, as evidenced by YouTube comments posted under the video for "Akit a hazája nem szeretett."[88] For example:

---

85   MGA May 14, 2021.
86   Ibid.
87   György Farkas, "Bródy János tesztje a hazaszeretetről," *24.hu*, March 29, 2019. https://24.hu/szorakozas/2019/03/29/brody-janos-tesztje-a-hazaszeretetrol/.
88   "János Bródy – Akit a hazája nem szeretett," *YouTube*. November 5. 2018. https://www.youtube.com/watch?v=sM_lhkcaoKg.

One day, when you are no longer here this song will stay, as an encouragement, as an eternal memento. You put into words, into song, what is in people's hearts and minds. You will be with us forever, even without this song, but this song complements your guidance! I love you; it is good that you are here for us, this encouragement gives us all strength. Thank you, János Bródy. Your name, your work, your worldview are to me a phenomenon.

János Bródy is a teacher to our generation and for those who are older … as [the famous Hungarian poet] Attila József said, "'cause it's beyond a high school education, I'll be teaching the whole nation, watch me, you'll see."[89] Bródy, Zsuzsa Koncz and Presser and his band[90] did this … if only more were willing to learn.

The positions of Zsuzsa Koncz and János Bródy in Hungarian popular music are intertwined with their political and broader cultural activity, and in both of their cases we can observe a continuity from the 1960s to the present day. The two songs we have analyzed depict two distinct means of resistance towards the Orbán regime through their aesthetics, namely the more combative rock-fantasy metal fusion and the rhythmically complex but steady, melancholic political chanson, yet both lyrics use similar concepts to the songs affording the populist discourse of the hegemonic power. Our analysis therefore indicates that rather than the songs embodying an anti-populist discourse, they create affordances for the hegemonic populist discourse.

9 Conclusions

In populism research, it has become increasingly important not to view the relation between politics and the masses as one of supply-demand, but as a complex phenomenon embedded in culture and power structures. A methodology we developed based on Adorno's popular music theory and analysis, and its rethinking by contemporary scholars such as Middleton and DeNora, along with Hall's theorization of popular culture and hegemony, has enabled us to grasp the issues of populism and hegemony-building beyond a narrowly interpreted sphere of politics. Moreover, moving beyond seeking simplistic, even

---

89 Translation by Michael Castro.
90 Gábor Presser is a Hungarian musician, songwriter and singer, a prominent figure of Hungarian popular music since the 1960s.

deterministic cause-and-effect relations, it has allowed us to interrogate the ways in which cultural texts afford specific social meanings.

In the chapter, we investigated the new hegemony-building that has taken place from 2010 in Hungary through popular music. We asked how the restructuring of power generated by the Orbán governments is present in popular music, and how popular music enables the spreading of populist discourses. Firstly, we looked at the affordances created by songs achieving mainstream success after 2010 in relation to concepts and ideas that form a crucial part of the new hegemony-building, in particular those relating to the idea of national unity and the polarizing logic. Secondly, we looked at what kind of affordances are created by songs produced and consumed within the framework of the liberal opposition. We have concluded that the four analyzed songs simultaneously play a part in the reinforcing of political polarization and the mobilization of political sides. Despite the different positionings of the artists in relation to the new hegemony, in all four cases, the political and social instrumentalization is clear: while "Nélküled" was transformed into an alternative national anthem from a radical right-wing subcultural context after 2010, the song "Tizenötmillióból egy" was utilized as promotion for voluntary reserves by the Ministry of Defense. "Ne mondd (hogy nincs remény)" and "Akit a hazája nem szeretett" were inserted into the symbolic politics of the opposition. While the first two songs create affordances that parallel the framework of Fidesz' nation-building and the notion of ethnic solidarity symbolized by the "fifteen million," the latter two perform the embodiment of intellectual positions (self-)defined as the opposition and enemies of the new regime, simultaneously incorporating a position of victimhood and a sense of cultural-intellectual superiority.

The new regime of capital accumulation has involved a transformation of power relations in the field of culture as part of structural and institutional transformation, reinforcing existing social divisions, and affecting various segments of everyday life. We have interpreted this process of transformation from the perspective of Critical Theory, renewing the methodological apparatus Adorno used to study popular culture to provide a complex interpretation of various popular songs and the shifting political, and in some cases social, positions of the artists performing them. This complexity includes questions regarding the musical structure, genre, and aesthetics of the musical text, the social aspects of their position in hierarchies of taste, as well as the social status of the artists and their relation to power. We believe that uncovering these aspects brings us closer to understanding the ways in which populist discourses are permeated in the cultural sphere, as well as to a system critique that takes popular culture seriously.

Bibliography

Adorno, Theodor W. "On the Fetish Character in Music and the Regression of Listening." In *The Culture Industry: Selected Essays on Mass Culture*, edited by Jay M. Bernstein, 29–60. London: Routledge, 1991.

Adorno, Theodor W. (1941) "On Popular Music. III. Theory about the Listener," https://ia800507.us.archive.org/26/items/ZeitschriftFrSozialforschung9.Jg/ZeitschriftFrSozialforschung91941.pdf.

Adorno, Theodor W., and Max Horkheimer. "The Culture Industry: Enlightenment as Mass Deception." In *The Cultural Studies Reader. Second Edition*, edited by Simon During, 31–41. London and New York: Routledge, 1999.

Barna, Emília, Mária Madár, Kristóf Nagy, and Márton Szarvas. "Dinamikus hatalom. Kulturális termelés és politika Magyarországon 2010 után." *Fordulat* 26 (2019): 225–251.

Barna, Emília, Kristóf Nagy, and Márton Szarvas. "COVID-19 Crisis in Hungarian Cultural Production – Vulnerability and deepening authoritarian control." *LeftEast*, February 12, 2019. https://lefteast.org/covid-19-crisis-in-hungarian-cultural-production-vulnerability-authoritarian-control.

Barna, Emília, and Ágnes Patakfalvi-Czirják. "'We are of one blood': Hungarian Popular Music, Nationalism and the Tajectory of the Song "Nélküled" through Radicalization, Folklorization and Consecration." *Journal of Contemporary Central and Eastern Europe* (2022).

Bourdieu, Pierre. *The Field of Cultural Production*. New York: Columbia University Press, 1993.

Brubaker, Rogers. "Why Populism?" *Theory and Society* 46, no. 5 (2017): 357–385.

Brubaker, Rogers. "Between Nationalism and Civilizationism: The European Populist Moment in Comparative Perspective." *Ethnic and Racial Studies* 40, no. 8 (2017): 1191–1226.

Csatári, Bence. "'Agyamban kopasz cenzor ül': A könnyűzenei élet politikai ellenőrzése a Kádár-korszakban." *Kommentár* 1 (2013): 55–70.

Csigó, Péter. *The Neopopular Bubble. Speculating on "the People" in Late Modern Democracy*. Budapest: CEU Press, 2016.

DeNora, Tia. *Music in Everyday Life*. Cambridge: Cambridge University Press, 2000.

DeNora, Tia. *After Adorno: Rethinking Music Sociology*. Cambridge: Cambridge University Press, 2003.

Doehring, André, and Kai Ginkel. "Popular Music and the Rise of Populism in Europe." GfpM Conference "One Nation Under a Groove," Mainz, 1–3 November 2019.

Éber, Márk, Ágnes Gagyi, Tamás Gerőcs, and Csaba Jelinek. "2008–2018: Válság és hegemónia Magyarországon." *Fordulat* 26 (2019): 28–75.

Egry, Gábor. "Beyond Electioneering: Minority Hungarians and the Vision of National Unification." In *Brave New Hungary. Mapping the "System of National Cooperation,"* edited by János Mátyás Kovács and Balázs Trencsényi. Lanham, MD: Lexington Books, 2019.

Farkas, György. "Egy rádió mégis leadta Bródy János új dalát." *24.hu*, August 11, 2018. https://24.hu/kultura/2018/11/08/egy-radio-megis-leadta-brody-janos-uj-dalat/.

Farkas, György. "Bródy János tesztje a hazaszeretetről." *24.hu*, March 29, 2019. https://24.hu/szorakozas/2019/03/29/brody-janos-tesztje-a-hazaszeretetrol/.

Feischmidt, Margit, and Gergő Pulay. "'Rocking the Nation': The Popular Culture of Neo-Nationalism." *Nations and Nationalism* 23, no. 2 (2017): 309–326.

Foucault, Michel. "Technologies of the Self. Lectures at University of Vermont Oct. 1982." In *Technologies of the Self*, 16–49. Amherst, MA: University of Massachusetts Press, 1988.

Gagyi, Ágnes. "Populism or People's Movements? Interview with Mary Taylor." *LeftEast*, April 11. 2018. https://lefteast.org/populism-or-peoples-movements-interview-with-mary-taylor.

Gramsci, Antonio. *Selections from the Prison Notebooks*. New York: International Publishers, 1971.

Hall, Stuart. "The Great Moving Right Show." *Marxism Today* 23, no. 1 (1979): 14–20.

Hall, Stuart. "Notes on Deconstructing 'The Popular'." In *People's History and Socialist Theory*, edited by Raphael Samuel, 231–239. London: Kegan Paul-Routledge, 1981.

Hall, Stuart. *Representation: Cultural Representations and Signifying Practices*. London: Sage Publications and The Open University, 1997.

Hall, Stuart, and Paddy Whannel. *The Popular Arts*. Durham, NC: Duke University Press, 2018.

Hennion, Antoine. "Music Lovers. Taste as Performance." *Theory, Culture and Society* 18, no. 5 (2001): 1–22.

Kovács, János Mátyás, and Balázs Trencsényi. "Conclusion: Hungary: Brave and New? Dissecting a Realistic Dystopia." In *Brave New Hungary. Mapping the "System of National Cooperation,"* edited by János Mátyás Kovács and Balázs Trencsényi, 379–432. Lanham, MD: Lexington Books, 2019.

Laclau, Ernesto, and Chantal Mouffe. *Hegemony and Socialist Strategy*. London: Verso, 1985.

Maiguashca, Bice. "Resisting the 'Populist Hype': A Feminist Critique of a Globalising Concept." *Review of International Studies* 45, no. 5 (2019): 768–785.

Marx, Karl. *Capital: Volume One*. Mineola, NY: Dover Publications, (1867) 2019.

Middleton, Richard. *Studying Popular Music*. Philadelphia: Open University Press, 1990.

Moffitt, Benjamin. *The Global Rise of Populism: Performance, Political Style, and Representation*. Redwood City, CA: Stanford University Press, 2016.

Moffitt, Benjamin, and Simon Tormey. "Rethinking Populism: Politics, Mediatisation and Political Style." *Political Studies* 62, no. 2 (2014): 381–397.

Moffitt, Benjamin. *Populism*. Cambridge, MA: Polity Press, 2020.

Moore, Allan. "Authenticity as Authentication." *Popular Music* 21, no. 2 (2002): 209–223.

Mudde, Cas. "The Populist Zeitgeist." *Government and Opposition* 39, no. 4 (2004): 541–563.

Nora, Pierre. *Realms of Memory. The Construction of the French Past, Volume 1*. New York: Columbia University Press, 1996.

Ostiguy, Pierre. *The High and the Low in Politics: A Two-Dimensional Political Space for Comparative Analysis and Electoral Studies*. Working Paper. Kellogg Institute, 2019. https://kellogg.nd.edu/sites/default/files/old_files/documents/360_0.pdf.

Palonen, Emilia. "Political Polarisation and Populism in Contemporary Hungary." *Parliamentary Affairs* 62, no. 2 (2009): 318–334.

Pogonyi, Szabolcs. *Extra-Territorial Ethnic Politics, Discourses and Identities in Hungary*. Cham: Palgrave Macmillan, 2017.

Scheiring, Gábor. *The Retreat of Liberal Democracy: Authoritarian Capitalism and the Accumulative State in Hungary*. Cham: Palgrave Macmillan, 2020.

Sengel, Ferenc. "Szembesültünk a hazugságokkal." *Origo.hu*, November 25, 2018. https://www.origo.hu/kultura/20181120-nyerges-attila-interju.html.

Szemere, Anna. *Up from the Underground: The Culture of Rock Music in Postsocialist Hungary*. University Park, PA: Pennsylvania State University Press, 2001.

Szemere, Anna. "'But he has nothing on at all!' Underground videos targeting Viktor Orbán, Hungary's celebrity politician." *Celebrity Studies* 11, no. 3 (2020): 320–335.

Taggart, Paul. *Populism*. Birmingham: Open University Press, 2000.

Taylor, Mary N. *Movement of the People: Hungarian Populism, Folk Dance, and Citizenship*. Indiana Bloomington, IN: University Press, 2021.

Williams, Raymond. "Base and Superstructure in Marxist Cultural Theory." *New Left Review* 82 (1973): 3–16.

Witkin, Robert W. *Adorno on Music*. New York: Routledge, 1998.

Wodak, Ruth. *The Politics of Fear: What Right-Wing Populist Discourses Mean*. Los Angeles: Sage, 2015.

Discography and Videos

Bródy, János. "Akit a hazája nem szeretett." *Gáz van babám!* [LP]. Grund Records, 2020.

Bródy, János. *Akit a hazája nem szeretett/ Magyarok közt európai* [7" single]. Grund Records, 2019.

"Bródy János – Akit a hazája nem szeretett" *YouTube*. November 5. 2018. https://www.youtube.com/watch?v=sM_lhkcaoKg.

Ismerős Arcok. "Nélküled." *Éberálom* [LP]. Grund Records, 2007.

"Ismerős Arcok – Nélküled." *YouTube.* January 3, 2010. https://www.youtube.com/watch?v=KmUMvShEq-E.

Koncz, Zsuzsa, and János Bródy. "Ne mondd (hogy nincs remény)." *Vadvilág* [LP]. Hungaroton, 2016.

"Koncz Zsuzsa – Ne mondd (hogy nincs remény)." *YouTube.* June 18, 2019. https://www.youtube.com/watch?v=NTsU3qHTmlg.

Koncz, Zsuzsa, Péter Gerendás, and János Bródy. "Százéves pályaudvar." *Ne veszítsd el a fejed* [LP]. EMI-Quint, 1993.

Kowalsky meg a Vega. "Tizenötmillióból egy" *Kilenc* [LP]. MFM Music, 2017.

"Kowalsky meg a Vega – Tizenötmillióból egy (official klip + werk)" *YouTube.* November 21, 2017. https://www.youtube.com/watch?v=iApofrBykkA.

CHAPTER 2

The Plague of Bannonism

Ronald Beiner

[Bannon] turned to what was driving the Tea Party, which didn't like elites. Populism was for the common man, knowing the system is rigged …

'I love that. That's what I am,' Trump said, 'a popularist.' He mangled the word.

'No, no,' Bannon said. 'It's populist.'

'Yeah, yeah,' Trump insisted. 'A popularist.'[1]

∴

Did we really need a new ideology in the second half of the second decade of the 21st century?[2] "Trumpism," it might be said, isn't really a candidate for such an ideology; it is too focused on the whims and vanity and egomania and greed and other character flaws of Donald J. Trump really to count as political at all. Bannonism arguably *is* such a new ideology.[3] That's not to say that it is a coherent doctrine or body of thinking. Errol Morris, in an interview with Frank

---

1 Bob Woodward, *Fear: Trump in the White House* (New York: Simon & Schuster, 2018), 4. It's easy to imagine that Bannon had this episode in mind when he famously referred to Trump as "a blunt instrument for us."
2 This chapter is a revised and expanded version of an article originally published in *Critical Review* 31, no. 3–4 (2019): 300–314.
3 For anyone who might wonder why I describe as "plague-like" Bannon's efforts as an ideologue, I think the shocking events of January 6th, 2021, suffice as an explanation: Bannon and other hard-core Trumpites seem determined to spread a contagion that, left unchecked, will surely poison and ultimately extinguish American democracy. As goes without saying, Bannon did his utmost to stoke up the conspiracy-minded frenzy that fed into and fueled the Trumpite insurrection on January 6th. According to a *Newsweek* report dated September 22, 2021 (Andre J. Ellington, "Steve Bannon Confirms His Involvement in January 6 Insurrection on 'War Room' Podcast"), Bannon was directly involved in a January 5th meeting to help plan the insurrection, and in the days leading up to January 6th urged Trump "to kill the Biden presidency in the crib."

Bruni in the *New York Times* concerning Morris's film-length Bannon interview, *American Dharma*, said:

> [Bannon is] well-read. He is obviously smart. But when you examine the philosophy, it's just – calling it incoherent or inchoate is too kind. It's just a mess: a little bit of the Crusades, a little bit of Thucydides, some crazy, Catholic right-wing theology. Add a dash of movies.[4]

My professional judgment as a political philosopher coincides exactly with Morris's encapsulation. Still, ideologies don't have to be coherent to have a significant impact. Those who are on the receiving end of a given ideology are not professional philosophers or political theorists, and how they respond to the buttons someone like Bannon pushes doesn't depend on how impressively his pronouncements satisfy robust standards of intellectual coherence.

The closest we have to a "doctrinal" statement of Bannonism is the transcript of the Skyped-in remarks at a Vatican right-wing-Catholic conference that received a fair amount of publicity around the time Bannon first came on the scene in a visible way.[5] Since it is the closest thing we have to a "text" laying out how Bannon thinks politically, what his policy agenda is, and what might define his vision of a desirable politics, we offer the following summary of leading themes in the Vatican remarks.

Bannon claims that there is both a crisis of capitalism and a crisis of Judeo-Christian values, and the two crises are interwoven. Bannon endorses a Christian rejection of liberal secularization; in fact, the contempt for Christianity on the part of ruling elites constitutes proof, for him, of the cultural arrogance of those elites. He suggests that Christianity was a key part of what sustained the health of capitalism, so secularization is simultaneously anti-religious and anti-capitalist.

Again and again, Bannon rails against "crony capitalism," (This from a former investment banker working for Goldman Sachs). At the same time, he attacks what he calls "state-sponsored capitalism" (in China and Russia). Bannon endorses a quasi-Marxist critique of the kind of Wall St. capitalism that treats people like commodities. But this doesn't deter him from also saying: "We are strong capitalists; the harder-nosed the capitalism, the better." He claims that God favors capitalism ("divine providence" intends for us to be

---

4 Frank Bruni, "The Devil in Steve Bannon," *New York Times*, August 26, 2018, p. SR3.
5 J. Lester Feder, "This is how Steve Bannon Sees the Entire World." *BuzzFeed.news*. November 16, 2016. https://www.buzzfeednews.com/article/lesterfeder/this-is-how-steve-bannon-sees-the-entire-world.

committed job-creators and wealth-creators). But Christian capitalists must support 'putting a cap on wealth creation and distribution.'

Bannon endorses a Samuel Huntington-type thesis of a clash of civilizations between the Judeo-Christian West and Islam. He suggests that the coming fight between Christianity and Islam will be of the same order of magnitude as the civilizational cataclysms associated with the First and Second World Wars. He assumes that jihadi versions of Islam are what represent Islam in this coming civilizational struggle.

Bannon aligns himself with a Tea-Party critique of the Republican establishment (the fight against which is more urgent than the fight against the Democrats); with right-wing Catholic anti-abortion and pro-traditional-marriage politics; and with far-right European populist parties like UK Independence Party (UKIP) and National Rally (formerly *Front National*). He repeatedly refers to the latter as "center right" because they represent a backlash of 'the middle class, the working men and women in the world' against arrogant cosmopolitan elites.[6] Washington, Beijing, and Brussels all belong to the same international elite that disdains ordinary people and bosses them around. Bannon even goes so far as to suggest that the centralized U.S. government matches the E.U. in its elitism and detachment from the ordinary citizenry. Should both be disbanded? Bannon clearly gestures in that direction. Tellingly, when Bannon allegedly called himself a "Leninist,"[7] he elaborated what he meant as follows: 'Lenin wanted to destroy the state, and that's my goal too. I want to bring everything crashing down and destroy all of today's establishment.' As is fairly clear, many of the people who Trump put in his cabinet soon after Bannon became his chief strategist were suggestive of this agenda.

While conceding that Putin's Russia is a kleptocracy, Bannon defends far-right ("center-right") populist movements in Europe with respect to admiring Putin because Putin stands for a firm concept of committed nationality.[8]

---

6 Bannon will invoke the same "center right" label in *American Dharma*.

7 Michael Wolff, "Ringside with Steve Bannon at Trump Tower as the President-Elect's Strategist Plots 'An Entirely New Political Movement' (Exclusive)." *The Hollywood Reporter*, November 18, 2016. http://www.hollywoodreporter.com/news/steve-bannon-trump-tower-interview-trumps-strategist-plots-new-political-movement-948747.

8 This alt-right-like partiality for Putin's Russia is also expressed in Bannon's activities vis-à-vis Bosnia: 'The Serb politicians whom Bannon supports want to secede from [Bosnia], oppose the European Union, and ally themselves closely with Russia.' See Krithika Varagur, "Why Bannon is Meddling with Bosnia," *The New York Review*, September 5, 2018. https://www.nybooks.com/daily/2018/09/05/why-bannon-is-meddling-with-bosnia/.

   In an interview given in March of 2019 (as reported in an Associated Press story entitled "Bannon Says Russia Probe Set Back Efforts to Work with Moscow"), Bannon sticks to

Insofar as Putin's nationalism draws sustenance from fascist sources (notably, the thought of Ivan Ilyin), that doesn't seem objectionable to Bannon. Bannon cites the Italian fascist, Julius Evola, and alludes to the Russian fascist, Alexander Dugin. Overall, Tea-Party themes (particularly outrage at the complicity between big government and the bankers responsible for the 2008 financial crisis) seem much more salient than alt-right themes, though Bannon puts a lot of emphasis on the "Judeo-Christian" foundation of the West. He believes (or *says* that he believes) that racial and ethnic aspects of contemporary populism will fade as populism attains its ends, which largely consist in the humbling of ruling elites.

The reference to Evola and the veiled reference to Dugin invites further elaboration. People on the alt-right took it as a signal that he was part of their club, and people rightfully fearful of the alt-right interpreted it in a similar way. For instance, Richard Spencer, soon after earning notoriety with his infamous "Hail Trump" speech in the fall of 2016, released a provocative podcast in which he offered the following response to Bannon's Vatican remarks: 'Bannon has made gestures towards us; he's said Breitbart is a platform for the alt-right. He's apparently read Julius Evola and Alexander Dugin.'[9]

---

the same Russia-friendly line. He says that "the Judeo-Christian West" is in an existential struggle with China and needs to align itself with Russia to prevail in that struggle.

9   For a slightly fuller version of Spencer's judgment on Bannon, see pp. 11–12 of my book, *Dangerous Minds* (Philadelphia: University of Pennsylvania Press, 2018). On October 5, 2017, Buzzfeed posted a long report on the Bannon-Milo Yiannopoulos relationship that included a damning series of e-mails between the two of them, one of which featured the following line from Bannon: 'I do appreciate any piece that mentions Evola,' referring to Yiannopoulos's notorious article, "An Establishment Conservative's Guide to the Alt-Right." Joseph Bernstein, "Here's how Breitbart and Milo Smuggled White Nationalism into the Mainstream." *Buzzfeed.com*, October 5, 2017. https://www.buzzfeednews.com/article/josephbernstein/heres-how-breitbart-and-milo-smuggled-white-nationalism#.savKN91xP These e-mails made available by Buzzfeed are as close as one is ever likely to get to glimpsing the real Bannon. Two helpful and intelligent surveys of the alt-right devote a fair bit of discussion to Bannon's oblique relation to this disturbing ideology: see George Hawley, *Making Sense of the Alt-Right* (New York: Columbia University Press, 2017), Chapter 5; and Thomas J. Main, *The Rise of the Alt-Right* (Washington: Brookings Institution Press, 2018), Chapter 9. For a collection of reactions to Bannon from alt-right figures themselves, see pp. 212–222 of Main's book. Especially telling are assessments of Bannon by two of the alt-right figures contacted by Main, namely Hunter Wallace and Greg Johnson. Wallace states that Breitbart under Bannon's direction 'popularized a diluted version of our beliefs. ... [Bannon] is far closer to us in spirit than to the "conservatives" ... Steve Bannon isn't one of us, but he isn't an enemy either. He has gone out of his way to stick up for the Deplorables. If politics is about friend vs. enemy, then we definitely count Steve Bannon as a friend. ... His enemies are our enemies' (Main, p. 213). Johnson's view is similar: 'Bannon is a civic nationalist. We're racial nationalists. There are overlaps but disagreements on fundamental values. But Bannon is not stiffing us because his life is an experiment. He's

Julius Evola (1898–1974) was a ferocious racist and anti-egalitarian who characterized his politics as being to the *right* of European fascism and who helped inspire far-right terrorism in Italy; Alexander Dugin (born 1962) is a Russian fascist who despises liberal democracy and believes in Russian imperial expansion far beyond anything aspired to by Putin.[10] Clearly, Spencer refers to Bannon's awareness of Evola and Dugin because he sees it as a further indication that Bannon is with "us." (Spencer is an English-language publisher of Dugin.) Spencer, in the podcast, goes on to say that the final video ad of the Trump campaign (surely inspired by Bannon) "reminded me quite a bit" of videos produced by N.P.I. (National Policy Institute, Spencer's far-right, white-nationalist outfit). A recent book on Bannon and his ideological sources and influences by Benjamin Teitelbaum contains stunning new revelations about Bannon, including the incredible bombshell that Bannon had an eight-hour secret rendezvous with Dugin in Rome in the fall of 2018.[11] The evident purpose

---

living as if the future he is fighting for has already arrived: a world where the Left has no power. ... Bannon wants to win and actually roll back the Left. That makes him a radical and revolutionary conservative' (Main, pp. 212–213). To these one may add John Morgan's assessment of Bannon as reported in the following Hope Not Hate blogpost: https://hopenothate.com/2018/03/23/hindu-mysticism-alt-right/ See also the Southern Poverty Law Center's report on how Bannon relates to the far right: https://www.splcenter.org/hatewatch/2017/03/01/breitbart-under-bannon-how-breitbart-became-favorite-news-source-neo-nazis-and-white.

10 For a fuller discussion, see my essay, "Russia's Ecumenical Jihadist," *Inroads*, no. 37 (Summer/Fall 2015): 92–100. Bannon's interest in or sympathy for Dugin is apparently reciprocated. Harrison Fluss and Landon Frim, in an essay entitled "Behemoth and Leviathan: The Fascist Bestiary of the Alt-Right," draw attention to a 2017 interview with Dugin in which Dugin, despite having soured on Trump, "praised [Bannon] as Washington's 'last hope'": https://www.academia.edu/35542784/Behemoth_and_Leviathan_The_Fascist_Bestiary_of_the_Alt-Right_Salvage_2017_.

11 Benjamin R. Teitelbaum, *War for Eternity: Inside Bannon's Far-Right Circle of Global Power Brokers* (New York: Dey Street, 2020). For a commentary on the book, see my review essay: "Life among the far-right Rasputins," *Inroads*, Issue No. 48, pp. 137–143. Teitelbaum's book highlights not only Bannon's relationship to Dugin but also his relationship to Olavo de Carvalho, the Rasputin of Jair Bolsonaro's right-populist regime in Brazil. Relevant to this, one can find on the Internet a photo posted on Facebook by Carvalho: https://www.facebook.com/carvalho.olavo/photos/visitante-ilustre-steve-bannon-na-minha-casa-ontem-foto-josias-te%C3%B3filo/1211297179022354/ Bannon is paying a visit to Carvalho (Carvalho calls him "a distinguished visitor"), and both men appear in high spirits. Bannon stands over Carvalho, holding up a copy of a publication with pictures of Carvalho and Dugin on the cover. The book is entitled *The USA and The New World Order: A Debate between Olavo de Carvalho and Aleksandr Dugin* (published by the Inter-American Institute for Philosophy, Government, and Social Thought, a think-tank run by Carvalho). The New World Order is a far-right conspiracy theory.

of the rendezvous from Bannon's side was to convince Dugin that China, not the United States, is the real enemy. Dugin hates the U.S. with every fiber of his being. Bannon claims to be an American patriot. The question is unavoidable: What kind of patriot of the American republic would even think of doing business with a fascist like Dugin, let alone expressing admiration for Dugin's writings, as Bannon does very explicitly in his interviews with Teitelbaum?[12]

Putting it all together, Bannon's worldview comes across as an incoherent hodge-podge of incompatible ideologies whose common thread is hatred of (liberal) elites. One can speculate that Trump was drawn to Bannon because Bannon shared Trump's sense of the political opportunities ripe to be exploited of European-style right-wing populism; whatever is driving the rise of populism in Europe can drive populism in America as well.[13] Hence, Bannon in conversations reported by Teitelbaum, depicts the United States as a land of "roots, spirit, destiny," indeed of *völkisch* "blood and soil" – the very opposite of what its founders intended the American civic community to be.[14] Beyond this strategic instinct or insight, neither Bannon nor Trump seems to have any particularly coherent idea of what they believe in, apart from the notion of a conspiracy on the part of a sinister liberal-cosmopolitan elite ("the party of Davos") against common folk in Kansas and Colorado. As the statement of a political philosophy, one has to say that it is pretty shallow and poorly thought-through. How do Bannon's professed Christian beliefs comport with his commitment to hard-nosed capitalism (the harder-nosed the better)? How does his vehement anti-statism mesh with his forbearance for authoritarian Putinite nationalism? Why are Bannon and Trump themselves exempt from membership in the despised elite? It suggests to me that people whose whole life revolves around the making of money and the consolidating of power (including media power) – and this is true of Bannon no less than Trump – haven't had the time

---

12   Teitelbaum, *War for Eternity*, 96.
13   Cf. Jason Jorjani, as quoted in the following article in *The Atlantic*: '[what] we will see hopefully in the next few years, maybe sooner than that, [is] a total integration of the European New Right and the North American alt-right.' Rosie Gray, "A 'One-Stop Shop' for the Alt-Right." *The Atlantic*, January 12, 2017. https://www.theatlantic.com/politics/archive/2017/01/a-one-stop-shop-for-the-alt-right/512921/ Arguably, Bannon in the years following his exit from the Trump Administration pursued his own version of just that kind of agenda. The Bannonite project to remake America's civic identity in the image of European ethnic nationalism is also intimated in a comment he supposedly made to a French official in 2016: 'We are at the end of the Enlightenment. Have you read Charles Maurras?' See Marc Weitzmann, "Code Yellow," *The Globe and Mail*, March 16, 2019, p. 08. Here is the online version: https://www.theglobeandmail.com/opinion/article-france-already-has-a-problem-with-anti-semitism-america-must-not/.
14   Teitelbaum, *War for Eternity*, 158, 193.

to reflect on what their actual political principles are, or didn't think it was worth bothering about.[15] Of course, one wouldn't dispute that Bannon has very strong opinions, and that those opinions follow various patterns; what's less clear is whether those opinions (the nefariousness of ruling elites, the evil of the dominant liberal-secular culture, the threat posed to the West by "Islam," the need to shake up the political culture in a thoroughly radical way) gel into something that's particularly coherent, with intelligible or predictable policy implications. To be sure, there is a distinctive Bannonite ideology, but it is, to say the least, a highly tension-ridden ideology, and all the various contradictions between thought and practice in Bannon's career (Harvard Business School, Goldman Sachs, Hollywood, and membership in the ruling elite, at least during his days as part of the Trump regime) express those very tensions.

It should not be assumed that speech and deeds, logos and praxis, will be in harmony. Bannon and Trump are ruthless operators, playing the political game in a hyper-Machiavellian fashion. (Bannon, in *American Dharma*, referred to both himself and Trump as "killers.") Words are not used primarily to express political intentions or to articulate a sincerely held political vision. To a much greater extent, they serve to keep people guessing, or to provide active smokescreens for their real designs, or to manipulate people by pushing the right buttons (or maybe it's just a question of getting a "buzz" from knowing that one has the power to stir up millions of people with one's words and images).[16]

---

15 Another contradiction in Bannon's thinking presents itself quite starkly in *American Dharma*. Bannon clearly reveres the ethos of a military sense of duty and adores the existential drama of war. Yet he also inherits the foreign-policy isolationism that runs through the American far right from the original America First people through the paleoconservatives to the contemporary alt-right. How can one yearn for civilizational conflict with Islam and China (as appears to be the case with Bannon) if actual wars are illegitimate impositions on the working class by evil liberal elites? One possible way of squaring this circle is suggested by Bannon's response to Trump's (conspicuously Bannonite) Syria and Afghanistan troop withdrawals, as reported in *The New York Times International Edition*, Dec. 29–30, 2018, p. 4: 'Mr. Trump, [Bannon] said, wanted to end these military campaigns [in Syria and Afghanistan] so he could focus on the economic and geopolitical contest with China, which he views as America's biggest foreign threat. "This is not about a return to isolationism," Mr. Bannon said. "It's the pivot away from the humanitarian expeditionary mentality of the internationalists."' Unlike Trump, Bannon can articulate a reason for the policy; but it still doesn't add up. How will withdrawing 2,000 Special Ops from Syria contribute to an eventual geopolitical showdown with China? Ultimately, it's hard to engage with Bannon's political postures because one can never really take what he says at face value.

16 In the article in the following link, it's reported that the Bannon-led Breitbart News had 45 million readers. Scott Shane, "Combative, Populist Steve Bannon found his man in Donald Trump." *New York Times*, November 27, 2016. http://www.nytimes.com/2016/11/27/us/politics/steve-bannon-white-house.html That's a lot of power! Especially so when

If Bannon insists that he's not "alt-right,"[17] yet also says that he was content to turn Breitbart into "the platform of the alt-right," then that in itself is a clear acknowledgement that purposes were being served other than the expression of actual political commitments (the pursuit of truth not being one of those purposes). Bannon the political agitator rails against what the bankers got away with during the crisis of 2008; yet the White House for which Bannon served as chief strategist supported a relaxation of post-2008 regulatory controls on Wall Street. The political activist Bannon casts "crony capitalists" as the root of all evil, yet the Trump cabinet put together when Bannon was chief strategist exhibited no lack of crony capitalists. On the contrary, they seemed to predominate. "Globalism" is supposedly the enemy, but that apparently didn't rule out appointing Goldman Sachs and ExxonMobil executives to positions of consummate power.

One can watch YouTube videos of Bannon bitterly condemning the scale of government debt, but of course the chosen blunt instrument of Bannonite populism severely accentuated the problem of ballooning debt with reckless tax cuts. Bannon famously told the *Wall Street Journal* that the onset of his whole commitment to populist politics flowed directly from the plunge in his father's AT&T stocks owing to the 2008 financial crisis.[18] But it would require twisted political reasoning to see the personnel or policies of the Trump Administration as a reasonable redress for Marty Bannon's anguish about his ravaged savings. Errol Morris, in *American Dharma*, basically put the same challenge to Bannon: namely, that Bannon's "populism" is really an utterly fake populism, since the actual reality of Trumpite policies is better designed for promoting the interests of the super-rich than for securing working-class interests. Bannon, someone who seems never lacking for words, was for once virtually silent. In his November 2, 2018, Munk Debate in Toronto with David Frum, Bannon again and again spoke of populism's championing of "the little

---

one considers that less than 63 million votes sufficed for Trump to win the presidency. For more detailed information on the scope of Breitbart's readership relative to other political publications, see Main, *The Rise of the Alt-Right*, Chapter 2. On p. 211, Main refers to Breitbart's 'monthly average of 64 million visits between September 2016 and February 2018.'

17 For Bannon's denial that he is a white nationalist, see the interview in the following link as well as the one cited in note 5: Kimberely A. Strassel, "Steve Bannon on Politics as War." *Wall Street Journal*, November 18, 2016. http://www.wsj.com/articles/steve-bannon-on-politics-as-war-1479513161.

18 Michael C. Bender, "Steve Bannon and the Making of an Economic Nationalist," *Wall Street Journal*, March 14, 2017. https://www.wsj.com/articles/steve-bannon-and-the-making-of-an-economic-nationalist-1489516113#.

guy." But how exactly does the little guy benefit from the "deconstruction of the administrative state" that Bannon so zealously desires? From the evisceration of affordable health care? From climate-change denialism? From a Trump cabinet stacked with plutocrats? From tax cuts serving the interests of billionaires? In truth, the disparate balls being juggled in Bannon's juggling act – Tea-Party libertarianism, compassionate conservatism, Christian piety and moralism, European-style populist nationalism (not excluding its Putinophile aspects), clash-of-civilizations Islamophobia, with ominous "gestures" to the alt-right – are much too eclectic to be taken at face value. But again, the unstable hodgepodge character of the ideological components of Bannonism doesn't preclude its efficacy in securing uptake on the ideological plane.

Trust in Bannon's populist credentials was obviously not helped by his arrest on August 20th, 2020 (aboard a billionaire's yacht) for wire fraud and money laundering – basically, swindling money out of people who subscribe to his ideology. These charges were later nullified when Bannon was granted a pardon by Trump in the waning hours of his presidency. Nevertheless, an interview with Joshua Green shortly after Bannon's arrest highlights the reasons for skepticism about whether Bannon is as committed to the interests of the little guy as he professes.

> How sincerely he held [his commitment to economic populism] was always an open question. I think he is sincere in his anti-immigration, nativist fervor, but in all the time I spent talking to him, publicly and privately, his passion was on the immigration front. It wasn't on pushing populist economics that would filter more income down to working people. When he was in the White House, he did make a push, briefly, with Mark Meadows, to try and raise marginal tax rates for people making more than five million dollars per year, and I think this push maybe lasted for a couple of days, and then everybody in the White House leaked on him and he got embarrassed. And that was the sum total of his efforts on economic populism. If you just look at where the focus of his energy has been in the last four or five years, it is all immigration. ... Pushing economic populist policies has been nowhere on his agenda for years and years.[19]

---

19 Isaac Chotiner, "The 'Narcissism and Ego' That Led to Steve Bannon's Arrest," *The New Yorker*, Aug. 20, 2020. https://www.newyorker.com/news/q-and-a/the-narcissism-and-ego-that-led-to-steve-bannons-arrest.

There's another "text" that Bannon is widely thought to have had a significant hand in drafting. I refer to Trump's Inaugural Address, which can be viewed as tacitly insinuating alt-right themes. The speech's slogan of "America First" is fairly disturbing. Trump himself may have been too historically clueless to know or care about the slogan's unpleasant lineage, but Bannon was surely fully aware of its lineage. It's as if Bannon, as co-author of the speech (Stephen Miller is believed to be the other co-author), was going out of his way to tell people that Philip Roth's *The Plot Against America* had finally, eighty years later, come true. Also, the phrase in the speech that made the biggest impression – the phrase "American carnage" – could easily be interpreted as reflecting the alt-right view of liberal-democratic America as beyond redemption. It was clearly the Bannonite aspects of the Trump Inaugural that elicited the discerning commentary on the speech reportedly offered by George W. Bush: "That was some weird shit." Samuel Francis, a "paleoconservative" who along with Paul Gottfried laid the groundwork for what became the alt-right, apparently advised Patrick Buchanan, at the time he commenced his 1992 campaign for the presidency, to identify himself as "a nationalist, an America Firster."[20] This "America First" branding, which informed the three Buchanan presidential campaigns (in 1992, 1996, and 2000), was revivified by Trump in 2016 and was officially inscribed in the 2017 Inaugural Address. That is: Trump quite clearly presented himself as the anointed successor to the paleoconservative movement whose standard-bearer was Buchanan. The Bannon/Miller speech announces that the overthrow of the established political order (liberal *and* conservative) yearned for by the paleoconservatives had been affected by the election of Trump. This is what Bannon memorably referred to as 'the birth of a new political order.'

At the start of this chapter, I quoted an Errol Morris interview concerning the lack of coherence in Bannon's worldview. Morris also did an interview with the *Boston Review*, which offers further help in getting a handle on what drives Bannon. The interviewer points out that 'Bannon contradicts himself often and sometimes just seems to be bullshitting,' to which Morris responds:

> I'm often asked whether Bannon is a true believer or an opportunist: does he believe in all of this stuff? I don't have a definitive answer; I can't give you a pie chart. But I think there are definitely elements of both. He's

---

20   Main, *The Rise of the Alt-Right*, p. 83. Main offers a quote from a 1996 article by Francis in which Francis complains that Buchanan never advanced the "Middle American Revolution" with the radicalism that Francis desired. Chapter 3 of Main's book is particularly helpful because the more one educates oneself about the paleoconservative roots of the alt-right, the more one begins to discern significant ways in which those ideological precursors anticipated what became Trumpism and Bannonism.

a snake oil salesman and he is a true believer. You can't be an effective salesman unless you believe in the product you're selling.[21]

The Vatican correspondent for Breitbart News, Thomas Williams, gave his then-boss, Bannon, the following excellent advice: 'If you are going to tear down, you better know what you are building.' Yet Williams knew that Bannon was incapable of taking that advice: 'I think he prefers tearing down to building up, honestly.'[22] Bannon's overriding purpose is not to achieve anything positive but rather to throw a brick through the window of the political establishment. Trump is one such brick. Nigel Farage is another. Victor Orbán is another. Again, Morris is quite effective at capturing the nub of the matter. Bannon "would say to me, 'I think there's a revolution coming unless we do X, Y, and Z. And my hope is that the revolution won't come.'" But it's not at all clear when you talk to him at other times that he's working against that revolution and not for it. It's him saying "P and not-P."'[23] Bannon is a man who transparently yearns for cataclysm while pretending that he is helping to fend off the coming catastrophe.

Make no mistake, Bannon's identification with the working class, even if one makes the generous assumption that it is sincere, does nothing to lessen the centrality of xenophobia and racism to his ideological project.[24] We don't

---

21 Deborah Chasman, Errol Morris, "Errol Morris on Steve Bannon's Dangerous 'Dharma.'" *Boston Review*, August 24, 2018. http://bostonreview.net/politics/errol-morris-interview-american-dharma.

22 As regards the possibility that Bannon is at bottom an opportunist, there's an interesting line about Alexander Dugin in Charles Clover's important book on Duginite ideology that may apply to Bannon as well. Referring to Dugin and a fascist comrade of his, Gaidar Dzhemal, Clover quotes Igor Dudinsky, another member of their circle, as follows: 'Those two, they wanted power. They were looking for any sort of elevator to the top, and they found it in fascism.' Charles Clover, *Black Wind, White Snow: The Rise of Russia's New Nationalism* (New Haven: Yale University Press, 2016), 162. Cf. Ben Shapiro as quoted by Thomas Main: 'I think Steve's a very, very power-hungry dude who's willing to use anybody and anything in order to get ahead' (*The Rise of the Alt-Right*, p. 215).

    Jason Horowitz, "Breitbart's Man in Rome: A Gentle Voice in a Strident Chorus." *The New York Times*, January 10, 2017. https://www.nytimes.com/2017/01/10/world/europe/breitbarts-man-in-rome-a-gentle-voice-in-a-strident-chorus.html.

23 See note 21. This formulation by Morris illustrates what I flagged in note 20, namely Bannon as the present-day version of paleo-conservative revolutionism (viz., the view of the status quo of contemporary liberal democracy as irredeemable, and the willingness to see it all burn to the ground rather than continue as it currently exists within the liberal dispensation).

24 Consider this telling commentary by Michelle Goldberg: 'Shaggy, pretentious and endlessly cynical, Bannon presented himself as a man with a limbic connection to Trump's base. But few people had more disdain for the members of the right-wing grass

lack for opportunities to glimpse Bannon in his true colors. One such occasion was a radio interview with Bannon in the U.K. when he was challenged about his support for the anti-Muslim extremist, Tommy Robinson (a.k.a. Stephen Yaxley-Lennon). When the interview was over, he directed the following arresting remarks at his interlocutor: 'Fuck you. Don't you fucking say you're calling me out. You fucking liberal elite. Tommy Robinson is the backbone of this country.'[25] Also relevant here is something to which Errol Morris, in his interview with the *Boston Review*, rightly draws attention, namely Bannon's dismissal of Emmanuel Macron as "a little Rothschild banker," as if Macron were a puppet of Jewish "globalists."[26] Last but not least: Bannon famously boasted about turning Breitbart into "the platform of the alt-right." Why would any sane and well-meaning person want to turn *anything* into a platform for the alt-right?

In fact, there is something even more damning: Charlottesville. On September 7, 2018, Barack Obama gave a speech in Illinois in which he lambasted Trump for his appallingly inadequate response to the ugly "Unite the Right" event in August 2017: "How hard can that be, saying that Nazis are bad?"

---

roots – whom Bannon sometimes referred to as "hobbits." In "The Brink," a 2019 documentary about Bannon, there's a scene in which he speaks to supporters in a modest living room stuffed with furniture and bedecked with crosses. As his small audience sits rapt, he lauds the room's similarity to one in his grandmother's house and pays homage to the "working-class, middle-class" people who make up nationalist movements everywhere. Then he and a young man traveling with him walk out and step into their chauffeured car. "You couldn't pay me a million dollars a year to live in that house," sneers Bannon's associate. They head to a private airport. Bannon starts to make a crack about the luxurious locale. "This is the populist ..." Then he thinks better of it and shoves some popcorn into his mouth'; Michelle Goldberg, "Trumpism's a Racket. Steve Bannon Knew It," *New York Times*, Aug. 20, 2020, p. SR 9. Benjamin Teitelbaum (*War for Eternity*, p. 188) rightly calls Bannon "a limousine populist," a characterization very much vindicated by his indictment for defrauding the credulous so that he and his friends could spend their time on luxury yachts like the one on which Bannon was arrested. As goes without saying, the same thing is true of Donald Trump. In the famous words of Howard Stern: 'The people Trump despises most love him the most.'

25 Sarah Marsh, "Steve Bannon calls for Tommy Robinson to be Released from Prison." *The Guardian*, July 15, 2018. https://www.theguardian.com/us-news/2018/jul/15/steve-bannon-tommy-robinson-released-from-prison-trump-strategist-lbc-radio-interview.

26 See note 21. On September 9th, 2018, I attended a Q&A with Morris at the North American premiere of *American Dharma* during which Morris quoted a conversation with Noah Feldman in which Feldman said that Bannon's line about Macron was not a "dog whistle" but a "whistle whistle." Cf. Franz Neumann's striking dictum: 'Whenever the outcry against the sovereignty of banking capital is injected into a popular movement, it is the surest sign that fascism is on its way' (*Behemoth* [New York: Oxford University Press, 1942], p. 322).

These comments came shortly after advance excerpts from Bob Woodward's book *Fear* revealed that Trump regarded the speech in which he *did* (briefly) concede that Nazis are bad as 'the biggest fucking mistake I've made.' No one doubts that Bannon (who was then still in the White House) was a big, and probably the decisive, influence on Trump's outrageous stance towards Charlottesville.

Michael Sandel, in common with many others, has tried to trace populism back to the "legitimate grievances" that lead people to fall prey to the Trumpist temptation:

> Before they can hope to win back public support, progressive parties must rethink their mission and purpose. To do so, they should learn from the populist protest that has displaced them – not by replicating its xenophobia and strident nationalism, but by taking seriously the legitimate grievances with which these ugly sentiments are entangled. Such rethinking should begin with the recognition that these grievances are not only economic but also moral and cultural; they are not only about wages and jobs but also about social esteem. … Liberal neutrality flattens questions of meaning, identity, and purpose into questions of fairness. It therefore misses the anger and resentment that animate the populist revolt; it lacks the moral and rhetorical and sympathetic resources to understand the cultural estrangement, even humiliation, that many working class and middle class voters feel; and it ignores the meritocratic hubris of elites.[27]

While I'm fully sympathetic to the aspiration to articulate a new vision of social democracy, or socialism, or whatever one wishes to call it, capable of winning back the support of the white working class, Sandel's judgment strikes me as altogether too generous. People who vote for someone who they know to be racist are complicit in racism. There's no way around that. A presidential campaign that was kick-started by deliberate and self-conscious appeals to racism says something no less damning about its own supporters than Hillary Clinton's line about "deplorables." Donald Trump knew potential Trump voters to be deplorables when he began his quest for the presidency by putting himself at the leadership of birtherism.[28] Equally, Bannon knew his target audience to be

---

27 Michael J. Sandel, "Populism, Trump, and the Future of Democracy." *OpenDemocracy*, May 9, 2018. https://www.opendemocracy.net/michael-j-sandel/populism-trump-and-future-of-democracy.

28 To what extent has contemporary right-populism in America been fueled by a racist backlash against the experience of having had a black president for eight years? Without

deplorables when he built Breitbart around the project to mobilize xenophobia and racism.²⁹ There is nothing innocent about any of this, no matter how many times and no matter how insistently Bannon (or Trump for that matter) professes his non-racism. Sandel says that "disentangling the intolerant aspects of the populist protest from its legitimate grievances is no easy matter." I would say that it's well-nigh impossible. That's because Sandel abstracts from the ethnic/racial dimension of the aggrieved sense of humiliation that he acknowledges: namely, the fear of a shift in the demographic balance within contemporary America, and the recoil back to a defensive white identity in reaction to the perception of being under siege by immigrants and ascendant minorities. If that weren't the case, it's hard to see how Trump's demagogic rhetoric acquired the purchase that it had and continues to have.

It would be easy to dismiss Bannonism as the flaky concoction of someone with an overweening desire to be in the limelight who happens to have a high IQ and a voracious appetite for books. He's also an instinctive bomb-thrower bent on stirring up a maximum degree of tumult and conflict, seemingly just for the sake of causing tumult and conflict, and he's come on the scene at a particularly dangerous moment for liberal democracies built on cooperation and generosity. Could someone as smart and as widely read as Bannon really believe that Trump's reality-TV brand of politics is a way of doing politics worthy of support and admiration? If the answer to this question is no, which I think it's obvious that it is, then there's an essential dishonesty at the very heart of Bannon's project. Bannon clearly knows that Trump is a politically ill-equipped clown, but this knowledge (the impolitic communication of which contributed to his losing his job in the White House) doesn't deter him from celebrating Trump as the avatar of "a new political order."

---

question, Donald Trump was betting on such a phenomenon when he heartily embraced birtherism back in 2011 to begin pursuing his presidential ambitions. And we know that the bet paid off. Henry Louis Gates put the point well when he told Stephen Colbert: 'I think that having a beautiful, brilliant Black family in the White House for eight years absolutely drove a lot of people crazy.'

29   Bannon never hesitates to refer to the Trump base as "the deplorables," as if Clinton's characterization of Trump-supporting racists is a perfectly appropriate, and even welcome, way of characterizing these voters. As Gadi Taub rightly notes in a profile in *Haaretz*, Bannon sees the term as "a rhetorical gift" to be warmly adopted 'in the same way that black rappers appropriated the N word': Gadi Taub, "Steve Bannon tells Haaretz why the Russians aren't Bad Guys and the Why he can't be an Anti-Semite." *Haaretz*, July 30, 2018. https://www.haaretz.com/world-news/.premium.MAGAZINE-steve-bannon-tells-haaretz-why-he-can-t-be-anti-semitic-1.6316437 The quote from Hunter Wallace in note 9 proves that white nationalists also happily embrace the term.

Has the Bannon movement fallen flat? Consider an interesting exchange in an interview Bannon gave to the *Sunday Times Magazine*.[30]

> It's tempting to dismiss Bannon as a braggart who uses one narrow electoral victory to justify a lifetime of xenophobic bleating. After all, this "carnivore" operative was edged out of the White House by the spoilt lightweights Jared and Ivanka. "Did I lose out to them?" he bristles. "Let's google what they are doing. Do we have every trade deal in play? Are we out of the Iran deal? Are we in a geostrategic fight with China? Are we working on immigration at the southern border? Are we out of the Paris [climate] agreement? Do we have a travel ban? I don't know any policy that the president has not full-on hammered down that is not a policy of the populist nationalist movement. Tell me where I'm losing."

Bannon said basically the same thing in another interview with Gabriel Sherman in *Vanity Fair*:

> Bannon was giddy. ... 'Populist nationalism is on the move everywhere in the world,' Bannon boasted. Events seemed to be breaking his way in Washington too. 'It's like my white board's there and Trump is checking shit off,' Bannon said. He marveled at a border crackdown and decision to launch a global trade war. 'Trump is on the full MAGA agenda,' he said.[31]

Is this all just bluster? Bluster, after all, is Bannon's middle name. It's far too soon to console ourselves with such a comforting judgment. Another way of re-stating the argument that Bannon is making in these interviews is to say that Trump became far more Bannonite after Bannon was ejected from the Trump circle than he was when Bannon was in the White House, and that observation would seem to be correct. Many thought that Bannon's career as a right-populist agitator would be over when the retired U.S. Marine Corps general John Kelly managed to evict him from the White House, when Trump soured on him after his indiscreet remarks about Don Jr. and the July 2016 meeting with the Russians was published by Michael Wolff, and finally and perhaps

---

30   Josh Glancy, "The Magazine Interview: The Former White House Chief Strategist Steve Bannon on Nigel Farage, populism in Europe and Trump's visit to London." *The Sunday Times*, July 8, 2018. https://www.thetimes.co.uk/article/the-magazine-interview-the-former-white-house-chief-strategist-steve-bannon-on-nigel-farage-populism-in-europe-and-trumps-visit-to-london-h6vbzc5g3.

31   Gabriel Sherman, "All the King's Rivals," *Vanity Fair*, September 2018, pp. 159–160.

most decisively when the Mercers stopped funding and employing him. So far, those predictions of Bannon's demise have all been premature. He seems to have nine lives.

If Bannon is right that Trump, Orbán, Bolsonaro, Salvini, and Farage herald the birth of a new political order (which cannot be ruled out), what characterizes this new political order? Its outlines have been well sketched by Roger Cohen in a *New York Times* op-ed:

> The [Bannonite] new right has learned from the past. It does not disappear people. It does not do mass militarization. It's subtler. It scapegoats migrants, instills fear, glorifies an illusory past (what the Polish sociologist Zygmunt Bauman called 'retrotopia'), exalts machismo, mocks do-gooder liberalism and turns the angry drumbeat of social media into a minute-by-minute mass rally.

Bannon, in an observation made to Cohen, made clear that he is perfectly comfortable with a new anti-liberal ethos that privileges rabble-rousing over deliberation: 'This is not an era of persuasion. It's an era of mobilization. People now move in tribes. Persuasion is highly overrated.'[32]

Someone might ask: why populism now? The short answer is that populism is a reaction to globalization. I would define globalization as a ramped-up version of capitalism where national borders come to mean virtually nothing, with the result that the typical anxieties associated with a capitalist way of life become even more dire. As Bannon's dreaded liberal elites probably should have foreseen, this could not have failed to produce political consequences. Again, the best one-paragraph encapsulation of the fundamental dynamic is offered by Roger Cohen in another *New York Times* op-ed, this one devoted to the topic of Brexit:

> Liberalism worked well for a while. It was good at freeing people from bigotry, sexism, racism, nationalism and prejudice. It was less good at providing people with meaning to their lives, beyond hedonism and materialism. In 2008, with the financial crisis, the wheels came off. Those responsible walked away. A lot of people felt empty, and were drowning

---

32   Roger Cohen, "Steve Bannon Is a Fan of Italy's Donald Trump," *New York Times*, May 19, 2019, p. SR 4. What's truly scary for anyone committed to the idea of a healthy democracy is that Bannon's judgment about the current state of things may be entirely accurate.

in debt. What had the elite ever done for them? Bigotry and nationalism made a storming comeback.[33]

But leaving aside its function as an instrumentality for expressing widespread social frustration, what can the new ideology actually do to supply meaning or the possibility of a better life? The late John McCain hit the target when he characterized Bannonism as a 'half-baked, spurious nationalism cooked up by people who would rather find scapegoats than solve problems.'[34]

Bibliography

Associated Press. "Bannon Says Russia Probe Set Back Efforts to Work with Moscow." *Bloomberg*, March 26, 2019.

Beiner, Ronald. "Russia's Ecumenical Jihadist." *Inroads* no. 37 (Summer/Fall, 2015): 92–100.

Bender, Michael C. "Steve Bannon and the Making of an Economic Nationalist." *Wall Street Journal*, March 14, 2017. https://www.wsj.com/articles/steve-bannon-and-the-making-of-an-economic-nationalist-1489516113#.

Bernstein, Joseph. "Here's How Breitbart and Milo Smuggled White Nationalism into The Mainstream," *Buzzfeed News*, October 5, 2017. https://www.buzzfeednews.com/article/josephbernstein/heres-how-breitbart-and-milo-smuggled-white-nationalism#.savKN91xP.

Bruni, Frank. "The Devil in Steve Bannon." *New York Times*, August 26, 2018: SR 3.

Chasman, Deborah, and Errol Morris. "Errol Morris on Steve Bannon's Dangerous 'Dharma.'" *Boston Review*, August 24, 2018. https://www.bostonreview.net/articles/errol-morris-interview-american-dharma/.

Chotiner, Isaac. "The 'Narcissism and Ego' That Led to Steve Bannon's Arrest," *The New Yorker*, Aug. 20, 2020. https://www.newyorker.com/news/q-and-a/the-narcissism-and-ego-that-led-to-steve-bannons-arrest.

Clover, Charles. *Black Wind, White Snow: The Rise of Russia's New Nationalism.* New Haven: Yale University Press, 2016.

Cohen, Roger. "The Official British Policy? Mayhem." *New York Times*, March 3, 2019: SR 5.

---

33   Roger Cohen, "The Official British Policy? Mayhem," *New York Times*, March 3, 2019, p. SR 5.
34   John McCain, "Speech at the Liberty Medal Award Ceremony," *TIME*, October 16, 2017. http://time.com/4985185/john-mccain-liberty-medal-speech/.

Cohen, Roger. "Steve Bannon Is a Fan of Italy's Donald Trump." *New York Times*, May 19, 2019: SR 4.

Feder, J. Lester. "This Is How Steve Bannon Sees the Entire World." *Buzzfeed*, November 16, 2016. https://www.buzzfeednews.com/article/lesterfeder/this-is-how-steve-bannon-sees-the-entire-world.

Freedman, Samuel G. "'Church Militant' Theology Is Put to New, and Politicized, Use." *New York Times*, December 30, 2016.

Glancy, Josh. "The Magazine Interview: The Former White House Chief Strategist Steve Bannon on Nigel Farage, populism in Europe and Trump's visit to London." *The Sunday Times*, July 8, 2018. https://www.thetimes.co.uk/article/the-magazine-interview-the-former-white-house-chief-strategist-steve-bannon-on-nigel-farage-populism-in-europe-and-trumps-visit-to-london-h6vbzc5g3.

Goldberg, Michelle. "Trumpism's a Racket. Steve Bannon Knew It," *New York Times*, Aug. 20, 2020, p. SR 9. https://www.nytimes.com/2020/08/20/opinion/sunday/trump-steve-bannon-fraud.html.

Gray, Rosie. "A 'One-Stop Shop' for the Alt-Right." *Atlantic*, January 12, 2017. https://www.theatlantic.com/politics/archive/2017/01/a-one-stop-shop-for-the-alt-right/512921/.

Hankes, Keegan. "Breitbart Under Bannon: How Breitbart Became a Favorite News Source for Neo-Nazis and White Nationalists." *Southern Poverty Law Center*, March 1, 2017. https://www.splcenter.org/hatewatch/2017/03/01/breitbart-under-bannon-how-breitbart-became-favorite-news-source-neo-nazis-and-white.

Hawley, George. *Making Sense of the Alt-Right*. New York: Columbia University Press, 2017.

Horowitz, Jason. "Breitbart's Man in Rome: A Gentle Voice in a Strident Chorus." *New York Times*, January 10, 2017. https://www.nytimes.com/2017/01/10/world/europe/breitbarts-man-in-rome-a-gentle-voice-in-a-strident-chorus.html.

Horowitz, Jason. "The 'It' '80s Party Girl Is Now a Defender of the Catholic Faith." *New York Times*, December 7, 2018.

Hosenball, Mark. "Steve Bannon Drafting Curriculum for Right-Wing Catholic Institute in Italy." *Reuters*, September 14, 2018. https://www.reuters.com/article/us-eu-politics-bannon-catholics/steve-bannon-drafting-curriculum-for-right-wing-catholic-institute-in-italy-idUSKCN1LU176/.

Landler, Mark. "Trump Unites Left and Right Against Troop Plans, but Puts Off Debate on War Aims." *New York Times*, December 27, 2018.

Lui, John. "Read the Full Text of John McCain's Speech at the Liberty Medal Award Ceremony." *Time*, August 19, 2019.

Main, Thomas J. *The Rise of the Alt-Right*. Washington, DC: Brookings Institution Press.

Mammone, Andrea. 2019. "Europe's Far Right Seems Determined to Hijack Christianity in Its Bid for Power." *The Independent*, January 13, 2018.

Marsh, Sarah. "Steve Bannon calls for Tommy Robinson to Be Released from Prison." *The Guardian*, July 15, 2018. https://www.theguardian.com/us-news/2018/jul/15/steve-bannon-tommy-robinson-released-from-prison-trump-strategist-lbc-radio-interview#:~:text=Steve%20Bannon%2C%20the%20former%20adviser,radio%27s%20political%20editor%2C%20Theo%20Usherwood.

McCain, John. "Speech at the Liberty Medal Award Ceremony," *TIME*, October 16, 2017. http://time.com/4985185/john-mccain-liberty-medal-speech/.

Neumann, Franz. *Behemoth*. New York: Oxford University Press, 1942.

Sandel, Michael J. "Populism, Trump, and the Future of Democracy." *OpenDemocracy*, May 9, 2018. https://www.opendemocracy.net/en/populism-trump-and-future-of-democracy/.

Shane, Scott. "Combative, Populist Steve Bannon Found His Man in Donald Trump." *New York Times*, November 27, 2016. http://www.nytimes.com/2016/11/27/us/politics/steve-bannon-white-house.html.

Sherman, Gabriel. "All the King's Rivals." *Vanity Fair*, September, 2018: 159–160.

Strassel, Kimberley. "Steve Bannon on Politics as War." *Wall Street Journal*, November 18, 2016. https://www.wsj.com/articles/steve-bannon-on-politics-as-war-1479513161.

Taub, Gadi. "Steve Bannon Tells *Haaretz* Why the Russians Aren't the Bad Guys and Why He Can't Be an anti-Semite." *Haaretz*, July 30, 2018. https://www.haaretz.com/world-news/2018-07-30/ty-article-magazine/.premium/steve-bannon-tells-haaretz-why-he-cant-be-anti-semitic/0000017f-dc61-db22-a17f-fcf1dbf00000.

Teitelbaum, Benjamin R. *War for Eternity: Inside Bannon's Far-Right Circle of Global Power-Brokers*. New York: Dey Street, 2020.

Varagur, Krithika. "Why Bannon Is Meddling with Bosnia." *New York Review Daily*, September 5, 2018. https://www.nybooks.com/online/2018/09/05/why-bannon-is-meddling-with-bosnia/.

Weitzmann, Marc. "Code Yellow." *The Globe and Mail*, March 16, 2019: O8.

Wolff, Michael. "Ringside with Steve Bannon at Trump Tower as the President-Elect's Strategist Plots 'An Entirely New Political Movement' (Exclusive)." *Hollywood Reporter*, November 18, 2016. https://www.hollywoodreporter.com/news/general-news/steve-bannon-trump-tower-interview-trumps-strategist-plots-new-political-movement-948747/.

Woodward, Bob. *Fear: Trump in the White House*. New York: Simon & Schuster, 2018.

CHAPTER 3

The Populist Persona: a Jungian Approach to the Populism of Donald Trump

Dustin J. Byrd

On March 4th, 2023, while running to regain the presidency, Donald Trump spoke at a Conservative Political Action Committee (CPAC) meeting, wherein he articulated his essential campaign theme:

> In 2016 I declared: I am your voice. Today I add: I am your warrior; I am your justice; and for those who have been wronged and betrayed, I am your retribution … I will totally eliminate the deep state; I will fire the unelected bureaucrats and shadow forces who have weaponized our justice system … I will put the people back in charge of this country again, the people will be back in charge of our country.[1]

While this image of himself wasn't entirely new, it was a new variation on his 2016 populist theme: Make America Great Again (MAGA). In order to carry out his political promises, he would seek revenge not only on those who supposedly wronged his aggrieved devotees, but also seek revenge for their additional sins, i.e., the defeat of Trump in the 2020 election. This enhanced form of MAGA populism, known as "Ultra-MAGA," promised to be even more vicious to the enemies of Trump and his movement than it was during his first term as president (2017–2021). Nevertheless, just like the first iteration of MAGA populism, the second form was just as manufactured, phony, and devoid of substance. Trump, as he had been doing since he glided down his golden escalator in Trump Tower in 2015, was *performing;* he was no more a man-of-the-people in 2023 than he was when he began his first run for the presidency. Nevertheless, the self-declared "nationalist," "stable genius," and "voice of the forgotten," had to advance the image of himself as the people's tribunal against the society that wronged the "real Americans" to advance his own ambitions. In other words, he created a "persona" of himself as being the long-awaited

---

1 C-Span, "CPAC Conference," March 4, 2023. https://www.c-span.org/video/?c5060238/pres-trump-i-justicei-retribution.

savior of the American White working class to gain power in the multi-ethnic, multi-lingual, and secular democratic United States. Without such a populist persona, he risked being perceived as what he truly is: A highly insecure and frightened *puer aeternus* (eternal child), who is deathly afraid to be perceived as a "loser," a "fraud," a "nobody."[2] This "tough guy for the masses" persona thus camouflages Trump's psychological reality – the "True Self" he does not display to his devoted followers, lest they perceived him the same way that he perceives himself when not absorbed by his fictive persona.

With the aid of analytical psychology, particularly the work of Carl Gustav Jung and his notion of the "Persona," this chapter will deconstruct the "Populist Persona" that Trump has created since he began his political career. It will demonstrate that Trump's psychological realities are far different that the confident, bold, and uncompromising picture that he paints of himself. It will show that the Populist Persona has numerous functions: (1) to convince his would-be followers that he is the only person who can advance their interests in the state, i.e., be their avenging champion – their political messiah; (2) to advance his political career, which in itself is an attempt to advance his own self-interests – a means to escape his self-doubt, and (3) to conceal the reality of his own psychological turmoil and vulnerabilities, especially his intransient insecurities, his abiding self-doubt, and his diminished sense of self-worth.

1   What Is the Persona?

In ancient Rome, the "persona" was a theatrical mask worn by actors to portray a given character. Through the persona, the audience understood the individual and their role in the performance, whether they were the protagonist, villain, hero or heroine, or even anti-hero, etc. In this way, the mask had a dual function: it first exported messages about the nature of the character being performed, and second it simultaneously hid the true identity of the actor performing behind the mask. For good actors, when the mask was dawned, they transformed into their character; their true identity was temporarily displaced and/or suspended. This notion that the identity of an individual can

---

2   For a discussion of the "puer aeternus," See C.G. Jung, "The Psychology of the Child Archetype," in *The Architypes and the Collective Unconscious* (Vol. 9.1 of the *Collected Works of C.G. Jung*) (Princeton, NJ: Princeton University Press, 1969), 151–181. Also see Dustin J. Byrd, *The Dark Charisma of Donald Trump: Political Psychology and the MAGA Movement* (Kalamazoo, MI: Ekpyrosis Press, 2023), 111, 136, 191.

temporarily disappear behind a mask, whether that is a physical mask or through an alter-ego, was important for Jung's conception of the Self, as his own experiences with analysands demonstrated to him that many in society often regressed behind a strategic mask. In fact, he realized that such a mask was a social norm, not an individual anomaly. In Jung's essay, "The Relations between the Ego and the Unconscious," he states,

> The Persona is a complicated system of relations between individual consciousness and society, fittingly enough a kind of mask, designed on the one hand to make a definite impression upon others, and, on the other, to conceal the true nature of the individual.[3]

Here, Jung argues that the concealing nature of the Persona also serves a dual function. In the first instance, the True Self does not reveal itself to society, for it is not entirely at home within itself. In other words, there are aspects within everyone that they do not feel comfortable with exposing to society's gaze. Such things are often the individual's vulnerabilities, insecurities, emotional scars from previous traumas, neuroses, and aspects of themselves that they despise or are ashamed of. Such aspects must stay hidden behind the Persona as not to invite outside scrutiny, which would inevitably cause additional mental anguish. The Persona, in this sense, is a defense mechanism against social inquisition.

The second function is related to the first, but slightly different; the Persona is an attempt to form and/or manipulate others into believing that the person on display publicly is the same as the person in private – that the "mask" is in fact the "True Self," i.e., their "individuality," when in reality it is camouflage constructed from societal expectations and the individual's own "ideal self." Through the Persona, others come to "know" the perceived person as they are presented publicly and develop their own assessment of them. They come to know the person's temperament and personality, their values, their core principles, and their patterns of behavior, etc. As Jung states:

> When we analyze the persona we strip off the mask, and discover that what seemed to be individual is at bottom collective; Fundamentally the persona is nothing real: it is a compromise between the individual and society as to what a man should appear to be. He takes a name, earns a

---

3   C.G. Jung, "The Relations between the Ego and the Unconscious," in *Two Essays on Analytical Psychology* (Vol. 7 of the *Collected Works of C.G. Jung*) (Princeton, NJ: Princeton University Press, 1977), para. 305, pg. 192.

title, represents an office, he is this or that. In a certain sense all this is real, yet in relation to the essential individuality of the person concerned it is only a secondary reality, a product of compromise, in making which others often have a greater share than he. The persona is a semblance, a two-dimensional reality.[4]

Additionally, Jung writes:

> Every calling or profession has its own characteristic persona ... A certain kind of behavior is forced on them by the world, and professional people endeavor to come up to these expectations. Only, the danger is that they become identical with their personas – the professor with his text-book, the tenor with his voice. Then the damage is done; henceforth he lives exclusively against the background of his own biography ... One could say, with a little exaggeration, that the persona is that which in reality one is not, but which oneself as well as others think one is.[5]

Thus, in Jung's schema of the Self, the Persona lies between the Ego and society. By "collectivizing" its outward appearance, i.e., making congruent with social expectations, the Persona protects the delicate core of the Self from social scrutiny by influencing how members of society perceive the individual.[6] If the individual's Persona conforms to societal expectations, i.e., it falls within the range of socially acceptable behavior, their Persona achieves an *effective* camouflage of the Self. In this sense, we perform Personae (plural) because society demands that of us; effective Personae makes human relations operate more smoothly, and thus more efficiently, as it removes potential friction points between social actors, as patterns of behavior between Personae are pre-determined to integrate better than the fractious realities of the True Selves. When Personae are ineffective, others will perceive that there's

---

4 C.G. Jung, *Two Essays on Analytical Psychology* (Vol. 7 of the *Collected Works of C.G. Jung*) (Princeton, NJ: Princeton University Press, 1977), para. 246, pg. 158.
5 C.G. Jung, *Archetypes of the Collective Unconscious* (Vol 9.1 of the *Collected Works of C.G. Jung*) (Princeton, NJ: Princeton University Press, 1971) para. 221, pg. 122–123.
6 By "collectivizing," I refer to Jung's claim that the Persona is but a "mask of the collective psyche." Jung writes: 'It is only because the persona represents a more or less arbitrary and fortuitous segment of the collective psyche that we can make the mistake of regarding it *in toto* as something individual. It is, as its name implies, only a mask of the collective psyche, a mask that *feigns individuality,* making others and oneself believe that one is individual, whereas one is simply acting a role through which the collective psyche speaks.' C.G. Jung, *Two Essays on Analytical Psychology*, para. 245, pg. 157.

something "off" about an individual; they are uneasy with their environment, they are difficult to "get along with," they are ill-fit with their social role, and are unable to do what society has tasked them to do. The effective Personae deconflicts the tensions between individual and society; the ineffective Persona fails to adequately lubricate the tensions and demands between the individual and society's expectation associated with the role the individual is performing.

In addition to Jung's two primary functions of the Persona, Jung perceived that there was a third aspect that was also integral: the mitigation of the inner-confrontation of the Self. He writes:

> Whoever looks into the mirror of the water will see first of all his own face. Whoever goes to himself risks a confrontation with himself. The mirror does not flatter, it faithfully shows whatever looks into it; namely, the face we never show to the world because we cover it with the persona, the mask of the actor. But the mirror lies behind the mask and shows the true face.[7]

This function of the Persona is to rescues the Ego from facing its Shadow – those aspects of itself that it has repressed, that it finds embarrassing, shameful, and worthy of banishment.[8] The Persona that emerges from this psychological dynamic is especially neurotic, as the Self creates a Persona that means to assassinate the True Self and replace it with the Persona. Although Jung believed that the Persona was comprised primarily of collective expectations of the individual, we can add that in some extreme cases, the Persona is comprised not solely of what society demands of the individual, but what the individual wishes for itself, i.e., the total of what it wishes it truly was – the Ego Ideal (*Ichideal*). In other words, when an individual finds themselves weak yet wishes themselves to be strong, their Persona projects unmitigated strength; when the individual finds themselves insecure, their Persona projects an abundance of confidence; when the individual finds themselves doubting their abilities, talents, and intelligence, their Persona projects supernatural-like abilities, talents, and intelligence, i.e., the "charisma" that is inaccessible to "originary" people.[9] As such, one can think of this form of Persona as the "overcompensating" Persona, a specific form of psychological mask that is composed from the individual's

---

7   C.G. Jung, "Archetypes of the Collective Unconscious," in *The Archityes and the Collective Unconscious* (Vol. 9.1 of the *Collected Works of C.G. Jung*) (Princeton, NJ: Princeton University Press, 1969), para. 43, pg. 20.
8   We will visit Jung's concept of the Shadow and how it relates to Trump later in this essay.
9   Byrd, *The Dark Charisma of Donald Trump*, 29–65.

ideal type, which both hides the reality of the psychic life of the individual as well as manipulates others into believing their Persona is in fact who they are: an *Übermensch* (Superman).[10]

Most psychologically healthy individuals construct some form of Persona for themselves, as they are social beings subjected to social expectations. We know that our Personae are not the totality of our being but are rather a small element of our Self. As such, we are aware that there is a distance between our Ego and our Persona(e) – a space that we remain cognizant of even when we are performing the Persona. However, the "Ego-Ideal" Persona, as mentioned above, often fails to maintain that cognitive distance. Because of their perpetual fear of succumbing to their own inner-doubts, insecurities, and self-loathing, they will do nearly anything to avoid confronting their fractured Self. Thus, the pathologically insecure individual will often collapse into an over-identification with the "Ego-Ideal" Persona, which leaves them with little to no exit from the confines of their superlative ideals.

2   Identification, Disintegration, Individualization

For Jung, most people remain conscious of the fact that when in public, and therefore subject to social demands, that they are performing at least one of their Personae. Even if in the moment a connection between Persona and Ego appears to be lost, there remains an abiding recognition that the Persona is not the Ego, but rather a camouflage for the Ego, concealed from public demands. Thus, the space between Persona and Ego is not lost, but rather is temporarily set in abeyance amidst the Persona's performance. The continued consciousness of the space (and connection) between Persona and Ego is what Jung describes as "identification," and such an identification is an important aspect in what Jung sees as a central feature in Analytical Psychology: Individualization. For Jung, the process of individualization is a painful yet emancipatory process. It is an attempt to "divest the Self of the false wrappings of the Persona." Jung states:

---

10   Here, I use the term *Übermensch* in much the same way that Nietzsche understood it: those who rise above all limitations, social expectations, etc., and become the masters of their own fate, no longer subject to the expectations of society's norms and demands. They are the creative geniuses in the arts, in history, in world affairs. It is not being used here in the perverse racial sense, as was developed and deployed in Nazi ideology.

> Individuation means becoming a single, homogeneous being, and, in so far as 'individuality' embraces our innermost, last, and incomparable uniqueness, it also implies becoming one's own self. We would therefore translate individuation as 'coming to selfhood' or 'self-realization.'[11]

Additionally, Jung writes: "I use the term 'individuation' to denote the process by which a person becomes a psychological 'in-dividual,' that is, a separate, indivisible unity or 'whole.'"[12]

If the process of individualization, in the perspective of Analytic Psychology, is the central task in the process of becoming a "single, homogeneous being," and such individualization can only be realized if one makes conscious that which is unconscious, then the Persona must be seen as a hinderance to such a task, as it attempts to spare the individual from such a confrontation with the unconscious. As Jung says,

> *One cannot individuate as long as one is playing a role to oneself;* the convictions one has about oneself are the most subtle form of persona and the most subtle obstacle against any true individuation. One can admit practically anything, yet somewhere one retains the idea that one is nevertheless so-and-so, and this is always a sort of final argument which counts apparently as a plus; yet it functions as an influence against true individuation.[13]

If individuation is successful, a radical reckoning and possible reconciliation within the Self occurs, wherein the individual becomes an authentic Self that is true to themselves: the individual's "self-realization." In the individuation process, the person relinquishes their pathological narcissism (a psychological defense mechanism that stands against the self's interrogation of itself), as well as the demands (sometimes irrational) of group attachments and society at large. In this sense, they live as a True Self, no longer concealed behind the Persona.

However, there are some that lose consciousness of the space between the Persona and the Ego, and begin to *over-identify* with their Persona, thus causing a break with (or at least a severe repression of) the Ego. The repression of the Ego and the augmentation of the Persona within the Self creates a situation

---

11   C.G. Jung, *Two Essays in Analytical Psychology*, para. 266, pg. 173.
12   C.G. Jung, *The Archetypes and the Collective Unconscious*, para. 489, pg. 275.
13   C.G. Jung, *Visions: Notes of the Seminary Given in 1930–1934*, ed. Claire Douglas (Princeton, NJ: Princeton University Press, 1997), 821.

wherein the Persona becomes the new master of the Self. These Personae are not situational, as most Personae are. Rather, these are abiding, recalcitrant, and thus rarely recede. Such intractable Personae's job is not to just lubricate momentarily social interactions or temporarily shield the Ego from social scrutiny, but rather their job is much more intractable: it is to psychologically create another person altogether; to create a personality bunker from which one does not emerge. Thus, we may call them the "pathological Personae."[14]

3   The Pathological Persona

Ego-weakness, or an underdeveloped Ego, allows for the Self to over-identify with the Persona, thus resulting in the dissolution of the Ego within the now "pathological" Persona. This is psychologically unhealthy, as the Persona is superficial and narrow; it inherently lacks the psychological depth and richness of a eudemonic life. Reducing the Self to the myopathy of the Persona results in a psychologically myopic individual. Such individuals can only identify with a narrow slice of reality, as the particularities of their pathological Persona dictate to them what they are in their totality. In the case of Trump, a malignant narcissist who is obsessed with his own greatness and success, all aspects of his life will be processed through the lenses of that narrow social role: the man that can't help but to be successful, as if it were his preordained fate. Thus, he cannot escape that social role even when it would be socially necessary to do so: in family life, in accordance with the dialogical nature of political life, in the life of a comforting and compassionate leader, especially in times of national crises: pandemic, economic collapse, war, etc. In this case, the pathological Persona engulfs the entire personality; the True Self is dissolved into the Persona, and like a "fanatic," all libidinal energy is directed towards the maintenance, reproduction, and defense of the Persona, against all that would (or could) call its legitimacy into question.

This over-bearing pathological Persona often emerges from severe traumas experienced by the individual, especially childhood, where the child was subject to persistent attacks upon its emerging and fragile Ego. Such attacks are accompanied by strong social demands and conformance-expectations from others, most often the parents, who look for their children to be narcissistic mirrors of themselves.[15] The exports of these fractured childhood, i.e.,

---

14   The "pathological Persona" is not a Jungian concept, but one that I have developed out of Jung's thought.
15   See Eric Berne, *Sex in Human Loving* (New York: Simon & Schuster, 1970), 99.

acute neuroses, pervasive insecurities, self-perceived weaknesses, nagging self-doubt, and miserable self-loathing, etc., are radically suppressed via the domination of the all-encompassing pathological Persona. Indeed, one of the pathological Persona's most important tasks is to eradicate any attempt of the Self to consciously engage with the sources of such neuroses: the traumas they've repressed. As such, the pathological Persona is not only informed by past traumas, but rather is determined by them. The pathological Persona is constituted by characteristics that are the opposite of their repressed condition; it is created from the opposite characteristics of what they would see in themselves if they were to look. Thus, if the individual's Ego perceives itself to be weak, the pathological Persona will project infinite strengths; if the individual's Ego perceives itself to be unintelligent, the pathological Persona will project infinite intelligence; if the individual's Ego perceives itself to be unworthy of admiration, the pathological Persona will project a grandeur that is worthy of all admiration *in perpetum*. Thus, the pathological Persona is the sum of oppositional characteristics to the weaknesses that are perceived to saturate the Ego. Thus, in contradistinction to Personae that all healthy individuals have as part of their overall Self, corresponding merely to the episodic social demands of the public sphere, the "pathological Persona" is an "ideal type" meant to address the world entire at all times. In other words, it is what the individual *wishes themselves to be in perpetuity* in opposition to *what they are in reality*. It is the most radical rejection of the Jung's notion of individualization, which begins with the "disintegration" of the Persona – the breakdown of its falsity. Rather, the pathological Persona is anti-individualization, as it attempts to fortify the protective and defensive nature of the Persona, thus replacing the reality-Ego with the wish-fulfilled-idealized Self.

Through the construction and outward projection of the pathological Persona, the wished-for ideals are falsely actualized: they are beings without flaws; they are beings without insecurities, without the kind of small imperfections, pains, and self-doubts that all mentally healthy people struggle with. In their minds, they *are* the sum of all their wished-for perfections, and thus project that false image of themselves toward society at large. As such, they do not need to confront the unconscious; they cannot be burdened by the dark night of the soul; they do not subject themselves to criticism from others or themselves; they are fully integrated into that which they wish they were, to the point that they are convinced that they are what their pathological Persona publicly projects them to be. In the end, this collapse of the Ego into the pathological Persona spares them the painful experiences of admitting the knowledge that they repress: they *are not* what they appear to be, but rather the opposite.

4   Donald Trump's Ultra-Persona: King Midas

When Donald Trump descended on his golden escalator in Trump Tower on June 16, 2015, very few political pundits and political analysts took his entrance into the race for the White House seriously. Why would they? There were numerous other Republican nominees who were serious contenders, and one of them would most likely square up against Hillary Clinton, the most qualified Democratic candidate to run for the presidency in decades. Surely, Trump would be crushed by her if not by one of the establishment Republicans in the primaries. He was a political novice, having no experience in elected office; he was bizarre looking – with hair dyed platinum blonde, a bad-combover, and skin painted orange; he was a billionaire in a time of growing disdain for the 1%; he showed disdain for the U.S. military – including for men like Senator John McCain; he was misogynistic, racist, and unabashedly narcissistic, among many other oddities that made his candidacy unserious. This campaign, like his other previous presidential campaigns, appeared to be a Trump Organization marketing stunt, no more, no less. Millions of Americans simply could not take him seriously. He was known as a self-promoting "carnival barker" for decades, one who was "famous for being famous," not for any other great feats of business genius. Historically, most of his business enterprises went bust, including the following: Trump Steaks, GoTrump, Trump Water, Trump Shuttle (Airlines), Trump Air (helicopter service), Trump: The Game, Trump Vodka, Trump Mortgage, Trump University, Trump Magazine, Trump Ice, Tour de Trump, Trump Network, Trumped! (radio show), Trump Taj Mahal, Trump Castle, Trump Plaza Casinos, Trump Plaza Hotel, Trump Entertainment Resorts, etc. He had filed for bankruptcy so many times that American banks refused to give him loans. Nevertheless, despite all his business failures, Trump had an uncanny ability to project to the world that he was hyper-successful in all his ventures, even when he clearly failed at most of them. This "success" image was cemented when he became the star of the NBC gameshow, "The Apprentice," wherein he play-acted a business mogul with unimpeachable business skills who mercilessly judged contestants on whether their business acumen lived up to his ruthless standards. With the signature line, "You're Fired," Trump's character fired anyone who failed to ascend to the heights of his demands in their weekly assigned business projects. Although it was not the intent of the producers to deify Trump, in the minds of millions, this "reality" TV show established him as a demigod of action; a man who could get the job done and ruthlessly so. He was a "self-made" billionaire, an American success story, who was not capable of failure. He was an unapologetic "alpha male" in an age where the "betas," "soy boys," and "Pajama Boys" seemed to be running the world.¹⁶ Therefore, when he descended on his escalator, and the "establishment" saw Trump as a political clown, millions of working-class others saw precisely what they believed the country desperately needed: A ruthless businessman who could bring about a rebirth of America for "real" Americans.

This image of the successful business mogul was only one iteration of what I call Trump's "Ultra-Persona": the King Midas Persona. Building on Jung's conception of the Persona, I argue that an Ultra-Persona is the penultimate pathological Persona from which all other sub-variant Personae descend. It is the *universal abstract* "ideal" Persona that gives birth to a variety of *particular* ideal Personae, which reveal themselves depending on the social-environment. Trump's Ultra-Persona reflects the story of King Midas: Just as King Midas in Greek mythology was cursed with the "Midas Touch," so too is Trump; whatever he touches will "turn to gold." In other words, his penultimate Persona is one that projects Trumpian fatalism: he cannot be anything other than successful; it is his destiny to succeed in all things.¹⁷ Almost magic-like, whatever Trump touches will be the greatest of all greats; the best of the best; the most tremendous, most beautiful, most perfect. This penultimate Persona manifests itself within particular variants, which are often times contradictory, as they are dependent on the social context. Among the variants are: (1) his *Playboy Persona* – which portrays him as being the ultimate woman's man, thus authorizing him to "grab them by the pussy" and commit other sexual aggressions; (2) the *Youth Persona,* which continues to reinforce the false-idea that he still embodies his idealized self – the 1980s alpha male

---

16   The Hungarian American right-wing idealogue and one-time political advisor to Trump, Sebastian Gorka, made the phrase "Pajama Boys" famous after the election of Trump in 2016, stating: "The message I have is a very simple one, it's a bumper sticker: the eras of the Pajama Boy is over January 20th and the alpha males are back." See Ian Schwartz, "Dr. Sebastian Gorka: The Era of the Pajama Boy is over and the Alpha Males are Back," *Realclearpolitics.com* December 17, 2016. https://www.realclearpolitics.com/video/2016/12/17/dr_sebastian_gorka_the_era_of_the_pajama_boy_is_over_and_the_alpha_males_are_back.html.

17   One should remember that Trump was counted out of the 2016 race from the beginning, yet he won – beating out the Democrats' own "fated" candidate: Hillary Clinton. Trump was twice impeached, yet he was not convicted by the Senate in either case. He was able to appoint three Supreme Court Justices in just four years, and dozens of other hyper-conservative judges. The economy was stable and growing during his four years, even if not at the same pace as it was under Obama (which was systematically ignored by his devotees). He would have repealed Obamacare if it wasn't for the treachery of his Republican opponent, Sen. John McCain. As evidence for his "winning" mounted, so too did the belief in his fated greatness increase. To the horror of much of the country, there was a lot of perceived evidence to back the claim that he could not fail, at least until the 2020 election.

that is not subject to time, aging, and mental decline; (3) *Family-man Persona*, which he utilizes when it's necessary for him to appear to be an embodiment of traditional "family values"; (4) his *Genius Persona*, which portrays him to be naturally smarter than all experts in all fields, which he deploys whenever he feels outsmarted or intellectually inadequate amidst experts, and (6) his *Political-Messianic Persona*, which can be encapsulated in his political phrase, "I alone can fix it," and "I'm the greatest president of all time." Lastly, Trump's default Persona is his *Business Persona*, which of all the Personae is the dearest to him, as it falsely depicts him as a "self-made" multi-billionaire – the Midas man of business. This Persona is also the most important to his psychological stability, as it masks his abiding imposture syndrome, which itself is the result of his feeling inadequate regarding his father, Fredrick Trump, whose claim to being a "self-made man" is certainly truer than Donald's, who historically relied on his father's money and business connections to not only lay the foundation for Donald's businesses, but also to bail him out when they failed.[18] Since his sense of self-worth is tightly wedded to his business success, confessing his dependency on his father undermines his fragile sense-of-self; thus the extreme grandiosity of the Business Persona overcompensates for the psychologically undermining memory of his father.

All of these particular sub-Personae embody, develop, and deploy in their own unique way the essence of the "Midas touch" – the core element of Trump's Ultra-Persona. In other words, they all radiate the same grandiosity and fatalism that structures and animates Trump's penultimate Persona. They exist both for public consumption and to mask the harsh psychological realities that Trump refuses to confront: the fact that he is the opposite of what such Personae publicly portray.

Yet, while all these Persona(e) should be further studied, especially in relation to how they forward authoritarian demagoguery, we want to focus our attention on one particular Persona for this study: Trump's *Populist Persona*.

5   The Populist Persona

From the beginning of his political career, Trump portrayed himself as the "voice of the voiceless," the "champion of the little guy," the man who would "drain the swamp" of corruption in Washington D.C. Singlehandedly, he

---

18   For a good overview of Trump's dependency on his father's business skills, see Michael D'Antonio, *The Truth about Trump* (New York: Thomas Dunne Books, 2016).

would return the country to the people who believed they had been wronged, neglected, and exploited by both establishment political parties. In effect, he would "Make America Great Again." Trump was successful at this. Through his anti-establishment demagoguery, he was able to detach millions of Obama voters and traditional Republican voters (including Evangelicals) from their parties, the loyalties of which then shifted to him personally. During his years in politics, it was common to hear such devotees make statements similar to the following: "he has everything, he's a billionaire, he doesn't need to do this. He is doing this for us." Indeed, even after his presidency, while facing mounting criminal indictments, Trump would tell his followers that "They're not coming after me, they're coming after you. I'm just standing in their way," thus extending his grip on their loyalty.[19]

Trump's Populist Persona was the strategic mask that he wore to elicit support, loyalty, and devotion from millions of disaffected, alienated, and aggrieved Americans, especially among the White working- and middle-classes. This Persona publicly radiated a double message: first, that Americans, especially White Americans, have been systematically denied that which they are entitled to: the full and complete benefits of being a White American. A "retrotopian" impulse saturated this message, especially when Trump invoked the "good old days," drawing upon popular nostalgia for an imagined innocence and justness thought to reside only in America's pre-1960s past. This imagined past was juxtaposed to the dysgenic and chaotic present, with its multiculturalism, cultural liberalism, and global tendencies. Tied to this message was the idea that the present state-of-being, both in government and society, did not have to continue, but rather could be turned around; time could be reversed. America could be made "great" again if only the righteous indignation of the aggrieved masses could be channeled into a political champion. Thus, the second message expressed through Trump's Populist Persona was that he, the man of the Midas Touch, and he alone, could reverse the collapse of America, and restore it to its former greatness, thus delivering the full benefits of being a White American to the "forgotten man."

While performing the role of the populist, Trump becomes synonymous with his populist persona, at least in the minds of his devotees. As a manifestation of the Midas Touch Persona, Trump's Populist Persona adopted as its own the stereotypical characteristics exemplified by the great populists of Western

---

19   Matt Dixon, "Trump delivers fiery post-indictment speech: 'They're coming after you,'" *NBC News*, June 10, 2023. https://www.nbcnews.com/politics/donald-trump/trump-deliver-fiery-post-indictment-speech-georgia-rcna88561.

history, which are always available within the collective unconscious.[20] His Populist Persona was not unique in any meaningful way, but rather was a repetition and manifestation of the collective psyche, the same from which other Western populists drew from. In this sense, the *minutia*, the personal colorings of Trump's populism reflected the particularities of Trump's personality, biography, as well as the time and place he operated within, but the populist patterns he displayed where easily identifiable, as they are normative patterns of populists throughout history. For example, in my book, *The Dark Charisma of Donald Trump: Political Psychology and the MAGA Movement*, I detail how Trump's populist rhetoric mirrors that of previous American populists and demagogues, especially as they were studied in Leo Löwenthal and Norbert Guterman's 1949 psychosocial study *Prophets of Deceit: A Study of the Techniques of the American Agitator*.[21] This seminal work of the Frankfurt School studied the ways in which populists, including Gerald L.K. Smith, Carl H. Mote, William Dudley Pelley, Joe McWilliams, and the fascist Catholic radio Priest Father Charles Coughlin, utilized characteristic rhetorical forms to "agitate" pro-fascists, anti-Semites, and other American authoritarians into signing onto their rightwing political projects. From dehumanizing the "others" to exaggerating the outside threats; from portraying the great leader as being both persecuted and the messianic strongman; from peddling in conspiracy theories to gaslighting with the "firehose of lies," the populist agitator's behavior patterns and techniques remain the same; only the particular content changes over time (and in some cases remains eerily consistent). Populists of all times are skilled in converting genuine "social malaise" into political grievances, on the backs of which the Populists advance their own agenda, self-interests, etc.[22] Yet, because the populist agitator needs the social malaise to remain relevant to his devotees, he does nothing that would fundamentally change the conditions from which such malaise originates. Rather, he works to cement the malaise or even accelerate it. The worse it gets, the more the

---

20   On the topic of the collective unconscious, Jung writes, 'It is only because the persona represents a more or less arbitrary and fortuitous segment of the collective psyche that we can make the mistake of regarding it *in toto* as something individual. It is, as its name implies, only a mask of the collective psyche, a mask that *feigns individuality,* making others and oneself believe that one is individual, whereas one is simply acting a role through which the collective psyche speaks.' (C.G. Jung, CW Vol. 7: "Two Essays on Analytical Psychology"), para. 245, pg. 157.
21   Byrd, *The Dark Charisma of Donald Trump*, 223–292; Leo Löwenthal and Norbert Guterman, *Prophets of Deceit: A Study in the Techniques of the American Agitator* (New York: Harper & Brothers, 1949).
22   Ibid., 11–19.

aggrieved masses need their champion. Additionally, the populist agitator's ideological claims function like opium; it placates the aggrieve masses' alienation, social pain, etc., by giving them a cause, an object of derision, a scapegoat, and a leader to adore, but in the process this turns them into "junkies" for the opiate of the populists' ideology and rhetoric, which in reality fails to address the true causes that give birth to the need for the ideological opium. Trump, like the populist agitators before him, fell comfortably into this same pattern before, during, and after his presidency. He, like agitators before him, would profit from the social malaise, both politically and economically, while simultaneously changing nothing substantively.

Trump never lowered the intensity of the Populist Persona during his presidency as many had hoped he would. Rather, it only intensified, especially after the Democrats won the House of Representatives in 2018 and began their investigations into his long and assorted ties with Russia.[23] Throughout all four years, the image of the charismatic "savior" of America would serve to mask Trump's anti-democratic agenda, i.e., building his anti-immigrant border wall, instituting the child-family separation plan, ordering the "Muslim ban," pulling the U.S. out of the Iran Nuclear Agreement, pulling the U.S. out of the Paris Climate Agreement, attempting to repeal the Affordable Care Act (Obamacare), nominating hard-right jurists in the Federal judiciary, undermining reproductive rights for women, undermining the Free Press – which he called "the enemy of the people," and many other policies that were popular with his rightwing authoritarian base.[24] Such measures were popular not because they would benefit the working- and middle-class, but popular because such people and policies were dehumanized, demonized, and emotionally instilled with invectiveness. These were the people (immigrants, Muslims, Journalists, RINOs, etc.) and policies that harmed the "real Americans," and thus they were targeted by the "champion of the forgotten man." Nevertheless, Trump's signature piece of legislation as President was his Tax Cut and Jobs Act of 2017 (TCJA), which further cemented the trickle-down economics of Ronald Reagan that had yet to benefit (if that was ever the intent) the very people Trump claimed to represent, the "forgotten" little man. Thus, despite all his campaign promises to bring jobs back to America, to bring back coal production, to make Americans wealthy like him, his economic policies resulted in no significant change for

---

23 See The Washington Post, *The Mueller Report* (New York: Scribner, 2019). Also see Michael Isikoff and David Corn, *Russian Roulette: The Inside Story of Putin's War on American and the Election of Donald Trump* (New York: Twelve, 2018).

24 See John W. Dean and Bob Altemeyer, *Authoritarian Nightmare: Trump and his Followers* (Brooklyn: Melville House, 2020).

middle-class and working-class Americans, but the ultra-wealthy did receive a massive tax cut.

When he was defeated in the 2020 election, and soon after left the presidency, the public started to witness the disintegration of his presidential Populist Persona. He had been demoted to "citizen" Trump, as opposed to the "most powerful man in the world." To fight against this fall from grace, he declared that he had actually won the election despite his resounding loss to Joe Biden; he demanded that he continue to be called "Mr. President" and not to be referred to as the "former president"; he stole thousands of government documents – some highly classified – that would continue to remind him that he was President (or still was in his mind), etc. Nevertheless, the painful reality that undermined his personal reality, i.e., his "psychosis" (his detachment from reality), was that he was no longer president, he had been defeated, he was what his authoritarian father demanded he never be: a "loser." With his loss, his charismatic appeal began to wane among some, especially after his coup d'état attempt on Congress on January 6th, 2021. Among his most devoted, his post-presidency troubles, including his numerous indictments, both Federal and in the state of Georgia, only proved to them that he was the victim of a corrupt system – the very "establishment" corruption he had warned them of.

Despite his loss to Joe Biden in the 2020 election, Trump did not regress into a confrontation with his True Self, as many do when their Persona is shattered by the loss of their job, position, status, etc. Rather, he doubled down on his Populist Persona: he augmented his claim that he was unjustly victimized by a "stolen election," thus sparing him the painful admission that he was the actual "loser," the very admission that his True Self desperately fears. Over the course of the next few years, Trump retreated into the Persecuted Strongman Persona, which allowed him to both claim that he was cheated out of his second term and was now being treated "unfairly" by a "corrupt" government. Prosecution was not the result of his own nefarious doings, but rather it was a case of a nefarious government protecting itself from the "champion of the people." Some of his devotees would even liken his post-presidency legal troubles to that of Jesus of Nazareth; Trump too was unjustly persecuted by the establishment for doing nothing other than offering salvation to his followers.[25] These claims of persecution allowed him to consistently remind his followers that he remained their champion, their fighter, the messiah, the only hope they have for defeating the globalists, democrats, communists, deep state, immigrants, etc.

---

25   David Klepper, "Trump Arrest Prompts Jesus Comparisons: 'Spiritual Warfare,'" *Associated Press*, April 5, 2023. https://apnews.com/article/donald-trump-arraignment-jesus-christ-conspiracy-theory-670c45bd71b3466dcd6e8e188badcd1d.

This shift into the Persecuted Strongman Persona was not an exit from the Populist Persona, but rather a difference in emphasis *within* the Populist Persona. The man with the Midas Touch did not lose the 2020 election, rather it was stolen from him by evil forces. His success-in-everything-fate wasn't proven false by his loss, rather it was thwarted by evil forces acting against the American people. Despite his election loss, Trump remains in his own mind and in the mind of his most devoted followers, the man who cannot help but to be successful. To evidence that claim, all he needs is to be reinstated and/or reelected as President of the United States. As such, it was psychologically imperative that he run for the presidency again in 2024. He had to prove to himself that he was not the "loser" he was told he was after the 2020 election, he had to show his naysayers that they were always wrong about him, and he had to demonstrate to his followers that he was still worthy of their devotion.

6 Trump's Populist Shadow

According to C.G. Jung, all individuals have what he describes as a "Shadow." He defines the Shadow as such:

> The shadow personifies everything that the subject refuses to acknowledge about himself and yet is always thrusting itself upon him directly or indirectly for instance, inferior traits of character and other incompatible tendencies.[26]

Like other aspects of the unconscious, which appear through a variety of behaviors, the shadow is made identifiable through the individual's "projections." In other words, the individual perceives in others what they unconsciously (or sometimes consciously) do not like about themselves, feel uncomfortable with in themselves, or even despise in themselves. Additionally, the Shadow can embody what the individual refuses to admit about themselves to themselves. When such characteristics appear in others, the other becomes a target, an ersatz-self, against which the individual attempts to suppress their unliked or unadmitted characteristics by attacking those perceived characteristics in others. Jung goes on to define the Shadow in the following way:

---

26   C.G. Jung, *The Archetypes and the Collective Unconscious*, para. 513, pg. 284–285.

the shadow [is] that hidden, repressed, for the most part inferior and guilt-laden personality whose ultimate ramification reach back into the realm of our animal ancestors and so comprise the whole historical aspect of the unconscious ... If it has been believed hitherto that the human shadow as the source of all evil, it can now be ascertained on closer investigation that the unconscious man, that is, his shadow, does not consist only of morally reprehensible tendencies, but also displays a number of good qualities, such as normal instincts, appropriate reactions, realistic insights, creative impulses, etc.[27]

In this sense, it is not what society deems to be "morally reprehensible" that necessarily populates the shadow, but rather the content of the shadow is dependent on what the individual believes about any given characteristics. If society believes a particular characteristic is morally good, but the individual believes otherwise, such socially determined "goodness" can populate the shadow, while the socially determined "morally reprehensible tendencies" can determine the consciousness and identity of the individual. While this seems counterintuitive, it is the case in extreme cases, and as we'll see, Trump is one of those extreme cases.

For Jung, the existence of the Shadow is a "moral problem," as it "challenges the whole ego-personality," since "no one can become conscious of the shadow without considerable moral effort."[28] Jung argues, "to become conscious of it involves recognizing the dark aspects of the personality as present and real. This act is the essential condition for any kind of self-knowledge, and it therefore, as a rule, meets with considerable resistance."[29] Understanding that the Shadow is comprised of what the Ego refuses to admit about itself, or has repressed deeply within the unconscious, we can ascertain to a large degree of certainty what characteristics comprise Trump's shadow by examining what he constantly and consistently attacks in others. In other words, by focusing our attention on stated reasons why Trump attacks individuals, such attacks reveal that which Trump despises in himself. The hated other is the mirror of

---

27   C.G. Jung, "Conclusion," in *Aion: Researches into the Phenomenology of the Self* (Vol. 9.2 of the *Collected Works of C.G. Jung*) (Princeton, NJ: Princeton University Press, 1970), para. 422, 423, pg. 266.
28   C.G. Jung, "The Shadow," in *Aion: Researches into the Phenomenology of the Self* (Vol. 9.2 of the *Collected Works of C.G. Jung*) (Princeton, NJ: Princeton University Press, 1970), para. 14, pg. 8.
29   Ibid.

Trump's unconscious Self – a mirror that he tries to verbally destroy and in doing so symbolically destroys the despised content of his Shadow.

It is well known in psychology that certain personality traits often elicit negative feedback and punishment from others, beginning with the parents, through the education and socialization process, and even into the maturity of adulthood. Because the social demand to abandon such traits conflicts with the fact that such traits are integral part of the individual's personality, they are often repressed. In doing so, they form the Shadow. What repressed personality traits comprise Trump's shadow? In most people, the dark side of their personality, i.e., their Shadow, is comprised of traits that conventional society rejects, such as aggressiveness, vengefulness, hostility towards others, obsessive pride, racial and sexual prejudices, etc. These are the characteristics that society and conventional morality condemns and demands to be repressed. In Trump, his Shadow – the dark side of his personality – is not comprised of such things. Rather unconventionally, he has been praised for such "negative" characteristics, both in the world of corporate business and later in rightwing populist politics. What his Shadow is comprised of is what conventional morality approves of: generosity, forgiveness, compassion, humility, forgiveness, altruism, etc. In other words, Trump's "dark side" shadow is constituted by the morally good, i.e., those things that he was conditioned to reject as being the virtues of the "losers." Such traits are what Nietzsche called "slave morality," the morality of the *untermenschen*, with which Trump fully agrees.[30] In public, Trump frequently attacks individuals who display such virtues, calling them "losers," "suckers," "incompetent," and "weak." This even includes members of the United States Military, who in their deaths on the battlefield, displayed the altruism that Trump's perceives as weakness.[31] Indeed, Trump's all-mighty penultimate

---

30   Friedrich Nietzsche, *Beyond Good and Evil and On the Genealogy of Morality,* trans. Adrian Del Caro (Stanford, CA: Stanford University Press, 2014), 170–173.
31   Jeffrey Goldberg, "Trump: Americans who died in War are 'Losers' and 'Suckers,'" *The Atlantic,* September 3, 2020. https://www.theatlantic.com/politics/archive/2020/09/trump-americans-who-died-at-war-are-losers-and-suckers/615997/ It should be noted that Donald Trump never served in the U.S. Armed Forces, but he did enjoy being in the presence of military generals during the early days of his presidency. As support for him from the military leadership began to wane, and many retired military men began to speak out against him, he often accused them as well of being incompetent, disloyal, etc. This "bad blood" culminated in Trump's violent suppression of protesters during the summer of 2020, wherein many Americans took to the streets to protest the brutal killing of George Floyd, an African America in Minnesota. While Trump wanted to invoke the Insurrection Act against the protesters, he settled for a vicious removal of the assembly via police. Once the area adjacent to Washington D.C.'s Lafayette Square was cleared of protesters, Trump and many in his cabinet made their way to St. John's Episcopal Church

Persona demands nothing less than the assassination of his perverse "good" Shadow. He must convince himself that he is the "killer" his father continually – even post-mortem – demands of him. To do so, he cannot see value in the "slave morality" of the conventional good. His Shadow is thus populated by "goodness," whereas his Ego if constructed of what he believes is "strength," i.e., domination, bulling, aggressiveness (sexual and otherwise), loyalty only to self, i.e., his malignant narcissism, Machiavellianism, and psychopathy.

Trump's Shadow is partially revealed by his abiding sense of inferiority. His pathological sense of inferiority was instilled in him by his father, Frederick Trump Sr., who demanded his sons be bourgeois "killers," i.e., predators devoid of sympathy, empathy, and compassion. Indeed, this over-powering paternal demand, the fulfillment of which was the only way to gain Fred Sr.'s approval, led to the psychological destruction of Donald Trump's older brother, Freddy Crist Trump Jr., who could not satisfy his father's demands of him. Freddy simply could not be the "narcissistic mirror" that his father demanded he be.[32] Donald's sense of inferiority, that he is a success "imposter," sits at the root of his insecurities – his emotional fragility, his famous thin skin – and fuels his constant need to conceal his own abiding psychological weakness with aggressive attacks in public. His Shadow also drives his acute paranoia, as he often suspects that others perceive the same qualities in him that he perceives in himself, i.e., those qualities that must be repressed. Trump's extreme narcissism, his self-apotheosis, mirrors in intensity his self-doubt, his self-loathing, his sense of always being under the shadow of his father. In this way, Trump is a psychological *puer aeternus* – an "eternal child" that deals with his childlike insecurities and qualities by camouflaging them with bravado, with aggression, with his Midas Touch Persona.

Additionally, Trump's deep-seated feeling of incompetence, stupidity, and his sense of being an imposter, leads him to attack those who are competent, intelligent, authentic, and justifiably confident. In the presence of such people Trump's paranoia regarding others' ability to see through his Persona is stimulated. He cannot allow himself to be perceived by others in the same way that he unconsciously perceives himself, and so he attacks them for being the opposite of what they are. Those who are extremely competent are dubbed

---

for photo-op of Trump holding a Bible. This led to a cascade of public denouncements from former military leadership. See Dustin J. Byrd, *The Dark Charisma of Donald Trump*, 421–455.

32   See Mary L. Trump, *Too Much and Never Enough: How my Family created the World's Most Dangerous Man* (New York: Simon & Schuster, 2020). Mary L. Trump is not only the niece of Donald Trump, the daughter of Donald older brother "Freddy," but also a clinical psychologist.

"incompetent"; those who are experts in their fields are labeled "stupid"; those with a strong work ethic are deemed "lazy," etc. These accusations reveal the opposite: Trump knows them to be competent, smart, and hardworking, as do others, thus he must characterize them as the opposite, even though he often previously praised them for being the "best people." Such attacks shield him from their critiques (spoken or unspoken), as it artificially inflates his competence, intelligence, work ethic, above theirs. Once those false assertions saturate his consciousness, it momentarily opiates his insecurities, and he can continue to go on believing in the delusion that his psychological realities are invisible to others.

Instead of doing the difficult task of integrating the shadow into consciousness and achieving what Jung called "self-knowledge," it is more than likely that Trump has achieved what can be called "Shadow exile" (the permanent exile of the Shadow from consciousness) through the over-identification of the Self with the penultimate Persona. It is often the case that individuals can be "seized" by their Shadows. Since the Shadow is an integrated factor in the psyche of most, it maintains the potential to break through the Ego's repression, and momentarily dominate the individual, leading them to do such things that they secretly want to do, but cannot do due to the repression that their society demands. However, the near deceased (or exiled) Shadow in Trump cannot "seize" him; it is either too weak or it has atrophied to the point of being powerless, a discarded psychological corpse. It can only haunt him. If it were to seize Trump, ironically, it would cause him to be good, moral, and ethical – a social and political death sentence for Trump. Nevertheless, there is no evidence that he has ever suffered from such a seizure, as public goodness would undermine the iron cage of his predatorial Persona. Over-identification with the persona would suggest that Trump's public identity is pure fiction; it is a manufactured identity designed to do two things: first, hide the True Self from others, and second, paradoxically, hide the True Self from the consciousness, which fears the mirror. Trump, when reflecting upon himself, cannot stand to confront himself; such is too horrifying. In an August 2023 interview with the philosopher and psychoanalyst, Slavoj Žižek, he argued that the absence of a confrontation between the True Self and the Shadow leads to the absence of "individualization," as Jung called it.[33] Žižek reminded his listeners that for psychoanalysis, and additionally for Jungian Analytical Psychology, the goal of the Self is wholeness (or authenticity), and that individualization is the way to

---

33   Renitzc Kantart, "Slavoj Žižek: 'I am totally against authenticity." *Youtube.com* https://www.youtube.com/watch?v=1x2aETEoc-I&t=58s.

become a "single, homogenous being."³⁴ However, for Žižek, the authenticity of the True Self is what must be avoided, for the True Self in all its authenticity is horrifying. It is better to retreat into the goodness, acceptableness, of the socially conscious Persona than to forward the True Self into a society that will not accept it. For Trump, amidst an age yearning for dictators and authoritarianism, the safest avenue for his psychological well-being is to remain hidden behind the politically longed-for Midas Touch Persona, the champion of the aggrieved masses, for it is a refuge against the painful indictments emanating from the unconscious. And while rightwing society demands such a Populist Persona of him, there is no reason for him to abandon it – it both protects his fragile psychological disposition and gives the yearning masses their messiah, albeit a false one.

7 Conclusion

The election of Donald Trump to the presidency of the United States of America was an extreme stress test for the Republic. Already fractured at its core, the Republic just barely survived the presidency of a man who was uniquely unqualified to wield such awesome power. As many psychoanalysts, clinical psychologists, and other mental health professionals routinely made known, Trump's psychological matrix was a present and abiding danger to the nation and therefore to the world.[35] It will take decades to undo the damage done by electing someone who wholly embodies the traits of the Dark Triad (Pathological Narcissism, Machiavellianism, and Psychopathy), tied to the perception that he is a charismatic leader who cannot fail, but rather is fated for success in all things. Indeed, as this chapter is being written, Trump is once again seeking the presidency for a second time. Even his failed coup d'état on January 6th, 2021, have not cleaved his most fanatical devotees from his orbit; he remains their "champion," and they are determined to reinstall him into the White House. "The first time as tragedy, the second time as farce," said G.W.F. Hegel. Understanding Donald Trump and the falsity of his Populist Persona is to understand that the first time Trump was elected was farce; if it happens again, the second time would be the tragedy. Through his concept of the Persona, C.G. Jung has given us the psychoanalytic tools to understand a very important aspect of Trump's psychological realities and its political export: Trumpist populism.

---

34 C.G. Jung, *Two Essays in Analytical Psychology*, para. 266, pg. 173.
35 Bandy X. Lee, Ed., *The Dangerous Case of Donald Trump: 27 Psychiatrists and Mental Health Experts Assess a President* (New York: St. Martin's Press, 2017).

His Populist Persona is merely one manifestation of his Ultra-Persona: King Midas – the man whose touch turned everything into gold. Yet, we cannot forget the implicit message of the King Midas story: that which appears to be "successful" is ultimately a catastrophe. And just like King Midas, who could not eat his gold, Donald Trump cannot eat the political success gained through his Populist Persona. As he faces just under one-hundred criminal indictments in four different jurisdictions, most of which having to do with his behavior while in office, his political gold will also be his downfall.

Bibliography

Berne, Eric. *Sex in Human Loving.* New York: Simon & Schuster, 1970.

Byrd, Dustin J. *The Dark Charisma of Donald Trump: Political Psychology and the MAGA Movement.* Kalamazoo, MI: Ekpyrosis Press, 2023.

C-Span. "CPAC Conference." March 4, 2023. https://www.c-span.org/video/?c5060238/pres-trump-i-justicei-retribution.

D'Antonio, Michael. *The Truth about Trump.* New York: Thomas Dunne Books, 2016.

Dean, John W., and Bob Altemeyer. *Authoritarian Nightmare: Trump and his Followers* Brooklyn: Melville House, 2020.

Dixon, Matt. "Trump delivers fiery post-indictment speech: 'They're coming after you.'" *NBC News,* June 10, 2023. https://www.nbcnews.com/politics/donald-trump/trump-deliver-fiery-post-indictment-speech-georgia-rcna88561.

Goldberg, Jeffrey. "Trump: Americans who died in War are 'Losers' and 'Suckers.'" *The Atlantic,* September 3, 2020. https://www.theatlantic.com/politics/archive/2020/09/trump-americans-who-died-at-war-are-losers-and-suckers/615997/.

Isikoff, Michael, and David Corn. *Russian Roulette: The Inside Story of Putin's War on American and the Election of Donald Trump.* New York: Twelve, 2018.

Jung, Carl Gustav. *Archetypes of the Collective Unconscious* (Vol 9.1 of the *Collected Works of C.G. Jung*) Princeton, NJ: Princeton University Press, 1971.

Jung, Carl Gustav. "Conclusion." In *Aion: Researches into the Phenomenology of the Self* (Vol. 9.2 of the *Collected Works of C.G. Jung*) Princeton, NJ: Princeton University Press, 1970.

Jung, Carl Gustav. "The Psychology of the Child Archetype." In *The Architypes and the Collective Unconscious* (Vol. 9.1 of the *Collected Works of C.G. Jung*) Princeton, NJ: Princeton University Press, 1969.

Jung, Carl Gustav. "The Relations between the Ego and the Unconscious." In *Two Essays on Analytical Psychology* (Vol. 7 of the *Collected Works of C.G. Jung*) Princeton, NJ: Princeton University Press, 1977.

Jung, Carl Gustav. "The Shadow." In *Aion: Researches into the Phenomenology of the Self* (Vol. 9.2 of the *Collected Works of C.G. Jung*) Princeton, NJ: Princeton University Press, 1970.

Jung, Carl Gustav. *Two Essays on Analytical Psychology* (Vol. 7 of the *Collected Works of C.G. Jung*) Princeton, NJ: Princeton University Press, 1977.

Jung, Carl Gustav. *Visions: Notes of the Seminary Given in 1930–1934*. Edited by Claire Douglas. Princeton, NJ: Princeton University Press, 1997.

Kantart, Renitzc. "Slavoj Žižek: 'I am totally against authenticity." *Youtube.com* https://www.youtube.com/watch?v=1x2aETEoc-I&t=58s.

Klepper, David. "Trump Arrest Prompts Jesus Comparisons: 'Spiritual Warfare.'" *Associated Press*, April 5, 2023. https://apnews.com/article/donald-trump-arraignment-jesus-christ-conspiracy-theory-670c45bd71b3466dcd6e8e188badcd1d.

Lee, Bandy X., Ed. *The Dangerous Case of Donald Trump: 27 Psychiatrists and Mental Health Experts Assess a President.* New York: St. Martin's Press, 2017.

Löwenthal, Leo, and Norbert Guterman. *Prophets of Deceit: A Study in the Techniques of the American Agitator.* New York: Harper & Brothers, 1949.

Nietzsche, Friedrich. *Beyond Good and Evil and On the Genealogy of Morality*. Translated by Adrian Del Caro. Stanford, CA: Stanford University Press, 2014.

Schwartz, Ian. "Dr. Sebastian Gorka: The Era of the Pajama Boy is over and the Alpha Males are Back." *Realclearpolitics.com,* December 17, 2016. https://www.realclearpolitics.com/video/2016/12/17/dr_sebastian_gorka_the_era_of_the_pajama_boy_is_over_and_the_alpha_males_are_back.html.

Trump, Mary L. *Too Much and Never Enough: How My Family Created the World's Most Dangerous Man.* New York: Simon & Schuster, 2020.

The Washington Post, *The Mueller Report.* New York: Scribner, 2019.

CHAPTER 4

Algorithmic Populism

Samir Gandesha

"We are all populists now" – to adapt a slogan from culture warrior Nathan Glazer's broadside attack against multiculturalism from the early 1990s.[1] What this means is that we are living through a period in which not just a particularized political antagonism but rather a generalized anger and hostility towards "elites" is palpable and can be discerned across the political spectrum, from the post-modern Left to the authoritarian Right. How are we to understand such hostility?

In a recent book, *Society of the Singularities*, German sociologist Andreas Reckwitz has argued that it is possible to grasp such a division in terms of a large-scale transformation of modern industrial society into a "society of singularities." While the former embodied a logic of formalization and rationalization emphasizing conformity to the *general*, the latter emphasizes a neo-romantic break with the general and an emphasis on the *particular*. Reckwitz argues the way the transition from the modern to *late* modern form of society is due to a three-fold crisis: of recognition, of self-actualization, and of politics.[2]

The political crisis is particularly interesting insofar as the society of singularities, according to Rechwitz, entails not just a simple process of the liberation of the individual but rather the retrenchment of collective often *essentialized* singularities, such as ethno-national identities, which has the effect, *inter alia*, of fracturing the public sphere, consequently further exacerbating the eclipse of the general. Reckwitz, moreover, shows the pronounced role of digital media in these crises. His framing of the problem in terms of a tension within modernity between formalization and rationalization (the general) and a romantic response (the particular), however, is not especially helpful when considering a key dimension of the opposition between the general and the particular today, namely: the politics of populism. It is precisely in the opposition between Left and Right forms of digitally inflected populism that the opposition between the general and the particular plays itself out in an especially acute fashion.

---

1   Nathan Glazer, *We Are All Multiculturalists Now* (Cambridge, MA: Harvard University Press, 1997).
2   Andreas Reckwitz, *Society of the Singularities* (Cambridge, MA: Polity Press, 2020).

In contrast to Reckwitz's account of a transformation of the relation between general and particular in the shift from industrial society to a society of singularities, the ubiquitous populism we see today is perhaps better thought of as resulting less from crises of recognition, self-actualization, and politics, than from a crisis of the very legitimacy of the institutions comprising the neoliberal-democratic order. This crisis has to do with the following contradiction: Given its nominal commitment to *democracy*, the state must secure legitimacy by meeting, or at least *appearing* to meet, the demands of the *demos*, on the one hand, and in its commitment to *(neo)liberalism,* the state must foster the conditions within a competitive global economy to maximize capital accumulation, on the other. Authoritarian states, arguably, can better solve this crisis through reinventing themselves as what Hungarian President Victor Orban and Russian President Vladimir Putin have called "illiberal democracies" by meeting the latter at the expense of the former, which is compensated for by a mythical notion of "the people."[3] Material needs and demands are satisfied by their symbolic proxies.

The liberal-democratic state's increasing inability to both satisfy the needs of its citizens and the demands of shareholders, for example, in the realms of housing, job security, healthcare and so on, is symptomatic precisely of such a legitimation crisis. This crisis, moreover, has been dramatically exacerbated by the COVID-19 pandemic but also clearly antedates it. The legitimation crisis became especially clear as the post-9/11 geopolitical and refugee crises collided with the near implosion of the foundations of the architecture of the global financial order in 2008–09. This provided the opening for a massive resurgence of populist politics throughout the West. Such a crisis of legitimacy can be seen to have elicited two very different kinds of populist responses.

On the one side, the crisis led to the emergence of a Left populism inflecting a democratic politics that took inspiration from the Arab Spring and that sought to, at least symbolically, bring the neoliberal order under control via Occupy Wall Street, and ultimately bolstered Bernie Sanders' presidential nominations in 2016 and 2020. A similar dynamic can be discerned in the relationship between the Indignados and Podemos in Spain and Momentum and the rise of Jeremy Corbyn as the leader of the British Labour Party. On the other side, it led to a countertendency towards a Right populism, first in the form of a libertarian Tea Party faction within the GOP, which then laid the groundwork

---

3   See Zsuzsanna Szelényi, "How Viktor Orbán Built his Illiberal State," *The New Republic.* April 5, 2022. https://newrepublic.com/article/165953/viktor-orban-built-illiberal-state; Helier Cheung, "Is Putin Right? Is Liberalism really Obsolete," BBC. June 28th, 2019. https://www.bbc.com/news/world-europe-48798875.

for Donald J. Trump's election as the 45th President of the United States. This would amount to a frontal attack on the institutions of the US democratic order in the favor of oligarchic interests, yet one that purported to act in the name of the "people." Characterizing the latter is a fervent anti-intellectualism, a hatred of thinking, an increasingly conspiratorial mind-set or what US historian Richard Hofstadter calls the "paranoid style" of politics, and the unleashing of violent and potentially destructive emotions.[4]

The most egregious recent example of the authoritarian populist challenge to the legitimacy of the liberal-democratic order was the storming of the US Capitol on January 6, 2021, with the express aim of preventing the certification of the Electoral College vote in favor of Joseph R. Biden as President of the United States. The insurrectionists acted at the behest of the out-going president and his allies such as Rudolph Giuliani and Steve Bannon, among others who perpetuated the "Big Lie" that the election had been fraudulent. The insurrectionists' numbers included ordinary Trump supporters, active-duty servicemen and women, as well as members of well-organized far-right groups such as the Oath Keepers and the Proud Boys. These groups were by no means mutually exclusive.[5]

---

4   Richard Hofstadter, *Anti-Intellectualism in American Life, The Paranoid Style in American Politics, Uncollected Essays 1956–65* (New York: Library of America, 2020). Racist political forces in the US, particularly in the Southern states, have been attacking the basic principle of liberal democracy, which is to say, equality, since the end of the Civil War and the era of Reconstruction, notably through Jim Crow legislation. See W.E.B. du Bois, *Black Reconstruction in America: An Essay Toward a History of the Part Which Black Folk Played in the Attempt to Reconstruct Democracy in America, 1860–1880* (Oxford: Oxford University Press, 2014). "Separate but equal" was precisely geared to disguise the obscene forms of inequality between Whites and Blacks. The aim was to systematically disenfranchise African Americans socially and politically. It has also led to increasingly restrictive voter legislation which its critics argue is part and parcel of a strategy of "voter suppression" by conservative forces that feel embattled by demographic shifts, thus fueling the fears of a "Great Replacement." The latter idea of a demographic takeover or indeed occupation by an alien culture has been popularized by the former socialist-turned-conservative thinker Renaud Camus in his eponymously titled book *You Will Not Replace Us*. It notoriously came to prominence during the so-called "Unite the Right" rally in which marchers chanted chillingly "Jews will not replace us!" An earlier version of the "Great Replacement" idea was first articulated by Enoch Powell in his infamous "Rivers of Blood" speech. In 1973, Jean Raspail published *Camp of the Saints*, which was an important influence on Renaud. See, Thomas Chatterton Williams, "The French Origins of 'You Will not Replace Us.'" *The New Yorker.* November 27, 2017. https://www.newyorker.com/magazine/2017/12/04/the-french-origins-of-you-will-not-replace-us.

5   See Alan Feuer, Luke Broadwater, Maggie Haberman, Katie Benner, and Michael S. Schmidt, "Jan. 6: The Story So Far," *The New York Times*. June 9, 2020. https://www.nytimes.com/interactive/2022/us/politics/jan-6-timeline.html?searchResultPosition=1.

It was to the Proud Boys that Trump made a notorious direct appeal in his first debate with Joe Biden, saying they should "stand down but stand by." They seemed to heed Trump's implicit suggestion that, were he to lose the election, the misogynist, White Supremacist organization should be prepared ("stand by"), to take action ("stand up"). On January 6th, 2021, they did precisely that. Such a challenge to the liberal-democratic order subsequently, in the guise of a so-called "Truckers' Protest," spread via Canada – what some are calling the country's own January 6th, 2021 – to New Zealand, Australia, Belgium, France (already profoundly roiled by the *Gilets jaunes* movement) and beyond.

What is especially significant about the assault on the Capitol is that it crystallized an assault on two related aspects of the liberal-democratic order: evidence-based truth claims and on the legitimacy of not just this election but arguably on the symbolism and substance of the US constitutional order itself, central to which is the sanctity of the peaceful transfer of power. And it did so not on the basis of utter chaos and lawlessness or the creation of a vacuum of authority, but rather on an appeal to a form of "charismatic authority," grounded in the unique qualities of Donald Trump. Indeed, it was such charisma that authorized the antinomian transgression of January 6th.

This means that incontrovertible evidence that there simply were no significant election irregularities could be disregarded in favor of claims by the former President and reinforced and amplified not only by a raft of his acolytes, as suggested above, but also, shockingly, sitting members of the Congress, that in fact the election had been "stolen." That this Trumpian narrative has all but captured the Republican Party is made clear by its subsequent censure of Liz Cheney and Adam Kinzinger and the claim that the January 6th attack was "legitimate political discourse."[6]

What this event amounted to, then, was a profound abjecting and undermining of public reason if we understand this to entail the capacity to present arguments and counterarguments grounded in logic and factual evidence. Democracy is premised upon a conception of the very public reason that has been undermined by both the Right and as well as aspects of the post-modern Left, which is increasingly inclined, it seems, to bypass reason and evidence and appeal to the identity and subjective experiences of those articulating truth claims and political demands. Admittedly, while arguments and evidence in the political field are never presented in an abstract and dispassionate way, the question emerges about the role of the logic of digital media in undermining

---

6 Jonathan Weisman and Reid J. Epstein, "G.O.P. Declares Jan. 6 Attack 'Legitimate Political Discourse,'" *The New York Times*. February 4, 2022. https://www.nytimes.com/2022/02/04/us/politics/republicans-jan-6-cheney-censure.html.

public *logos* itself. We have seen in the past decade or so, the dramatic unleashing and exacerbation of powerful and often negative effects that have accompanied and indeed increasingly governed political discourse.[7] Could it be that this is the very digital media that has made us all into populists now?

The assault on the US Capitol raises questions about the role of digital technology not simply in the crisis of liberal-democratic political and scientific institutions, but more specifically about whether the form of post-internet subjectivity is uniquely susceptible to the affective politics of Identitarianism?[8] In order to begin to try to answer this question, this chapter will first provide a sketch of populist politics from the dawn of the neo-liberal order through its current consolidation. It will then provide a framework that addresses the relation between totality, technological form, and ideology within which to survey recent work done on the increasingly pervasive role of digital capitalism in our lives. It argues that while the internet provides a space for new forms of contestation between Left and Right, given the very business model of platform capitalism based on the capture of attention, the maximization of "clicks" and therefore advertising revenue, it seems to lead to a proliferation of negative effects such as anxiety and fear, and this can then be more easily and effectively mobilized by contemporary authoritarian movements than it can by the Left.[9]

1   The Roots of Contemporary Populism

It is hardly deniable that populism has become an increasingly influential form of politics in recent decades. It has a long history stretching all the way back to the Narodnik politics in Russia in the 19th century,[10] as well as forms of agrarian opposition to banking and railway interests in North America. It is also worth noting that Canada's nominally social democratic party, the New Democratic Party, began its life as the populist CCF (Cooperative Commonwealth Federation) in the early 1930s.[11] Populism was also, of course, ancillary to democratization in

---

7   See Shoshona Zuboff, *The Age of Surveillance Capitalism: The Fight for a Human Future at the New Frontier of Power* (New York: Public Affairs Books, 2020).
8   Sam Moore and Alex Roberts, *The Post-Internet Far Right: Fascism in the Age of the Internet* (London: Dog Section Press, 2021).
9   Zuboff, *The Age of Surveillance Capitalism*.
10 Gavin Kitching, *Development and Underdevelopment in Historical Perspective: Populism, Nationalism, Industrialization* (London: Methuen, 1982).
11 J.F. Conway, "Populism in the United States, Russia, and Canada: Explaining the Roots of Canada's Third Parties". *Canadian Journal of Political Science Via Wikipedia Library* 11, no. 1 (March 1978): 99–124.

the Latin American southern cone.[12] It has enjoyed a powerful resurgence in the past decades, possibly in unrecognizable form in comparison to its historical antecedents.

Given this wide range of nominally "populist" politics, populism is one of the slipperiest concepts in the vocabulary of politics and therefore, as many commentators have noted, notoriously difficult if not impossible to define satisfactorily. A recent conception, however, that has proven especially influential is that offered by Cas Mudde in a series a books, articles, and interviews. Mudde defines populism in "ideational" terms that is, defined as a "discourse, and ideology or a world-view." Writing with Cristóbal Rovira Kaltwasser, Mudde defines populism as

> a thin-centered ideology that considers society to be ultimately separated into two homogeneous and antagonistic camps, "the pure people" versus "the corrupt elite," and which argues that politics should be an expression of the volonte générale (general will) of the people.[13]

Kaltwasser and Mudde go on to insist that populism is to be understood as a "thin" ideology, which is to say morphologically restricted in its substantive commitments and therefore dependent upon other ideologies from across the spectrum such as socialism or fascism, hence can take a left-wing and a right-wing form. Kaltwasser and Mudde argue that populism ought to be understood as a "'mental map' through which individuals comprehend and analyze political reality."[14]

A strikingly similar definition is set forth by Jan-Werner Müller in his book *What is Populism?* In Müller's view, populism has three dimensions, it is: (1) anti-elitist; (2) anti-pluralist and therefore a species of morality rather than politics; and, finally, (3) a form of "identity politics." He elaborates on this definition in his conclusion with seven intriguing theses on populism: (1) Populism is a unique feature of representative democracy, which paradoxically it challenges for being insufficiently representative of the "people." (2) Like Mudde and Kaltwasser, Müller reiterates the view that populist politics hinge on

---

12 Ernesto Laclau, *Politics and Ideology in Marxist Theory: Capitalism, Fascism, Populism* (New York: New Left Books, 1977); Nicos Mouzelis, *Politics in the Semi-Periphery: Early Parliamentarianism and Late Industrialization in the Balkans and Latin America* (London: Palgrave Macmillan, 1985).
13 Cas Mudde and Cristobal Rovira Kaltwasser, *A Very Short Introduction to Populism* (Oxford: Oxford University Press, 2017), 6.
14 Ibid.

the opposition between a "pure people" and a "corrupt elite." (3) Populists are less interested in effecting the genuine formation of popular will than in a symbolic representation of its idealized form from which policy can be deduced. (4) Populists typically govern and write or rewrite constitutions in terms favorable to themselves on the assumption that they, and they alone, understand the needs of the people. (5) While they ought to be understood as a threat to democracy and not just to liberalism, populists nonetheless ought to be engaged in debate and discussion. (6) Populism ought not to be regarded as a corrective to liberal democracy, however, it should be seen as a symptomatic of failures of representation. (7) Populism also raises important questions, in Müller's view, of the conditions of inclusion/exclusion in liberal democracies, provides a negative example reinforcing the intrinsic value of pluralism, and so on. Müller, correctly wanting to avoid pathologizing supporters of populist movement, insists on treating them as free and equal citizens and not driven by "frustration, anger and resentment."[15]

There is much of value in both of these overlapping accounts of populism, such as populism's internal tie to the very representative democracy with which it seeks to break; its symbolic rather than real or aggregate representation of the will of the people grounded in identity claims; the way it functions as a symptom of the increasingly apparent short-comings of liberal-democracy, as well as the prescription to engage with, rather than pathologizing, populists.[16]

Several criticisms can also, however, be levelled at Müller as well as Mudde and Kaltwasser's key definition of populism. Müller's contention that populists are less interested in engaging in popular will formation than in symbolically representing the people seems dubious insofar as in Latin America in the 19th century, populism was the means by which the "people" were integrated into politics, though in a subordinate and dependent manner.[17]

Moreover, the key definition of populism as turning on the opposition between a morally "pure people" and a "corrupt elite" is also deeply questionable. Indeed, even if one looks at that recent exemplary form populism, namely

---

15   Jan-Werner Müller, *What is Populism?* (Philadelphia: University of Pennsylvania Press, 2016), 102–03.
16   Such a pathologization has marked a good deal of liberal-left commentary on the Truckers protest. An important debate in the pages of *Canadian Dimension Magazine* in February 2022, centered precisely around the limits and possibilities of a Left populist response that would attempt to re-articulate some of their demands within the context of a genuine working-class movement while, of course, leaving aside its unsavory elements such as White supremacy and misogyny that seemed to be present in the protest. One wonders why no genuinely working-class movement was built.
17   See Mouzelis, *Politics in the Semi-periphery*.

Trumpism, can it really be maintained that it appeals to a morally "pure" representation of the people? A strong argument could be made that the opposite is, in fact, the case.

After Hillary Clinton's disastrous decision to turn her back on disaffected, impoverished Whites from the "rustbelt," labeling them as "a basket of deplorables," many of them, in fact, enthusiastically *embraced* the label. Trump has moreover celebrated the fact that he is popular among the "uneducated." Trump, himself, gave the "people" license to adopt and express explicitly racist, misogynist, and homophobic views in the public sphere.

Perhaps in her epithet, Clinton flips Mudde and Kaltwasser as well as Müller's definition of populism on its head. Is she not the most obvious representative of the "morally pure" *elite* that sneeringly opposes itself to a "corrupt people,"[18] many of whom had been long-standing Democratic Party voters? This becomes especially important when we consider the fact that increasingly the political class has sought to appropriate the moralizing social justice rhetoric of liberal identitarianism by emphasizing race, gender, and sexual orientation while eliding class.

The real source of moralism, it could be argued, is not *populism* per se but the *identity politics* it opposes on both Left as well as the Right. Indeed, it could be maintained that while in the past, the far-right was the party of traditional morality, today it appears to have become the party of transgression. Can any better example of this be cited than the smearing of human feces in the offices of Congress during the January 6th, 2021, insurrection? How could such an act be meaningfully claimed to have been done in the name of a morally "pure" people. The liberal-left has, moreover, with its speech codes and safe spaces, in contrast, become increasingly the upholders of moral rectitude in speech and action.[19] In fact, it could be the case that Trumpism represents a new form of what I call "transgressive populism," by which the "people" are constituted not as a collective moral agent in opposition to a corrupt elite, but, rather, precisely in its capacity to radically transgress what it construes as "politically correct" norms. The pain those interpellated as "the people" experience in the form of the diminishing provision of material goods, i.e., real wages, housing security, healthcare, is *over-compensated* by the profound although regressive pleasures

---

18 One is reminded of Brecht's quip in response to the East German regime's claim that it was disappointed with the "people" that it should then dissolve it and elect another.

19 See Bannon's infamous lecture in Europe where he says racism ought to be regarded as a "badge of honor" by Europeans. "Steve Bannon: Wear 'Racist' label as a Badge of Honor," CNN. March 10, 2018. https://www.youtube.com/watch?v=SYysrAg8Yfo.

of symbolic transgression. Such regression is no better signaled than by the cosplay, scatological apotheosis of January 6th.

In contrast, the Left populism of Bernie Sanders, Podemos, and Jeremy Corbyn, far from construing the people in moral terms, sought to do so explicitly in terms of a class analysis of existing socio-economic inequalities and hierarchies: the 1% versus the 99%. It sought to do so based on a clear-headed strategy of alliance building of the sort that is precisely ruled out by the identitarian moralization of politics, precisely because of its profoundly fragmenting effects, as previously suggested.[20]

What is even more questionable is Müller's injunction against regarding populism being fueled by "frustration, anger and resentment." To draw attention to the affective dimension of political life doesn't *necessarily* lead to a pathologization of those who express negative emotions in public life and who are indeed often encouraged to do so by Right populist leaders.[21] To take up what Mudde and Kaltwasser call an "ideational" approach to populism has the advantage of grasping its protean nature.[22] However, at the same time, like Müller, such an approach can have the effect of eliding precisely the profoundly affective dimension of populism, particularly in its right-wing form. And insofar as they are unable to grasp the affective dimension of populism, they are unable to understand the threat represented by digital or algorithmic populism in establishing, sharpening and aggravating the opposition between "friend and enemy," as it is an in-built feature of the business model of "platform capitalism," on which more later.

The key problem in the "ideational" definition of populism is that it fails to distinguish between Left and Right forms of populism. Left populists draw

---

20   Bernie Sanders' supporters, such as *Jacobin Magazine*, criticize liberal-left identity politics specifically for moralizing political categories. In fact, the endorsement of Bernie Sanders by the now especially controversial podcast host, Joe Rogan, sparked an enormous amount of debate on the identitarian Left because of some of the unsavory things that Rogan had said about transgender people. Subsequently, it has come out that he had repeatedly used the "N" word and has also provided a platform to vaccine skeptics and had himself spread false information about negative health impacts of vaccines on young people. While Rogan's comments and stances on vaccines are reprehensible and worthy of condemnation, his endorsement of Sanders could have delivered considerable support to the latter's Presidential nomination campaign. Political strategy cannot allow itself to run aground on the shoals of moral purity.

21   For a similar argument viz *The Authoritarian Personality*, see Martin Jay, "*The Authoritarian Personality* and the Problematic Pathologization of Politics," *Polity* 54, no. 1 (January 2022): 124–145.

22   Or to understand the notion of the people as an "empty signifier" as Ernesto Laclau puts it. See his *On Populist Reason* (London and New York: Verso, 2005), Chapter 4.

attention in a more-or-less *rational* manner to socio-economic inequality, which contradicts the basic principle of the liberal-democratic order, namely: the idea of the *equality* of citizens.[23] In other words, it points towards the legitimacy crisis of the liberal-democratic order and argues for a new set of economic and social arrangements. Right populists, on the other hand, present the political field not in the analytical terms of a structural form of inequality between the 99% and the 1% or between the "many" and the "few," but in a profoundly affectively-charged idiom in which the "people" are confronted by nefarious, inscrutable, and implacable existential "enemies," that is, forces that call into question the "people's" very existence, typically through demographic threats such as immigration and the supposed rising birth-rates of immigrant populations. Right populists claim that elites seek to manage these dynamics by way of "social justice" discourse and "political correctness," which they construe, misguidedly, as threatening White privilege. They foster a strong state and a free market (Schmitt).[24]

While Left populists also, to be sure, challenge the authority of elites, they nonetheless draw a distinction between *legitimate* and *illegitimate* forms of authority. By and large, Left populists tend to accept the legitimacy of scientific reason and the liberal-democratic order even as they defend oversight over the former and propose ambitious programs to further "democratize" the latter by redistributing wealth and power. As the left-liberal turned socialist economist, Thomas Piketty has argued: "We need to turn our backs on the ideology of absolute free trade," he writes, in favor of "a model of development based on explicit and verifiable principles of economic, fiscal and environmental justice."[25]

---

23   One of the first leftist theorists of populism, or what he called the "national-popular," Antonio Gramsci, saw demystification of social relations in terms of a transformation of "common sense" into "good sense" or a historically grounded understanding of social relations. This would be central to building proletarian hegemony. The influence of the republican political theory of the Renaissance thinker par excellence, namely Niccolo Machiavelli, is well known. See Samir Gandesha, "The Aesthetic Politics of Hegemony," *Studi di estetica, anno XLVI, IV serie, 3/2018*.

24   The evidence for this is suggested by Thomas B. Edsall in a series of interviews with political operatives and academics in this article. While those on the left of the Democratic Party seek to pursue an ambitious legislative agenda, those on the right of the GOP engage in little more than "bullying" and attention seeking. Thomas B. Edsall, "How much Damage have Marjorie Taylor Greene and the 'Bullies' done to the G.O.P.?," *The New York Times*. June 8, 2022. https://www.nytimes.com/2022/06/08/opinion/maga-caucus-squad-congress.html?searchResultPosition=1.

25   See Robert Kuttner's review of Thomas Piketty's *A Time for Socialism*, "Thomas Piketty: The Making of a Socialist," *The New York Times*, October 28, 2021. https://www.nytimes.com/2021/10/26/books/review/time-for-socialism-thomas-piketty.html Accessed Dec 9, 2023.

The form of authority upon which liberal-democracy is based is what Max Weber called "legal-rational authority."[26] The idea which could be said to encompass not just political and legal institutions but also the authority of claims to truth and moral rightness is the legitimacy of the procedures that constitutes their ground. In other words, the recognition of the authority of governments and scientific bodies, such as, for example, centers for disease control, resides not in the *personalities* of their leaders but in the *soundness of the procedures* they follow, which is to say: methods, rules, and laws.

The moment elected representatives and scientists cease following such procedures, they forfeit the authority invested in them. Each of the substantive claims made according to such procedures is contestable by definition via rational means. Governments are considered to be legitimate (even or perhaps especially by those who didn't cast a vote for them) because the procedure by which they are elected is held to be sound, which is to say, "free and fair." This means the very same procedures can be used at the time of the next election to vote the incumbents out of office. And the assumption is that if they lose an election these *incumbents will peacefully transfer power to the newly elected representatives*.

Science, moreover, is grounded in a logic of Popperian "conjecture and refutation" or systematic, controlled, and precise skepticism within the ambit scientific inquiry itself. But this makes scientific inquiry inherently fraught insofar as the dynamic nature of scientific research, the very revisability of its claims in light of the best available evidence, is often taken as grounds for its untrustworthiness and opens it to the kind of summary dismissal that has become ubiquitous in our age.

In contrast to Left populism, which seeks to further *democratize* the liberal-democratic order by directly tackling socio-economic inequality, Right populism launches an attack on democratic institutions, although often disingenuously in the form of a democratic appeal to the "general will" of the people, for example, in the form of what Richard Nixon called the "silent majority." It does so – in a tradition that can be traced back to the conservative critic of the French Revolution, Edmund Burke – within the context of more general criticism of the increasingly *abstract* nature of social life in the interest of lived experience and forms of identity grounded in such meaningful experience.[27]

---

26   Max Weber, *Economy and Society: An Outline of Interpretive Sociology Volume 1*, ed. Guenther Roth and Claus Wittich (Berkeley: University of California Press, 1978), 215.
27   For example, a placard at a recent anti-vaccine rally read: "Better to die at the hand of God than an artificial vaccine." The claim, of course, is that while the former constitutes a *meaningful* death, latter a *meaningless* one. This is reminiscent of the existential decisionism that lies at the heart of political theology.

Rather than contesting specific elections or scientific findings – call this a logic of "immanent skepticism" – Right populism increasingly tends to bring skepticism to bear from the outside and challenges the legitimacy of institutions that governed by abstract and formal procedures *per se*. In doing so, it rejects the fundamental principles of liberal order and moves increasingly in the direction of "illiberal democracy"[28] based on exclusionary forms of nationalism (ethno-nationalism rather than civic nationalism), majoritarianism or Reckwitz's "collective singularity." As previously suggested, its solution, *pace* Orban and Putin, is "illiberal democracy."[29]

Rather than addressing the crises by way of bringing the social systems of money and power increasingly under the sway of the communicative rationality of the social lifeworld, according to the deliberative social democratic option favored by Habermas, or through a radical democratic option whereby both state and economy are "democratized" by transcending the law of value, Right populism launches general attacks on "elites" defined predominantly in *cultural* rather than *socio-economic terms*.[30] Moreover, it constructs an opposition between friend and foe as the basis for a concrete grounding of politics in polemical opposition to the abstract, universalist principles of liberalism. In other words, rather than mediating these abstract logics, by embedding them in *genuinely* egalitarian and democratic institutions, Right populists simply seek to negate these logics in the interest of a supposedly concrete form of identity. The appeal to such a form of identity is inherently authoritarian.

2   Authoritarianism Populism

As I have argued elsewhere, it is possible to regard Right and Left forms of populism less in terms of their opposition between a supposedly "pure people" and

---

[28]   A rejection that is increasingly common on the "decolonial" liberal-left, which appears to want to throw the proverbial rational baby out with the colonial bathwater.

[29]   This explains why an Alt-Right commentor such as Tucker Carlson is so enamored of Orban and Putin and also why this love is clearly requited. See Anne Applebaum, "The American Face of Authoritarian Propaganda," *The Atlantic*. September 21, 2023. https://www.theatlantic.com/ideas/archive/2023/09/tucker-carlson-putin-orban-propaganda/675380/.

[30]   Populist leaders, themselves typically drawn from elite strata, such as Boris Johnson, play up an image that makes them appear to be rather uncouth or rough around the edges and hence easy for ordinary people to identify with as an enlarged or inflated version of themselves. See Samir Gandesha, "A Composite of King Kong and a Suburban Barber: Revisiting Adorno's "Freudian Theory and the Pattern of Fascist Propaganda," in Samir Gandesha (ed.) *Spectres of Fascism: History and Theory in International Perspective* (London: Pluto Press, 2020), 120–141.

"corrupt elite" but in their approach to affect or, more precisely, *disaffection*. Far from being "pathological," frustration and anger can be regarded a structural feature of capitalist civilization as psychoanalysis suggests.[31] Objective socio-economic crisis which is endemic to capitalist societies lead to subjective psychological responses such as frustration, anger, anxiety, and fear. Capitalist civilization necessitates what Herbert Marcuse calls "surplus" repression, which is to say, a form of repression required by a capitalist social order to maximize the rate of exploitation but that could be made obsolete in a post-capitalist one in which only "basic" repression would be present.[32] Such disaffection exacerbates the democratic paradox and the crisis of meaning identified by Weber. It provokes, moreover, what Erich Fromm called a "fear of freedom" insofar as freedom becomes experienced less as liberation and more as a sense of disempowerment that propels individuals in the direction of an identification with the aggressor.[33] Such disaffection is exacerbated by contemporary neoliberal-democracy insofar as it, on the one hand, holds out the promise of the equality of citizens and genuine self-determination, however, on the other, insofar as such an order is a *capitalist* democracy, and therefore based on social and economic inequality, these promises are inevitably and often cynically broken.[34]

After forty years of neoliberal policies, *Les Trente Glorieueses* seem increasingly anomalous.[35] What comes to the fore is the heightened contradiction, alluded to above, between the conflicting imperatives faced by the liberal-democratic state of fostering capital accumulation, on the one hand, and democratic legitimation, on the other.[36] Populism arises as a result of such

---

[31] Indeed, from a Weberian perspective, the emotion of fear in the form of fear of damnation lies at the heart of the "spirit" of capitalism and could be said to be present at its very origin. Hobbes of course before Weber shows the way in which the naturalized image of the early capitalist order is suffused with insecurity, anxiety, and fear of violent death. We might say that the dialectic of enlightenment creates a radical form of anxiety that is mobilized as fear of the other by forces fostering a mythological construction of the "people."

[32] See Herbert Marcuse, *Eros and Civilization: A Philosophical Inquiry into Freud* (Boston: Beacon Press, 1974).

[33] Erich Fromm, *Escape from Freedom* (New York: Henry Holt & Co., 1994).

[34] This has been well documented by the British film-makers Ken Loach and Mike Leigh.

[35] See Thomas Piketty, *Capital in the Twenty-first Century* (Cambridge, MA: Belknap Press, 2017).

[36] Neoliberals such as Milton Friedman and Friedrich Hayek notoriously chose the former over the latter and embraced authoritarian solutions such as the Pinochet dictatorship. See Samir Gandesha, "The Brazilian Matrix: Between Fascism and Neo-Liberalism Vladimir Safatle and Samir Gandesha in Conversation," *Krisis* 40, no. 1 (November 2020): 215–233. https://krisis.eu/article/view/37054.

contradiction particularly in moments of particularly acute crises of legitimation, for example in the late 19th century, in the 1930s, the mid-1970s, and so forth. While legitimation crises of advanced capitalist societies have been frequent throughout the 20th century, the first one of the 21st century can be discerned in the aftermath of the 2008–09 financial crisis in the US, one with global ramifications. The legitimation crisis of democratic institutions became especially clear in the idea that private financial institutions would be rescued with public funds; members of the public, whose tax dollars funded the bailout, would be left to their privatized, individualized fates, insofar as they were abandoned to default on their mortgages and consequently would lose their homes. So, again, the anger and frustration that arises out of the legitimation crises of neoliberal-democracy is not to be conceived in any sense as *pathological* but as an understandable subjective response to objective or structural feature of contemporary capitalist societies. In other words, disaffection is a predictable response to the repeated breaking of promises by the liberal-democratic order, which are experienced with especial intensity during its legitimation crises.

Right populism tends to take up the disaffection of its followers, "the people," magnifies it, and finally directs such disaffection towards the people's ostensible "enemies." In many cases, this enemy is two-fold: it is comprised of both the established elites as well as what we could call the downtrodden or the marginalized whom they supposedly champion: immigrants, refugees, migrant workers, members of the LGBTQ+ communities and so forth. The establishment's embrace of identity politics was made clear in Clinton's moralizing dismissal of the "basket of deplorables" and her rather cynical embrace of the language of "intersectionality." The culture war becomes a distraction that permits class inequalities to only deepen. Insofar as the neo-liberal state has increasingly embraced identity politics in a manner that elides class, Right populists typically articulate their politics in terms of an increasingly violent transgressive violation of "politically correct" norms emphasizing a nostalgic discourse that highlights the importance of traditional, White, patriarchal, and hetero-normative values as was crystalized by the notorious slogan "Make America Great Again."

Left populism, in contrast, far from magnifying the disaffection of its followers, seeks to provide determinate policy solutions to its causes. While the perfect storm created by the migration crisis following from the wars resulting from the US response to 9/11 and then, seven years later, the financial crisis, created an opening for the Tea Party to push the GOP far to right, ultimately preparing the ground for Trump's version of existential politics, the response by the Left was to "Occupy Wall Street." This movement, however, was perhaps correctly criticized for refusing or being unable to engage in what Ernesto Laclau would call an equivalential articulation of heterogenous demands against an antagonistic frontier.[37] Drawing on the powerful yet anarchic energies of Occupy, Bernie Sanders was able to clearly articulate a set of democratic socialist demands including universal healthcare, the abolition of student debts, the inclusion of workers' representatives on corporate boards, etc. Additionally, he famously argued that if the banks were "too big to fail," they should be broken up. So, in contrast to the attempt to *weaponize* the justifiable sense of grievance experienced by those who were negatively impacted by globalization and its socio-economic consequences, Sanders and increasingly those on the left or progressive wing of the Democratic Party *offered concrete policy solutions to such greivances.*

There was a resurgence of populism at the beginning of the neo-liberal era, most notably with Margaret Thatcher's brand of what Stuart Hall, drawing upon Antonio Gramsci, calls "authoritarian populism." What is key in Hall's account is that such a form of populism was a response to the "organic crisis" of the Keynesian state that was beset by "stagflation," which now appears to be haunting our present once again. In contrast to a limited or merely "conjunctural" crisis, Gramsci defined such a crisis as one of hegemony, which implied an opening for the creation of a new "power bloc" and new forms of "common sense." The latter pitted the individual, now defined principally as a rate- or taxpayer rather than citizen, against a putatively unresponsive, ossified bureaucratic state that was inextricably linked with an equally oppressive, bureaucratic laborism or social democracy. What was more is that it successfully portrayed the social welfare state as pandering to "special," which is to say "ethnic" or "multicultural," interests while supposedly denigrating "authentic" British or English values, typically by fostering immigration from the formerly colonized world such as South Asia and Africa, which, in turn, fed into crises of education and "law and order." With the dramatic rise of unemployment, workers and their families who had been encouraged to emigrate from the Caribbean – the "Windrush Generation" – now began to fall out of favor and were increasingly subjected to the accusation that "they" were taking "our" jobs.

An important flashpoint, moreover, was the arrival of Asians from Uganda after their expulsion in 1972, at which point the racism that had already found visceral expression in the Enoch Powell's infamous "Rivers of Blood" speech four years earlier, exploded and led to the meteoric rise of neo-fascism amidst socio-economic crisis of historic proportions. Powell's racist invective was echoed in only a slightly more measured way in Margaret Thatcher's own political discourse. In a widely viewed and cited television interview, she suggested

---

37   Laclau, *On Populist Reason*, 74.

that "ordinary" (read: nativist or White) Britons were concerned about being "rather swamped by a different culture."[38] In this statement, one finds a key trope that would come to animate contemporary authoritarian populism: the White supremacist fear of being "replaced" by "inferior" brown and black races or what has come to be called the "Great Replacement" or even more provocatively "White genocide."[39]

In fact, the rightward turn of the Conservative Party under Thatcher had a profoundly adverse impact on neo-fascist parties such as National Front and the British Movement as their agendas were increasingly appropriated by the Tories. What was at issue here is a worry about the replacement of human labor power by machines and automation (today we would add AI and machine learning) is expressed not in universalist terms, i.e., the replaceability by constant of variable capital but the replacement of a particular "people" defined specifically in ethno-nationalist terms by its malevolent enemy or enemies.[40] The formula of authoritarian populism was therefore set: the atmospheric *anxiety* created by a major socio-economic crisis was transformed by figures such as Powell, Thatcher, Tebbitt, and others into a *fear*

---

38   "1978: Le 'swamped' de Margaret Thatcher." https://www.dailymotion.com/video/x28votz.
39   Renaud Camus, *You Will not Replace US* (Plieux, France: Chez l'auteur, 2018); Jean Raspail, *The Camp of the Saints,* ed. Norman Shapiro (Petoskey, MI: The Social Contract Press, 2015).
40   One finds this shrewdly captured in Joel Schumacher's 1993 film *Falling Down,* in which the protagonist, anti-hero William Foster (played by Michael Douglas), is beset by a series of minor misfortunes (his car breaks down, he doesn't have the change to call his ex-wife, hilariously he can't get breakfast at Whammy Burger, etc.), which magnifies the frustration and anger he feels at losing both his family and his job as a technician helping to build missiles in the defense industry (he is identified by Robert Duval's character Prendergast by his car license plate that reads D-fens, which also of course has psychoanalytical meaning). The vocabulary Foster employs to describe his situation is, significantly, borrowed from a Black man he sees earlier in the day protesting histrionically outside of a bank for deeming him to be "No longer economically viable." Foster, whose predicament is the product of the very neo-liberal mantra "greed is good" famously uttered by his alter-ego, so to speak, Gordon Gekko (also of course played by Michael Douglas) in Oliver Stone's *Wall Street* seven years earlier, understands himself to be similarly obsolete. Rather than making common cause across the "color line" with others in the same position based on class, he harkens back to the good old days when White men like him possessed incontestable power. The reason for his disorientation and anger is a result of the increasing realization that he now shares the same fate of a Black man. Foster is therefore clearly bewildered amidst a multicultural, polyglot Los Angeles, beset with crime and homelessness due to the very forces that have turned his own life upside down, as profoundly alien, and therefore threatening. Not only is his whiteness called into question but so is his masculinity understood not only in terms of sexual virility but also ability to provide for his estranged wife and daughter. Foster has no choice but to move back home and live with his mother, whom he wishes to murder, in a strange inversion of the Oedipus complex.

of an identifiable object – the immigrant, refugee, "mugger" – who in the process is turned into a political "enemy" who threatened a certain way of life (Britishness).[41]

Contemporary populism, in contrast to that of Thatcher's brand of authoritarian populism, is marked not by opposition to the welfare state, but rather represents a deeply ambivalent response to the managerial elites steering neo-liberal globalization. It now responds to the organic crisis of the neo-liberal capitalist order it helped to forge. Although it is tempting to conjecture that perhaps with the transformation of Keynesian state, with each crisis now-liberalism falls forward, that is, it occasions not a retreat from but a deepening of neo-liberalism itself.[42]

An important reason for this is that unlike in the late-1970s, there are seemingly no alternatives to the neo-liberal order such as an admittedly deeply flawed form of state socialism. The alternative, unacceptable though it was, of the Soviet bloc nevertheless kept Western capitalist states honest insofar as they were forced to adhere to basic legal protections for unions, workplace health and safety, progressive taxation, the redistribution of wealth, and so forth. This meant that authoritarian populists had to at least pay lip-service to liberal-democracy to contrast it to the supposed "tyranny" of the Eastern Bloc.

So, it could be that what we witness is a transformation in the very nature of crisis itself: from acute to chronic, from episodic events to an enduring syndrome on the backdrop of ecological collapse.[43] This perception has been reinforced by the COVID-19 pandemic. Moreover, while nominally social democratic parties, such as the British Labor Party under Blair and Brown and now under Starmer, have made clearly their peace with neo-liberalism, a form of Left populism has emerged, in the form the Corbyn Interregnum as well as Bernie Sanders' candidacy in 2016 and 2020 for the Democratic ticket, which has also propelled other progressive figures within the Democratic Party such as the so-called "Squad," and has enormously energized the DSA and also vehicles of socialist ideas such as the publication *Jacobin*. Left populism is resurgent in other parts of Europe such as Spain with Podemos as well as in Germany with Die Linke, specifically, Sara Wagenknecht's BSW. Left populism has also found its critics such as in the French commentator Eric Fassin, who has suggested that in attempting to challenge

---

41 Samir Gandesha, "The Political Semiosis of Populism," *The Semiotic Review of Books* 13, no. 3 (2003): 1–7.
42 See Jamie Peck, *Constructions of Neo-Liberal Reason* (Oxford: Oxford University Press, 2010).
43 See Samir Gandesha, "Introduction," in *Spectres of Fascism*, 1–26.

right-populism on its own terms, Left populism, inadvertently perhaps, reinforce xenophobic and nativist ideas.⁴⁴

What most separates the populism of the late 1970s from contemporary populism, however, is the key role of digital technologies in its communication strategies. As I have already alluded to, populism is more than just a discourse whose fulcrum is the opposition between the "people" and the "elites." Rather, the internet itself has in a certain sense "democratized" knowledge and therefore contributed profoundly to the conditions within which populism as a political discourse can succeed by weaking the hold of traditional elites, not least in academia as well as in the so-called "legacy" media. In releasing powerful effects, digital media has also contributed to a logic of Left-liberal attempts to capture and discipline such affects through the moralization of politics (policing of language, creation of safe spaces, callouts, etc.) and a Right populist counterstrategy of radical transgression. If the Left has fallen prey to a morose and melancholic enjoyment of victimhood, of what Sara Ahmed has termed "Killjoy Feminism," then what the populist right offers is a politics of pleasure in transgression, which had historically been central to a certain left-wing avant-garde.⁴⁵

Populism has therefore become at a certain level inescapable. And this raises the question of whether it is possible to speak of what we might call an "algorithmic populism," which is to say, a populism that is to be distinguished from all previous forms insofar as the rhetorical elements of previous forms of authoritarian populism are increasingly replaced by technologically-mediated forms of communication, which are increasingly pervasive in all aspects of our lives, themselves increasingly played out in virtual spaces.⁴⁶ While perhaps not exactly replacing but displacing what Löwenthal and Guterman call the "agitator's" invective against ostensible "enemies" of the "people," is the more subtle and insidious role algorithms play in imperceptibly multiplying, amplifying, and accelerating negative affects directed against particular, denigrated out-groups.⁴⁷

---

44 See Martina Tazzioli, "Left-wing Populism A legacy of Defeat: An Interview with Eric Fassin with Martina Tazzioli, Peter Hallward and Claudia Aradau," *Radical Philosophy* 202 (June 2018): 79–92. https://www.radicalphilosophy.com/article/left-wing-populism. Given the anti-immigration and xenophobic turn of BSW, this seems like a prescient analysis.

45 Think, for example, of Brecht's epic theatre, the Russian avant-garde, Dada, Surrealism and the détournement of the Situationist International. Today their work and practices would no doubt be shut down as "offensive" or "triggering."

46 With the advent of the so-called "metaverse," this is poised to become even more pronounced in the near future.

47 See Leo Löwenthal and Norbert Guterman, *Prophets of Deceit: A Study in the Techniques of the American Agitator* (London and New York: Verso, 2021).

3 Algorithmic Populism?

Let us think about the three dimensions – objective, subjective, institutional – of the new authoritarian populism. To explain the *objective* conditions that give rise to authoritarian potential, it is necessary to go beyond mere historical events, such as 9/11 or the 2008 financial crisis and their complex consequences, to underlying structural factors. These have to do, as I've already suggested, with the profound tension lying at the heart of bourgeois society between the principle of *democratic self-governance* and the actuality of a negative *account of freedom*, the long-standing conflict between equality and liberty. In "The Meaning of Working Through the Past," Theodor W. Adorno argues that an understanding of fascism cannot be reduced to "subjective dispositions," but rather must be rooted in an analysis of an economic system in which the majority of people are dependent upon forces beyond their control and therefore in a state of what he calls, in a bow to Kant, "political immaturity," or a condition in which they are unable to think or speak for themselves. He suggests:

> If they want to live, then no other avenue remains but to adapt, submit themselves to the given conditions; they must negate precisely that autonomous subjectivity to which the idea of democracy appeals; they can preserve themselves only if they renounce their self ... The necessity of such adaptation, of identification with the given, the status quo, with power as such, creates the potential for totalitarianism.[48]

And if there were any doubt that this logic applies only to the Global North then such doubt is dispelled by Jawaharlal Nehru University political scientist, Ajay Gudavarthy, who writes in his 2018 book, *India After Modi: Populism and the Right:*

> This unique historical moment has been one where the formal reach of the political discourse of equality, dignity, recognition, and representation has spread to all quarters and sections of human society, while the conditions to realize them have become cumulatively contained and dissipated.[49]

---

48 Theodor W. Adorno, "The Meaning of Working Through the Past," in *Critical Models: Interventions and Catchwords*, trans. Henry W. Pickford (New York: Columbia University Press, 1998), 98–99. See also Theodor W. Adorno, *Aspekte des neuen Rechtsradikalismus* (Frankfurt am Main: Suhrkamp, 2019), 39.
49 Ajay Gudavarthy, *India After Modi* (New Delhi: Bloomsbury, 2018): xii.

The neoliberal, financialized form of capitalism, which has been in place roughly since the mid-1970s, has dramatically sharpened this contradiction insofar as what Wendy Brown calls *homo politicus* has become eclipsed by *homo economicus*, understood as the "entrepreneur of himself."[50] The latter is forced to take more responsibility for himself, yet, at the same time, has access to fewer resources with which to actualize this responsibility in any meaningful sense. On average, rates of growth in high-income countries have dropped precipitously since the 1960s. At the same time, since the 1970s, wages for the vast majority have remained stagnant, not even keeping pace with inflation,[51] while welfare state provisions have declined considerably, and social services as well as higher education have become more costly. What has filled this vacuum is growing financialization and debt.[52] Individuals cannot but fall drastically short of their subjective aspirations and ideals, and as a result there is a corresponding proliferation of guilt, anxiety, frustration, and ultimately anger.[53] For Samo Tomsic, this leads to the production of what he calls the "capitalist unconscious," which is to say capital's colonization of fantasy. Nick Dyer-Witheford and Svitlana Matviyenko develop an analysis of cyberwar "in political–economic terms, as a manifestation of the class antagonisms of global high-technology capitalism, and psychoanalytically, as a field where these contradictions are charged with fantasies and imaginary misrecognitions, production of affect and capitalization of fears, and symptoms of users"[54]

Far from guarding against authoritarianism as per the justification of its advocates, then, the contradictory inner logic of neoliberalism generates a profound subjective tendency towards such authoritarianism; that it first emerged

---

50 See Wendy Brown, *Undoing the Demos: Neo-Liberalism's Stealth Revolution* (Princeton: Zone Books, 2015); Michel Foucault, *Birth of Biopolitics: Lectures at the College de France 1978–79* (New York: Picador, 2010), 226.

51 See Thomas Piketty, *Capital in the Twenty-First Century*, trans. Arthur Goldhammer (Cambridge, Mass: Belknap Press, 2014) in which he shows that the average return on capital far outstrips the increase in the rise of wages leading to a logic of widening socio-economic inequality, which reverses the anomalous trend of the *trente glorieuses*.

52 See Costas Lapavitsas, *Crisis in the Eurozone* (London: Verso, 2012) and Maurizio Lazzarato, *The Making of the Indebted Man: An Essay on the Neoliberal Condition* (Cambridge, MA: Semiotext(e) Books, 2012) and *Governing by Debt* (Cambridge, MA: Semiotext(e) Books, 2015).

53 As Jay Frankel and Lynne Layton have argued, this also leads to shame – a common response to trauma that results from the feeling that there is something wrong with oneself. See Jay Frankel, "The persistent sense of being bad: The moral dimension of identification with the aggressor," in *The Legacy of Sandor Ferenczi: From Ghost to Ancestor*, ed. Adrienne Harris and Steven Kuchuck (New York: Routledge, 2015), 204–222.

54 Nick Dyer-Witheford and Svitlana Matviyenko, *Cyberwar and Revolution: Digital Subterfuge in Global Capitalism* (Minneapolis: University of Minnesota Press, 2019), 28.

under the supervision of the Chicago Boys under the watch of Pinochet dictatorship is no coincidence, as the Brazilian philosopher, Vladimir Safatle has recently reminded us.[55] This was not a "stealth" revolution at all, but an all-too open and transparent one.

Neoliberalism, in other words, creates conditions for authoritarian potential to be activated by contemporary "agitators" who can transform such guilt, anxiety, and frustration into fear and hatred of an increasingly dehumanized other. The condition for the possibility of "people being transformed into a mass," as Adorno put it, is the passivity that follows from the gradual but steady weakening of the critical function of the ego. The individual is no longer capable of genuine experience, which is to say, encounter *otherness* in a receptive and transformative way.

In their account of the culture industry, Horkheimer and Adorno show the way in which it replaces what Kant called the "transcendental schema," according to which the sensible manifold is related to concepts through the activity of the imagination, by

> ready-made thought models, the termini technici which provide them with iron rations following the decay of language. *The perceiver is no longer present in the process of perception.* He or she is incapable of the active passivity of cognition, in which categorial elements are appropriately reshaped by preformed conventional schemata and vice versa, so that justice is done to the perceived object.[56]

This is what Herbert Marcuse calls in his synthesis of historical materialism and phenomenology the "technological a priori."[57] Such a passive structure of experience creates the conditions in which agitators can appeal directly to the affects by circumventing critical, rational mediation.

Through a propagandistic appeal to an exclusionary conception of the "people" combined with the claim to manifesting its will, executive authority embodied in a "strong man" seeks to undermine liberal democracy's system of checks

---

55 See Vladimir Safatle, "Fascist Neoliberalism and Preventive Counter-Revolution: The Second Round of the Latin American Laboratory," in Gandesha, *Spectres of Fascism*, 179–190.
56 Max Horkheimer and Theodor W. Adorno, *Dialectic of Enlightenment: Philosophical Fragments* (Stanford, CA: Stanford University Press, 2002), 167. Emphasis added.
57 Herbert Marcuse, "Some Social Implications of Modern Technology," in *The Essential Frankfurt Reader*, ed. Andrew Arato and Eike Gebhart (New York: Continuum, 1985), 138–162.

and balances via the autonomy of legislative, and particularly the judicial, branches of government and the rule of law more generally.[58] Institutionally, the "transcendental schema" has become replaced by what Ed Finn, in his book *What Algorithms Want*, calls the "algorithmic imagination" in organizing the manifold of sensible intuition.[59] Jaron Lanier likens such an imagination, at least as it manifests itself in social media platforms, to a gigantic virtual Skinnerian box.[60] In place of Fordist mass production and standardization, the culture industry now generates difference and heterogeneity tailored specifically to the whims and tastes of each individual, which are, themselves, subjected to unending modification, manipulation, and monetization.

Three of the most visible populist leaders in the current era, Donald J. Trump, Narendra Modi, and Jair Bolsonaro, use social media platforms such as Twitter/X and WhatsApp with great effect to communicate directly with their supporters. They are able to circumvent in-principle critical institutions such as the so-called "legacy" media and the academy, whose role as sites of historically informed, systematic expertise is to scrutinize the claims of political leaders, parties, and governments and, in the process, to hold them accountable. If liberal democracy embodies a constellation of institutions and laws (constitutions) designed to limit majoritarian governments in their capacity to dominate the minority, then social media is a multifaceted tool that enables an authoritarian or even fascistic rejection of liberal democratic limits on sovereign power. We have seen this, as I have already suggested, in the January 6th, 2021, insurrection on Capitol Hill as well as in the more recent Truckers' protest originating in Canada and subsequently fanning out to other continents.

Populist leaders' use of social media to create a spectacle of power and domination, through which they construct enduring bonds with their followers through shared conspiratorial fantasies, a sense of persecution and victimhood, and negative effects of frustration, anger, even hatred, goes hand in hand with attacks on the mainstream media and the university, which then become characterized as nefarious and elitist "enemies of the people." In respect to the latter, there is a pattern in the previously mentioned examples of attacks on universities as bastions of "cultural Marxism" and "political correctness."

The parallels with the Nazis' attacks on the "lying press" (*Lügenpresse*) and Leftist intellectuals ought to be clear. This was shown strikingly in Volker

---

58 See Gandesha, "Introduction," in *Spectres of Fascism*.
59 Ed Finn, *What Algorithms Wand: Imagination in the Age of Computing* (Cambridge, MA: MIT Press, 2017).
60 Jaron Lanier, *Ten Arguments for Deleting Your Social Media Accounts Right Now*, epub (New York: Henry Holt, 2018), 12.

Schlöndorff's adaptation of Gunter Grass's arresting rise of National Socialism in *The Tin Drum* in the scene in which the bust of Beethoven that rests on the piano is replaced by a radio that broadcasts Hitler's speeches directly into the sphere of intimate private life. This dramatically anticipates the way in which social media works today. What the film suggests is a remarkable shift in culture from the active relationship towards art, signified by the piano and the mimetic relationship to music; that is, the inextricable connection between playing and listening to the increasingly passive consumption of the speeches of the *Führer*, which in their own way set the mold for patterns of consumption of commodified products of what Horkheimer and Adorno would call the "culture industry."

However, the culture industry has become even more ubiquitous than the technologies of cultural reproducibility. In the early 20th century, the culture industry began to colonize the private sphere, the bourgeois interior, with its consolidation, and to transform the very structure of subjectivity itself. As Marx noted in the *Grundrisse*, "production thus not only creates an object for the subject, but also a subject for the object."[61] The culture industry evinces the same logic: its products transform subjectivity and in not just a figurative way. It is likely that the highly addictive nature and compulsive use of social media profoundly affects brain plasticity insofar as it alters neural networks and, in the process, can negatively impact, for example, length of attention spans and the ability to concentrate over sustained periods of time.

Yet today social media platforms such as Facebook, Instagram, and Twitter/X don't simply form part of the entertainment or the culture industry. Given the context, we present different aspects of ourselves through social media: we present our professional selves on LinkedIn, where we share news about a new position or a promotion; our social selves on Instagram, where we share photos of a recent dinner party or vacation; our public selves on Facebook and Twitter/X, where we share our views, news (fake and otherwise) with "friends" as well as strangers across the world.

If within neoliberalism's all-pervasive ethos of "possessive individualism" persons are made to become increasingly responsible for their own fates and must, therefore, constantly invest and reinvest in their own "human capital," which becomes, as it were, their "brand," then social media enables this across the increasingly blurred private, public, and professional domains of their lives. It contributes to what Morelock and Narita call, up-dating Guy Debord,

---

61   Karl Marx, *Grundrisse: Introduction to the Critique of Political Economy*, trans. Martin Nicolaus (New York: Vintage Books, 1973), 92.

"the society of the selfie."[62] As a result, social media becomes increasingly inescapable. Choosing to opt out of it often entails embracing marginalization and exclusion. Social media encourages and monetizes a scripted form of authenticity in which users show themselves, paradoxically, in a highly staged and artificial way, being "true to themselves."[63] Taken together, social media becomes key to what sociologist Erwin Goffman calls the "presentation of self in everyday life" insofar as it entails a form of dramaturgy, stage-setting, and definition of the situation.[64] All of these are components of social media, from individual page design and creation through often exaggerated, histrionic staking out of moral and political positions for the benefit of an audience (friends, followers, networks). The growing authoritarianism on the Left (identity politics) and on the Right (the Alt-Right) is often closely linked to specific social media platforms: Tumblr for the former, 4- and 8-Chan and YouTube for the latter.[65]

At one level, digital technology is much more active than the analog technology it replaced. For example, YouTube makes it possible for consumers to produce and curate their own content to generate likes, attract viewers and subscribers, and eventually advertisers, revenue, and income. Yet at a deeper level, that of the very design of the technology itself, passivity, uniformity, and identity is built in. If I typically watch a particular band or follow particular YouTubers, then the algorithm, which is essentially a digital flowchart, directs the me to other, similar "products." Like the Kantian notion of transcendental apperception, it *pre-selects* content for me, the consumer.

The pivotal role of social media can help us understand, in part, why its ubiquity should be structurally biased towards authoritarianism as opposed to liberal much less radical democracy. Each of these sites has become a conduit of political messaging or propaganda, as we know from the Cambridge Analytica scandal that showed the mass manipulation during the 2016 US Presidential Election and the UK Brexit referendum. While the politically deleterious effects of communications technologies have been widely remarked upon, there has been little attention to their specific role within the rise of authoritarian populism, although Timothy Snyder notes that the contemporary far-right has reflexively learned the lessons of the 1930s and has adopted

---

62   Felipe Ziotti Narita and Jeremiah Morelock, *The Society of the Selfie: Social Media and the Crisis of Liberal Democracy* (London: University of Westminster Press, 2021).
63   See Catherine Fieschi, *Populocracy: The Tyranny of Authenticity and the Rise of Populism* (New York: Columbia University Press, 2019).
64   Erving Goffman, *The Presentation of the Self in Everyday Life* (New York: Doubleday, 1956).
65   See Angela Nagle's insightful though flawed book, *Kill All Normies* (UK: Zero Books, 2017).

them in the age of social media and "fake news."⁶⁶ While social media played a key role in the 2009 Iranian Presidential elections, as well as the Arab Spring and Occupy Movements, and was once thought to enable radical democratic movements, there's a sense today that social media is particularly fraught for the Left.⁶⁷

The algorithm is a code that locks into place an inherently authoritarian logic of repetition and stereotypy, often confirming, deepening, and reinforcing subjective prejudices through the creation of so-called "echo chambers." As Richard Seymour has argued in his book *The Twittering Machine*:

> There must be something in some viewers waiting to be switched on. The algorithms, by responding to actual behaviour, are picking up on user desires, which may not even be known to the user. They are digitalizing the unconscious. The platforms thus listen intently to our desires, as we confess them, and give them a numerical value. In the mathematical language of informatics, collective wants can be manipulated, engineered and connected to a solution.⁶⁸

Just as 20th century fascists used radio and film to spread their propaganda, contemporary agitators evince a predilection for the use of Twitter/X, Facebook, Instagram, and WhatsApp, which amongst other things, enables them to effectively bypass institutional "critique": the in-principle rational and systematic scrutiny of expert cultures of professional journalists, scientists, intellectuals, and academics, and communicate often unconscious wishes and desires directly to their followers themselves.

One could say that according to Löwenthal and Guterman, the agitator relies on and contributes to the accelerated circulation of negative effects, unlike the reformer and revolutionary, who both provide a reasoned analysis of a given historical conjuncture and offer a program to address the fears and anxieties (as well as hopes and dreams) of their followers. And, in this, social media has come to play an increasingly automated role insofar as algorithms are written in such a way as to optimize what is referred to as "rage bait." Social

---

66   See Timothy Snyder, *On Tyranny: Twenty Lessons from the Twentieth Century* (New York: Crown, 2017).
67   Reflecting on her experiences with Occupy Wall Street, the Dene writer and artist, Leanne Simpson, refers to this in *As We Have Always Done* (Minneapolis: University of Minesota Press, 2020), 221, as "digital dispossession," which signifies the lack of trust in on-line communities. I'm indebted to Morgan Young for bringing this to my attention.
68   Richard Seymour, *The Twittering Machine*, (London and New York: Verso, 2020), 182.

media creates new virtual types of Freud's "artificial groups" that increasingly weaken and undermine the reality-testing, rational, and critical capacities of the ego.[69] In other words, what Seymour calls "social industry" functions as both the medium and the expression of what Adorno refers to as the "turning the outward of the unconscious" *en mass*.[70] Seymour argues,

> The 'networked individualism' of the internet is both social and a machine. It binds social interactions to protocol. Information, far from wanting to be free, as Californian folk wisdom has it, desires control. It wants hierarchy and infallible instruction: the smack of firm leadership.[71]

To conclude, then, the all-too common comparisons between the recent rise of authoritarian populism in the West with the 1930s are somewhat misplaced. A more fitting antecedent, in contrast, is Britain in the late 1970s, which laid the groundwork for the installation of neoliberalism via Thatcher's "authoritarian populism," which had already undergone a trial-run in Chile after the coup d'état in 1973. In the contemporary period, authoritarian populism is in theory poised against this order although in practice it seems only to tighten its hold. There is, it would seem as Thatcher gleefully remarked, "no alternative." What must not be forgotten is that the subjective authoritarian tendencies are ones that are not peculiar to neoliberalism but are present in the deep and psychologically lacerating contradiction within liberal democracy. This is the contradiction between, on the one hand, egalitarianism, and its promise of a self-determining or autonomous life, and, on the other, the pervasive powerlessness and dependence or heteronomy engendered by social order based on the private ownership appropriation of property and wealth. While remaining largely implicit in the three decades after the end of the Second World War, this contradiction is made increasingly explicit with neoliberalism's emphasis

---

69   Richard Seymour has this to say about the new Brexit Party led by Nigel Farage: "Unlike older party models, it doesn't invest in lasting infrastructure. It is nimble-footed, expert at gaming social media – the stock market of attention. It won the battle for clicks and made a killing in this election. Such online frenzies are akin to destabilizing flows of hot money, forcing legacy parties to adapt or die. But when Parliament is so weak, its legitimacy so tenuous, they can look like democratic upsurge." Richard Seymour, "Nigel Farage is the Most Dangerous Man in British Politics," *The New York Times*, 28 May 2019. www.nytimes.com/2019/05/28/opinion/nigel-farage-brexit.html.

70   Theodor W. Adorno, "Freudian Theory and the Pattern of Fascist Propaganda," in *The Essential Frankfurt School Reader*, ed. Andrew Arato and Eike Gebhardt (London: Bloomsbury Publishing, 1982), 118–180.

71   Richard Seymour, *The Twittering Machine*, 183.

on possessive individualism and extreme self-reliance coupled with an abjection of institutionalized forms of social solidarity. This contradiction lies at the heart of the legitimacy crisis of contemporary liberal democracy, which has created an opening for new algorithmic forms of populism. Such self-reliance drives the deepening and intensification of social media which, itself, amplifies powerful effects that are weaponized by authoritarian populist leaders and movements. The digitized culture industry with its myriad social media platforms, both produce an increasingly docile citizenry as well as provide tools for authoritarian leaders to circumvent the institutional, critical scrutiny of the expert cultures of academy, science, and serious journalism, and make affective appeals in such way as to transform socio-economic anxieties into fear of the political "enemy." While promising an expanded public sphere of critical debate and dialogue, such a refashioned culture industry has contributed enormously to possibly irreversibly undermining such a sphere.

Bibliography

Adorno, Theodor W. *Aspekte des neuen Rechtsradikalismus.* Frankfurt am Main: Suhrkamp, 2019.

Adorno, Theodor W. "Freudian Theory and the Pattern of Fascist Propaganda." In *The Essential Frankfurt School Reader.* Edited by Andrew Arato and Eike Gebhardt (London: Bloomsbury Publishing, 1982).

Adorno, Theodor W. "The Meaning of Working Through the Past." In *Critical Models: Interventions and Catchwords.* Translated by Henry W. Pickford. New York: Columbia University Press, 1998.

Applebaum, Anne. "The American Face of Authoritarian Propaganda." *The Atlantic.* September 21, 2023. https://www.theatlantic.com/ideas/archive/2023/09/tucker-carlson-putin-orban-propaganda/675380/.

Camus, Renaud. *You Will not Replace US.* Plieux, France: Chez l'auteur, 2018.

Cheung, Heiler. "Is Putin Right? Is Liberalism really Obsolete." BBC. June 28th, 2019. https://www.bbc.com/news/world-europe-48798875.

CNN. "Steve Bannon: Wear 'Racist' label as a Badge of Honor." *CNN.* March 10, 2018. https://www.youtube.com/watch?v=SYysrAg8Yfo.

Conway, J.F. "Populism in the United States, Russia, and Canada: Explaining the Roots of Canada's Third Parties." *Canadian Journal of Political Science Via Wikipedia Library* 11, no. 1 (March 1978): 99–124.

du Bois, W.E.B. *Black Reconstruction in America: An Essay Toward a History of the Part Which Black Folk Played in the Attempt to Reconstruct Democracy in America, 1860–1880.* Oxford: Oxford University Press, 2014.

Dyer-Witheford, Nick, and Svitlana Matviyenko, *Cyberwar and Revolution: Digital Subterfuge in Global Capitalism.* Minneapolis: University of Minnesota Press, 2019.

Edsall, Thomas B. "How much Damage have Marjorie Taylor Greene and the 'Bullies' done to the G.O.P.?" *The New York Times.* June 8, 2022. https://www.nytimes.com/2022/06/08/opinion/maga-caucus-squad-congress.html?searchResultPosition=1.

Feuer, Alan, and Luke Broadwater, Maggie Haberman, Katie Benner, and Michael S. Schmidt, "Jan. 6: The Story So Far." *The New York Times.* June 9, 2020. https://www.nytimes.com/interactive/2022/us/politics/jan-6-timeline.html?searchResultPosition=1.

Fieschi, Catherine. *Populocracy: The Tyranny of Authenticity and the Rise of Populism.* New York: Columbia University Press, 2019.

Finn, Ed. *What Algorithms Wand: Imagination in the Age of Computing.* Cambridge, MA: MIT Press, 2017.

Foucault, Michel. *Birth of Biopolitics: Lectures at the College de France 1978–79.* New York: Picador, 2010.

Frankel, Jay. "The Persistent Sense of Being Bad: The Moral Dimension of Identification with the Aggressor." In Adrienne Harris and Steven Kuchuck, eds., *The Legacy of Sandor Ferenczi: From Ghost to Ancestor.* New York: Routledge, 2015.

Fromm, Erich. *Escape from Freedom.* New York: Henry Holt & Co., 1994.

Gandesha, Samir. "The Aesthetic Politics of Hegemony." *Studi di estetica, anno XLVI, IV serie, 3* (2018).

Gandesha, Samir. "The Brazilian Matrix: Between Fascism and Neo-Liberalism Vladimir Safatle and Samir Gandesha in Conversation," *Krisis* 40, no. 1 (November 2020): 215–233. https://krisis.eu/article/view/37054.

Gandesha, Samir. "The Political Semiosis of Populism." *The Semiotic Review of Books* 13, no. 3 (2003): 1–7.

Gandesha, Samir. (ed.) *Spectres of Fascism: History and Theory in International Perspective.* London: Pluto Press, 2020.

Glazer, Nathan. *We Are All Multiculturalists Now.* Cambridge, MA: Harvard University Press, 1997.

Goffman, Erving. *The Presentation of the Self in Everyday Life.* New York: Doubleday, 1956.

Gudavarthy, Ajay. *India After Modi.* New Delhi: Bloomsbury, 2018.

Hofstadter, Richard. *Anti-Intellectualism in American Life, The Paranoid Style in American Politics, Uncollected Essays 1956–65.* New York: Library of America, 2020.

Horkheimer, Max, and Theodor W. Adorno. *Dialectic of Enlightenment: Philosophical Fragments.* Stanford, CA: Stanford University Press, 2002.

Jay, Martin. "*The Authoritarian Personality* and the Problematic Pathologization of Politics." *Polity* 54, no. 1 (January 2022): 124–145.

Kitching, Gavin. *Development and Underdevelopment in Historical Perspective: Populism, Nationalism, Industrialization.* London: Methuen, 1982.

Kuttner, Robert. "Thomas Piketty: The Making of a Socialist," *The New York Times*, October 28, 2021. https://www.nytimes.com/2021/10/26/books/review/time-for-socialism-thomas-piketty.html

Laclau, Ernesto. *On Populist Reason*. London and New York: Verso, 2005.

Laclau, Ernesto. *Politics and Ideology in Marxist Theory: Capitalism, Fascism, Populism*. New York: New Left Books, 1977.

Lanier, Jaron. *Ten Arguments for Deleting Your Social Media Accounts Right Now*. New York: Henry Holt, 2018.

Lapavitsas, Costas. *Crisis in the Eurozone*. London: Verso, 2012.

Lazzarato, Maurizio. *Governing by Debt*. Cambridge, MA: Semiotext(e) Books, 2015.

Lazzarato, Maurizio. *The Making of the Indebted Man: An Essay on the Neoliberal Condition*. Cambridge, MA: Semiotext(e) Books, 2012.

Löwenthal, Leo, and Norbert Guterman. *Prophets of Deceit: A Study in the Techniques of the American Agitator*. London and New York: Verso, 2021.

Marcuse, Herbert. *Eros and Civilization: A Philosophical Inquiry into Freud*. Boston: Beacon Press, 1974.

Marcuse, Marcuse. "Some Social Implications of Modern Technology." In *The Essential Frankfurt Reader*. Edited by Andrew Arato and Eike Gebhart. New York: Continuum, 1985.

Moore, Sam, and Alex Roberts. *The Post-Internet Far Right: Fascism in the Age of the Internet*. London: Dog Section Press, 2021.

Mouzelis, Nicos. *Politics in the Semi-Periphery: Early Parliamentarianism and Late Industrialization in the Balkans and Latin America*. London: Palgrave Macmillan, 1985.

Mudde, Cas, and Cristobal Rovira Kaltwasser. *A Very Short Introduction to Populism*. Oxford: Oxford University Press, 2017.

Müller, Jan-Werner. *What is Populism?* Philadelphia: University of Pennsylvania Press, 2016.

Nagle, Angela. *Kill All Normies*. UK: Zero Books, 2017.

Narita, Felipe Ziotti, and Jeremiah Morelock. *The Society of the Selfie: Social Media and the Crisis of Liberal Democracy*. London: University of Westminster Press, 2021.

Peck, Jamie. *Constructions of Neo-Liberal Reason*. Oxford: Oxford University Press, 2010.

Piketty, Thomas. *Capital in the Twenty-first Century*. Cambridge, MA: Belknap Press, 2017.

Raspail, Jean. *The Camp of the Saints*. Edited by Norman Shapiro. Petoskey, MI: The Social Contract Press, 2015.

Reckwitz, Andreas. *Society of the Singularities*. Cambridge, MA: Polity Press, 2020.

Safatle, Vladimir. "Fascist Neoliberalism and Preventive Counter-Revolution: The Second Round of the Latin American Laboratory." In *Spectres of Fascism: History and Theory in International Perspective*. Edited by Samir Gandesha. London: Pluto Press, 2020.

Seymour, Richard. "Nigel Farage is the Most Dangerous Man in British Politics." *The New York Times*, 28 May 2019. www.nytimes.com/2019/05/28/opinion/nigel-farage-brexit.html.

Seymour, Richard. *The Twittering Machine*. London and New York: Verso, 2020.

Snyder, Timothy. *On Tyranny: Twenty Lessons from the Twentieth Century*. New York: Crown, 2017.

Szelényi, Zsuzsanna. "How Viktor Orbán Built his Illiberal State." *The New Republic*. April 5, 2022. https://newrepublic.com/article/165953/viktor-orban-built-illiberal-state.

Tazzioli, Martina. "Left-wing Populism A legacy of Defeat: An Interview with Eric Fassin with Martina Tazzioli, Peter Hallward and Claudia Aradau." *Radical Philosophy* 202 (June 2018): 79–92. https://www.radicalphilosophy.com/article/left-wing-populism.

Thatcher, Margaret. "1978: Le 'swamped' de Margaret Thatcher." https://www.dailymotion.com/video/x28votz.

Weber, Max. *Economy and Society: An Outline of Interpretive Sociology Volume 1*. Edited by Guenther Roth and Claus Wittich. Berkeley: University of California Press, 1978.

Weisman, Jonathan, and Reid J. Epstein. "G.O.P. Declares Jan. 6 Attack 'Legitimate Political Discourse.'" *The New York Times*. February 4, 2022. https://www.nytimes.com/2022/02/04/us/politics/republicans-jan-6-cheney-censure.html.

Williams, Thomas Chatterton. "The French Origins of 'You Will not Replace Us." *The New Yorker*. November 27, 2017. https://www.newyorker.com/magazine/2017/12/04/the-french-origins-of-you-will-not-replace-us.

Zuboff, Shoshona. *The Age of Surveillance Capitalism: The Fight for a Human Future at the New Frontier of Power*. New York: Public Affairs Books, 2020.

CHAPTER 5

"Kultur ist ein Palast der aus Hundescheisse gebaut ist": Right-Wing Populism, Social Media and the Failure of Eurocentric Humanism

Mlado Ivanovic

1   Introduction

In the contemporary Western socio-political landscape, a discernible shift toward anti-immigration sentiment and humanitarian skepticism has emerged as a dominant aspect of our political and moral culture, reshaping public discourse and policy across the "developed" industrialized world. This phenomenon has not occurred in isolation but is symptomatic of broader cultural and political currents that have gained momentum over recent years. The current climate is characterized by a growing disillusionment with global humanitarian efforts, as the Western public increasingly questions the efficacy and motives behind such initiatives. This skepticism often translates into a reluctance to engage with the problems of "distant others," leading to a retrenchment of aid and a reevaluation of what constitutes moral and political responsibilities on a global scale. Simultaneously, anti-immigration sentiment has become a staple of political rhetoric, fueled by fears of cultural dilution and economic competition. Right-wing populist movements have successfully tapped into these fears, painting immigration as an existential threat to national identity and security. This narrative has been particularly potent amid vast waves of migration spurred by conflicts in the Middle East, Africa, and Latin America, coupled with the perceived failure of inclusive multicultural policies.

As this chapter embarks on exploring this climate and narratives further, it is pertinent to pose a foundational question: *Has the influx of migrants significantly fueled the ascent of right-wing populism in Europe and the US?* This question, seemingly trivial at the outset, becomes significant when we consider the strategic positioning of immigration at the heart of the European (and American) "right-wing" and "right-leaning" populist agenda. These parties, most notably *the Republican Party* mobilized behind the persona of Donald Trump and his recent political rise, Germany's *Alternativ für Deutschland* (AfD) and Austria's *Freiheitspartei Österreichs* (FPÖ) among others, have meticulously crafted their political agenda to exploit public fears around the perceived erosion of cultural identity and the escalation of violence and crime – all aspects of which they associate with uncontrolled immigration. Unfortunately, this discourse seems not to be merely a political tactic but reflects a broader, more pervasive shift within the socio-political realm of Western industrialized nations. The anti-immigration rhetoric has not only permeated public discourse but has also instigated a wave of skepticism towards humanitarian values that were once important in these societies. It has ushered in a new era where the once-celebrated ethos of open borders and collective global responsibility is being questioned and, in many instances, outright rejected. The prevailing scholarly discourse posits that economic distress and cultural unease, particularly among those who feel marginalized by the relentless pace of modernization, fuel populist sentiments, thereby bolstering the prospects of right-wing populist (RWP) parties.[1] The concurrence of heightened public aversion to immigrants with the swelling ranks of RWP party supporters underscores the perception of immigration as a pivotal factor in the political triumph of these parties within affluent, developed nations.[2]

The rise of such sentiments has had tangible implications, with right-wing populist parties gaining unprecedented traction and transforming immigration policy into a litmus test for national security and cultural preservation. These parties have adeptly amplified the societal undercurrents of discontent and disaffection, resonating with a significant segment of the population that feels besieged by the rapid pace of globalization and demographic shifts. However serious and real these predicaments may be, the empirical evidence to substantiate a direct causal relationship between immigration and the electoral fortunes of RWP parties remains elusive and subject to ongoing debate. Rather than asserting a straightforward cause-and-effect dynamic, contemporary research is increasingly oriented toward uncovering the contextual factors that render immigration a more pronounced political issue. This includes examining the impact of unemployment rates, the socio-economic texture of

---

1 Hans-Georg Betz, *Radical Right-wing Populism in Western Europe* (New York: St. Martin's Press, 1994); Herbert Kitschelt and Anthony J. McGann, *The Radical Right in Western Europe: A Comparative Analysis* (Ann Arbor: University of Michigan Press, 1995).
2 Kai Arzheimer, "Contextual Factors and the Extreme Right Vote in Western Europe, 1980–2002," *American Journal of Political Science* 53, no. 2 (2009): 259–275; Martin Halla, Alexander F. Wagner, Josef Zweimüller, "Immigration and Voting for the Far Right," *Journal of the European Economic Association* 15, no. 6 (December 2017): 1341–1385; Eric Kaufmann, "'It's the demography, stupid": Ethnic Change and Opposition to Immigration," *The Political Quarterly* 85, no. 3 (2014): 267–276.

local communities, and the frequency of new migrant influxes.³ Despite this growing body of work, there is a conspicuous gap in the literature concerning a comprehensive analysis of how the cultural and economic profiles of migrant-origin countries, along with varied immigrant demographics, might shape the attitudes of native populations and influence their support for RWP parties.⁴ A deeper understanding of these dimensions is crucial for a more holistic grasp of the connection between migration and populism in contemporary Europe. The juxtaposition of these developments against the backdrop of increasing global inequalities, environmental crises, and forced migration underscores a pressing need to interrogate the material conditions and ideological constructs that have led to such a profound transformation in public sentiment. It raises critical questions about the future trajectory of Western societies and their willingness to engage with the complex realities of a globalized world.

In what follows, this chapter sets the stage for a deeper exploration of the cultural, political, and ethical dimensions of this socio-political shift, and the role that critical theory might play in both understanding and potentially countering this trend. The following pages explore the multi-faceted nature of this socio-political phenomenon, examining the extent to which migration has acted as a catalyst in the resurgence of right-wing populism. It contends that the rise of right-wing populism and its accompanying rhetoric has been significantly bolstered by developments in communication technologies (i.e., internet, social media, etc.) and the incapacity of Western public discourse to humanize distant others, which act as important catalysts in the dissemination and normalization of anti-immigrant sentiment. This tendency is not isolated but is symptomatic of a failure in Eurocentric humanism, which has traditionally championed universal values and inclusive solidarity. To address these challenges, this chapter's aim revolves around two pivotal, interconnected dimensions: *First,* it revisits the extensive work of the Frankfurt School to draw parallels between historical media influences on nationalism and the modern dynamics of social media as tools for populist propaganda. One of the claims here is that *the echo chambers* created by social media platforms have facilitated a revival of nationalist populism and authoritarian tendencies by manipulating narratives and exploiting public fears. *Second,* it investigates the

---

3 Eric Kaufmann, "Complexity and nationalism," *Nations and Nationalism* 23 (2017): 6–25; Alkis Otto and Matt Steinhardt, (2014), "Immigration and Election Outcomes – Evidence from City Districts in Hamburg," *Regional Science and Urban Economics* 45 (2014): 67–79; Rune Jørgen Sørenson, "After the Immigration Shock: The Causal Effect of Immigration on Electoral Preferences," *Electoral Studies* 44 (2016): 1–14.
4 Matt Golder, "Far Right Parties in Europe," *Annual Review of Political Science* 19 (2016): 477–497.

decline in global humanitarian sentiments, suggesting a correlation with the strategic exploitation of public anxieties by right-wing populist parties. These parties have effectively utilized such anxieties to implement and justify restrictive immigration and asylum policies, which have increasingly gained political legitimacy. Ultimately, the aims of this analysis are modest, as the main goal is to see if critical philosophy can help us alter our political and ethical landscape, as their true value lies in their potential to illuminate the underlying dynamics and pitfalls of our political (and moral) culture. Hope persists that understanding these dynamics represents the first step towards initiating the social change and personal transformation necessary to counteract the growing trend of right-wing populism and the erosion of humanitarian values.

2   The Rise of Right-Wing Populism

The historical context and growth of right-wing populism in Europe and the United States can be traced through a complex web of socio-economic changes, cultural shifts, and political evolution that have collectively fueled its ascent. Namely, following the devastation of World War II, Europe embarked on a path of reconstruction and reconciliation, largely embracing liberal democratic values. However, the Cold War era saw the emergence of a right-wing undercurrent as a reaction to the perceived threat of communism. In the United States, the fight against communism also saw the rise of conservative movements, which, while not populist in the current sense, laid the groundwork for a more individualistic and nationalist rhetoric. The 1980s marked a significant turn with the advent of neoliberal policies, which emphasized deregulation, privatization, and a reduction in state intervention. The economic restructuring led to deindustrialization and the decline of traditional industries in both Europe and the United States. This economic upheaval disproportionately affected the working class, creating a sense of loss and disenfranchisement. Such a trend continued during the 1990s, which witnessed the effects of globalization intensifying, with a more significant movement of goods, capital, and people across borders. In Europe, the formation of the European Union and the Schengen Area facilitated this movement, which some perceived as a threat to national sovereignty and identity.

The attacks on September 11, 2001, and subsequent terrorist attacks in Europe shifted the focus to issues of national security and immigration. This period saw the securitization of immigration policy and the association of immigrants, particularly from Muslim-majority countries, with security threats. This fear was instrumentalized by right-wing populists who framed themselves as protectors of national security and cultural identity. The financial crisis of 2007–2008 and the subsequent European sovereign debt crisis led to severe economic downturns, austerity measures, and high unemployment rates. These crises further undermined trust in the political establishment and the European Union, providing fertile ground for right-wing populist narratives that blamed economic woes on the political elites and immigrants. The influx of refugees and migrants during the Syrian Civil War and other conflicts intensified the debate on immigration, wherein right-wing populist parties gained prominence by arguing that the influx of refugees threatened social cohesion and overburdened already vulnerable welfare systems. This sentiment resonated with a substantial portion of the population, leading to significant electoral gains for populist parties in Europe and the election of Donald Trump in the United States in 2016.

Today, right-wing populism remains a potent political force, with its leaders portraying themselves as the true representatives of the people against a corrupt elite. The historical trajectory of right-wing populism shows that it is not an aberration but a persistent political phenomenon that adapts to and capitalizes on the anxieties of each era.

Throughout this analysis, I build upon Mudde and Kaltwasser's comprehensive articulation of populism, which they elucidate through three foundational components. *First* and foremost, populism asserts its moral authority by claiming to embody the voice and interests of "the people." This notion of "the people" can be interpreted in various ways, but it invariably stands central to the populist ethos.[5] *Second*, populism inherently positions "the people" in opposition to "the elite," who are typically depicted as the morally corrupt architects of societal woes.[6] *Lastly*, populism champions what it perceives as the "general will" of "the people," a rallying cry to dismantle the perceived injustices wrought by "the elite."[7] It is critical to contextualize this framework not as a rigid definition but as a flexible lens through which we can examine the contours of political movements.

While populism itself is not inherently aligned with any political spectrum, it frequently manifests in right-wing contexts, especially within recent European history.[8] When considering the socioeconomic factors closely associated with

---

5 Cas Mudde and Cristóbal Rovira Kaltwasser, *Populism: A Very Short Introduction* (New York: Oxford University Press, 2017; online edition), 8–10.
6 Ibid., 12–13.
7 Ibid., 16–17.
8 Mudde and Kaltwasser clarify that the essence of populism is not wedded to left or right ideologies; rather, it is a malleable construct that can be adopted by diverse political factions (2017, p. 9). They cite instances of right-wing populist movements such as subsets of the U.S.

the rise of right-wing populism, one cannot deny their significant overlap with the immigration narrative. The socio-economic approach is a prevalent lens through which scholars examine the underpinnings of right-wing populism in Europe, and this perspective compellingly argues that the economic disruptions caused by globalization have indeed laid the groundwork for the rise of right-wing populist movements.[9] Yet, such an overwhelming focus on degrading living standards and the volatile economy does not entirely capture the political complexities tied to increasing public presence of populist movements. For example, the emergence of parties like the AfD in Germany and Vox in Spain occurred notably after the advent of economic globalization but closely followed the surge of refugees entering Europe from Africa and Western Asia. Hence, such timing suggests a strong correlation between migration patterns and the burgeoning support for right-wing populist agendas.

3   The Role of Social Media in Amplifying Right-Wing Populist Narratives

The evolution of communication technologies, particularly the rise of social media, has marked a significant departure from traditional media outlets and has had a substantial impact on the spread and influence of right-wing populism. To understand this, it is essential to contrast traditional media with these new forms of communication. Namely, traditional media outlets functioned as gatekeepers, with editors and journalists deciding which stories were newsworthy and how they were presented to the public. This centralized control often ensured that content met certain standards of veracity and objectivity, albeit not without biases and editorial slants. Traditional media is characterized by a one-to-many model where information flows from a single source to a wide audience, what in itself limits interactivity between the audience and the content provider. When we consider how traditional media accounts are subject to regulatory frameworks and standards that hold them accountable for the content they broadcast or publish, we can see how important recent developments in communication technologies and changes in how information

---

  Republican Party, Bulgaria's Attack, and Hungary's Jobbik, illustrating the adaptability of populism (Ibid., 14–16).
9 Matthias Diling, "Two of the Same Kind?: The Rise of the AfD and its Implications for the CDU/CSU," *German Politics & Society* 36, no. 1 (2018): 84–104; Davide Vampa, "Competing Forms of Populism and Territorial Politics: The Cases of Vox and Podemos in Spain," *Journal of Contemporary European Studies* 28, no. 3 (2020): 304–321.

has been disseminated are to the general public. In traditional media, space (in print) and time (in broadcasts) are limited resources, meaning that not all viewpoints or stories can be covered. Hence, the necessity of editorial decisions meant that only the most newsworthy content made it to the public.

In contrast, social media removes the gatekeeping role of traditional media, allowing anyone to create and share content. This democratization of content creation means there is no filtering process for accuracy or newsworthiness, allowing false information to spread as easily as factual reporting. Unlike the editorial decisions of traditional media, social media platforms use algorithms to determine what content to show users. These algorithms often prioritize content that engages users the most, which can favor sensationalist, emotionally charged, or divisive content – a boon for populist messaging. Furthermore, social media operates on a global scale and in real-time, allowing right-wing populist movements to spread their message quickly and to a worldwide audience. This immediacy can galvanize support and mobilize action more effectively than traditional media. Considering the design of social media to optimize user engagement, it is natural that content eliciting strong emotional responses tends to be more widely shared and discussed. Given this dynamic, it is not surprising that populist messages, which frequently carry an emotional punch, have a higher propensity to spread rapidly on social media compared to traditional media platforms. This tendency amplifies the reach and impact of such messages, fueling their propagation across digital networks.

Social media platforms have empowered populist figures to circumvent the limitations imposed by conventional media, allowing them to communicate directly with the populace. This direct line of communication ensures their narratives are disseminated without the moderation of fact-checkers or editors, significantly enhancing their ability to rally and engage with their supporter base. This has led to the creation of parallel discursive spaces where populist ideas can spread unchecked and unchallenged, significantly altering the public discourse and contributing to the polarization of society. The shift from traditional to new media has not just changed how information is disseminated; it has transformed the very nature of political communication, with right-wing populism being one of the primary beneficiaries of this new media landscape.

The role of social media in amplifying right-wing populist narratives is an indispensable facet of contemporary political dynamics. Its ascendancy as a communicative force has coincided with the recent political success of different populist political agendas, suggesting more than mere correlation; social media has fundamentally altered the manner in which populist messages are disseminated and received. At the heart of social media's influence is its ability to circumvent traditional gatekeeping institutions of information, such as mainstream news media. Right-wing populist groups have exploited this to great effect, directly reaching out to the public with their ideologies. This direct line to the electorate allows for the crafting of tailored messages that resonate on a personal level, often appealing to emotional and identity-based aspects of politics. Moreover, the algorithmic nature of social media platforms further entrenches users within echo chambers, where the content they encounter often reinforces pre-existing beliefs and biases. This effect is particularly advantageous for right-wing populists, who thrive on narratives of division and conflict. The "us versus them" mentality inherent in populist rhetoric finds a fertile breeding ground in the personalized feeds of social media, where complex political issues are reduced to simplistic, digestible content.

In addition to fostering echo chambers, social media provides the tools for virality, ensuring that provocative content can achieve unprecedented reach and influence. Populist leaders and movements harness this feature to spread their messages quickly, often employing sensationalist and polarizing content to capture the attention of users and drive engagement, which in turn feeds the algorithms that prioritize content visibility. Another significant aspect of social media's role is the way it has democratized content creation. Anyone with a social media account can potentially contribute to the populist narrative, blurring the lines between consumers and producers of information. This has led to the proliferation of grassroots populist movements, where supporters not only consume content but actively participate in its propagation, creating a participatory form of political campaigning that can operate independently of the political party's formal structure.

Furthermore, social media platforms serve as key spaces for shaping collective identities, a process that right-wing populist movements deftly utilize. These groups often promulgate a vision of national identity steeped in nostalgia and marked by exclusion, employing social media to propagate and normalize cultural symbols and narratives that resonate with those disaffected by societal diversity. Moreover, the global nature of social media facilitates the spread of populist ideologies beyond borders, fostering a transnational populist dialogue that exchanges and replicates strategies across nations. This digital connectivity has given rise to an international populist wave, capable of synchronizing messages and tactics across the globe.[10]

---

10 One notable instance is the 2016 U.S. Presidential Election, where Donald Trump's campaign utilized social media platforms to great effect. Trump's Twitter account, characterized by its direct and unfiltered communication style, resonated with many voters. The campaign also employed data analytics companies to target voters with personalized

4 The Frankfurt School and Media Influence on Nationalist Populism and Authoritarianism

The Frankfurt School's pioneering philosophical inquiry critically dissects the pervasive power of media in molding human agency, societal norms, and political ideologies. Rooted in a deep philosophical and critical examination, the Frankfurt School's approach reshaped our understanding of the intricate interplay between media, culture, and politics. Their incisive analysis of mass communication's impact on the fabric of society sheds light on the powerful ways in which media acts not just as a conduit of information but as a significant force in shaping political thought and cultural norms. This exploration, far from being purely academic, unveils the undercurrents of power and ideology embedded within media structures, providing essential insights into the mechanisms through which media can shape public consciousness and influence political landscapes. Through their rigorous scrutiny of the media's role within the cultural and political spheres, they have provided a comprehensive framework for understanding how mass communication influences and intersects with the currents of politics and culture. Their scholarship, which delves into the nuances of how media serves as both a reflection and an architect of societal values and power relations, remains remarkably relevant, particularly as we confront the challenges posed by nationalist populism and authoritarian regimes. Hence, the Frankfurt School's analysis transcends the time in which it was written, offering tools for dissecting the symbiotic relationship between media practices and the consolidation of political ideologies that continue to resonate in the age of digital media and global communication networks.

Max Horkheimer and Theodor Adorno introduced the concept of the "culture industry" in their groundbreaking critical treatise, *Dialectic of Enlightenment*. Their thesis contended that culture, once a sphere of creative human activity, had been transformed into an industry with mass production lines akin to other acute aspects of capitalism.[11] This industry churned out not just innocuous entertainment but also ideologies that served to indoctrinate

---

        content, thus leveraging social media's micro-targeting capabilities. In Europe, the Brexit campaign is another prime example. Campaigns like "Leave.EU" made extensive use of social media to disseminate their message, utilizing platforms like Facebook to target voters with bespoke messages. The campaign was marked by the viral spread of slogans and memes that simplified complex political and economic arguments into highly shareable content, often appealing to emotional reactions over factual accuracy.

11   Theodor W. Adorno and Max Horkheimer, *Dialectic of Enlightenment: Philosophical Fragments* (Stanford: Stanford University Press, 2002), 94.

and mollify the populace. They observed that the products of this industry – be it cinema, radio, or later television – were designed to inculcate a passive acceptance of the prevailing order, reducing the critical faculty of individuals and lulling them into a state of complacency. Along these lines, the concept presents a scathing critique of how mass media and culture under capitalist systems contribute to social domination. The central tenet of it is that these cultural products are not created to enlighten or educate the masses but to perpetuate the interests of the capitalist system. Adorno and Horkheimer observed that this standardization of culture leads to the pacification of the masses, as individuals are less likely to engage in critical or divergent thinking. Instead of social actors actively interpreting their world, they become passive consumers of media content that is carefully designed to shape their perceptions in subtle ways.

Seeing the mass culture as a tool of social control, Horkheimer and Adorno were particularly concerned with how this process contributed to the erosion of individual autonomy and the capacity for self-determination. The homogenization of cultural outputs stifled diversity of thought, marginalizing unconventional ideas and promoting a uniform worldview. The culture industry, through its pervasive influence, perpetuated the status quo by portraying societal conditions as natural or inevitable, thus diminishing the likelihood that individuals would challenge or envision alternatives to the existing power structures.

When applied to the phenomenon of rightwing/nationalist populism, the theory of the culture industry suggests that media – extended now to include digital platforms – plays a pivotal role in disseminating and entrenching nationalistic and authoritarian ideologies. By framing the narrative in a way that appeals to emotions, simplifies complex issues, and vilifies the "other," the culture industry creates an environment where populist rhetoric can thrive and propagate unchallenged. It also implicates media not just as a passive conveyor of the populist message but as an active participant in crafting a reality that favors authoritarian politics. Hence, Horkheimer and Adorno's insights shed light on the mechanisms through which contemporary media can continue the culture industry's legacy, using technology and digital algorithms to reinforce certain political narratives while marginalizing others.

Another way to understand the relationship between the culture industry and right-wing populism is by focusing on ways in which media influences societal norms and values. Right-wing populist movements have often capitalized on the "culture industry's" ability to reach wide audiences with emotionally charged content that resonates with latent fears and prejudices. Utilizing the media's reach and its penchant for emotionally potent content, these movements disseminate narratives that tap into societal anxieties. Such content often bypasses rational analysis, appealing directly to emotions and reinforcing simplistic, nationalistic perspectives. Right-wing populists leverage this dynamic to bolster authoritarian ideals, crafting media portrayals that favor strong, homogeneous leadership, often to the detriment of diverse or dissenting voices. The dramatization of political issues in line with populist ideologies through the mass media thus cements such values in the collective consciousness, paving the way for these ideologies to grow and persist within society. This is particularly effective when nationalistic and xenophobic sentiments are woven into the fabric of cultural narratives, creating a fertile ground for populist ideologies to take root and flourish. Finally, Adorno and Horkheimer's theory does not leave us without hope. They suggest that through critical engagement with cultural products and an awareness of the culture industry's effects, individuals can resist the passivity and domination that the industry seeks to impose. In the context of right-wing populism, this means fostering a culture that values critical thought, open debate, and the questioning of simplistic narratives that populist movements often promote.

5 Adorno and the Pathological Shifts in Public Agency

The early Frankfurt School's diagnosis of the culture industry as a mechanism for perpetuating dominant ideologies finds a disturbing echo in Adorno's exploration of authoritarian and fascist personalities. The same mass-produced cultural narratives that the Frankfurt theorists saw as reinforcing the status quo also play a critical role in shaping the authoritarian and fascist dispositions in individuals that Adorno later delineates. The culture industry, with its potent capacity to influence and manipulate through media, serves as a breeding ground for the authoritarian personality, which thrives on the simplistic, conformist, and uncritical narratives that such an industry propagates. This connection between the culture industry and the authoritarian personality becomes particularly salient when considering the insidious ways in which right-wing ideologies can seep into the fabric of society. As we can see from previous pages, media, as a central pillar of the culture industry, disseminates more than just entertainment – it conveys and normalizes the values and beliefs that can lead to the acceptance of authoritarian and fascist ideologies. In his two lectures "The Meaning of Working Through the Past" and "Aspects of the New Right-Wing Extremism" the impact of fascist or authoritarian ideologies on the personalities and agency of social actors is profound.[12] As insightfully identified by Adorno, some people are especially receptive to this form of cultural conditioning, being predisposed to submit to authoritarian figures and to hostile attitudes towards those who are portrayed and conceived as different. The seamless integration of cultural production and ideological indoctrination underlines the power of media as a force that can either challenge or uphold authoritarian tendencies within a democracy. As Adorno cautions, the survival of fascism within a democratic society – insidiously woven into the very threads of everyday life through the culture industry – poses a far greater threat than its overt resurgence against the backdrop of a challenged democracy. It is the cultural underpinnings of fascism, perpetuated through media and accepted by the authoritarian personality, that we must vigilantly scrutinize and address if we are to understand and dismantle the conditions that allow such ideologies to flourish.

In these two short treatises, Theodor Adorno insightfully observed that the endurance of National Socialist ideology within democratic frameworks could pose a greater threat than overtly fascist movements opposing democracy. He contended that the persistence of fascism, and the failure of society to fully confront and process its historical legacy – regressing instead into a superficial and indifferent form of forgetting – is rooted in the continuation of the very societal conditions that once gave rise to fascism.[13] Remarkably, what stands out in retrospect about Adorno's lecture is not solely his prescient identification of resurgent right-wing tendencies that are all too familiar in the current day, but the precision, efficacy, and foresight with which he dissected these trends decades ago. What is worrisome is that despite his analysis, contemporary society still grapples with conceiving and implementing effective countermeasures to mitigate the harmful potential of right-wing ideologies and politics. The enduring difficulty in addressing these issues suggests that the allure of fascist ideologies may be emblematic of deeper, more ingrained problems within the fabric of modern societies. These problems include a range

---

12 Theodor W. Adorno, "The Meaning of Working Through the Past," in *Can One Live after Auschwitz: A Philosophical Reader,* eds. Rolf Tiedemann, Mieke Bal, and Hent de Vries. Trans. Rodney Livingstone (Stanford: Stanford University Press, 2003), 3–18; Theodor W. Adorno, *Aspects of the New Right-wing Extremism,* trans. Wieland Hoban (Medford, MA: Polity Press, 2020).

13 Theodor W. Adorno, "The Meaning of Working Through the Past," in *Critical Models: Interventions and Catchwords.* Trans. Henry W. Pickford (New York: Columbia University Press, 2005), 90, 98.

of social inequalities that are not peripheral but central to the structural and functional aspects of these societies.

Furthermore, Adorno's reflections imply that the challenges we face also speak to the inadequacies of formal democratic systems. There is a prevalent, albeit mistaken, belief that the mere existence of democratic institutions is an adequate representation or near – realization of a profound and substantive democracy. This misconception overlooks the importance of a democracy that is felt and lived – the kind that extends beyond the procedural and into the substantive realm, one that is deeply understood and experienced by its constituents. Adorno's insights suggest that without such a substantive democracy, the societal conditions that enable the resurgence of authoritarianism and right-wing extremism cannot be effectively countered. It is this profound and empathetic understanding of democracy that needs to be cultivated and protected to ensure that democracy itself does not become a mere facade under which authoritarian tendencies thrive.

Engaging with Adorno's lectures from late 1950s and 60s in today's climate – a time when democratic institutions globally are facing challenges and experiencing erosion – necessitates an understanding of the lectures' original socio-historical and political milieu. It was both a product of its time and a critical commentary on the societal trends of the era. To fully appreciate the relevance of Adorno's insights, we must contextualize them within the sociopolitical landscape that they were addressing and the interventionist role they intended to play. The recent political climate in the US and Germany provides a vivid illustration of the pertinence of Adorno's work. The rise of Donald Trump and *Alternativ für Deutschland* (AfD) and their subsequent successes came as a shock to many across the political spectrum in the US and Germany. Characterized by a staunchly xenophobic and anti-immigrant stance, both political figures gained momentum particularly during and in the aftermath of the refugee crisis that peaked in 2015 and continued to hold a steady trend of movement. Angela Merkel's administration, with its policy of openness and the Chancellor's rallying cry of "Wir schaffen das!" (We can handle it!), initially found widespread support, particularly in the western states that had formed the Federal Republic of Germany (BRD) post-1949.

However, this sentiment was not uniformly held, especially in the former East Germany – the erstwhile German Democratic Republic (DDR) – where, following its integration into the BRD in 1990, resistance quickly coalesced, notably in Dresden with the emergence of PEGIDA (Patriotic Europeans Against the Islamization of the Occident). This movement, characterized by its anti-Islamic and far-right ideology, began demonstrating in 2014 and quickly became a pan-European phenomenon. The synergy between the AfD and

PEGIDA, while strained and informal, saw members of the AfD participating in PEGIDA demonstrations, indicating a level of cooperation and shared ideology between the two groups.

This contemporary example underscores the ongoing relevance of Adorno's reflections on authoritarianism and the conditions that enable its resurgence. The rise of right-wing political figures exemplifies the very dangers that Adorno warned against – the re-emergence of fascist ideologies in democratic societies, not as fringe elements, but as significant political forces. These movements exploit socio-political fissures and capitalize on fears stemming from economic uncertainty and cultural change, demonstrating that the "objective conditions of society" that once gave rise to authoritarianism persist, perhaps in evolved forms, to this day. Adorno's work situates these developments within a broader historical and global framework, recognizing them as part of a wave of comparable trends across various democracies. It has become increasingly evident that rapid social transformations and the accompanying uncertainties, along with the real or perceived threats they bring, have generated fear and disquiet among many. This anxiety has made a growing segment of the population receptive to reductionist narratives that offer seemingly straightforward solutions to the complex challenges presented by an interconnected and globalized world. These narratives often manifest in a distinct form of resentment and anger, which finds targets in established political entities, specific demographic groups such as immigrants, or elite decision-makers accused of harboring hidden and harmful intentions.[14]

---

14 Considering this, Adorno's lectures, when revisited, not only elucidate the authoritarian undercurrents that can exist within a democracy but also serve as a sobering reminder of the need for vigilance and proactive engagement in the defense of democratic values against such regressive forces. These tendencies, the agitations, and the appeal of simplistic explanations by right-wing tainted agencies, have been particularly visible during times of crisis, such as the Coronavirus pandemic. Right-wing factions in the US, Germany, and indeed globally, have capitalized on the chaos and uncertainty, propagating conspiracy theories about the establishment of a totalitarian world government among other sensationalist claims. These assertions, while lacking evidence, have nonetheless found fertile ground in a society grappling with the pandemic's unsettling effects on normalcy and order. Adorno's insights into the psychology behind this susceptibility to extreme right-wing ideologies become even more relevant in such times.

6 The Authoritarian Personality

Theodor Adorno's penetrating lectures frequently circled back to a theme that was also central to his co-authored work, *The Authoritarian Personality*, a seminal study that has garnered both acclaim and controversy since its research in the 1940s and its subsequent publication in 1950.[15] Adorno, responsible for the introduction and various chapters, highlighted a disturbing reality within the fabric of liberal democracies: a notable portion of the populace might not truly endorse the foundational values of liberal democracy and may, in fact, harbor opposition to these principles, often without overt acknowledgment or even conscious awareness of this opposition. This conclusion disrupts the comfortable assumption that the benefits and freedoms offered by liberal democracies are universally appreciated and upheld within such societies. It calls into question a fundamental premise – that all rational individuals would naturally support a system that affords them personal and collective liberties and opportunities unmatched by any other form of governance on such a large scale.

Recent developments and the historical record alike point to a more nuanced reality: the faction of the population with ambivalent or outright negative sentiments towards democracy, particularly when it ceases to cater to their direct, personal interests, may be larger than previously recognized. This is not a marginal phenomenon but a substantial and critical issue, revealing the precariousness of democratic stability. It underscores the uncomfortable truth that the principles of democracy are not self-sustaining but require active engagement and support – a support that cannot be taken for granted. From the perspective of liberal democracy and its advocates, the revelation that democracy is not an unchallenged ideal is indeed unsettling. Yet, it is precisely this realization that Adorno's work illuminates, urging a deeper examination of democratic society's assumptions and the vulnerabilities that can be exploited by anti-democratic forces. Understanding this paradox – that the freedoms of democracy may also enable the growth of sentiments and movements that fundamentally oppose it – was central to Adorno's critical approach and remains vital to any attempt to safeguard democratic structures against the rise of authoritarianism.

For advocates of liberal democracy, the idea that a significant number of citizens within democracies might actively resist the democratic framework is profoundly disconcerting. The very blueprint of democratic institutions and regulations is to prevent exploitation, harm, and denigration by establishing

---

15   Theodor W. Adorno et al, *The Authoritarian Personality* (London: Verso, 2019).

a robust legal framework. Yet, it is within the confines of this legal structure that such detrimental practices can persist – legally yet unjustly – reflecting the inherent contradictions and injustices of modern social organization. Moreover, the capitalist economic underpinning of these societies inadvertently sanctions and even encourages behaviors that, while ostensibly within legal limits, essentially involve exploiting, harming, or belittling others to maintain the social order and ensure the smooth operation of its economic systems. These activities, often carried out under the guise of competition or efficiency, reveal the complexities and darker undercurrents that lie beneath the surface of the democratic facade, challenging the integrity of the democratic ideal.

7 Diminishing Global Solidarity

The decline of empathy and solidarity with "distant others" marks a critical juncture in the social consciousness of contemporary societies. This gradual retreat from a globally empathetic mindset to one that is increasingly localized points to a deeper transformation within collective moral fabric of our time. The proliferation of media has paradoxically brought images of distant suffering into the immediate purview of millions, yet the response is often one of detachment rather than engagement. This detachment raises probing questions about the role of societal and political currents in shaping our responses to the suffering of others. It is within this complex milieu that populism emerges as a force – its narratives and policies potentially contributing to a decline in humanitarian impulses or capitalizing on an existing trend to bolster its own political agenda. The subtle yet profound interconnectedness between the decline of global empathy and the tactics of populism underscores a reciprocal relationship that challenges the foundations of international solidarity.

Traditionally, humanitarian impulses and general sentiments regarding solidarity relied on the concept of compassion. Unfortunately, when scrutinized, this concept exhibits frailties that problematize its function as a pillar of human solidarity. I have written on this topic extensively elsewhere,[16] but for the purposes of this chapter it will suffice to say that compassion is inherently selective and unpredictable – it can be easily kindled for some and withheld

---

16   See Mlado Ivanovic, "Stubborn Realities, Shared Humanity: The State of Humanitarian Ethics Today," *Ethics and Economics* 16, no. 1 (2019): 71–87; Mlado Ivanovic, "Humanitarian Melancholia: Humanitarianism and the Need for Morality of Thinking," in *Refugees Now: Rethinking Borders, Hospitality, and Citizenship*, eds. Kelly Oliver et al. (London: Rowman and Littlefield International Ltd., 2019): 43–63.

from others based on proximity, identity, or perceived worthiness. This selectivity not only perpetuates but also deepens power disparities, casting those who suffer as objects of pity rather than subjects with rights and agency. Thus, the overarching tendency of our humanitarian culture to consider compassion as the primary moral engine overlooks ways in which the narrative of compassion becomes a means of inequality and power, where the dispensers of compassion retain control over whom to help and how. Not only, can it create a hierarchical relationship where the person in need is seen not as an equal but rather as an "other" to be saved, but it also perpetuates a cycle of dependency and disempowerment that leaves an increasing impact on the humanitarian resilience of those affected. In this way, compassion, rather than being a steadfast drive for solidarity, becomes a tool that maintains the status quo, offering intermittent relief rather than advocating for systemic change and justice.

Right-wing populism exacerbates the selectivity of compassion by framing it as a zero-sum game. It employs a rhetoric that often pits the "national" community against the "foreign" other, framing acts of humanitarian aid or acceptance of refugees as threats to the well-being of the in-group. Populist leaders craft narratives that valorize the protection of the co-nationals over the needs of "distant others," thereby transforming compassion from a universal humanitarian response into a politically charged instrument of social negotiation. The anti-immigration stance of many right-wing populist movements is emblematic of this approach, effectively shutting the doors of empathy and painting those outside national borders as undeserving of support or concern.

Transitioning from this broader societal context to the realm of individual emotions and responses, it becomes evident that compassion itself is subject to these same forces of politicization and social change. Compassion, in its essence, should be a boundless, inclusive emotion, driving individuals toward altruistic actions. However, in reality, it often manifests in a more selective and conditional form. This limitation in how compassion is experienced and expressed has profound implications, as it influences who we see as worthy of our empathy and assistance. The selective nature of this moral sentiment is particularly evident in the context of humanitarian crises. Responses to such crises are often filtered through lenses of national interest, cultural affinity, or media representation, leading to an uneven distribution of empathy and aid. This selective aspect of compassion not only undermines the principle of universal humanitarianism but also reinforces existing power dynamics, inadvertently contributing to the dehumanization and marginalization of those who are most in need of help. This forces us to confront the uncomfortable truth that our empathetic impulses are not only naturally limited but are also shaped and constrained by broader societal and political forces. Understanding this dynamic is crucial for addressing the challenges of fostering genuine solidarity in a world increasingly influenced by neo-liberal ideologies, populist rhetoric, and the insular tendencies they promote.[17]

8   Role of Populism in Eroding Solidarity

Right-wing populist parties have become adept at exploiting public anxieties, often employing the politics of fear to bolster their nationalist agendas. Fear is a potent political tool, and it is wielded with strategic precision by right-wing leaders by playing on common anxieties, they can mobilize support and galvanize public opinion in their favor. Hence, populism, particularly of the right-wing variety, often thrives on the delineation of "us" versus "them." It harnesses narratives that can engender a sense of besiegement and foster a protective stance towards the inner group (i.e., co-nationals, members of political party, etc.). This can actively lead to a decline in empathy as it frames distant others as potential threats to the well-being and purity of the national community. Immigration is a particularly salient issue, often presented as a triple threat to the economic stability, public safety, and cultural identity of the nation. Populist leaders often stoke fears about immigration, portraying migrants as a threat to jobs, public safety, and cultural identity.[18] In a world increasingly defined by rapid globalization, economic uncertainties, and cultural shifts, individuals may naturally withdraw into more insular, local identities. Populism harnesses this inward turn, exploiting it to advance its political narrative. Anxieties about job security, cultural identity, and safety concerns may shift priorities inward,

---

17   This strategic narrowing of empathetic responses serves a dual purpose for populism: it consolidates in-group solidarity by defining a common "enemy" in the form of the outsider, and it diverts attention from the systemic causes of global suffering by focusing on the preservation of national interests. As a result, the very notion of solidarity is at risk of becoming not just atrophied but weaponized, wielded as a tool to further nationalist aims rather than to address the common vulnerabilities that bind humanity.

18   A common strategy is to amplify incidents that can be used to support their narratives, thus magnifying fears that may be disproportionate to the actual risks involved. Populist rhetoric claims that immigrants take jobs from native-born citizens and undercut wages. Despite economic studies often showing the benefits of immigration, populist leaders exploit economic uncertainties by attributing unemployment and financial insecurity to the influx of foreign workers. Right-wing populists also exploit isolated incidents of crime involving immigrants to create an exaggerated sense of danger. By presenting these incidents as part of a pattern, they argue that immigration poses a direct threat to public safety, advocating for restrictive immigration policies as a solution.

lessening the impetus to address broader, international concerns and instead focusing energies on immediate, nationalistic goals.

The relationship between populism and declining empathy is not merely one of cause and effect; it is deeply interconnected. Conversely, as populist rhetoric becomes more mainstream, it further entrenches the erosion of solidarity by normalizing indifference and hostility towards outsiders. This cycle creates a feedback loop where the decline in moral and political considerations provides fertile ground for populism to grow, which in turn further diminishes the space for empathy and solidarity in public discourse and policy. The consequences of this interconnected decline in empathy and solidarity are profound for humanitarian action. The reluctance to assist distant others or to engage with global issues can lead to a reduction in aid, support for restrictive policies on refugees and immigrants, and a general turning inwards of societies. This poses challenges for international cooperation and for the support of global institutions tasked with addressing humanitarian crises as most of these programs rely on public support and advocacy.

Observing what is going on in Western world in recent years, one can see that the ascension of right-wing populist politics across the globe has had a profound impact on the policies and attitudes toward asylum seekers and humanitarian issues. This connection is not incidental but is deeply rooted in the ideological fabric of right-wing populism, which often prioritizes national interest and homogeneity over global humanitarian commitments. Acknowledging how right-wing populism is anchored in a strong sense of nationalism and sovereignty, means recognizing the state as the ultimate arbiter of who is allowed to enter and who is not. This worldview often translates into restrictive asylum policies, where the rights and needs of refugees and asylum seekers are secondary to the perceived interests of the nation. The rhetoric used by populist leaders frames the arrival of refugees as an invasion or threat to the cultural and social fabric of the host country, thus justifying stringent measures to control and limit their entry. Furthermore, populist politics frequently emphasize the importance of cultural homogeneity as a pillar of national identity, which in itself creates friction within society that often leads to violence and exclusion. As the arrival of individuals from diverse backgrounds is portrayed as a challenge to this homogeneity, it is inevitable that right-wing populist agendas or governments rely on policies that are not only restrictive but also selective, favoring immigrants who are seen as culturally similar to the host population and placing barriers in front of those who are not.

As most right-wing populist outlooks tap into economic fears, the general public often understands the presence of asylum seekers and refugees as competition for scarce resources and jobs. This argument is often used to garner support for policies that curtail the rights of refugees to work, access public services, or receive financial aid.[19] The protectionist stance extends to humanitarian aid, with claims that resources devoted to foreign aid would be better spent on domestic concerns regardless if such funds would be directed toward national needs or not. Another major theme in right-wing populist narratives that impacts public reception of humanitarian targets is security, as most nationalist frameworks argue in one way or the other that refugees and migrants pose essential security risks. In turn, policies are crafted with the ostensible aim of protecting the public from terrorism and crime, which are unfairly and inaccurately associated with asylum seekers and immigrants.[20] Such policies often lead to increased surveillance, detention, and deportation of refugees and migrants. In practice, right-wing populist governments enact legislation and administrative barriers that make it difficult for refugees to obtain asylum or use their international rights. These barriers can include fast-track deportation proceedings, the detention of asylum seekers, and the imposition of strict legal requirements for asylum that are difficult to meet. Furthermore, right-wing populism challenges the international legal framework designed to protect those most vulnerable layers of humanity (i.e.,

---

19   Economic insecurity, especially in the wake of globalization, has been a prime catalyst for right-wing populist narratives. Populists frame job losses, declining industries, and economic downturns as the direct result of free trade policies, outsourcing, and immigration. They present themselves as the champions of the 'ordinary' citizen against the 'elites' who benefit from global economic structures, promising to reverse these trends through protectionist policies and the prioritization of native-born citizens in the job market. These parties frequently invoke a glorified version of the past, suggesting that the nation's cultural purity and historical identity are under siege. They rally support by asserting that they alone can preserve the nation's heritage against the supposed threats posed by globalization and multiculturalism. Economic downturns and the loss of traditional industries provide fertile ground for right-wing populists, who blame economic woes on international trade agreements and immigration policies. They promise to restore economic stability and job security through protectionist policies.

20   In the context of global terrorism and transnational crime, right-wing populists often conflate these security threats with the presence of immigrants and refugees. By painting these groups as potential harbors of terrorists or criminals, they create a climate of fear that they claim can only be mitigated through hardline security measures and stringent immigration controls. In the face of global terrorism, right-wing populists often draw direct lines between immigration policies and national security threats. They advocate for strict border controls and aggressive security measures, suggesting that such actions are necessary to protect citizens from harm. The political strategy of exploiting public anxieties creates a climate where fear overrides reasoned debate, and policies are enacted that may compromise democratic values and human rights. This politics of fear undermines trust in institutions and divides societies, as it fosters a narrative of constant threat that can only be alleviated by adopting nationalist, often exclusionary policies.

refugees, asylum seekers, etc.). Populist agenda often criticizes international agreements and cooperation on refugees as infringements on national sovereignty. Consequently, we see how such sentiments lead towards withdrawal from international accords, refusal to participate in refugee resettlement programs, or reduction of funding for international humanitarian organizations. Right-wing populism influences public sentiment and discourse, regardless of whether we accept that or not. Their ideologies and political presence shape how society views refugees and humanitarian issues and dictate patterns of conduct in the face of such influence. Populist media campaigns can dehumanize refugees, while populist politicians use incendiary language that stigmatizes them. This rhetoric not only affects policy but also contributes to a hostile environment for refugees already in the country, impacting their ability to integrate and receive necessary community support.

Considering such a situation, populist rhetoric tends to portray migration in a monolithic, negative light, ignoring the nuanced realities of why people migrate. These oversimplified claims overlook the fact that migration is often a symptom of larger global issues that require comprehensive, collaborative solutions, not just tightened borders. Unfortunately, populism simplifies this complexity, often presenting migration as a voluntary act, ignoring the often-desperate circumstances that force people to leave their homelands. Such a misrepresentation fuels nationalist fervor and justifies restrictive policies while failing to acknowledge the global interconnectedness that these crises reveal. This not only reinforces nationalistic ideologies but also leads to restrictive policies while neglecting the interconnected nature of global crises and migration. Faced with such a predicament, the challenge lies in countering these populist narratives with informed, empathetic policies that recognize the historical and present dimensions of migration, addressing its root causes while upholding the dignity and rights of those compelled to leave their homes.

9 Conclusion: Critical Theory and the Possibility of Change

One of the important claims of this chapter is that the rise of right-wing populist narratives and agendas represents a significant challenge to the norms and institutions that have traditionally governed the international humanitarian response. I have called to attention the need for a robust and principled defense of the rights and dignity of refugees and asylum seekers in the face of such ideological developments that continue to dehumanize and reduce individual experiences and hardship to a political slogan. In reflecting on the ascent of right-wing populism and the associated decline in humanitarian values, this chapter hints at the potential of critical theory in dissecting and interpreting these interconnected trends. By applying critical scrutiny to the discourse and policies propagated by right-wing populists, we can discern their influence on our collective moral compass, with particular regard to humanitarian solidarity and justice in general. Hopefully, this examination not only enhances the understanding of the waning of humanitarianism but also prompts a reassessment of our political and moral strategies, with the objective of cultivating a more inclusive global community. To expand on the case for critical theory, especially early Frankfurt School work, as a tool for social change and individual transformation, critical theory not only provides an analytical framework to critique and deconstruct these phenomena but also offers insights into how individual and collective consciousness can be reshaped towards more empathetic and inclusive viewpoints. By challenging the prevailing narratives and encouraging a deeper awareness of underlying issues, critical theory paves the way for societal and individual transformation, promoting values of empathy, solidarity, and justice in the face of divisive populist rhetoric. This approach, therefore, stands as a beacon of hope and a practical pathway to effectuate meaningful change in both the public discourse and private beliefs.

Especially as the Frankfurt School's critical philosophy remains pivotal in confronting the rise of right-wing populism and the ensuing erosion of humanitarian dispositions. It still offers a critical lens that allows us to scrutinize how populist narratives manipulate societal fears and prejudices, thus impacting collective ethics. This scrutiny is not merely academic; it has practical implications, encouraging a reevaluation of the moral compass guiding public policies and social attitudes. By fostering a critical consciousness, we can counter the divisive effects of populism, advocating for policies rooted in inclusion and justice. The critical theory thus emerges as an essential tool in the quest to rekindle a humanitarian spirit within the global community, challenging us to transcend the narrow confines of populist discourse and to strive for a society that upholds the dignity and rights of all its members. The Frankfurt School's insights into authoritarian tendencies and the impact of the commodification of art and culture on societal structures are crucial for dissecting the narratives that bolster populist ideologies and individual dispositions of social actors. In contemporary contexts, this framework assists in understanding not just the allure of populist messages but also the systemic societal issues that give rise to such movements.

Future research on right-wing populism, informed by insights of the Frankfurt School thinkers, should delve into the ethical ramifications of populist strategies and their impact on international law and humanitarian efforts in general. Such research should aim to uncover the ways in which right-wing populism undermines social inclusion and the ethical principles of solidarity, potentially leading to policies that marginalize vulnerable groups. The challenge will be to develop ethical frameworks and political solutions that effectively counteract the divisive nature of populist politics while reaffirming a commitment to global humanitarian standards. Exactly here is the space for the transformative power of critical philosophies, as they can help society redefine their perception and understanding of contemporary socio-political events. Challenging social actors to look beyond surface-level narratives and urging a deeper exploration of the underlying forces shaping politics, culture, and ethics. By encouraging this level of critical engagement, we gain a more nuanced understanding of current political dynamics and the ability to envisage alternative, more inclusive futures.

For this goal to be something more than just dead letters on the paper, any further critical analysis of the relationship between right-wing populism and atrophy of humanitarian standards and disposition needs to bridge the theoretical insights of critical theory with practical, actionable strategies. There's a pressing need to explore the psychological foundations that drive support for populist ideologies and understand the social and emotional factors at play. Additionally, identifying effective methods to promote and sustain humanitarian ethics within the public discourse is crucial, as we can see that oversaturation in media just leads to humanitarian fatigue and further indifference. This call to action is not just for scholars and theorists but for every individual. Embracing critical insights as a lived practice can catalyze the transformation toward a more equitable and inclusive world, encouraging a collective movement against the divisive currents of our time.

Bibliography

Adorno, Theodor W. *Aspects of the New Right-wing Extremism*. Translated by Wieland Hoban. Medford, MA: Polity Press, 2020.

Adorno, Theodor W. "The Meaning of Working Through the Past," in *Can One Live after Auschwitz: A Philosophical Reader,* edited by Rolf Tiedemann, Mieke Bal, and Hent de Vries. Translated by Rodney Livingstone, 3–18. Stanford: Stanford University Press, 2003.

Adorno, Theodor W., et al, *The Authoritarian Personality*. London: Verso, 2019.

Adorno, Theodor W. and Max Horkheimer. *Dialectic of Enlightenment: Philosophical Fragments.* Stanford: Stanford University Press, 2002.

Arzheimer, Kai. "Contextual Factors and the Extreme Right Vote in Western Europe, 1980–2002." *American Journal of Political Science* 53, no. 2 (2009): 259–275.

Betz, Hans-Georg. *Radical right-wing Populism in Western Europe*. New York: St. Martin's Press, 1994.

Dilling, Matthias. Two of the Same Kind?: The Rise of the AfD and its Implications for the CDU/CSU. *German Politics & Society* 36, no. 1 (2018): 84–104.

Golder, Matt. "Far Right Parties in Europe." *Annual Review of Political Science* 19 (2016): 477–497.

Halla, Martin, Alexander F. Wagner, Josef Zweimüller, "Immigration and Voting for the Far Right." *Journal of the European Economic Association* 15, no. 6 (December 2017): 1341–1385.

Ivanovic, Mlado. "Stubborn Realities, Shared Humanity: The State of Humanitarian Ethics Today." *Ethics and Economics* 16, no. 1 (2019): 71–87.

Ivanovic, Mlado. (2019). "Humanitarian Melancholia: Humanitarianism and the Need for Morality of Thinking." In *Refugees Now: Rethinking Borders, Hospitality, and Citizenship*, edited by Kelly Oliver et al., 43–63. London: Rowman and Littlefield International Ltd., 2019.

Kaufmann, Eric. "Complexity and Nationalism." *Nations and Nationalism* 23 (2017): 6–25.

Kaufmann, Eric. ""It's the demography, stupid": Ethnic Change and Opposition to Immigration." *The Political Quarterly* 85, no. 3 (2014): 267–276.

Kitschelt, Herbert and Anthony J. McGann. *The Radical Right in Western Europe: A Comparative Analysis*. Ann Arbor: University of Michigan Press, 1995.

Mudde, Cas, and Cristóbal Rovira Kaltwasser. *Populism: A Very Short Introduction*. New York: Oxford University Press, 2017. Online edition.

Otto, Alkis, and Matt Steinhardt. "Immigration and Election Outcomes – Evidence from City Districts in Hamburg." *Regional Science and Urban Economics* 45 (2014): 67–79.

Sørenson, Rune Jørgen. "After the Immigration Shock: The Causal Effect of Immigration on Electoral Preferences." *Electoral Studies* 44 (2016): 1–14.

Vampa, Davide. "Competing Forms of Populism and Territorial Politics: The Cases of Vox and Podemos in Spain." *Journal of Contemporary European Studies* 28 no. 3 (2020): 304–321.

CHAPTER 6

Who Is Afraid of the People? The Entanglement of Democracy, Populism and Stupidity

Yonathan Listik

> So why address these issues through a discussion of populism? Because of the suspicion, which I have had for a long time, that in the dismissal of populism far more is involved than the relegation of a peripheral set of phenomena to the margins of social explanation. What is involved in such a disdainful rejection is, I think, the dismissal of politics *tout court*, and the assertion that the management of community is the concern of an administrative power whose source of legitimacy is a proper knowledge of what a "good" community is.
>
> LACLAU, *On Populist Reason*

∴

> Because "the people" does not exist. What exist are diverse or even antagonistic figures of the people, figures constructed by privileging certain modes of assembling, certain distinctive traits, certain capacities or incapacities: … a democratic people putting to use the skills of those who have no particular skills; an ignorant people that the oligarchs keep at a distance; and so on. The notion of populism itself constructs a people characterized by the formidable alloy of a capacity – the brute force of great number – and an incapacity – the ignorance attributed to that same great number.
>
> RANCIÈRE, *The Populism That Is Not to Be Found*

∴

1 Introduction

In his essay on stupidity, Robert Musil argues that in order to comment on stupidity, one must not be stupid:

> the best place might be with the initial difficulty, which is that anyone who wants to talk about stupidity, or profitably participate in a conversation about it, must assume about himself that he is not stupid; and he also makes a show of considering himself clever, although doing so is generally considered a sign of stupidity![1]

Still, this account sets a challenge for any engagement with stupidity when considering that claiming to be intelligent is commonly taken to be a sign of its inverse. A situation emerges where only the intelligent can comment on stupidity but, in doing so, they turn themselves stupid hence invariably delegitimizing their account.

If one adopts this assessment, just as a working definition for now, it seems stupidity has two main features. First, it is always the category of some other who is a threat to us despite being inherently inferior to us. Second, it is impossible to comment on stupidity since this would require an unchecked *hubris* associated with stupidity; *hubris* being that improper grasp of reality that disavows one from being intelligent. This situation makes it an object that cannot be tampered with, despite its obvious inferiority. Stupidity seems to be a trap for intelligence (to outsmart it in some sense even!). In that sense, intelligence never occupies itself with stupidity or never seriously. It remains this ultimate unvanquishable challenge. Hence the question "who is afraid of stupidity?" can be easily answered: only the intelligent.

Moreover, rightly so since it seems only the intelligent are aware of stupidity's destructive power. The stupid invariably believe themselves to be carriers of reason or else they would be aware that they are stupid. This is perhaps the distinction between stupidity and evil, where only in the latter we encounter the clear intention and motivation for destruction, whereas in the former it is a collateral effect or an unintentional consequence. Intelligence is presented as the exclusive power capable of assessing reality and acting accordingly: accessing the facts and foreseeing the appropriate set of responses to it. As a response to this assumption, this chapter will argue that any conception of intelligence

---

[1] Robert Musil, *Precision and Soul: Essays and Addresses* (Chicago: University of Chicago Press, 1995), 270.

is already a political notion. More specifically, it is one that exists exclusively as the placeholder for a conception of objective/reasonable knowledge, which operates on life in order to cleanse it of non-objective/unreasonable elements that interfere in the implementation of a naturalized harmonious order, and hence intelligence is a politically charged construction.

Intelligence here will refer to the totalizing form of knowledge and reason. Thus, it is invariably a project of naturalizing (social) order and hierarchy.[2] It is fundamental to highlight what is being implied here but will be explicitly stated further in the text: intelligence refers to a structure of self-evident authority that emerges from knowledge/rationality/reason. Intelligence is not *employed* for any means (good or bad); it is itself the logic of employment that determines both what is and what should/could be, hence creating an imperative determination (i.e., a must). In that sense, it is both descriptive and normative without being either, since it is self-evident.

In *For a Left Populism,* Chantal Mouffe makes the argument that recent undemocratic phenomena are not extraordinary events inconsistent with the current political configuration, but rather, to a great extent, continuations of its logic.[3] This is perhaps an unconventional line to pursue but I will argue that her intuition is proven correct since even though recent undemocratic movements present themselves as protest movements, they are representatives of mainstream logic. I will show that despite what might seem to be the case, those are neither marginalized nor disruptive ideas. I will demonstrate that in fact they stand precisely on ideas of loyal and law-abiding citizenship that are consistent with the maintenance of the *status quo*, not its disruption.

For example, a central concept in Bolsonaro's campaign was the "good citizen" in the sense that his government would represent a return to legality rather than a break from it.[4] In other words, only the "bad citizens" would be damaged from his government and logically they should be damaged, considering that they are bad citizens. Like Trump, as perhaps the emblematic figure of the problem, or other undemocratic governments, undermocratic waves oppose the idea of a degeneration caused by the masses. Even when they allegedly advocate against the establishment, it is on behalf of a liberal

---

2   That includes conceptualizations such "street smarts," "people smart," "moral intelligence," "emotional intelligence," etc., or any "intelligent" combination of them. For example, to argue that one should know when to be calculative and when to be emotional is already a structure on intelligence since it relies on a reasonable organization of life – "knowing" when and where to be as one should.
3   Chantal Mouffe, *For a Left Populism* (New York: Verso Books, 2018), 22.
4   It is also important to emphasize that "The Good Citizen" was the name of KKK publication.

capitalist imperative to enjoy and be free which does not in any way represent a break with the establishment.[5] It is merely a reproduction of the neoliberal logic of opposing the scroungers and money-grabbing bureaucracy on behalf of the productive taxpaying citizen.

Based on this argument, this chapter will explore the extent to which the current political configuration is democratic via an investigation of the conditions for political legitimacy: the central axis will be the idea of "the people" and the conditions placed on the legitimacy of its political role. In this sense, the argument will explore the manner in which what is presented as democratic is in fact repressive and marginalizing. The central idea is that while political discourse presents itself as an open sphere of dispute, such logic is conditioned on a technocratic assumption that certain claims are politically reasonable while others are stupid. Even though the term "stupid" is not openly employed, one can collect several examples where politics is openly described as the activity of managing the "masses" who are unable to guide themselves. At this stage, I will limit myself to referring to the canonical figure of John Rawls who argues about unreasonable positions: 'This gives us the practical task of containing them – like war and disease – so that they do not overturn political justice.'[6] This is a clear statement of what Mouffe calls the "egalitarian precipice" to denote claims that democratic ideals are posing a threat to governability— that the democratic ideal of equality poses a threat to democracy itself. This underlying conditionality of democracy on governability is the object of the argument here. In this sense Jacques Rancière description of populism is relevant:

> Populism is the convenient name under which is dissimulated the exacerbated contradiction between popular legitimacy and expert legitimacy, that is, the difficulty the government of science has in adapting itself to manifestations of democracy and even to the mixed form of representative system. This name at once masks and reveals the intense wish of the oligarch: to govern without people, in other words, without any dividing of the people; to govern without politics. And it enables the expert government to rid itself of the old aporia: how can science govern those who do not understand it?[7]

---

5 The idea of "theft of enjoyment" is pertinent here but it requires a careful investigation that is beyond the scope of this chapter.
6 John Rawls, *Political Liberalism* (New York: Columbia University Press, 1993), 64.
7 Jacques Rancière, *Hatred of Democracy* (New York: Verso Trade, 2014), 62.

The argument here will show that this is not a new challenge to democracy but expressive of a repressive and undemocratic conception of politics that is fundamentally technocratic. This is evident considering the Greek conception assessed in Brown[8] that the *polis* is the public realm of intelligence where those capable of making decisions grounded on reason are free while those lacking the capacity to participate (*idios*) should be subjugated to the private realm. More specifically, in Brown's account, the relationship between manhood and politics constructs womanhood as an uncontrolled element only to have politics dedicated to its control. A similar account is present in Federici's assessment of the role of women and witches in the transition to capitalism (where the term "good citizen" is employed against the "chaotic masses"). One finds that the *Demos* (the masses or the people) are presented as an impediment to democracy, not its sovereign. It is at best a contingent element that has its power conditioned on proper participation as in Rawls' quote.

The analysis here therefore shows that one should revisit the portrayal of totalitarian politics as a form of populist stupidity. Fascism emerges, in fact, from within this controlling impetuous: this attempt to administer stupidity as unproductive and incapacity. To a large extent, the fear of the "stupid masses" enables undemocratic interventions, so perhaps the conceptualization of the political role of stupidity can offer an alternative. Or in Rancière's words:

> There is politics when this presupposition is broken by the affirmation that the power belongs to those who have no qualification to rule – which amounts to saying that there is no ground whatever for the exercise of power. There is politics when the boundary separating those who are born for politics from those who are born for the "bare" life of economic and social necessity is put into question.[9]

2 Aims and Limitations

In this chapter, I will provide a conceptual framework for understanding the relationship between intelligence, stupidity, and power. My contribution to the debate will be to provide a new account of the relation between intelligence and stupidity and develop the political implications of this relation. In

---

8 See Wendy Brown, *Manhood and Politics: A Feminist Reading in Political Theory* (Lanham, MD: Rowman & Littlefield Publishers, 1988).
9 Jacque Rancière, "The Thinking of Dissensus: Politics and Aesthetics," in *Reading Rancière*, ed. Paul Bowman and Richard Stamp, 1–17 (New York: Continuum, 2011), 3.

understanding the administrative logic of intelligence my aim is twofold: first, I will demonstrate that what is portrayed as democratic is in fact largely undemocratic. Second, I will attempt to provide an account of what *could be* democratic, exploring the way stupidity's disruptive power is a form of democratic intervention.

In this context it is fundamental to circumscribe the argument advanced here as well as its limitations. I will wisely refrain from defining stupidity, but I want to nevertheless pose the following question: why are we so afraid of being stupid? Considering the evilness of intelligence and the innocuousness of stupidity, why is it stupidity that we are afraid of? Before exploring the contours of stupidity, one must affirm the possibility that it can be an alternative to our current regime. I will make this claim by showing that intelligence is leading us nowhere, so we should consider stupidity as an alternative. To be honest, it is not a robust argument. It can be summarized by two trivial statements: (1) intelligence is bad, and (2) stupidity is not intelligent – which obviously leaves miles in theoretical work to be done. Yet, I would like to believe, perhaps stupidly, that it is a small initial step, nevertheless. In other words, I do not aim to describe what stupidity is but rather what it is not, whilst making the case that because it refuses the current logic, it must be considered an alternative prospect. Thus, this chapter aims merely to open a debate, not close one. It barely even asks the question of stupidity, much less closes it. I merely propose that we consider it a question in the first place, to consider it a worthy issue and not a problem to be resolved by intelligence.

I will argue that the political category of stupidity *could be* useful in opposing contemporary political issues since it offers some resistance to dominant logic. Considering that domination is the defining characteristic of civilization, then maybe (and no more than maybe) it is time to be *non*-civilized, to truly bring "degeneration" to civilization. It might be a "stupid" argument, but this is precisely the point. We *should* not be afraid of being stupid, "barbaric," or anarchic. To say it bluntly, I am not yet suggesting that we ought to be stupid, I am rather raising a question regarding the imperative to be intelligent. This text does not aim to convince nor provide any definite answers on the question. It is merely identifying what I believe is a serious question, one that is often overlooked or wrongly framed.

As stated previously, this text is merely an invitation to consider stupidity as a political category. Or in other words, to shift the essential political question from "who is the best?" or "what is the best way?", to the question "why the best?" Thus, all that is being proposed is (1) this is an interesting question and (2) a criterion for what will constitute a valid answer to this question: avoiding intelligence. The aim of this paper is not to defend undemocratic political interventions such as Trump and Bolsonaro by arguing that in their stupidity they are in fact enacting a democratic posture. Instead, the underlying thesis is that they still represent a continuation of hegemonic discourse (intelligence) so unless we revisit the political role of stupidity, we would not be able to face those challenges.

3   What Is Wrong with Intelligence?

When we reflect on some of the worst examples of extreme violence in our history such as colonialism and eugenics, can we say they were the result of stupid and outdated views? One is tempted to say "yes," but the answer should not be so clear. Maybe in hindsight it seems that way, yet even a superficial historical investigation proves otherwise. Colonial and eugenic logic were not the superstitious beliefs of the uneducated masses; they were upheld by scientific and reasonable scrutiny.

The colonization of America and Africa were not "unfortunate" steps in the development of civilization, nor was social Darwinism an error in the otherwise progressive evolution of science. John Marion Sims, "The Father of Modern Gynecology," legally experimented on enslaved black woman without anesthesia because it was believed they did not feel pain. In 1927, the United States Supreme Court ruled it was constitutional to perform sterilizations on its citizens, resulting in 70,000 women of "weak mind" being sterilized because they were "irresponsibly reproducing."[10] As recently as the 1990s, programs of mass enforced sterilization took place in Peru where women of native origins were vociferously targeted.[11] Looking at those cases, and the overarching history of civilization, violence is persistently an element of intelligence rather than stupidity.

A more sophisticated version of what was insinuated is Silvia Federici's Marxist opposition to Marx.[12] Marx argues that the development of capitalism is a violent step towards communism (he uses the metaphor of birthing

---

10   Fresh Air, "*The Supreme Court Ruling That Led To 70,000 Forced Sterilizations.*" March 7, 2016 Retrieved from NPR: https://www.npr.org/sections/health-shots/2016/03/07/469478098/the-supreme-court-ruling-that-led-to-70-000-forced-sterilizations
11   Carranza Ko, Ñ.. "Forcibly sterilized during Fujimori dictatorship, thousands of Peruvian women demand justice" March 3, 2021 Retrieved from *The Conversation:* https://theconversation.com/forcibly-sterilized-during-fujimori-dictatorship-thousands-of-peruvian-women-demand-justice-155086
12   See Silvia Federici, *Caliban and the Witch* (Chico, CA: AK Press, 2004).

as a violent event that creates something new). Federici argues against him, claiming that the development of capitalism was not a progressive event unfortunately embedded with the necessity of violence, but rather a counter-revolutionary event where struggles were repressed in order to impose domination i.e., pure dominating violence.[13] In line with Federici, we can think of the whole of history as a regressive movement driven by intelligence and reason.

Federici's argument is based on her demonstration that the notion of rationality and agency are not in any way objective but rather emerge exclusively within a disciplinary impetus in modernity and capitalism. Her main argument is that opposition to magic is not located in feudalism, but in the necessity of capitalism to root production in work, discipline, and obedience. To achieve that goal, capitalism had to eradicate the possibility of magic and inoperative production on behalf of a notion of agency that is mechanically constructed. In her understanding, this is the logic behind cartesian rationalism, as exemplary of a key moment in modernity with its division of body and soul. The parallel here being that in the same manner that spirit governs the mechanic body, the invisible hand governs, via the dominant class, the mechanic masses in the factories or the enslaved bodies, who themselves are purely mechanized. As the body does not think, it requires bourgeois intelligence and calculability: 'Like the land, the body had to be cultivated and first of all broken up … It was not sufficient, then, to decide that in itself the body had no value. The body had to die so that labor-power could live.'[14]

This same conclusion regarding modern subjectivity and its conception of rational agency, as a mode of violent subjugation, is found in Esposito's[15] and Brown's[16] assessment of the subject. In Esposito, the account is constructed via the conceptual framework of immunity and privatization. According to him, the idea of selfhood is not an enclosed windowless monad, but rather results from the process of immunization, where the privatized subject must gain autonomy by enclosing itself against pathological otherness. The individual autonomous agent exists only as the constant rejection of its openness and dependency on otherness, or translating into the cartesian terms proposed by Federici, the spirit exists only as the administration of the body.[17]

---

13   Ibid.
14   Ibid.
15   See Roberto Esposito, *Immunitas: The Protection and Negation of Life* (London: Polity Press, 2002); Roberto Esposito, *Bios: Biopolitics and philosophy* (Minneapolis, MN: University of Minnesota Press, 2008).
16   See Brown, *Manhood and Politics*.
17   Esposito, *Bios*, 85.

This dynamic is present in Brown's assessment of manhood's political construction.[18] In her account, manhood is determined by its taming and domestication of womanhood. The irrational and untamable object exists as an already pacified object, "mechanized" in the cartesian vocabulary, or an object to be pacified by the reasonable autonomous agents, as in the pathological element one must immunize against in Esposito's account. Again, in the three theories one finds that ideas of order, rationality, agency, autonomy, and citizenship are not objective standards one can impartially hold and employ as measurements for actions. They are invariably and inherently tainted by their violent and repressive constructions along with the naturalization of those dynamics as factual or objectively true.[19]

It is important here to emphasize how this logic differs from previous critiques of modernity, i.e., the synthesis of Enlightenment and capitalism. Even though there are several possible places to find such critique, *The Black Jacobins* by C.L.R. James for example (a text that is often forgotten in this context), the focus here will be exclusively on Adorno and Horkheimer's *Dialectics of Enlightenment*, as it is a canonical text.[20] Against what Adorno and Horkheimer argue, the idea advanced here is that the Enlightenment has not forfeited its realization.[21] Instead, one must realize that there is no other possible outcome to Enlightenment because there is no other possible outcome to intelligence.

As the *Dialectic of Enlightenment* explicitly argues, the totalization of Enlightenment does not concern its outcomes, but rather it involves the totality of control.[22] Hence, it makes no sense to hold it to its own standards. That is, to argue that it does not deliver on its promise of reason and productiveness, i.e., to point at its contradiction, as it would be naïve to expect that its goals

---

18 Brown, *Manhood and Politics*, 24.
19 Ibid., 26–27.
20 In the following, I will provide a reading of Adorno and Horkheimer as it is presented in some of its canonical followers, such as Axel Honneth, *Pathologies of Reason* (New York: Columbia University Press, 200); Peter Dews, *Logics of Disintegration: Poststructuralist Thought and the Claims of Critical Theory*. (London: Verso, 2007); Fabian Freyenhagen, *Adorno's Practical Philosophy: Living Less Wrongly* (Cambridge: Cambridge University Press, 2013). The critique of modernity is undoubtedly indebted to them, and I would argue that there is room for a reading of their texts that provides a more radical perspective than the one employed here. Still, this chapter does not aim to engage in a debate over this issue and it recognizes that the canonical interpretation is loyal to the original project.
21 Theodor W. Adorno and Max Horkheimer, *Dialectic of Enlightenment* (Redwood City, CA: Stanford University Press, 2002), 33.
22 Ibid., 69–70.

could be separated from its totalitarian methods. In this manner, the dialectics is not found in the fact that intelligence invariably results in stupidity or that reason becomes madness, but in the fact that intelligence is inherently "stupid" in being intelligent.[23] In other words, we are not witnessing the self-destruction of reason but merely its upmost realization in its opposite. The Enlightenment does not "shift" or "transform" into irrationality, or in the terms proposed here, intelligence into stupidity. There is no dynamic of control or balance between those two elements. In fact, any belief in such a possibility would already entail the possibility of an "intelligent" administration of that relation, which would itself be the object of the critique here.[24]

Reason is fully realized in its "stupid" domination of stupidity. In other words, in the fact that the unity/identity with itself is only possible via the constant sublimation of its opposite. So, one finds that reason is not undermined by the disastrous effects of its implementation, but rather, it is reaffirmed and reified as the objective truth of reality. As will be demonstrated in the sequence, despite what seems evident, the undemocratic movements that are portrayed as barbaric or unreasonable are never stupid since they are never the outcome of some improper otherness. They are consistent with hegemonic logic. Again, this chapter will not provide a positive definition of stupidity or the way it is a radical form of otherness. It will limit itself with the negative threshold that stupidity is 'not being part of the hegemonic discourse' and considering the argument that the hegemony is characterized by the totalitarian grasp of intelligence, anything that is consistent with intelligence/reason is automatically not stupid.

In this manner, the Enlightenment is undesirable precisely because it delivers on its promises.[25] In other words, the problem is not the triumphalism of reason but that it did in fact win. It has managed to liquidate any alternative and thus, it has ended history. It no longer has any alternative. As in Adorno and Horkheimer's example of the bank with glass walls, which exposes the reality of capitalism in a literal sense, the issue today is this domination of transparency.[26] Everything is public and accessible. We are permeated by intelligence and any possible conflicts can be solved or reconciled via reason. This totalitarian regime is problematic not because it is unable to eliminate the

---

23 Ibid., 169.
24 See Yonathan Listik, "A Biopolitical Account of Social Pathology: Viewing Pathology as a Political-Ontological Issue," in *Pathology Diagnosis and Social Research: New Applications and Explorations*, ed. Neal Harris, 163–189 (London: Palgrave Macmillan, 2021).
25 This is perhaps in friction with some of the traditional reading of Adorno and Horkheimer.
26 Adorno and Horkheimer, *Dialectic of Enlightenment*, 183.

place of stupidity, but because it manages to fully control it. As they recognize, the idea of Enlightenment is not problematic just because it is repressive, but rather because it is an absolutization of self-government and autonomy.[27] Any lamentation of capitalist selfhood as a form of pseudo-individuality is equivalent to believing in the enlighten promise that autonomy would be harmonious.[28] Instead, one must face the fact that what the authors are describing is not the loss of individuality but its very concretization. Put bluntly, there is no conception of individuality that is not inherently a form of enlighten agency.[29]

As mentioned earlier, the dynamic between intelligence and stupidity will not be elaborated upon here, but nevertheless it is fundamental to propose the question regarding this binary dynamic and the moral blackmail it entails. Regarding the first issue: is irrationality really the negative of rationality? As evidenced in Adorno and Horkheimer's argument about the cyclops, the Enlightenment is not threatened by the unjust repercussions of its productive force (i.e., irrationality), the real opposition to enlightenment lies in unproductiveness and incivility.[30] As unreasonable as it might be, the social hierarchy and order represented in the figure of Odysseus as a Robinsonian self-made agent are not problematic for capitalism. It is the cyclops' anarchic society, where satisfaction is not conditioned on discipline, that is treated as problematic within Enlightenment.

In this sense, the figure of the Cyclops hints at a possibility of a third option that is neither reasonable nor unreasonable, it is stupidly banal. Returning to the issue of moral blackmail, the imperative to adopt reason since its opposite is invariably worst, is precisely the self-evident normative power of intelligence, which this chapter aims to challenge. The fear that any abdication of reason will be a return to barbarism erases the fact that it is civilization that is violent.[31] The barbarian never came, it was civilization who came to them and imposed not barbarism, but rather civilization, rationality, and intelligence. In simple terms, I fear the *Dialectic of Enlightenment* remains a text that speaks on behalf of civilization against barbarism. The question that I propose is whether it has to? Whether or not this is the only way to deter destruction? The question is obviously hinting at a negative answer, since even if it does not provide

---

27 Ibid., 90.
28 Ibid., 125.
29 As it was hopefully established via Federici, Esposito, and Brown in the previous section.
30 Adorno and Horkheimer, *Dialectic of Enlightenment*, 50–51.
31 See Dews' reading of Adorno's "Subject and Object," in Peter Dews, *Logics of Disintegration: Post-structuralist Thought and the Claims of Critical Theory* (London: Verso, 2007).

a *definite* answer, in suggesting that the barbaric option, i.e., adopting stupidity and refusing civilization, should be at least considered, the argument here is at least implicitly stating that one does not have to be civilized.

4 Marginalizing Stupidity

This section will focus on the way the realistic and reasonable posture that emerges from the previous account of the Enlightenment reifies the elimination of politics via a self-evident logic where stupidity has no place in politics and should be prevented from taking any political role. In other words, this section explores the actual political ramification of upholding the Enlightenment. This section, along with the previous one, will be combined into an assessment of contemporary issues in the following section.

In the context established previously, one finds that the notion of democracy within mainstream theory is conditioned on a hermeneutic imperative where understanding (or any other instance of intelligence) conditions political participation. Besides the already mentioned Rawls, one could comment on David Estlund,[32] Joseph Raz,[33] or Ronald Dworkin,[34] but perhaps it is Jason Brennan's open opposition to democracy on behalf of epistocracy that is most revealing regarding this inherent condition. He states that politics is too important to allow it to be dangerous. If the requirement for a driver's license is grounded on the fact that driving creates life-threatening circumstances, the same logic should be extended to political participation as it has the same (if not greater) life-determining consequences. One might oppose the conclusions or the ethics of its applications, as most of the other authors referred to in this paragraph do, but his presupposition that stupidity should not be in charge remains self-evident. In a similar manner, most authors avoid directly opposing stupidity or

---

32 Even though he initially denies epistemic authority, he implicitly builds on it later via the concept of "democratic muster." See David Estlund, *Democratic Authority: A Philosophical Framework* (Princeton, NJ: Princeton University Press, 2009), 3.

33 See Joseph Raz' elaboration on mandatory norms and reasons for action. The basic idea is that one should not only be able to construct a normative framework but also a second-order normativity that would provide the reasons to prefer one set of values over another. Joseph Raz, *Practical Reason and Norms* (Oxford: Oxford University Press, 1999).

34 This is not a surprising accusation considering his book is entitled *Laws's Empire* and supports its arguments on idealized versions of judges based on Greek gods, such as Hercules and Hermes, who possess hermeneutic superpowers. For a more detailed criticism of Dworkin, see Paul Kahn, *Political Theology: Four New Chapters on the Concept of Sovereignty* (New York: Columbia University Press, 2011).

even using the term, but I want to argue that it remains the underling logic of their arguments.

If one considers the idea of democracy under its classic formulation as 'the government of the people, by the people, for the people,' the central idea is that democracy is essentially the possibility of the people's self-government. In the theories highlighted, this conception of "self-government" is conditioned on the possibility of proper agency: on determining proper political rationality and more importantly on avoiding the improper ones. On the one hand, democracy refers to the people's unconditional autonomy; on the other, the notion of autonomy and its constructions, as demonstrated in the previous section, restricts the unconditionality of democracy and imposes a control over possible political claims. This is emblematically illustrated by the way those theories attempt to frame the conditions for legitimate authority.[35]

In this manner, in mainstream political theories, the unconditionality of democracy is constantly permeated by the fear of ungovernability. For instance, the fear of the uncontrolled masses equipped with new technological avenues. This fear seems to be the common ground between the conspiracy theorist of the deep web, who believe society is overtaken by secret technological mechanisms of control, and those who point precisely at those deep web groups as secret mechanisms of control. In this way, the unconditionality that is proposed appears to be deeply rooted in the possibility of governing the uncontrolled element: on conditioning self-government. As much as self-government is good, it appears to be damaged precisely by the autonomy of the object whose autonomy we advocate for.

In this way, democracy is fundamentally challenged since it is not the people who govern but whatever authority is deemed legitimate on behalf of the people. This technocratic administration relies on the guise of democracy and supports itself precisely on the transparent violence of the self-evidence of intelligence. In simple words, the theory engenders the logic that even if it is not what the people want, it is what they *should* want, and the fact that they are not currently in that stance is just further proof that authority is required. The idea of "people" appears exclusively as the mass that must be shaped into citizens. Left to their own devices, they are a mass of individualistic whimsical consumers who recognize no order or authority.[36] The notion of "the people" is employed as a depository of energy always ranging from passivity to wild

---

35 See for example the argument about the creation of involuntary reasonable obligations in Ronald Dworkin, *Law's Empire* (Cambridge, MA: Harvard University Press, 1986).

36 The clear reference to the idea of technological devices and the fear-mongering roles it plays in contemporary political discourses is purposeful.

spontaneity that must be handled with care. Against this amorphic "people," the category of proper citizenship emerges. It is important to highlight that this category of proper citizenship that permeates authoritarian regimes is also present in the humanitarian and paternalistic attempt to educate the masses towards tolerance. Even if in a more inclusive project, it too demands intelligence as a condition for democratic participation.

In this way, the epitome of this logic is found in Brennan's argument that only White middle-class males should participate since that is the population that is most suited for making decisions.[37] Such an argument does not dignify a response since any engagement would already presuppose a level of legitimacy that it does not have.[38] Still, it illustrates a dynamic that is relevant to highlight as it already appeared and will appear in other parts of the essay: the non-radicality of conservative politics. In a sense, his proposal could be achieved by not writing it. The problem with his theory is not that it presents an alternative that is repulsive or unacceptable, but rather that it does not in any way do that while still being treated as doing so. Again, the presupposition that stupidity is the fundamental issue of democracy, and one should provide a theory of legitimate means to oppose it, is already present in Rawls and permeates traditional accounts of politics even if Brennan's solution is not supported.

This is a common feature of right-wing claim where they seem to fail precisely because they are already winning.[39] Moreover, this spectacular presentation of its radicality is not innocent. It serves a twofold normalization purpose of emptying politics of dispute on behalf of a moderate/intelligent position, by: (1) excluding actual radical alternatives by drawing a supposed equivalence between the so-called extremes, and (2) dismissing the continuity between capitalism (intelligence) and those undemocratic postures, and in that same movement normalizing them since they remain palatable/reasonable within the governing logic.[40] Or, as Rancière puts it:

---

37 Jason Brennan, *Against Democracy* (Princeton, NJ: Princeton University Press, 2016), 119, 193–194.
38 Yet, it does reinforce a dynamic that is being highlighted here: the way the discrimination against stupidity covers for more "traditional" structures of discrimination that are (supposedly) no longer tolerable but remain in place under its guise. In other words, since open discrimination (racism, homophobia, chauvinism, classism, etc.) is no longer tolerable, epistocracy is its acceptable version. This would be a way to explain how it has become so "fashionable" (the duality between high-end/prestigious/exclusive and common/acceptable in the term "fashion" is purposely invoked here).
39 As in the example of the January 6th, 2021, Capitol invasion that will be used in the following section.
40 For an account of how the term populism is employed in this process, see Jason Glynos and Aurelien Mondon, "The Political Logic of Populist Hype: The Case of Right-Wing

Beyond the polemics on immigrants, communitarianism, or Islam, their essential goal is to merge the very idea of a democratic people with the image of the dangerous masses. It is to draw the conclusion that we must leave matters up to those who govern us and that any contestation of their legitimacy and their integrity is the open door to totalitarianism. ... The current campaign on the mortal dangers of populism aims to justify in theory the idea that we have no other choice.[41]

Mouffe denotes this moral blackmail of adhering to normality, realism, and common-sense, as the imposition of a "radical center" position. It refers to a political scenario that erases the political dispute by claiming to no longer be ideological. Politics becomes a matter of technocratic and intelligent implementation of administration: capitalism is not optional as Thatcher argued. In this context, Rancière points to the irony of simultaneously reprehending the masses for their capitalist behavior while defending precisely the capitalist values of free market and interaction. This demonization, as Adam Kotsko calls it, of the people is characterized by this scheme where the people must fall in error only to have their behavior used to legitimate their repression.[42]

As Rancière argues, democracy in its actual implementation continuously appears as a mechanism of controlling the part that has no part, or in other words, the part that is unable to take part in *polis* must be under constant supervision of the *polis*. In this sense, he refers to this element that has no part as belonging twice: first, as being an integral part of the system, and second as being that part that must constantly have no part in the system.[43] Government exists exclusively as the administration of those who are unable to govern themselves by those who are self-governing and require no government. This administration is simultaneously overabundant, since the intelligent do not require it and it only restrains their self-sufficiency, yet is never sufficient, since it never manages to fully control stupidity as the masses insist on making themselves present, hence endangering the *status quo*.

Populism's 'Meteoric Rise' and Its Relation to the Status Quo.'" *POPULISMUS Working Paper Series*, 2016.

41 Jacques Rancière, "The Populism That Is Not to Be Found," in *What is a People?* Translated by Jody Gladding, 101–106 (New York: Columbia University Press, 2016), 105.

42 See Adam Kotsko, *Neoliberalism's Demons* (Redwood City, CA: Stanford University Press, 2018).

43 Jacques Rancière, *Disagreement: Politics and Philosophy* (Minneapolis, MN: University of Minnesota Press, 1999), 137.

As Rancière concludes his *Hatred of Democracy*, intelligence is always dominating. One can read it as a change in dynamic; it is not a fascist *must,* but a neoliberal *should* as a variation of the same disciplinary imperative of control. In this context, intelligence becomes equivalent to passivity and subjugation, to the innocuous preservation of the *status quo*. Intelligence is this dictatorship of devotion:

> This is most admirably consonant with the way cleverness easily "harnesses" the strong person. Cleverness in the submissive person is esteemed, but only so long as it is connected with unconditional devotion. The instant devotion lacks this certificate of good character and is no longer clearly serving the advantage of the dominant person, it is less often called clever than immodest, insolent, or malicious; and a relationship often arises that looks as if this devotion were at least opposing the dominating party's honor and authority, even if it poses no real threat to the latter's security.[44]

Musil's phrase resonates with the Rancierian assessment of the rhetorical question "do you understand?" According to Rancière, this is a void question since it presupposes common understanding only to draw a distinction between the speaker and the listener. The speaker invariably knows and can reason while the listener's ability is under question. Still, Rancière points to the fact that in drawing the asymmetry of inequality between the elements, one must assume equality: one must assume that the subject understands what is being asked only to impose the obedience of not-fully understanding. In this sense, there are two levels to this understanding: first, a literal understanding, which is accompanied by the second: an understanding of what one is expected to understand, which one must not understand since one must be unable to fully grasp the larger picture (even though one just did to some extents even better than the enunciators to whom the reality is often given to the point of invisibility). To these two levels, stupidity opens the possibility of a third response: of not understanding. This is the possibility of being unable to see the larger picture and make sense of it. If it is only through intelligence, through the understanding of the "do you understand?" interpellation, that a political structure is reified, stupidity might be a form of breaking with this logic.

In this regard, the concept of populism plays a central role as it refers to some form of surpassing the conditionality imposed on the people's participation.

---

44 Musil, *Precision and Soul*, 271.

Still, even though this chapter is suspicious of the manner that the concept is often employed – as a placeholder for the corruption of politics – populism does not automatically represent a model to be adopted. For instance, one finds that Mouffe's[45] and Laclau's[46] account remains limited to challenging the hegemonic account of intelligence rather than breaking with the presupposition that the intelligent should govern the stupid. In other words, their defense of populism, remains one that aims to alternatively organize the people rather than allow its unconditional disruptive power to emerge.

In Mouffe this comes about via her defense of an agonistic political dispute, that despite its heteronomy and heterogeneity, ultimately relies on a political consensus.[47] In other words, her project is aimed at disputing power with the hegemonic discourse to reclaim an alternative hegemonic construction. For Laclau, the notion of "empty signifier" operates as a regulative idea that organizes political disruption.[48] In his account, despite the contingency and even ephemeral nature of any political "name," it still plays a role in managing and directing the dispute. For both, political categories are ontologically empty but can be filled with meaning as a mechanism of political engagement. This dynamic relies on the possibility of political signification and understanding in order to claim a name for the un-nameable, or to employ the framework advanced by Rancière, to claim the acknowledgement of a new set of conditions.[49]

> In one sense, our analysis keeps within the field of Marxism and attempts to reinforce what has been one of its virtues: the acceptance of the transformations entailed by capitalism and the construction of an alternative project that is based on the ground created by those transformations and not on opposition to them. Commodification, bureaucratization, and the increasing dominance of scientific and technological planning over the division of labour should not necessarily be resisted. Rather, one should work within these processes so as to develop the prospects they create for a non-capitalist alternative.[50]

---

45 See Mouffe, *For a Left Populism*.
46 See Ernesto Laclau, *On Populist Reason* (New York: Verso, 2005).
47 Mouffe, *For a Left Populism*, 93.
48 Laclau, *On Populist Reason*, 66–68.
49 Rather than a politics of the unconditional as Rancière defends.
50 Laclau, Ernesto, *New Reflections on the Revolution of Our Time* (New York: Verso, 1990), 55–56. The text here diverges from his reading of Marx, but this falls outside the scope of the discussion proposed here.

An agonistic account argues that capitalism replaces political life with marketable ideas. The end of politics is symbolized by the end of political disputes. Still, as much as it opposes capitalism, the dispute for hegemony remains one over the interaction and exchanges between autonomous individual agents and the possibility of organizing them into a common political movement. In other words, it still respects the logic of the marketplace of ideas since it aims at being the hegemonic product.

A challenge to "radical centrism" must offer a response of a different nature all together: one that does not present a competing strategy or policy. Considering the description of the issues raised previously, the argument proposed here is that it is not enough to challenge political consensus without challenging the idea of dispute itself. For example, the neo-liberal conception of competition and unregulated circulation is largely a form of agonism. In that way, a dispute over political logic cannot be a form of competition if it aims at disrupting the existing logic.

Stupidity in that manner could offer us such an "unmarketable idea" since it does not compete with intelligence. It merely has the empty unsustained courage to claim power against order. As will be further elaborate in the following section, stupidity should not be framed as a set of alternative facts or as the belief in incorrect conceptions of reality. Those would still constitute iterations of an intelligent account of politics, even if factually incorrect ones. The strength of the stupid masses would come precisely from their unsustained and unconditional democratic claim in the sense proposed by Rancière. Or in other words, one that does not rely on a factual or correct account.[51] The actual construction of this claim requires further investigation that is beyond the scope of this chapter. Still, within the criterion offered here, one is able to formulate at least two ideas: (1) by its own definition this claim will prove to be unsustainable and require the construction of a hegemonic formation as a consequence. That is, it cannot be limited to a negative account. Still, (2) the positive cannot be constructed as a legitimate claim to hegemony within the hegemonic discourse. That is, as it is an unfounded political claim, it will be largely a "bad idea" or better yet, a stupid idea.

---

51 It is fundamental to emphasize here that the argument that the political claims should not rely on the factual precision does not entail that there is no such thing. In more concrete terms, the argument is that the strength of a political claim should not emerge from, or be conditioned by, the capacity the explored have regarding framing the injustice of their situation in a precise manner. The accuracy or inaccuracy of their awareness could be relevant but in a contingent rather than a determining or fatalistic manner.

5   The Issue Today

To translate this theoretical construction into concrete examples, it is comfortable to reflect on John Marion Sims and others "progressive" agents of violence like him as historical missteps we moved past, but it is vital to take full account of those events. Those were not foolish hang-ups we overcame as a civilization; those were the implementations of utmost rigor, determination, and assurance. In other words, it is important to take full account that intelligence would not have prevented those events. In fact, intelligence was *the* central motor driving those events. Thus, once again it appears that intelligence, order, morals, and so forth are in fact the causes for all that which is blamed on stupidity and evilness.

Beyond Musil's account where intelligence turns into stupidity, here the evilness of intelligence cannot be dismissed as merely accidental, i.e., as a form of stupidity. Dispossession, genocide, chattel slavery, ICE detention centers and the destruction of indigenous forms of knowledge and kinship relations (to name but a few) are *not* collateral damages but *the very aim* of the colonial, neocolonial, and eugenicist projects. In other words, those are not deviances in the overarching advancement of civilization, they are the very meaning of civilization. So, even though no one is purposely evil, evilness is *intentionally* enacted on behalf of intelligence (which is perhaps much worse).[52]

Consider briefly the logics of racism, homophobia, and even conspiracy theories. They are undoubtedly wrong. Yet these accounts are more consistent with approaches of intelligence than with stupidity even if we rely exclusively on the simple separation of intelligence as the privileging of knowledge and stupidity as marginalized otherness.[53] For instance, conversion therapy advocates, QAnon supporters, and "race scientists" do not ground their worldview on the absence of facts. Quite the opposite, they claim to be the ones holding the facts. They support their claim on statistics and information. Despite being wrong, they do not claim that we should ignore the facts.

The same is true for Trump and Bolsonaro. Again, it is not that they are "in fact" astute political characters. They are unquestionably bad politicians (and human beings in general) but they do not abdicate the privilege of intelligence and they do not challenge existing political structures. If anything, they are

---

52   The intention here is fundamental considering the short taxonomy in the introduction.
53   See Rancière, "The Populism that is not to be Found," 103–104, for an account of racism (i.e., uncivilized behavior) does not emerge from the immigrant suburbs but from the invisible and neutral hand of the state and its policies, often even from left/progressive sectors.

radical defenders of lawfulness. Unlike so-called liberal "snowflakes," they argue that the law is a *fact* and must be upheld against the stupid masses.[54]

Slogans such as "intolerance towards criminals," "when the looting starts the shooting starts," and "just don't break the law and you would have nothing to fear," are emblematic of that lawfulness. The cleverness of their common sensical imperativeness is something to be highlighted: there is no reasonable opposition to them.[55] To oppose it, means opposing legality and morality, hence supporting criminality. Only bad citizens, or idiots, would advocate that, so (1) they can be legitimately repressed, (2) they are always the figure of some other since no one thinks of themselves as idiots/bad people, and (3) one should support those repressive platforms since one is a good citizen who defends law and morality and has nothing to fear and only something to gain from them since they will persecute the bad elements exclusively.

Those who stormed the US Capitol on January 6th, 2021, were not doing so *against* the constitution but on its behalf. More specifically, the "sacred" second amendment not only allows the possession of firearms, also seems to even motivate citizens to take up arms to preserve any corrupt takeover of power: 'A well-regulated Militia, being necessary to the security of a free State, the right of the people to keep and bear Arms, shall not be infringed.'[56] Or the second paragraph of the declaration of independence:

> That whenever any Form of Government becomes destructive of these ends, it is the Right of the People to alter or to abolish it, and to institute new Government, laying its foundation on such principles and organizing its powers in such form, as to them shall seem most likely to affect their Safety and Happiness.[57]

---

54 See for instance reports on Trump's claims to superior intelligence by USNEWS, The Washington Post and CNN. This list is hopefully sufficient evidence of my claim, but it can easily be expanded by any research of the simple combination of words like "Trump" and "IQ" just to use the limited framework of intelligence and not its expanded semantic sphere explored here, which included themes of order, lawfulness, preservation, and so on.

55 As will be argued in the next two paragraphs, the opposition opposes specific implementations of that logic as unreasonable while reinforcing the reasonability of the principles.

56 Moreover, the fact that such a right is not extended to improper citizens such as felons and the "ill minded" is consistent with the overarching argument advanced here.

57 For the sake of the overarching argument, I would highlight that this is not exceptional. In fact, it is a common feature in several constitutions.

They were not trying to break the law but rather to prevent it from being broken. In other words, they were "stopping the steal." They are obviously wrong, but the argument here is that in calling them "stupid" we buy into the account that stupidity threatens normality, and in that sense, even if indirectly, reinforces the narrative: normality, intelligence, and "truth" must prevail.

The moral panic around post-truth relies on the possibility of a return to normality where facts and expertise guides politics against this degeneration. In other words, the dispute over the correct facts overshadows the overarching *common* presupposition: facts should govern. To put it as explicitly as I can, the lurking idea that our social fabric is threatened by elements that refuse to comply to its prerogatives is the cause not the outcome of destruction: it allows for destruction since it allows for an undemocratic logic to govern as the hegemonic common sense via a guise of "prevention," "protection," "return to normality," and so on. In simple words, facts never stopped governing, even if very often they are proven to be incorrect, and moreover, it is this common sensical self-feeding logic that creates the monster and is empowered by its creation, as it presents itself as the only "reasonable" alternative to it.

In this manner, we notice a reproduction of the dominant strategy in the attempt to oppose it. In making the case that the issue with Trump, Bolsonaro, the capitol invaders, or any other problematic ideology, is that they are breaking the law or another conceptualization of a social contract, one is merely directing the logic highlighted above towards them. It uncritically employs problematics accounts of criminality and normalcy that can never serve a counter-hegemonic purpose since it exists precisely to prevent any counter-hegemonic project.[58] The irony in this iteration being that the progressive alternative does the conservative's work by taking the position of the hegemonic posture and appealing to some form of legal authority. In other words, in treating them as marginals, the opposition not only grants them that their claims for order, morality, and lawfulness represent a disruption to the current situation, hence reinforcing their conservative posture, but it also places itself against those values while not fully adopting a radical posture of disruption with the *status quo*. It has the same conservative discourse as the extreme right of defending civilization against barbarism without being as strong and committed in its postures.[59] Even though the cases highlighted before are presented as stupid

---

58 As it was established in the previous section, ideas of normalcy, the individual agent, and its framing as a subject of society, are inherently the product of a dominating structure.

59 It cannot be more conservative than the conservatives and in trying to be it reduces the whole political dispute to the sphere of conservatism, hence eliminating any actual political debate or option of disruption. Moreover, since this is portrayed as the realistic and reasonable posture, the elimination of politics is naturalized. This logic, where the

in a spectacular and mediatic manner, which should already alert any counter-hegemonic stance, they are fundamentally "normal."[60] The issue with those so-called outrageous phenomena is not that they are criminal/outrageous, but rather that they are unable to be. They will repeatedly fall within the law or only on its edge since they are ultimately within the political common sense.

Nothing is more emblematic of this than the response to the capitol invasion that resulted in what can only be described as symbolic imprisonment that were immediately followed by a wide discussion over the constitutional rights of those people resulting in limitations to what was already a limited response.[61] One could mention anecdotal instances ranging from organic food demands to one woman being set free to go to her planned Mexico vacation, but in my opinion the most symbolic case was the fact that after some airlines put people who proudly associated to the invasion on the "no-fly list," this was proven to hurt their constitutional rights since no American can be placed there without being charged with terrorism. I argue this is the most symbolic because of the combination between the known leniency in using terrorist charges in the past together with the very unamerican intervention in the private sector on behalf of people who were publicly self-advertising their intention to invade a government building among other clear infringements of the law less the 48 hours before. Those people had no fear of becoming criminals and I would argue that it is no surprise that history has proven them right since they were in fact operating within the "law" (in the larger sense of a social contract) even when planning to infringe its literal sense.

Put plainly, on both sides of the discussion stupidity is a radical form of otherness that remains that which must be contained, or better yet, eliminated. As a way of illustrating the theory mentioned previously, the cases demonstrate that despite what might seem to be the case, stupidity has never taken over; the issue was and remains the rule of intelligence. As stupid as it might sound, Trump, QAnon, and conversion therapy remain of the regime which speaks to/from intelligence. Trump supporters and flat earthers are not stupid. They are

---

marginalization of stupidity results in elimination of politics and democracy, was the subject of the previous section.

60   As demonstrated in the previous section, this spectacle erases the possibility of any political dispute.

61   I am aware that a number of arrests were made but I insist on their symbolic nature considering that there is already the possibility of a pardon pending on the results of the next election. The sole fact that this is a topic of conversation makes it symbolic when this case is constrasted to the fact that there are people serving life sentences for much less significant crimes under the "three strike rule". This is further aggravated by taking into accoiunt the constrast in profile of the two groups.

simply wrong; just as eugenicist programs and the practices of colonization were and *are* wrong. In calling them stupid we adhere to and reproduce the same logic in our attempts to refute their claims.

The essential question that emerges when considering the theories along the contemporary case, is: what do we have to lose from abdicating intelligence? It is not that renouncing intelligence will disappear all evil; rather that we do not need such a promise. There is nothing to gain from upholding the imperative of intelligence. The politics of intelligence is *inherently* violent and not by accident. Moreover, one finds that intelligence is not only pure domination but also the self-evident privilege of this domination: the neutral violence of progress that cannot be refuted nor refused. Only idiots refuse the facts so there is no harm in repressing them. In fact, it is for their own good. This is the logic that engenders both the eugenics of sterilization and the IMF's worldwide imposition of neoliberal debt reconstruction policies (for example, in Argentina, Nigeria, and Trinidad & Tobago [the Budhoo case])[62] – yet only one of them is no longer a valid policy.[63]

6 The Case for Political Stupidity

> Et je proposerais donc, comme toute première définition de la critique, cette caractérisation générale: l'art de n'être pas tellement gouverné.
>
> [So, I would propose, as an initial definition of critique, this general characterization: the art of not being governed.]
> FOUCAULT[64]

Stupidity emerges as a central political category since it has both historically served as a mechanism of marginalization and in the current age of information and (supposedly) democratic inclusion. It continues to operate in similar iterations as a transparent self-evident political logic. In the neoliberal age of inclusion and tolerance, it serves as a legitimate mechanism of exclusion under a meritocratic discourse. My argument is that it is not enough to challenge the

---

62 For his impressive letter of resignation see, Davison L. Budhoo, *Enough is Enough* (Apex Press, 1990).
63 Even though both still take place.
64 Michel Foucault, *Qu'est-ce que la Critique? Suivie de la Culture de Soi* (Paris: Librairie Philosophique J. Vrin, 2015).

definition of stupidity without challenging the political structure that relies on its marginalization. The criticism that certain groups were wrongly defined as "stupid" or that the enlighten position does not entitle the authority to categorize another group as "stupid" (or even that it is itself a stupid stance) does not fully challenge the technocratic perspective if it is not accompanied by a rejection of an "intelligent" account of politics.

Returning to the Rancièrian definition, the stupidity of no matter who, whatever and whoever, opposes the meritocratic universalistic idea of everyone as a political principle. Those are two types of unconditional democracy. One is the accessibility of the Coca-Cola that becomes the universal common denominator between the president of the USA and the lowest of the workers. All cokes are the same and all cokes are good: it is the universality of the market and its possibilities. On the other hand, stupidity's unconditionality is its impossibility of participating. While normative democracy is one of equivalence, the democracy of stupidity is one of equality. Within the administrative logic, everyone is theoretically equivalent under a common denominator that imposes order. Under stupidity we are all equally incapable, there is no guarantee or order that sets the principle of politics. Stupidity is non-qualified or non-conditioned politics; it is one of equality in the absence of any value for equivalence.

Normative democracy is a form of de-bureaucratization and transparency where accessibility seems unconditioned since it seems unrestrained. But despite its inclusive approach (which is evidently false), it operates as a mechanism that reifies the self-evidence of the market via its positive implementation. In other words, the unconditionality is merely the transparency of capital as a form of universal equivalence between everything and everyone. What appears as an unconditional and self-governing sphere turns into an all-encompassing model of production. This marketization of reality reveals itself to be a stagnation of life rather than its realization: the supposedly unmediated logic of capitalism reveals itself to be an absolutely mediated interaction, only that capital becomes the invisible naturalized element.

Such structure is constructed via the relationship between democracy and intelligence: the transparency of the overwhelming abundance of information of the marketplace of ideas has no outside. Under the full exposure of an absolute knowledge, there is nothing else to be discovered. In this sense, intelligence creates a blindness of overwhelming visibility. Or in other words, one often forgets the self-evident (and quite trivial) truth that transparency is equivalent to invisibility. It is not that information and communication bring no light to darkness, but, more interestingly, they do, and it is precisely in doing it that they obfuscate the possibility of something appearing.

In this manner, the challenge that stupidity might pose to the neoliberal marketized implementations of "direct democracy" that equates what is popular (or can be made to be) with democratic via mechanisms of majority or elections, is to posit that democracy does not regard the empty neoliberal freedom of an autonomous agent capable of choosing or electing (as if reality was equivalent to a supermarket).

Stupidity is the courage of the impotent, or as Musil claims: 'If one were therefore looking for the most general notion of wisdom,[65] these comparisons would yield something like the notion of capability or soundness, and everything that is incapable or unsound might then, on occasion, also be called stupid'[66] and 'This notion of the diminution of achievement, which sticks like a burr, will later reveal itself to be the most universal notion of stupidity that we have.'[67] This is also the courage of the stupid student in Kafka's *Abraham* who mishears his name being called for an award. As he walks up to take the award, he unknowingly challenging his subjectification. This courage can also be found in the girl who stupidly shouts that the king is naked, thus destabilizing the social structure. As in this last case, one finds our reality being supported by a trivial pretense that everything is working or could work when the blatant and evident truth is that it is ruined. Still, intelligence demands that we be realistic and work through it rather than abandon it since there is no actual gain in realizing the king is naked. In fact, everybody already knew it. Only an idiot would state the truth rather than hold to such silly lie.

The interruption of the girl who shouts that the king is naked is not a sudden revelation that challenges the already established knowledge. In this manner, stupidity's political claim would not be the introduction of a new element but merely the affirmation of reality regardless of its consequences. In this context of hyperbolic transparency of information where nothing can be hidden anymore, the stupid fact, that which has no part, that which cannot be presented or represented, hides in plain sight: the evident and blatant fact that capitalism/enlightenment has exhausted itself. Still, the affirmation of such truth has no consequences regardless of its correctness: truth as appropriate knowledge is not sufficient to impact reality. As in the tale, everyone is already aware of reality so claiming that capitalism is ruined or pointing to the illusory force of money is a powerless and trivial statement. One needs the possibility of an enacted construction of truth.

---

65 The English text has "stupidity" rather than wisdom. Intelligence or wisdom are the appropriate translation of the original "Klugheit."
66 Musil, *Precision and Soul*, 276 [my emphasis].
67 Ibid., 273.

In other words, only an idiot misunderstands order and walks right through it. The Kafkian student does not wish to avoid or escape authority. In fact, within a meritocratic structure, there would be no explicit authority being exerted on him since one can extrapolate Kafka's account and assume that in the eyes of the school that student was just someone of no particular interest. A figure in the collective causing no harm or benefit, transparent in its overwhelming presence, i.e., so idiotically banal that it becomes invisible. Still, in its act of receiving the award, the act of not understanding the condition and requirements for participation, the student walks through the harmonious administration of his life and dismantles its logic. Again, not by demonstrating his worthiness according to those standards or the injustice of upholding unfair and arbitrary conditions, but by failing to uphold it to such a deeper extent that it crumbles.

Stupidity's impotency makes it ungovernable so it could serve as an uncoditionalpolitical act in the sense that it has neither interest nor strategy. It is incapable of being intelligent, and in its impotency, it serves neither a refusal nor a replacement of intelligence. It is the element that is truly independent from government unlike the supposedly self-sufficient administrators who rely on the labour of the masses they must subordinate. The ungovernability of stupidity would hopefully grant it the freedom to act politically as a truly desubjectified agent, not in the sense that it knows what it does and acts purposely, but in the sense that it is in no way conditioned or grounded, i.e., *it has no arche so it is* an-*archic*.

As in the tale where Lie deceives Truth into diving into the well only to run away with its clothes, leaving it horrifically naked and unable to show itself, the invitation proposed here is to think stupidity as a possible form of presenting this account of an unbearable truth. For example, one place of intersection could be a connection between Musil's account of failure and Heidegger's argument about errancy and truth:

> *Errancy* is the most concealed gift of truth – for in it is bestowed the essence of truth as the stewardship of the self-refusal and as the purest preservation of being in the unrecognizable protection of what always is. To be sure: errancy is here not "error," an established mistake, the failure of truth as correctness – but instead is that which belongs to the "there" – of Da-*sein*.[68]

---

68   Martin Heidegger, *Ponderings VII–XI: Black Notebooks 1938–1939* (Bloomington, IN: Indiana University Press, 2017), 14 [emphasis in original].

One can also look to Jacque Lacan's notion of "un-thinking":

> I think where I am not, therefore I am where I think not. ... I am not, wherever I am the plaything of my thought; I think of what I am wherever I don't think I am thinking.[69]

Additionally, we can consult Nancy's ontology of patency:

> The world is simply patent, if one may understand by that an appearance that does not "appear," no immanence of a subject having preceded its transcendence, and no obscure ground its luminosity. ... Truth, in fact, or sense of sense, is the patency of the world: that is, on the one hand, the appearing of the nonapparent, or the nonappearing of all "patency," and on the other hand, this, that there is only the world. ... Patency is related to itself-as if one were saying simply: *patet*, "it is manifest," "it is evident," not so as to initiate infinite reflexivity ('it is evident that it is evident'), but rather so as to make appear, to make heard, felt, and touched, the "subject" *it* of the obviousness. This *it* is uttered, on the one hand, as a "*there* is obviousness," putting the accent on the *there*, there is there, according to the multiplicity of places, spaces, zones, instants, and, on the other hand, as an "it is *it* that is obvious," "it" being neither a person nor a thing, nor a principle, nor a ground, but the singular plural of occurrences of existence, or presence, or passage.[70]

One still needs to work out exactly how and if those connections exist, and moreover, if within this context stupidity can serve the purpose framed here. This chapter hints in the direction of a positive answer but even if the answer is found to be negative, hopefully the questions opened here remain relevant. That is, the question of the conditions of democracy and the way that framework restrains democracy by creating a legitimated fear of popular participation, not just despite but also because of our intelligent efforts. In other words, by raising the question of stupidity, I propose that we reflect on the notion of democracy and the unconditionality that it entails, specifically in light of recent undemocratic claims and the responses that have been offered. Arguments such as "democracy has gone too far," or that "we live in an overly democratic time, and it is dangerous," and the logical implication that there

---

69   Jacques Lacan, "The Insistence of the Letter in the Unconscious," *Yale French Studies* 36/37 (1966): 136.
70   Jean-Luc Nancy, *The Muses* (Redwood City, CA: Stanford University Press, 1996), 33–34.

must be means to guarantee a sense of "normality," are traps that further reinforce the issues they aim to confront. In the counter direction of that logic, the only claim being made here is that we need more unconditional democracy rather than restrictions on it.

Hopefully, this text sets the agenda for opposing any form of realistic or conciliatory politics. In that manner, even if the positive side is not yet fully constructed, the negative claim that the contemporary logic must be replaced in a fundamental way is established; that any conception of agency, autonomy, rationality, and so on is inherently tainted and must be dismissed. To put it as directly as possible, considering what was established here, any legalistic or institutional avenues are to be taken not just as ineffective but counterproductive in any endeavor to change society. For instance, notions such as human rights, or for that matter any conception of rights either on a national or international level, becomes a dead end since it is grounded on the conception of autonomy and agency that develops into the idea of proper citizenship.[71] Briefly, the aim of this chapter is merely to convince its reader that the solution to our current crisis will be radical, or it will not be.

Bibliography

Brennan, Jason. *Against Democracy*. Princeton, NJ: Princeton University Press, 2016.

Brown, Wendy. *Manhood and Politics: A Feminist Reading in Political Theory*. Lanham, MD: Rowman & Littlefield Publishers, 1988.

Budhoo, Davison L. *Enough is Enough*. Apex Press, 1990.

Carranza Ko, Ñ. "Forcibly sterilized during Fujimori dictatorship, thousands of Peruvian women demand justice" March 3, 2021 Retrieved from *The Conversation:* https://theconversation.com/forcibly-sterilized-during-fujimori-dictatorship-thousands-of-peruvian-women-demand-justice-155086.

Dews, Peter. *Logics of Disintegration: Post-structuralist Thought and the Claims of Critical Theory*. London: Verso, 2007.

Dworkin, Ronald. *Law's Empire*. Cambridge, MA: Harvard University Press, 1986.

---

71 As Angela Mitropoulos states: 'Rights are not something one possesses even if many of us are reputed, by correlation, to possess our own labor in the form of an increasingly self-managed or self-employed exploitation. Rights, like power, are *exercised*, in practice and by bodies. As juridical codes, they are both bestowed and denied by the state, at its discretion.' Angela Mitropoulos, "Precari-us?" *Mute: Culture and Politics after the Net* 1, no. 29 (Spring 2005): 5.

Esposito, Roberto. *Immunitas: The Protection and Negation of Life*. London: Polity Press, 2002.

Esposito, Roberto. *Bios: Biopolitics and Philosophy*. Minneapolis, MN: University of Minnesota Press, 2008.

Estlund, David. *Democratic Authority: A Philosophical Framework*. Princeton, NJ: Princeton University Press, 2009.

Federici, Silvia. *Caliban and the Witch*. Chico, CA: AK Press, 2004.

Foucault, Michel. *Qu'est-ce que la Critique? Suivie de la Culture de Soi*. Paris: Librairie Philosophique J. Vrin, 2015.

Fresh Air, "The Supreme Court Ruling That Led To 70,000 Forced Sterilizations." March 7, 2016 Retrieved from NPR: https://www.npr.org/sections/health-shots/2016/03/07/469478098/the-supreme-court-ruling-that-led-to-70-000-forced-sterilizations.

Freyenhagen, Fabian. *Adorno's Practical Philosophy: Living Less Wrongly*. Cambridge: Cambridge University Press, 2013.

Glynos, Jason, and Aurelien Mondon. "The Political Logic of Populist Hype: The Case of Right-Wing Populism's 'Meteoric Rise' and Its Relation to the Status Quo.'" *POPULISMUS Working Paper Series*, 2016.

Heidegger, Martin. *Ponderings VII–XI: Black Notebooks 1938–1939*. Bloomington, IN: Indiana University Press, 2017.

Honneth, Axel. *Pathologies of Reason*. New York: Columbia University Press, 2009.

Horkheimer, Max, and Theodor W. Adorno. *Dialectic of Enlightenment*. Redwood City, CA: Stanford University Press, 2002.

Kahn, Paul. *Political Theology: Four New Chapters on the Concept of Sovereignty*. New York: Columbia University Press, 2011.

Kotsko, Adam. *Neoliberalism's Demons*. Redwood City, CA: Stanford University Press, 2018.

Lacan, Jacques. "The Insistence of the Letter in the Unconscious." *Yale French Studies* 36/37 (1966): 112–47.

Laclau, Ernesto, and Chantal Mouffe. *Hegemony and Socialist Strategy: Towards a Radical Democratic Politics*. New York: Verso Trade, 1985.

Laclau, Ernesto. *New Reflections on the Revolution of Our Time*. New York: Verso, 1990.

Laclau, Ernesto. *On Populist Reason*. New York: Verso, 2005.

Listik, Yonathan. "A Biopolitical Account of Social Pathology: Viewing Pathology as a Political-Ontological Issue." In *Pathology Diagnosis and Social Research: New Applications and Explorations*, edited by Neal Harris, 163–189. London: Palgrave Macmillan, 2021.

Mitropoulos, Angela. "Precari-us?" Mute: Culture and Politics after the Net 1, no. 29 (Spring 2005): 88–96.

Mouffe, Chantal. *For a Left Populism*. New York: Verso Books, 2018.

Musil, Robert. *Precision and Soul: Essays and Addresses*. Chicago: University of Chicago Press, 1995.
Nancy, Jean-Luc. *The Muses*. Redwood City, CA: Stanford University Press, 1996.
Rancière, Jacques. *Disagreement: Politics and Philosophy*. Minneapolis, MN: University of Minnesota Press, 1999.
Rancière, Jacques. "The Thinking of Dissensus: Politics and Aesthetics." In *Reading Rancière*, edited by Paul Bowman and Richard Stamp, 1–17. New York: Continuum, 2011.
Rancière, Jacques. *Hatred of Democracy*. New York: Verso Trade, 2014.
Rancière, Jacques. "The Populism that is not to be Found." In *What Is a People?* Translated by Jody Gladding, 101–106. New York: Columbia University Press, 2016.
Rawls, John. *Political Liberalism*. New York: Columbia University Press, 1993.
Raz, Joseph. *Practical Reason and Norms*. Oxford: Oxford University Press, 1999.

CHAPTER 7

Left-Wing Populism in Power in Argentina and Greece

Grigoris Markou

1   Introduction

The economic, social, and political crises of the early 21st century led to the rapidly growing popular distrust and anger against national and supranational organizations and institutions, technocrats and mainstream parties and leaders. The popular anger and indignation found shelter, most of the times, in political parties and leaders who spoke "on behalf of the people," opposing the strong politico-economic hegemony of the elites.[1] In European countries, such as Greece and Spain, popular classes provided their support to left-wing populist parties, which proposed new alternative paths that would protect societies from the "neoliberal danger" and austerity logic.[2] Even in countries where the crisis did not cause much upheaval (e.g., France, UK, etc.), the left found the opportunity to organize itself and create progressive alliances, standing against neoliberalism and the rise of the far-right through a populist discourse.[3] Hence, the European radical left found the appropriate circumstances to move away from the political margins and participate more actively in the political arena, shaping progressive and pro-popular proposals for governance.

In Latin America, critical events had unfolded a few years earlier, as neoliberal capitalism had already failed since the mid-1990s and the alternative

---

1   Yannis Stavrakakis, "The Return of 'the People': Populism and Anti-Populism in the Shadow of the European Crisis," *Constellations* 21, no. 4 (2014): 505–517.
2   Grigoris Markou, "The Rise of Inclusionary Populism in Europe: The Case of SYRIZA," *Contemporary Southeastern Europe* 4, no. 1 (2017): 54–71; Alexandros Kioupkiolis, "Podemos: the ambiguous promises of left-wing populism in contemporary Spain," *Journal of Political Ideologies* 21 no. 2 (2016): 99–120.
3   See Philippe Marlière, "Jean-Luc Mélenchon and France Insoumise: The Manufacturing of Populism," in *The Populist Radical Left in Europe*, eds. Giorgos Katsambekis and Alexandros Kioupkiolis (Oxon and New York: Routledge, 2019), 93–112; Bice Maiguashca and Jonathan Dean, "Corbynism, populism and the re-shaping of left politics in contemporary Britain," in *The Populist Radical Left in Europe*, eds. Giorgos Katsambekis and Alexandros Kioupkiolis (Oxon and New York: Routledge, 2019), 145–167.

proposal of left-wing populism began to be implemented in practice shortly after, in countries such as Venezuela, Argentina, and Bolivia.[4] Sebastián Ronderos highlights that in Latin America,

> the anti-neoliberal backlash was triggered by the systematic privatization of public assets (Bolivia, Argentina, Chile, Brazil), corruption scandals (Venezuela, Ecuador, Argentina), and ruthless institutional repression (Venezuela, Bolivia, Ecuador, Argentina, Chile).[5]

In Argentina, neoliberal policies of Carlos Menem (1989–1999) and Fernando de la Rúa (1999–2001) destroyed the country's economy, resulting in huge economic problems and social unrest.[6] When things began to calm down, a new era dawned upon the country, led by left-wing Peronist Néstor Kirchner, a period that marked the beginning of a left-wing hegemony that would last for twelve consecutive years.[7]

In this chapter, I deal with left-wing populism in power, namely with left-wing political parties and leaders that have come to the fore through a populist discourse, in response to the problems created mainly by economic crises (2001 in Argentina and around 2009 in Greece) and the neoliberal management. Specifically, I focus on two left-wing political forces in Latin America and Europe, *Front for Victory* (FpV) in Argentina, a political alliance of the historic Peronist Party, and *Coalition of the Radical Left* (SYRIZA) in Greece, analyzing their discourse and policies after their victory in the elections (2003 and 2015, respectively), with the aim of examining their successes and failures as populist governments of the Left.[8] I choose to compare Argentina and Greece as they present significant similarities in history, politics, and political culture, a fact that is also underlined by scholars, such as Nicos Mouzelis and Eleni

---

4 Susanne Gratius, "The "Third Wave of Populism" in Latin America," *FRIDE* (Fundación para las relaciones internacionales y el diámogo exterior), Working Paper no. 45 (2007): 1–26; Francisco Panizza, *Contemporary Latin America, Development and Democracy Beyond the Washington Consensus* (London and New York: Zed Books, 2009).

5 Sebastián Ronderos, "Hysteria in the squares: Approaching populism from a perspective of desire," *Psychoanalysis, Culture and Society* 26 (2021): 47.

6 Eduardo Silva, *Challenging Neoliberalism in Latin America* (New York: Cambridge University Press, 2009), 94.

7 See Marcela Levy Lopez, *Argentina under the Kirchners: The legacy of populism* (Warwickshire and Shropshire: LAB and Practical Action Publishing, 2017).

8 This piece builds on my PhD research at the Aristotle University of Thessaloniki. The analysis draws on many speeches, statements, announcements of the parties and leaders in both cases.

Kefala.⁹ Besides that, the politico-economic context (economic crisis and neoliberal management of the economy) and the emergence of two left-wing cases with "anti-neoliberal" narratives provides the ground for a comparative analysis that can provide us important insights into how left-wing populists govern in the semi-periphery.[10]

2   Discursive and Performative Approaches to Populism

The interpretation and conceptualization of populism has always been a demanding task. The complexity of the notion and the different populist experiences that have emerged over the years have hampered the attempt to produce a widely accepted definition with specific characteristics. Thus, today there are several theories and methodologies on populism, examining the phenomenon through different scientific prisms and theories, such as that of political communication style,[11] rhetoric,[12] discourse,[13] strategy,[14] mobilization,[15] performance,[16] ideology,[17] and others.[18]

---

9   Nicos Mouzelis, *Politics in the Semi-Periphery: Early Parliamentarism and Late Industrialization in the Balkans and Latin America* (New York: Macmillan, 1986), 219; Eleni Kefala, *Peripheral (Post) Modernity, The Syncretist Aesthetics of Borges, Piglia, Kalokyris and Kyriakidis* (New Yok: Peter Lang Publishing, 2007), 4.
10   See, for the notion of semi-periphery: Mouzelis, *Politics in the semi-periphery*.
11   Jan Jagers and Stefaan Walgrave, "Populism as political communication style: An empirical study of political parties' discourse in Belgium," *European Journal of Political Research* 46, no. 3 (2007): 319–345.
12   Kirk Hawkins, "Is Chavez Populist? Measuring Populist Discourse in Comparative Perspective," *Comparative Political Studies* 42, no. 8 (2009): 1040–1067.
13   Ernesto Laclau, "Populism: What's in a Name?," in *Populism and the Mirror of Democracy*, ed. Francisco Panizza (London and New York: Verso, 2005), 32–49.
14   Robert Barr, *The Resurgence of Populism in Latin America* (London: Boulder and Lynne Rienner Publishers, 2017).
15   Robert Jansen, "Populist Mobilization: A New Theoretical Approach to Populism," *Sociological Theory* 29, no. 2 (2011): 75–96.
16   Benjamin Moffitt, *The Global Rise of Populism, Performance, Political Style, and Representation* (California: Stanford University Press, 2016).
17   Cas Mudde and Cristobal Rovira Kaltwasser, *Populism: A very short introduction* (Oxford: Oxford University Press, 2017).
18   See more for different theories and methodologies on populism: Paris Aslanidis, "Ethnography of populism," In *Populism in History, Art and Politics* (Athens: The Moraitis School, 2016): 9–29 [Greek]; Cristóbal Rovira Kaltwasser, Paul Taggart, Paulina Ochoa Espejo, and Pierre Ostiguy eds., *The Oxford Handbook of Populism* (Oxford: Oxford University Press, 2017).

How do I analyze populism in this study? Following the theoretical tradition of the Essex School of Discourse Analysis, I perceive populism as a discourse that separates society into two opposing camps, the "people" and the "elites/establishment."[19] As Laclau argues, populism is characterized by 'the dichotomic construction of the social around an internal frontier' and 'the discursive construction of an enemy.'[20] Yannis Stavrakakis, Laclau's student and one of the main representatives of the Essex School in recent years, recognizes two main elements in populism: "people-centrism" and "anti-elitism."[21] Stavrakakis mentions that the signifier "the people" functions as a nodal point of populist discourse, while there is a dichotomic representation of the socio-political field between "us" (the marginalized, the underprivileged, the people) and "them" (the establishment, the 1%, the elite).[22] Furthermore, the Greek political theorist feels the necessity to respond to the anti-populist narratives and explain what populism is not, by supporting that populism is not equivalent to nationalism, nativism, fascism, clientelism, while it is not inherently based on charismatic leadership. Stavrakakis recognizes a democratic perspective within the populist phenomenon, while arguing that even if populism is detached from negative stereotypes, it should not be regardedas a "political panacea" and as something a priori positive.[23]

The Essex School of Discourse Analysis can be enhanced through its connection to *performative* theories that have been developed recently.[24] Two representatives of performativity in populism today are Pierre Ostiguy, with his *socio-cultural* approach, and Benjamin Moffit with his *performative* approach. According to Ostiguy, populism entails a specific form of political relationship between a leader and a social base, which is based on a politico-cultural "low" appeal and is accepted by certain social groups and classes for socio-cultural reasons.[25] In a few words, this means that a populist pursues politics in a specific (popular) way, trying to articulate the demands of specific parts of the society. In a similar perspective, Benjamin Moffitt defines populism as a

---

19 Laclau, "Populism: What's in a Name"; Yannis Stavrakakis, *Populism: Myths, Stereotypes and Reorientations* (Athens: Publications of the Hellenic Open University, 2019). [Greek].
20 Laclau, "Populism: What's in a Name," 38–39.
21 Stavrakakis, *Populism*, 94.
22 Stavrakakis, *Populism*, 94.
23 Stavrakakis, *Populism*, 107.
24 Pierre Ostiguy, Francisco Panizza and Benjamin Moffitt, *Populism in Global Perspective: A Performative and Discursive Approach* (New York: Routledge, 2021).
25 Pierre Ostiguy, "Populism. A Socio-Cultural Approach," In *The Oxford Handbook of Populism*, eds. Cristobal Rovira Kaltwasser, Paul Taggart, Paulina Ochoa Espejo and Pierre Ostiguy (Oxford: Oxford University Press, 2017), 73.

political style and emphasizes three main characteristics of a populist performance: (1) the appeal of the people against the elites, (2) the "bad manners," and (3) the crisis, breakdown, or threat.[26] Following quite the same logic with discursive analysis, performative approaches examine populism through a "neutral" value perspective, enabling the evaluation of the (positive or negative) effects of populism on democracy, society, and politics. The above performative approaches are particularly helpful in categorizing and differentiating political discourses and practices that lie near the boundaries between populism, non-populism, and anti-populism, offering a clearer understanding of the political landscape.

3 Left-Wing Populism in the Semi-Periphery: from Kirchnerism to SYRIZA

Argentina and Greece are two semi-peripheral countries with many aspects of culture, modern history, and politics in common.[27] A significant feature of these countries is populism and the emblematic populist leaders, such as Juan Domingo Peron and Andreas Papandreou. Besides that, Argentina and Greece share a common diachronic double political spectrum with left-right and low-high (populist and anti-populist) axes. Recently, I underlined the fierce and diachronic battle between populism and anti-populism in these countries and the presence of similar anti-populist narratives ("civilization or barbarism" in Argentina and "cultural dualism" in Greece).[28] The populist/anti-populist common spectrum appears to persist in our time, as following the recent economic crises in both countries, similar left-wing and right-wing (populist and anti-populist) examples and economic solutions against the neoliberal threat have emerged and been implemented.

Through the above discursive and performative approaches, I focus on the political discourse, performance and policies of two left-wing political alliances in Argentina and Greece after the economic crises, aiming to highlight their main characteristics in power and draw some conclusions on their impact on democracy, society, and political system. In addition, through the comparative study of these two cases, I highlight their positive and negative effects as well as the difficulties and obstacles that they faced in each case. Even though the

---

26 Moffitt, *The Global Rise of Populism*, 43–45.
27 Mouzelis, *Politics in the semi-periphery*; Kefala, *Peripheral (Post) Modernity*.
28 Grigoris Markou, "Anti-populist discourse in Greece and Argentina in the 21st century," *Journal of Political Ideologies* 26, no. 2 (2021): 202.

Argentine and the Greek case present many similar features, it seems that their different politico-social context affect their courses and choices.

4   The Argentine Case: Kirchnerism in Power (2003–2015)

Néstor Kirchner's surprisingvictory in the 2003 election brought the *Victory Front* (FpV) to power, at a time when many left-wing populist forces were gradually gaining ground in Latin America (during what is known as the"pink tide"), seeking a new economic model and a new democratic direction. This populist wave included leaders such as Chavez (Venezuela), Kirchner (Argentina), Morales (Bolivia) and Corea (Ecuador).[29] Specifically, Kirchner rose to power after the collapse of Argentina's economy and the social unrest that erupted in the country, as a "fresh" and dynamic political figure from the mainstream Peronist political camp, forming a new progressive left-wing alliance. According to Marcela Lopez Levy, 'Nestor Kirchner seemed to burst onto the national scene from nowhere in 2003 … He came to power thanks to the outgoing interim president, Eduardo Duhalde.'[30]

The FpV cannot be seen as a party with a strong ideological core. It was an alliance of parties that combined diverse ideas with a populist style that stemmed from the Peronist tradition. Néstor Kirchner (2003–2007) and Cristina Fernández de Kirchner (2007–2015), two Peronist politicians, managed to form a progressive politico-social alliance within the existing political system, advocated the implementation of a "nationalcapitalism" and declared allegiance to the constitution. However, at the same time, the two leaders created coalitions and special bonds with communist leaders (e.g., Fidel Castro) and left-wing populist and other politicians (e.g., Hugo Chavez, Evo Morales, Luiz Inácio Lula) in Latin America, opposing mainstream political forces and the elites both inside and outside the country.[31] In fact, Kirchnerism did not develop any Marxist class analysis, nor did it defend the revolutionary path to power, even though it collaborated with some communist organizations. Its main goal was to reconstruct a "national capitalism" through the formation of a large popular coalition.[32] As Nestor Kirchner argued after its first election: 'The

---

29   Gratius, "The "Third Wave of Populism" in Latin America."
30   Levy, *Argentina under the Kirchners*, 21.
31   Jerome Adams, *Liberators, Patriots and Leaders of Latin America: 32 Biographies* (Jefferson, North Carolina and London: McFarland and Company, 2010), 299.
32   Daniel Ozarow, *The Mobilization and Demobilization of Middle-Class Revolt: Comparative Insights from Argentina* (New York and Oxon: Routledge, 2019), 72.

central part of our plan is to rebuild national capitalism, which will generate alternatives that will allow us to restore upward social mobility. It is not a matter of shutting out the world, it is not a matter of reactionary nationalism, but of intelligence, observation, and commitment to the nation.'[33]

The question here is whether Kirchnerist discourse was presented as antagonistic and, thus "populist." Who were "the people" and who were "the enemies of the people" in its discourse? If we shed light on the governmental period of Kirchnerism (2003–2015), we can notice that the two leaders expressed a populist discourse, dividing society between "us" (the people) and "them" (the enemies of the people). The collective subject of "the people" does not seem to be narrowly defined by Kirchner and Fernández, including every Argentine citizen, the people of toil and labor, the young people, the people of *favela*, the people of sacrifices and struggles. In particular, the people of Kirchnerism included Peronists and non-Peronists, men and women, young and old, students, unemployed, workers, the poor, the indigenous, vulnerable social groups and every democratic citizen of the country. Furthermore, the notion of "the people" in Kirchnerist discourse included social and human rights organizations and movements, as well as much of the social movements that opposed the neoliberal policies of the 1990s and participated passionately in the social uprisings of the following years. It is no coincidence that Kirchner's administration tried to redress human rights violations of the past and developed a warm relationship with "Mothers and the Grandmothers of Plaza de Mayo" ("Madres").[34] Levy underlines the fact that Kirchner stood by Mothers, while, at the same time, he stood by 'the groups that had grown after the mid-1990s, organizing against neo-liberalism and the rise of poverty and unemployment in Argentina.'[35]

Who were "the opponents" of the people of Kirchnerism? The movement's enemies were not born out of nowhere but had a direct bond with the anti-establishment discourse of the 2001 social uprising, a discourse that opposed the corrupt political system, the banks, the IMF, the judges, and the privatized companies. Of course, the formation of the opposing camp is not a short and fast process, but it presents a continuum and is reshaped over the years, depending on the political, social, and economic situation. For Kirchner, some of the most prominent enemies of the popular classes was Menemism,[36] the

---

33   "Excerpts: Kirchner's inaugural speech," BBC.co.uk, May 26, 2003, http://news.bbc.co.uk/2/hi/americas/2938070.stm.
34   Barbara Sutton, *Surviving State Terror: Women's Testimonies of Repression and Resistance in Argentina* (New York: New York University Press, 2018), 8.
35   Levy, *Argentina under the Kirchners*, 30.
36   The ideas and policies of Carlos Menem, former president of Argentina (1989–1999).

neoliberal economy, the political establishment, the IMF that created many problems in country's economy, the privatized companies and the multinational corporations, parts of the military that were involved in the recent dictatorship, and the Supreme Court judges who were accused by Kirchner for corruption and favoritism.[37] Fernández maintained a similar antagonistic logic between "the people" and "the elites" during her rule, turning her criticism also on other opponents, such as the media. According to Ostiguy and Casullo, 'Néstor Kirchner sought to unify most of the social and political national actors under the banner of the fight against transnational economic actors: the International Monetary Fund (IMF), the foreign banks, the financial "vultures" …, and their domestic partners and economic gurus,' while Cristina Fernandez de Kirchner 'switched the direction of antagonism from the outside to the domestic scene: from foreign financial sectors to the old "oligarquía ganadera," urban upper middle classes … and very especially the media.'[38]

Moreover, Kirchner and Fernández expressed a populist performance, presenting themselves as part of "the people," while Kirchner often made references to his humble origins. In contrast to technocratic politicians who have almost no direct contact with the masses, the two leaders developed a close and warm relationship with the popular classes and social organizations, visited the favelas, hugged the workers, kissed poor peoples' hands and expressed their feelings through an emotional and passionate discourse. Besides that, they strengthen their popularity and simplicity through their popular expressions which, however, did not reach the intensity of the "bad manners" of Chavez and other populist leaders. Moreover, a key feature of their populist performance was the frequent references to God. In many of their speeches, the two leaders asked for God's help or felt the need to thank him.[39] The choice

---

37 See more for the division of the social field and "the enemies of the people" by Kirchner in: Paula Biglieri, "El retorno del pueblo argentino: entre la authorizacion y la asamblea. Argentina en la era K," In *En el Nombre del Pueblo: la emergencia del populismo kirchnerista*, eds. Paula Biglieri y Gloria Perelló (Buenos Aires: UNSAM Edita, 2007), 61–84. [Spanish].

38 Pierre Ostiguy and María Esperanza Casullo, "Left versus Right Populism: Antagonism and the Social Other," Presentation at the 67th PSA Annual International Conference, Glasgow, UK (10–12 April 2017): 20–21.

39 Nestor Kirchner, "Palabras del Presidente Néstor Kirchner en el acto de cierre de campaña del Partido Justicialista en la Provincia de Buenos Aires," *Casa Rosada*, 11/9/2003, https://www.casarosada.gob.ar/informacion/archivo/24413-blank-72709869 [Spanish]; Cristina Fernandez de Kirchner, "Asunción de Cristina Kirchner, 10 de diciembre de 2007," *Cfkargentina*, December 10, 2007, https://www.cfkargentina.com/asuncion-de-cristina-kirchner-10-de-diciembre-de-2007. [Spanish].

of invoking God in front of their audience and the general references to God are part of the Peronist tradition and "low" culture. Evita did the same with her frequent references to God.[40] It is important to note that Kirchner and Fernandez did not present exactly the same characteristics in their populist performance and specifically in the style of their clothes. Nestor Kirchner used to go "low," wearing large, unbuttoned jackets and tieless shirt, showing that he was part of "the people," while Fernández was always fashionably dressed with elegant clothes, following perhaps the tasteful style of Evita Peron.[41]

Additionally, a central element of their populist performance was the concept of crisis. Kirchnerist populist performance "took advantage" of economic and social crisis, understanding that the slogan of the social uprising of 2001 "que se vayan todos" ("let them all go") could support their project. This is the reason why they attempted to listen to the demands of the emerging movements and social organizations, came close to poor people, visited factories and schools, and conveyed a message of hope to workers and young people, identifying those responsible for the crisis and setting up a progressive framework for action. Nonetheless, they did not present the crisis as a simple and manageable situation during their rule.

What were the main axes of their political agenda? The Kirchnerist political program was based on the axes of memory, truth, and justice, as they defended human rights and justice for the victims of the bloody military dictatorship of the past, put special emphasis on the "memory" of the crucial events experienced by the people of Argentina in modern history, and defended justice.[42] As Sebastián Etchemendy and Candelaria Garay highlight, the Kirchners,

> established solid alliances with popular actors such as mainstream unions and some of the largest unemployed workers' organizations and community-based social movements, and they promoted a series of trials of the military accused of human rights violations during the 1976–83 dictatorship.[43]

---

40 See John Barnes, *Evita, First Lady: A Biography of Evita Peron* (New York: Grove Atlantic, 1978).
41 María Esperanza Casullo, "Populism as Synecdochal Representation: Understanding the Transgressive Bodily Performance of South American President," in *Populism in Global Perspective: A Performative and Discursive Approach*, eds. Pierre Ostiguy, Francisco Panizza and Benjamin Moffitt (New York and Oxon: Routledge, 2021), 84–87.
42 See Levy, *Argentina under the Kirchners*.
43 Sebastián Etchemendy and Candelaria Garay, "Argentina: Left Populism in Comparative Perspective, 2003–2009," In *The Resurgence of Latin American Left*, eds. Steven Levitsky and Roberts Kenneth M. (Baltimore: The Johns Hopkins University Press, 2011), 283.

Furthermore, one of its main goals was the economic recovery of the lower social class, while promoting nationalizations, repaying the debt to the IMF, and placing particular emphasis on health, education, and employment through a neo-developmental economic model.[44] Simultaneously, Kirchner and Fernández developed the investment and industry sectors, strengthened the Southern Common Market (MERCOSUR), developed good relations with Brazil, proceeded with debt restructuring, came into conflict with part of the elite and promoted policies in favor of the rights of the LGBTQ+ community.[45] Nonetheless, the country, during Kirchnerist rule, experienced major political scandals, high inflation, and massive anti-government demonstrations. Pablo Stefanoni has highlighted the two different images of the Kirchnerist period in a very apt way. As he argues, Kirchnerist legacy includes,

> progressive measures like same-sex marriage, improvements in real wages, increased consumption for popular sectors, important advances in the trials of military figures tied to the dictatorship. At the same time, that legacy includes meddling in national statistics and the manipulation of inflation figures, oftentimes authoritarian rhetoric (even if that rhetoric was never translated into practice, unlike in Venezuela), and above all, diverse claims of corruption linked to public works. The growth in Néstor and Cristina Kirchner's personal wealth is difficult to account for.[46]

Conclusively, Kirchnerism's discourse possesses the necessary characteristics to be considered a populist discourse, while its policies have been directed towards a humanitarian, progressive, and neo-developmental direction, trying to improve the lives of the "social majority" but being unable to meet all challenges that came on its way. The strong hegemony of Kirchnerism closed its first cycle in 2015 with the defeat in the presidential elections by the anti-populist Mauricio Macri, but the progressive political space managed to reorganize itself and return to power in a new form in 2019, with Alberto Fernandez as president and Cristina Fernández de Kirchner as vice-president.[47] Even if the left seemed to be weakening in Latin America, its recent great victories in Argentina, Bolivia, Mexico, and Peru prove that it remains strong.

---

44 See Levy, *Argentina under the Kirchners*, 32–44.
45 See Levy, *Argentina under the Kirchners*.
46 Stefanoni Pablo, "Kirchnerism for Centrists?," *Jacobinmag.com*, May 31, 2019, https://jacobinmag.com/2019/05/cristina-kirchner-alberto-fernandez-peronism-argentina.
47 Daniel C. Hellinger, *Comparative Politics of Latin America: Democracy at Last?* (New York and Oxon: Routledge, 2021), 403.

5   The Greek Case: SYRIZA in Government (2015–2019)

The Coalition of the Radical Left (SYRIZA) was founded in 2004 as a coalition of left-wing political forces. However, for many years it could not gain large electoral support.[48] The eruption of the international financial crisis (2007/08) and the rise of social movements against the political and economic establishment changed this situation. The newly elected president of the party, Alexis Tsipras, gave a new populist direction to the political style of the party, gaining more and more support from the Greek people. "The people," which became the nodal point of his discourse,[49] included workers and farmers, poor people and unemployed, youth, minorities, and every democratic citizen, while his criticism was mainly directed against the Greek and European political and economic establishment.[50]

In January 2015, SYRIZA won the elections through a strong populist discourse and performance. The people of Tsipras were not homogeneous but presented a special diversity and inclusiveness. At the same time, the adversary of the people was not formed on the basis of racist or nativist reasons (e.g., it was not a discourse against foreigners, immigrants, etc.), as SYRIZA mainly opposed neoliberalism and the neoliberal EU, the economic oligarchy, and the corrupt establishment.[51] Therefore, its populist discourse didn't have common features with right-wing populism. Nonetheless, due to SYRIZA's failure to get the necessary votes to form a majority government, the left-wing party decided to form a coalition government with Independent Greeks (*Anexartitoi Ellines* – "ANEL") of Panos Kammenos, a radical right party with conservative and xenophobic ideas,[52] which supported the return to Christian Orthodox values.[53] The cooperation between Tsipras and Kammenos was justified through their common anti-austerity agenda, a fact that was confirmed in practice, as the

---

48   Yiannos Katsourides, *Radical Left Parties in Government: The Cases of SYRIZA and AKEL* (Palgrave Macmillan, 2016), 53–67.
49   Yannis Stavrakakis and Giorgos Katsambekis, "Left-wing populism in the European periphery: the case of SYRIZA," *Journal of Political Ideologies* 19, no. 2 (2014): 119–142.
50   Markou, "The Rise of Inclusionary Populism."
51   Giorgos Venizelos, "Populism and the digital media: a necessarily symbiotic relationship?" In *Politics and populism across modes and media*, eds. Ruth Breeze and Ana María Fernández Vallejo (Bern: Peter Lang, 2020), 60.
52   Paris Aslanidis and Cristóbal Rovira Kaltwasser, "Dealing with populists in government: the SYRIZA-ANEL coalition in Greece," *Democratization* 23, no. 6 (2016): 1081.
53   Emmanouil Tsatsanis and Eftichia Teperoglou, "Greece's coalition governments: power sharing in a majoritarian democracy," in *Coalition Government as a Reflection of a Nation's Politics and Society: A Comparative Study of Parliamentary Parties and Cabinets in 12 countries*, ed. Matt Evans (Oxon and New York: Routledge, 2020), 232.

two governing parties presented many disagreements on human rights issues (e.g., gender change, cohabitation agreement, etc.) and national issues (e.g., Macedonia naming dispute), but not so much on other subjects related to austerity and Memoranda.[54]

The first "radical" period (January-September 2015) was characterized by the negotiations between the Greek government and institutions (*Troika*) for a new bailout agreement. The main actors of this period were, on the one side, Alexis Tsipras, the prime minister, and Yanis Varoufakis, minister of finance, and on the other side, the European Commission (EC), the European Central Bank (ECB), and the International Monetary Fund (IMF) (or the so-called "Institutions" or Troika).[55] The Greek government negotiated with the "institutions" to reach a new agreement that would reduce the strict anti-popular measures of Memoranda. The negotiation was presented by the prime minister as a fierce battle of a "government of the people" against the political and economic establishment of the country and Europe. Nevertheless, despite the predominance of "No" (61%) in the referendum of 2015, SYRIZA accepted a new Memorandum (austerity) package, leading to the departure of many MPs from the party and new elections that were won by Tsipras.[56]

After its second consecutive victory in the elections of September 2015, SYRIZA did not have the choice for a new partner in power. Thus, it cooperated again with ANEL, without drastically changing its political rhetoric and style. Tsipras promised to protect the "underprivileged people" through the implementation of a "parallel program" to the Memorandum.[57] "The people" continued to be a nodal point in his discourse until the end of his rule, while its populism presented an inclusive and progressive character. The president of SYRIZA called the Greek people, the workers, the unemployed, the low class, minorities, and all democratic citizens to participate in its effort to build a better future for the country and refuse the return of "the corrupt establishment." The notion of "the people" was also expressed in his discourse through connotations, such as "we," "the underprivileged," or "the many." For instance, during the election campaign for the European elections of 2019 the main slogan of

---

54 Tsatsanis and Teperoglou, "Greece's coalition governments," 239.
55 Diana Panke, "Greek-EU Debt Dueling in the Endgame," In *How Negotiations End: Negotiating Behavior in the Endgame*, ed. William Zartman (Cambridge: Cambridge University Press, 2019), 51.
56 Fernando Menden and Mario Mendez, "Referendums on European integration: crisis solving or crisis inducing?," in *The Routledge Handbook to Referendums and Direct Democracy*, eds. Laurence Morel and Matt Qvortrup (Oxon and New York: Routledge, 2018), 398–99.
57 "The parallel program of SYRIZA," *Avgi.gr*, September 6, 2015, https://www.avgi.gr/politiki/154641_parallilo-programma-toy-syriza.

the party was: 'For the Greece of the many, for the Europe of the peoples.'⁵⁸ However, the intensity of Tsipras' populist discourse has been decreasing over the years and the party has at best a lukewarm relationship with the Greek people, especially after its defeat in the 2019 elections and the beginning of the pandemic crisis. According to Antonis Galanopoulos, while 'SYRIZA is still correctly recognized as a left-wing populist party, its populist discourse was admittedly toned down during the pandemic.'⁵⁹ However, I consider it difficult to safely decide if SYRIZA in opposition (under Tsipras' leadership) continues to be a populist party or it is a party that flirts intensely with the abandonment of the populist element.⁶⁰

What about Tsipras' populist performance in power? The leader of SYRIZA presented himself as part of "the people" and as a prime minister who understood the problems of the Greek people, while placing his main opponent (president of New Democracy – "ND") on the side of the elites. Tsipras expressed a populist performative logic through his simple and popular political style in his public appearances, utilizing popular expressions in his statements and speeches, passionate gestures, and emotional rhetoric. He did not change his "humble" way of life, while he continued to live in Kypseli, a working-class area of Athens.⁶¹ Moreover, the leader of SYRIZA followed a casual fashion style, usually wearing a tieless shirt without a jacket.

Furthermore, SYRIZA based most of its agenda on how the country would put an end to Memoranda, relying on the "performance of the crisis." However, it is interesting that Tsipras did not attempt to spread "the sense of crisis" within the Greek society, presenting his party as a successful governmental party that won the battle against austerity and brought the country back to "normality."⁶²

---

58 "For the Greece of the many, for the Europe of the peoples," *Avgi.gr*, May 9, 2019, https://www.avgi.gr/politiki/311215_gia-tin-ellada-ton-pollon-gia-tin-eyropi-ton-laon. [Greek].
59 Antonis Galanopoulos, "Greece," In Populism and the Pandemic: A Collaborative Report, eds. Giorgos Katsambekis and Yannis Stavrakakis (Thessaloniki: Populismus, 2020), 28, http://populismus.gr/wp-content/uploads/2020/06/interventions-7-populism-pandemic-UPLOAD.pdf.
60 Grigoris Markou, "The systemic metamorphosis of Greece's once radical left-wing SYRIZA party," *openDemocracy*, June 14, 2021, https://www.opendemocracy.net/en/rethinking-populism/the-systemic-metamorphosis-of-greeces-once-radical-left-wing-syriza-party/.
61 Nick Squires, "The flat from where Greece's Che Guevara is planning Europe's downfall," *Telegraph*, January 25, 2015, https://www.telegraph.co.uk/news/worldnews/europe/greece/11368269/The-flat-from-where-Greeces-Che-Guevara-is-planning-Europes-downfall.html.
62 "Alexis Tsipras: We are returning back to normality," *Naftemporiki.gr*, June 24, 2018, https://m.naftemporiki.gr/story/1363943/al-tsipras-epistrefoume-stin-kanonikotita. [Greek].

Besides that, while SYRIZA in opposition presented the confrontation of the crisis and the end of the Memoranda as a simple and easy process,[63] it changed its attitude after its rise to power, as Tsipras accepted the fact that there are huge difficulties on dealing with the critical economic situation of the country and on negotiations with the institutions.[64]

What kind of policies did SYRIZA implement in power? The party's dominant narrative in opposition was to put an end to austerity policies, corruption, and neoliberalism, but it failed to achieve all its goals while in power. During its first "radical" period, SYRIZA tried to implement part of its agenda, revoking some unpopular decisions of the previous governments, such as the closure of Hellenic Broadcasting Corporation (ERT).[65] The government promoted a humanitarian aid program to tackle poverty, which included free electricity and social benefits for the poor, despite EU pressures against it.[66] In addition, it settled the debts of thousands of citizens with the tax authorities, social security funds, and municipalities, while enabling the acquisition of Greek citizenship to children of immigrants.[67]

Following its victory in the September 2015 election, the government's goal was to tackle corruption and tax evasion, as well as protect minorities and other social groups. The problem was that Tsipras had agreed to implement austerity policies (e.g., increases in many taxes, reductions in pensions, several privatizations, etc.), which adversely affected the lives of much of society and especially the middle class of the country. In fact, SYRIZA maintained austerity measures while trying to provide a few benefits to the people. The leader of SYRIZA considered that if the Greek government refused to sign a new agreement with "institutions" (EC, ECB, and IMF), then the consequences

---

63   Alexis Tsipras stated in his speech on November 11, 2012: "The only realistic and lifeline alternative is the abolition by a law and an article [...] of all the austerity measures that impoverish society and create even greater recession. "Tsipras' Speech," *Syn.gr*, November 11, 2012, http://www.syn.gr/gr/keimeno.php?id=29223. [Greek].
64   According to Tsipras, SYRIZA had a hard battle and fought to protect Greece. See: "Alexis Tsipras: We fought so much that they were afraid of everything we are capable of," *News247.gr*, September 1, 2015, https://www.news247.gr/ekloges/alexis-tsipras-paleps ame-toso-poy-fovithikan-gia-ola-osa-eimaste-ikanoi.6372747.html. [Greek].
65   See: Nicos Myrtou, Stamatis Poulakidakos and Panagiota Nakou, "Greece," In *A Trasnational Study of Law and Justice on TV*, eds. Peter Robson and Jennifer L. Schulz (Portland: Hart Publishing, 2016), 122.
66   "Greece adopts 'anti-poverty' law despite alleged EU row," *France24.com*, March 18, 2015, https://www.france24.com/en/20150318-greece-anti-poverty-law-eu-tsipras.
67   "The bill on citizenship has passed – ANEL voted against," *News.gr*, June 25, 2015, https://www.news.gr/politikh/esoterikh-politikh/article/226498/perase-to-nomoshedio-gia-thn-ithageneia-katapshfis.html.

would have been much worse for Greece.⁶⁸ As the country reached the end of its memorandum obligations, the Greek government devoted more attention to the welfare state, social benefits, and the basic salary. Moreover, it promoted much-discussed policies that created tensions on the political scene (some more, some less), such as the cohabitation agreement, the recognition of gender identity, the acceptance of adoption by same-sex couples, the law on television licenses, and the Prespa agreement (Macedonia naming dispute).⁶⁹ For example, the Macedonian issue became the central topic on the political agenda, directly affecting the political scene and the parties involved.⁷⁰ Even though SYRIZA lost its radicalism and succumbed to the demands of the political system, it continued to support the claim that its social agenda was a way to protect the social majority. As Tsipras stated in 2016, 'the old political establishment left a social majority unprotected in the vortex of the economic crisis,' while it is necessary 'to organize actions and interventions in the next steps, in what we call the reconstruction of the social state.'⁷¹

Tsipras' inability to simultaneously manage austerity policies and the protection of the vulnerable, the sketchiness of its governmental planning in many issues, the strong controversy with parts of the popular classes (e.g., in the occasion of the Prespa agreement), and the critical economic situation of some social groups and the middle class, seems to be what led to the defeat of SYRIZA in the 2019 elections. This defeat is part of a general decline of left-wing populist parties in Europe. Left-wing populists have failed to win the elections in Europe since the beginning of the crisis (with the sole exception of Tsipras), while Pablo Iglesias from Podemos decided to leave Spanish politics after the Madrid regional election.⁷² It seems that the left-wing populist vision of the post-crisis period is now closing.

---

68   John Gregson, "Socialism and Communism," in *Political Ideologies*, ed. Paul Wetherly (Oxford: Oxford University Press, 2017), 123.
69   The Prespa agreement was accepted by Greece and North Macedonia in 2018, under the auspices of the United Nations, resolving a long-standing dispute between the two countries on the name of the latter after almost three decades of unfruitful negotiations. See more, Athina Skoulariki, "Political Polarisation in Greece: The Prespa Agreement, Left/Right Antagonism and the Nationalism/Populism Nexus," *South European Society and Politics* 25, no. 3–4 (2021): 411–439.
70   Skoulariki, "Political Polarisation in Greece."
71   "Tsipras: The 7 pillars of action for the weakest," *Real.gr*, July 27, 2016, https://www.real.gr/archive_politiki/arthro/tsipras_oi_7_pylones_drasis_gia_tous_asthenesterous-74193/. [Greek].
72   Sam Jones, "Pablo Iglesias leaves Spanish politics, 'very proud' of Podemos legacy," *TheGuardian.com*, May 5, 2021, https://www.theguardian.com/world/2021/may/05/pablo-iglesias-leaves-politics-podemos-spain.

6   Common Trajectories, or Not?

Even though Argentina and Greece are two countries far apart from each other, they have experienced similar situations and critical events at the beginning of the 21st century, like economic crisis and huge anti-governmental social unrest and movements ("Argentinazo" and "Aganaktismenoi," respectively). In both countries left-wing populist parties rose to power as a response of neoliberalism and economic disaster, while their political scene was divided between populist and anti-populist forces.[73] In addition, as can be easily seen from my previous analysis, the two populist examples of our study had numerous discursive and performative features in common, although there were some differences that led to different results in the end.

First, Kirchnerism and SYRIZA both emerged in the context of an economic crisis, wherein they attempted to stop the destructive economic recipes and create new promising paths for their peoples. As political forces, they rose up to put an end to the failed austerity policies of previous governments, but without seeking a radical overthrow of the political system. They both expressed an inclusionary and progressive populist discourse, defended human rights, opposed neoliberalism, cooperated with politicians from other political areas, and attempted to implement a social agenda that would favor "the unprivileged people." Their populist logic brought the people back to the forefront of political life, supported social forces that had been left on the margins for years, and revealed the weaknesses and limitations of the dominant political system. Additionally, the two populist cases had to confront common anti-populist narratives with similar dualist cultural schemes, which underestimated populism and the popular classes.[74]

The Argentine and the Greek case present also significant differences. Kirchnerism, as a progressive political movement within Peronism, expressed a populist rhetoric, which, however, never reached the intensity of other Latin American populist leaders, such as Hugo Chavez and Evo Morales. This is something that some scholars point out. For example, Hawkins believes that 'Kirchner uses populist language very inconsistently' and that his 'campaign speech is the only one with a fairly populist discourse.'[75] Certainly, Cristina

---

73   Markou, "Anti-populist discourse"; Pierre Ostiguy, "Argentina's Double Political Spectrum: Party System, Political Identities, and Strategies, 1944–2007," *Kellogg Institute*, Working Paper no. 361, (2009).
74   Markou, "Anti-populist discourse."
75   Kirk Hawkins, *Venezuela's Chavismo and Populism in Comparative Perspective* (New York: Cambridge University Press, 2010), 79.

Fernández appears to increase the intensity of the populist discourse after Kirchner. On the other side, SYRIZA has been expressing a strong populist rhetoric since the beginning of the crisis and at least until the middle of its rule.[76] There is an interesting fact here: Kirchnerism's populism does not seem to come into FpV so much through Kirchner's (its first leader) personality and style, but rather through the populist tradition of Peronism. After all, Kirchner was a passionate Peronist politician with many progressive and pragmatist elements in his discourse and actions. In contrast, the Greek radical left had a close relationship with anti-populism for many years in Metapolitefsi,[77] due to the increasing popularity of the Panhellenic Socialist Movement (PASOK) of Andreas Papandreou, something that change in the beginning of the 21st century, especially after the rise of Tsipras to its leadership, a politician who followed new discursive paths for at least a decade.[78]

Another characteristic difference is the fact that Kirchnerism defended from the outset the implementation of a "national capitalism" in Argentina, highlighting the pragmatic aspects of its agenda, in contrast to the populist SYRIZA that contained anti-capitalist elements and harshly criticized (up to a point) capitalism and social democratic parties in the opposition. Beyond doubt, SYRIZA in power followed a more social-democratic and pragmatist rhetoric and action. As John Milios states, 'SYRIZA remains dominant on the Greek political scene, but today the party is better understood as a mainstream social democratic party, than as a movement of the radical left.'[79] Furthermore, it is crucial to underline that there was a significant difference between the two cases in their relationship with the popular classes. Kirchnerism had a more direct connection with the people and the popular and social organizations throughout the years of its governmental rule, while in the case of SYRIZA this relationship has been gradually weakened. This seems to be the result of the impact of their policies regarding the social majority. The two Argentine presidents had the opportunity, due to the size and independence of their national economy, as well as the important role of Argentina in Latin America, to change the political direction of their country relatively easily, applying a neo-development economic model that somewhat improved the lives of most of the people. At the same time, they were able to rely on a strong popular base

---

76   Stavrakakis and Katsambekis, "Left-wing populism in the European periphery."
77   Metapolitefsi is called the period after the fall of the military junta of 1967–74 and the 1974 legislative elections.
78   Markou, "The Rise of Inclusionary Populism'"; Venizelos, "Populism and the digital media."
79   John Milios, "SYRIZA: From Subversion to Pragmatism," *Global Dialogue* 6, no. 4 (2016) https://globaldialogue.isa-sociology.org/syriza-from-subversion-to-pragmatism/.

of Peronism, which helped them continue to pursue their agenda for years. Nevertheless, SYRIZA did not have many options to get out of the situation, as the economy of Greece operates as a member of the EU and the Eurozone and is essentially committed to following the orders of European partners.[80] Thus, it faced obstacles in its effort to implement a pro-popular agenda. Furthermore, SYRIZA has been strengthened electorally after the crisis and did not have the opportunity and the conditions to create a strong electoral base like Peronism or PASOK of the past. As shown in practice, the two populist cases of our study did not differ in their discursive and performative characteristics, but in the fact that they had to face different barriers on the road to change.

7 Conclusion

In this chapter, I shed light on my analysis on the political discourse, performance, and policies pursued by two left-wing parties in power following the outbreak of economic crises and the neoliberal management, aiming to examine whether they present populist characteristics and how they managed the critical political-socio-economic situation. Our study was based on the discursive and performative approaches, which offer us particularly useful tools in the study of populism, without adopting stereotypical perspectives.

Both Kirchnerism and SYRIZA expressed a progressive and inclusionary populist discourse in power, while attempting to implement a range of social and human rights policies. The political style of Kirchner, Fernández, and Tsipras came as a response to the technocratic anti-populist style, including common features in terms of language, manners, and passion. Kirchnerism was able to give more weight to the policies for the vulnerable people, thereby further improving to an extent the economic situation of the popular classes, without, however, avoiding economic problems (e.g., inflation). The "partial" success of Kirchnerism is confirmed by the important electoral successes of all the previous years and the popular support that Fernández (and her associates) continues to receive until today. In Greece, SYRIZA managed to improve the living conditions of some social groups (e.g., "the vulnerable," such as the unemployed and low-paid workers) but without avoiding the problems that arose mainly through its austerity policies.

---

80 For the different institutional framework of the Argentine and the Greek economy, see: Kostas Melas, *Argentina-Greece: A descriptive comparative analysis of economic developments in both countries after payment defaults* (Athens: Patakis, 2015), 9–11. [Greek].

Populism can sometimes improve the political situation and offer remarkable solutions to problems, but as Stavrakakis mentions 'it is not a political panacea.'[81] The Argentine and Greek left-wing populisms showed that at the same moment that populism manages to achieve important things, it faces its own limits. For instance, both political parties provided to the marginalized people new opportunities and a voice, putting them again at the heart of the political scene. Additionally, they supported some social forces that suffered at the beginning of the crisis, while they highlighted the anti-popular and cruel nature of neoliberal management. Nevertheless, while they managed to alleviate popular dissatisfaction, they did not pursue deeper democratization. Rather, they accepted and maintained the main characteristics of the political system and they did not radically change the lives of the popular classes. The two populist cases created the belief that the people would be able to defeat their tough opponents and change the bad situation for the social majority, but in practice, beyond some significant progressive and humanitarian interventions that have been extremely important to a part of the people, they did not allow the deepening of democratization and the reform of the political system.

Bibliography

Adams, Jerome. *Liberators, Patriots and Leaders of Latin America: 32 Biographies*. Jefferson, North Carolina and London: McFarland and Company, 2010.

"Alexis Tsipras: We are returning back to normality." *Naftemporiki.gr*, June 24, 2018, https://m.naftemporiki.gr/story/1363943/al-tsipras-epistrefoume-stin-kanonikotita. [Greek].

"Alexis Tsipras: We fought so much that they were afraid of everything we are capable of." *News247.gr*, September 1, 2015, https://www.news247.gr/ekloges/alexis-tsipras-palepsame-toso-poy-fovithikan-gia-ola-osa-eimaste-ikanoi.6372747.html. [Greek].

Aslanidis, Paris. "Ethnography of populism." In *Populism in History, Art and Politics*. Athens: The Moraitis School, 2016. [Greek].

Aslanidis, Paris and Cristóbal Rovira Kaltwasser. "Dealing with populists in government: the SYRIZA-ANEL coalition in Greece." *Democratization* 23, no. 6 (2016): 1077–1091.

Barnes, John. *Evita, First Lady: A Biography of Evita Peron*. New York: Grove Atlantic, 1978.

---

81 Stavrakakis, *Populism*, 107.

Barr, Robert. *The Resurgence of Populism in Latin America*. London: Boulder and Lynne Rienner Publishers, 2017.

Biglieri, Paula. "El retorno del pueblo argentino: entre la authorizacion y la asamblea. Argentina en la era K." In *En el Nombre del Pueblo: la emergencia del populismo kirchnerista*, edited by Paula Biglieri y Gloria Perelló, 61–84. Buenos Aires: UNSAM Edita, 2007. [Spanish].

Casullo María, Esperanza. "Populism as Synecdochal Representation: Understanding the Transgressive Bodily Performance of South American President." In *Populism in Global Perspective: A Performative and Discursive Approach*, edited by Pierre Ostiguy, Francisco Panizza and Benjamin Moffitt. New York and Oxon: Routledge, 2021.

Etchemendy, Sebastián and Candelaria Garay. "Argentina: Left Populism in Comparative Perspective, 2003–2009." In *The Resurgence of Latin American Left*, edited by Steven Levitsky and Kenneth M. Roberts. Baltimore: The Johns Hopkins University Press, 2011.

"Excerpts: Kirchner's inaugural speech." BBC.co.uk, May 26, 2003, http://news.bbc.co.uk/2/hi/americas/2938070.stm.

Fernandez Cristina de Kirchner. "Asunción de Cristina Kirchner, 10 de diciembre de 2007." *Cfkargentina*, December 10, 2007, https://www.cfkargentina.com/asuncion-de-cristina-kirchner-10-de-diciembre-de-2007. [Spanish].

"For the Greece of the many, for the Europe of the peoples." *Avgi.gr*, May 9, 2019, https://www.avgi.gr/politiki/311215_gia-tin-ellada-ton-pollon-gia-tin-eyropi-ton-laon. [Greek].

Galanopoulos, Antonis. "Greece." In *Populism and the Pandemic: A Collaborative Report*. Edited by Giorgos Katsambekis and Yannis Stavrakakis. Thessaloniki: Populismus, 2020. http://populismus.gr/wp-content/uploads/2020/06/interventions-7-populism-pandemic-UPLOAD.pdf.

Gratius, Susanne. "The 'Third Wave of Populism' in Latin America." FRIDE (Fundación para las relaciones internacionales y el diámogo exterior), Working Paper no. 45 (2007): 1–26.

"Greece adopts 'anti-poverty' law despite alleged EU row." *France24.com*, March 18, 2015, https://www.france24.com/en/20150318-greece-anti-poverty-law-eu-tsipras.

Gregson, John. "Socialism and Communism." In *Political Ideologies*. Edited by Paul Wetherly. Oxford: Oxford University Press, 2017.

Hawkins, Kirk. "Is Chavez Populist? Measuring Populist Discourse in Comparative Perspective." *Comparative Political Studies* 42, no. 8 (2009): 1040–1067.

Hawkins, Kirk. *Venezuela's Chavismo and Populism in Comparative Perspective*. New York: Cambridge University Press, 2010.

Hellinger, C. Daniel. *Comparative Politics of Latin America: Democracy at Last?* New York and Oxon: Routledge, 2021.

Jagers, Jan and Walgrave Stefaan. "Populism as political communication style: An empirical study of political parties' discourse in Belgium." *European Journal of Political Research* 46, no. 3 (2007): 319–345.

Jansen, Robert. "Populist Mobilization: A New Theoretical Approach to Populism." *Sociological Theory* 29, no. 2 (2011): 75–96.

Jones, Sam. "Pablo Iglesias leaves Spanish politics, 'very proud' of Podemos legacy." *TheGuardian.com*, May 5, 2021, https://www.theguardian.com/world/2021/may/05/pablo-iglesias-leaves-politics-podemos-spain.

Kaltwasser, Cristóbal Rovira, Paul Taggart, Paulina Ochoa Espejo, and Pierre Ostiguy, eds. *The Oxford Handbook of Populism*. Oxford: Oxford University Press, 2017.

Katsourides, Yiannos. *Radical Left Parties in Government: The Cases of SYRIZA and AKEL*. London: Palgrave Macmillan, 2016.

Kefala, Eleni. *Peripheral (Post) Modernity, The Syncretist Aesthetics of Borges, Piglia, Kalokyris and Kyriakidis*. New Yok: Peter Lang Publishing, 2007.

Kioupkiolis, Alexandros. "Podemos: the ambiguous promises of left-wing populism in contemporary Spain." *Journal of Political Ideologies* 21, no. 2 (2016): 99–120.

Kirchner, Nestor. "Palabras del Presidente Néstor Kirchner en el acto de cierre de campaña del Partido Justicialista en la Provincia de Buenos Aires." *Casa Rosada*, September 11, 2003. https://www.casarosada.gob.ar/informacion/archivo/24413-blank-72709869. [Spanish].

Laclau, Ernesto. "Populism: What's in a Name?" In *Populism and the Mirror of Democracy*. Edited by Francisco Panizza. London and New York: Verso, 2005.

Levy, Lopez Marcela. *Argentina under the Kirchners: The legacy of populism*. Warwickshire and Shropshire: LAB and Practical Action Publishing, 2017.

Maiguashca, Bice and Jonathan Dean. "Corbynism, populism and the re-shaping of left politics in contemporary Britain." In *The Populist Radical Left in Europe*. Edited by Giorgos Katsambekis and Alexandros Kioupkiolis. Oxon and New York: Routledge, 2019.

Markou, Grigoris. "The Rise of Inclusionary Populism in Europe: The Case of SYRIZA." *Contemporary Southeastern Europe* 4, no. 1 (2017): 54–71.

Markou, Grigoris. "Anti-populist discourse in Greece and Argentina in the 21st century." *Journal of Political Ideologies* 26, no. 2 (2021): 201–219.

Markou, Grigoris. "The systemic metamorphosis of Greece's once radical left-wing SYRIZA party." *OpenDemocracy*, June 14, 2021. https://www.opendemocracy.net/en/rethinking-populism/the-systemic-metamorphosis-of-greeces-once-radical-left-wing-syriza-party/.

Marlière Philippe. "Jean-Luc Mélenchon and France Insoumise: The Manufacturing of Populism." In *The Populist Radical Left in Europe*, edited by Giorgos Katsambekis and Alexandros Kioupkiolis. Oxon and New York: Routledge, 2019.

Melas, Kostas. *Argentina-Greece: A descriptive comparative analysis of economic developments in both countries after payment defaults.* Athens: Patakis, 2015. [Greek].

Menden, Fernando and Mario Mendez. "Referendums on European integration: crisis solving or crisis inducing?" In *The Routledge Handbook to Referendums and Direct Democracy.* Edited by Laurence Morel and Matt Qvortrup. Oxon and New York: Routledge, 2018.

Milios, John. "SYRIZA: From Subversion to Pragmatism." *Global Dialogue* 6 no. 4 (2016). https://globaldialogue.isa-sociology.org/syriza-from-subversion-to-pragmatism/.

Moffitt, Benjamin. *The Global Rise of Populism, Performance, Political Style, and Representation.* California: Stanford University Press, 2016.

Mouzelis, Nicos. *Politics in the semi-periphery: Early Parliamentarism and Late Industrialization in the Balkans and Latin America.* New York: Macmillan, 1986.

Mudde, Cas and Cristóbal Rovira Kaltwasser. *Populism: A Very Short Introduction.* Oxford: Oxford University Press, 2017.

Myrtou Nicos, Stamatis Poulakidakos and Panagiota Nakou. "Greece." In *A Trasnational Study of Law and Justice on TV.* Edited by Peter Robson and Jennifer L. Schulz. Portland: Hart Publishing, 2016.

Ostiguy, Pierre. "Argentina's Double Political Spectrum: Party System, Political Identities, and Strategies, 1944–2007." *Kellogg Institute*, Working Paper no. 361 (2009).

Ostiguy, Pierre and María Esperanza Casullo. "Left versus Right Populism: Antagonism and the Social Other." Presentation at the 67th PSA Annual International Conference, Glasgow, UK, 10–12 April, 2017.

Ostiguy, Pierre. "Populism. A Socio-Cultural Approach." In *The Oxford Handbook of Populism.* Edited by Cristobal Rovira Kaltwasser, Paul Taggart, Paulina Ochoa Espejo and Pierre Ostiguy. Oxford: Oxford University Press, 2017.

Ostiguy, Pierre, Francisco Panizza and Benjamin Moffitt. *Populism in Global Perspective: A Performative and Discursive Approach.* New York: Routledge, 2021.

Ozarow, Daniel. *The Mobilization and Demobilization of Middle-Class Revolt: Comparative Insights from Argentina.* New York and Oxon: Routledge, 2019.

Panizza, Francisco. *Contemporary Latin America, Development and Democracy Beyond the Washington Consensus.* London and New York: Zed Books, 2009.

Panke, Diana. "Greek-EU Debt Dueling in the Endgame." In *How Negotiations End: Negotiating Behavior in the Endgame.* Edited by William Zartman. Cambridge: Cambridge University Press, 2019.

Ronderos, Sebastián. "Hysteria in the squares: Approaching populism from a perspective of desire." *Psychoanalysis, Culture and Society* no. 26 (2021): 46–64.

Silva, Eduardo. *Challenging Neoliberalism in Latin America.* New York: Cambridge University Press, 2009.

Skoulariki, Athina. "Political Polarisation in Greece: The Prespa Agreement, Left/Right Antagonism and the Nationalism/Populism Nexus." *South European Society and Politics* 25, no. 3–4 (2021): 411–439.

Squires Nick. "The flat from where Greece's Che Guevara is planning Europe's downfall." *Telegraph*, January 25, 2015. https://www.telegraph.co.uk/news/worldnews/europe/greece/11368269/The-flat-from-where-Greeces-Che-Guevara-is-planning-Europes-downfall.html.

Stavrakakis, Yannis. "The Return of "the People": Populism and Anti-Populism in the Shadow of the European Crisis." *Constellations* 21, no. 4 (2014): 505–517.

Stavrakakis, Yannis and Giorgos Katsambekis. "Left-wing populism in the European periphery: the case of SYRIZA." *Journal of Political Ideologies* 19, no. 2 (2014): 119–142.

Stavrakakis, Yannis. *Populism: Myths, Stereotypes and Reorientations*. Athens: Publications of the Hellenic Open University, 2019. [Greek].

Stefanoni, Pablo. "Kirchnerism for Centrists?" *Jacobinmag.com*, May 31, 2019. https://jacobinmag.com/2019/05/cristina-kirchner-alberto-fernandez-peronism-argentina.

Sutton, Barbara. *Surviving State Terror: Women's Testimonies of Repression and Resistance in Argentina*. New York: New York University Press, 2018.

"The bill on citizenship has passed – ANEL voted against." *News.gr*, June 25, 2015. https://www.news.gr/politikh/esoterikh-politikh/article/226498/perase-to-nomoshedio-gia-thn-ithageneia-katapshfis.html. [Greek].

"The parallel program of SYRIZA." *Avgi.gr*, September 6, 2015. https://www.avgi.gr/politiki/154641_parallilo-programma-toy-syriza. [Greek].

Tsatsanis, Emmanouil and Eftichia Teperoglou. "Greece's coalition governments: power sharing in a majoritarian democracy." In *Coalition Government as a Reflection of a Nation's Politics and Society: A Comparative Study of Parliamentary Parties and Cabinets in 12 countries*. Edited by Matt Evans. Oxon and New York: Routledge, 2020.

"Tsipras' Speech," *Syn.gr*, November 11, 2012. http://www.syn.gr/gr/keimeno.php?id=29223. [Greek].

"Tsipras: The 7 pillars of action for the weakest." *Real.gr*, July 27, 2016. https://www.real.gr/archive_politiki/arthro/tsipras_oi_7_pylones_drasis_gia_tous_asthenesterous-74193/. [Greek].

Venizelos, Giorgos. "Populism and the digital media: a necessarily symbiotic relationship?" In *Politics and populism across modes and media*. Edited by Ruth Breeze and Ana María Fernández Vallejo. Bern: Peter Lang, 2020.

CHAPTER 8

A Dialectical Constellation of Authoritarian Populism in the United States and Brazil

Jeremiah Morelock and Felipe Ziotti Narita

We are long past the expansion of liberal democracy enjoyed in the middle to late 20th century.[1] In the wake of uncertainties following the 2007–2008 economic crisis, and deep crises of representation in contemporary politics, the current conjuncture is rife with uncertainty regarding the fates and promises of democratic regimes. Today, authoritarian populism poses a daunting challenge. "Toxic straws" (De Kadt), "anti-pluralism" (Galston), "cultural backlash" (Norris and Inglehart), and "new authoritarianism" (Bugaric) are some terms associated with these emerging illiberal movements, where established institutions and formal procedures are stretched, sidestepped, or overturned to make way for "free" autocratic action.[2]

However, the contemporary combinations of authoritarianism and populism reach beyond political offices and formal institutions. They involve many elements in the social terrain. The cultural war of the populist authoritarian revolt is not only about taking control of the state, but also about attaining cultural hegemony.[3] Polarization, empowerment of "the people," anti-pluralism, charismatic performance, vituperation of multicultural societies and scapegoating of subpopulations are only some of the components of populist mobilization in the contemporary authoritarian genre. Critical social theory might be useful to grasp the issue in a way that preserves its subtleties, contradictions and multiplicities, without collapsing into pure description. Rather than squeezing and cropping authoritarian populism so that it can fit into a

---

1 This chapter first appeared in Jeremiah Morelock (ed.) *How to Critique Authoritarian Populism: Methodologies of the Frankfurt School* (Leiden: Brill, 2021), 85-107.
2 Raphael De Kadt, "The End of the Liberal Democratic Era?" *Journal of the Helen Suzman Foundation* 2, no. 84 (2019): 3–10; William Galston. *Anti-Pluralism: The Populist Threat to Liberal Democracy* (New Haven: Yale University Press, 2018); Pippa Norris and Ronald Inglehart. *Cultural Backlash: Trump, Brexit and Authoritarian Populism* (Cambridge: Cambridge University Press, 2019); Bojan Bugaric, "The Two Faces of Populism: Between Authoritarian and Democratic Populism," *German Law Journal* 20, no. 2 (2019): 390–400.
3 Volker Weiß, *Die Autoritäre Revolte: Die Neue Rechte und der Untergang des Abendlandes*. Stuttgart: Klett-Cotta, 2017.

reductive, general theoretical overlay, and rather than fetishizing the particular so that no coherent dynamics or transferable tendencies are permitted voice, we seek to map out subtleties spread throughout the social terrain (inside and outside of formal channels), articulating them into broader contexts of ideological twists and historical transformation.

Our aim is to transpose Theodor Adorno's formulations concerning dialectics and constellations into contemporary socio-political scenarios in order to construct a broad critique of authoritarian populism. Adorno's constellation methodology is useful for illuminating the complex contexture of objects like authoritarian populism.[4] Attending to multiple theoretical angles, allowing discovered contradictions to sit rather than avoiding them or stretching to synthesize them, a dialectical constellation presents a development of conceptual moments (a process) that composes a larger view of objects instead of imposing unity. Adorno's argument about the lack of equivalence between concept and object is not purely negative – it is a claim that phenomena *can* be *approached* – rather than contained – by understanding. Adorno's constellation methodology consists of the juxtaposition of dialectically connected conceptual elements in which one element might shed light on the limitations of the other. Instead of pinning the object to a definition, the object is experienced in a process of dialectical exposition. This sort of directed yet non-systemic theorizing is especially useful for drawing connections between closely related yet differently constituted developments in different parts of the world. Instead of avoiding terms such as populism because of the many variations they refer to, constellations afford us the opportunity to name and explore a proposed class of phenomena – an abstract object – without confining ourselves to narrow, limiting designations. The choice between atheoretical empirical description on the one hand, and myopic conceptual oversimplifications on the other hand, is not necessary. This is one of the brilliances of Adorno's invention.

The argument will be voiced from various angles that this kind of decentered analysis introduces an anarchistic lack of accountability into the project of social theory. If concepts are no longer bound by limits nor by the prohibition of internal contradiction, then in theory anyone could invent any constellation just to give theoretical voice to their prejudices. But we argue that this is nothing new. Social theory must fit the "real world" enough to be illuminating, but beyond this vague stricture, we always evaluate it according to

---

4 David Kaufmann, "Correlations, Constellations and the Truth: Adorno's Ontology of Redemption," *Philosophy and Social Criticism* 26, no. 5 (2000): 62–80.

some combination of the impersonal dictates of logic and the personal/social dictates of resonance. Adorno incorporates both elements. The constellation is an expressive portrait structured by dialectical logic.

In our exploration here, we pull back some from Adorno's expressive emphasis and style. Our constellation is structured along dialectical lines, but instead of our theoretical thought "whirling" around our object, we move slower in order to explain more and illustrate with examples. Our sympathies are with Adorno, and we hold what he did in great esteem. But even if we wanted to and were able to, and even if somehow our publisher and peer reviewers were amenable, as a general rule the academic world is nowhere close to accepting theoretically dense, artful and expressive constellations as legitimate sources of knowledge – so it would be bogus and irresponsible of us to claim that constructing full-blown constellations in the style of Adorno is a working strategy to move social theory and research forward today. Yet it does have a very powerful "backbone," in the use of dialectics to unravel complex, abstract objects without apology. In this sense our analytical animal consists of a constellational skeleton under more familiar and orthodox flesh and skin. We *do* claim *this is* a working strategy to move social theory and research forward today.

Our analysis follows this basic structure – we move through dialectical moments that illustrate dimensions of the complex, abstract object authoritarian populism. There is no teleology or golden thread. Our exposition is part narrative, part socio-psychological. In describing authoritarian populism as a narrative phenomenon, we borrow from articulation theory.[5] While we find the theory of articulation to be a powerful and quite adept basis for critiquing the inflamed identity politics of authoritarian populism, we agree with Gandesha (2018) that the approach of Laclau and Mouffe is incomplete; staying on the level of discourse, it is bereft of social psychology. This limits both its explanatory scope and its insight into human motivation and experience.[6]

---

5 Stuart Hall, "Popular Culture, Politics and History," *Cultural Studies* 32, no. 6 (2018): 929–952; Ernesto Laclau and Chantal Mouffe. *Hegemony and Socialist Strategy: Towards a Radical Democratic Politics* (New York: Verso, 1985).

6 As for whether a discursive theory of articulation can be combined with theoretical social psychology in a way that is epistemologically sound (enough), our answer is "yes." The connecting link between the two can be summed up in the "Thomas theorem" that "if men define situations as real, they are real in their consequences." See William I. Thomas and Dorothy S. Thomas, *The Child in America* (New York: Alfred P. Knopf, 1928). For our purposes, we might emphasize that 'if people articulate social divisions as real, they are real in their socio-psychological consequences.' There remain many open questions about distinctions and relationships between discourse, experience and the unconscious. We reject the strong postmodernist stance that it is "discourse all the way down." Discourse is not the whole of human experience, but it is impossible to extract it from the non-discursive parts of

To frame our description of the socio-psychological dynamics that surround social articulations, we focus on recognition and power. Somewhat like our take on Laclau's theory of articulation, we see recognition theory as very important yet incomplete.[7] Honneth's elevation of recognition to an overarching and defining principle of all social struggle understates inequalities of power[8] and wealth,[9] prematurely subsuming them when they might be more appropriately represented using a more pluralist approach. These different domains of inequality can define themselves, so to speak, even as they inevitably overlap and intertwine. We assume that authoritarian populist political mobilization is generated from experienced deprivations and threats concerning recognition and power, in various combinations. And we view these developments through a specifically dialectical methodology. For instance, we say experienced disrespect generates desire for attaining recognition. And experienced political domination generates desire for political liberation. We posit recognition and domination as separate yet intrinsically intertwined issues. The full extent of their relations requires much more elaboration, and so is outside our scope here. Instead, we will present suggestions about how they operate together in different ways throughout our dialectical constellation.

To complicate this a little further, we emphasize that these threats and deprivations, and the social movements targeted against them, occur in both discursive and structural dimensions of social life. In other words, empirical conditions are interpreted discursively, and discourse always refers back to empirical conditions. Narratives influence [empirical] social action, and

---

ourselves. When Kristeva posits the intermingling of prerational, preverbal "semiotic" cognition with rational, verbal, "symbolic" cognition, this points in a very important direction. See Noëlle McAfee, *Julia Kristeva* (London: Routledge, 2004). We suggest that this murky area of distinctions and relationships between discourse, experience and the unconscious is central to human existence, and yet we can only offer tentative observations and hypotheses. We should not ignore this area because of its murkiness. Its significance outweighs its difficulty. Any theory worthy of its salt contains speculation and risks error. See Jeremiah Morelock, "Resuscitating Sociological Theory: Nietzsche and Adorno on Error and Speculation," in *Nietzsche and Critical Social Theory: Affirmation, Animosity, and Ambiguity*, ed. Michael Roberts and Christine Payne (Leiden: Brill, 2019). It is up to each reader to decide if and to what extent what we present seems resonant and fitting.

7 Charles Taylor, "The Politics of Recognition," *New Contexts of Canadian Criticism* 98 (1997): 25–73; Axel Honneth, *The Struggle for Recognition: The Moral Grammar of Social Conflicts*. Cambridge: MIT Press, 1996.
8 Amy Allen, "Recognizing Domination: Recognition and Power in Honneth's Critical Theory," *Journal of Power* 3, no.1 (2010): 21–32.
9 Nancy Fraser and Axel Honneth, *Redistribution or Recognition?: A Political-philosophical Exchange* (New York: Verso, 2003).

changes in [empirical] social relations influence popular discourse. The connections we draw are influenced threefold: empirical trends, social theories, and dialectical logic. Although Adorno disliked empirical examples because using them falsely implies that particulars can be subsumed within the logic of general categories, we construct a model of critique in which examples are intended in illustrative rather than denotative spirit, to clarify and lend support to the theoretical exposition.

We frame authoritarian populism as the meeting of two domains: authoritarianism and populism. This logical and analytical separation of two domains is important because it avoids the deterministic reduction of one domain to the other (as if every populist movement would be condemned to be authoritarian), yet in many places they overlap or intertwine, making a strict separation of them difficult if not impossible. In our discussion, we will treat them in this separate-but-related fashion – as forces or tendencies that merge in the "object" of our analysis. In each domain considered separately, one can identify dialectical movements that pertain to power or recognition. In the domain of authoritarianism arise relationships between power and resistance, domination and freedom, since we understand authoritarianism as an attempt at imposing unity in heterogeneous societies. In the domain of populism are the drawing of social distinctions and conflicts over recognition between "the people" and what we will call the "non-people," the latter including elites and outsiders. "The people" operate as non-elites when contrasted with elites, and as insiders when contrasted with outsiders. The people are often articulated as an actual or potential authentic community, pitted against the alienated establishment. In our constellation, these dialectical elements often overlap, mix and merge as the domains of authoritarianism and populism run together.[10] Finally, in the meeting of the two domains, other elements frequently emerge, namely the association of authenticity with decisionism and the myth of recreating a lost golden age. We also discuss some social and narrative dialectical dynamics in the emergent trends.

---

10   The mixing of authoritarianism and populism is not a determinate negation; this step is synthetic, not dialectical. Yet when the two domains are combined, their respective internal contradictions interface, for example in dialectics of domination and freedom of insiders and outsiders.

1   Dialectical Constellations

In the 1960s, when Adorno published his most important theoretical work, *Negative Dialectics*, he was also interested in political issues in general and German politics in particular. He was perfectly aware of latent regressions in democratic political systems and the intimate relationship between capitalist modernization and far-right extremism. His 1967 public lecture on the presence of the far-right in post-war German politics, for example, pointed to the failures of modern democracies in light of class societies vulnerable to declassification (*Deklassierung*), the aggressive defense of lost privileges and crisis of representation within bureaucratic apparatuses (political system) as the preconditions (*Voraussetzungen*) of (neo)fascist movements and authoritarian revolt against the established institutions.[11] Instead of a linear history of progress in which democracy would be the reconciliation of enlightenment premises, Adorno warned that new forms of domination and barbarism become latent in contemporary societies.

It is well known that Adorno was a pessimist. He saw no grand political solution, as his essay on "resignation" attested. His lamentation in *Minima Moralia* that 'wrong life cannot be lived rightly' speaks of the negative core of his "melancholy science," as well as of a similar temperament if not assessment as his broad historical diagnosis of Enlightenment turning to myth, this time applied to everyday experience in late capitalism.[12] And yet, one could argue that Adorno had an unshakeable faith in humanity. Despite all his pessimistic assessments, he continued to write and to theorize, to critique forms of domination. Believing that philosophy was falling into ruin, he invested astounding intellectual resources in composing his *Negative Dialectics* – a venture intended to rescue philosophy from its demise by helping it move beyond itself. On the one hand, for Adorno there could be no poetry or metaphysics after Auschwitz. Hegel's optimistic dictum that the real is the rational and the rational is the real had become indefensible, and 'any appeal to the idea of progress would seem absurd given the scale of the catastrophe' that had already taken place in the course of capitalist history.[13] The early twentieth century socialist liberation movements found their consummation in authoritarian regimes, e.g.,

---

[11]   Theodor W. Adorno, *Aspekte des neuen Rechtsradikalismus: ein Vortrag* (Frankfurt am Main: Suhrkamp Verlag, 2019).

[12]   Theodor W. Adorno, *Minima Moralia: Reflexionen aus dem beschädigten Leben* (Frankfurt am Main: Suhrkamp Verlag, 2003), 43.

[13]   Theodor W. Adorno, *History and Freedom: Lectures 1964–1965*. Translated by Rodney Livingstone (London: Polity, 2006), 14.

under Stalin in the Soviet Union. On the other hand, in the face of the proliferated dogmatic and determinist "vulgar Marxism" – which converted dialectics into a "thoughtless theory" – administrated by the socialist bureaucracy of the Eastern bloc, Adorno forged on to work out his own "modified version of dialectics."[14] The importance of Adorno's work goes well beyond his persistence, his finesse with dialectics, and his iconoclasm. Adorno also offers a powerful positive vision of how philosophy can outgrow its straitjacket. Rather than skepticism, Adorno offers us a way forward without illusions.[15]

For Adorno, dialectics must deal with objects not simply as given and final truths. Dialectics needs to consider the conceptual contexture of objects: 'because the entity [*Seiende*] is not immediate, but only through [*durch*] and via [*hindurch*] the concept,' it would be useful 'to begin with the concept and not with the mere datum.'[16] As a contradictory relationship between the dynamic parts and the whole, the fundamental ontological concepts always require their opposites and their mediations to constitute the contours of the process.[17] In other words, Adorno's *démarche* might be useful to make explicit the contradictory trends that underlie the appearance of unity imposed by any concept in its effort at producing an immediate identity between reason and effective reality (*Wirklichkeit*). Adorno's dialectic is a process in which the confrontation between the concept and the object implies that 'a contradiction in reality [*Realität*] is a contradiction against reality.' In this sense, he states:

> But such dialectics is no longer compatible [*sich vereinen*] with Hegel. Its motion [*Bewegung*] does not tend to the identity in the difference between each object and the concept; on the contrary, this dialectics turns the identical suspect [*beargewöhnt*]. Its logic is one of disintegration [*Zerfall*]: disintegration of the constructed [*zugerüsteten*] and objectified image [*Gestalt*] of the concept that the cognitive subject faces immediately [*unmittelbar*].[18]

---

14   Theodor W. Adorno, *Três Estudos sobre Hegel*. Translated by Ulisses Vaccari (São Paulo: São Paulo State University Press, 2007), 79.
15   Yvonne Sherratt, *Adorno's Positive Dialectic* (Cambridge University Press, 2002).
16   Theodor W. Adorno, *Negative Dialektik / Jargon der Eigentlichkeit* (Frankfurt am Main: Suhrkamp Verlag, 2003), 156.
17   Adorno, *Três Estudos sobre Hegel,* 82.
18   Adorno, *Negative Dialektik / Jargon der Eigentlichkeit,* 148.

Adorno does not seek to subsume objects under a dialectical reason that covers them absolutely. Against the "strong form of identity" that subsumes dissonances and conflicts under a concept, Adorno advocates the consistent consciousness (*Bewußtsein*) of nonidentity between concepts and the objects they refer to.[19] For Adorno, there is no absolute equivalence between concepts and their objects because concepts cannot exhaust (*Aufgehen*) the complexities of the objects they point toward.[20] In other words, the differences cannot be reconciled into a homogeneous whole, but rather co-exist as differences and contradictions, that is, the whole is not prior to its parts.[21]

Instead of being a blockade to the thought, contradiction is the very motion of critical theory since it depicts (*Herrstellen*) the barriers that lead to a transformation of the concept without losing its determinations (*Bestimmungen*).[22] Adorno's negative dialectic is not merely a dialectical logic without the rational moment of synthesis, but rather a consistent theoretical rearrangement within Hegelian idealist assumptions in which Adorno rejects any positive identity that falsely reconciles the heterogeneous conceptual moments under a synthetic, unitary "construction [*Aufbau*] against the disintegration [*Zersetzung*]" of the concept.[23] This implies that,

> Objectively, dialectics means to break the forced identity [*Identitätszwang*], and to break it through the energy stored in that compulsion and congealed in its objectifications [*Vergegenständlichungen*] … Since the concept is experienced [*Erfährt*] as nonidentical, as inwardly in motion [*in sich bewegt*], it is no longer purely itself; in Hegel's terminology, it leads to its otherness without absorbing [*Aufzusaugen*] that otherness. It is defined by that which is outside it, because on its own it does not exhaust itself [*sich erschöpft*].[24]

---

19   Fredric Jameson, *Late Marxism: Adorno, or, the Persistence of the Dialectic* (New York: Verso, 1990), 20.
20   Adorno, *Negative Dialektik / Jargon der Eigentlichkeit*, 17. Adorno also says that particular objects cannot account for the formal, general and abstract qualities that are intrinsic to concepts. This assertion is important in the sense that Adorno's methodology cannot be collapsed into an empiricism that rejects theoretical concepts in favor of pure particularity. Adorno preserves the sense found in Hegel that concepts and objects constitute one another. The key difference is that Adorno sees the relationship as inherently dissonant.
21   Alison Stone, "Adorno, Hegel and Dialectic," *British Journal for the History of Philosophy* 22, no. 6 (2014): 1118–1141.
22   Theodor W. Adorno, *Einführung in die Dialektik*, ed. Christoph Ziermann – Nachgelassene Schriften, 2/IV. (Frankfurt am Main: Suhrkamp Verlag, 2010), 18.
23   Adorno, *Negative Dialektik / Jargon der Eigentlichkeit*, 158.
24   Ibid., 159.

Adorno's effort is put in motion via the liberating potential of determinate negation and the critique of the immediate adequacy of identitarian reason. This approach is far from falling into unproductive pessimism or any kind of *naïve* irrationalism, as it appears in the critique expanded by the late Georg Lukács against Adorno, in the sarcastic conclusion of the 1962 preface to *The Theory of the Novel*, arguing that Adorno's philosophy flirted with the 'abyss of nothingness,' that is, 'the disconsolate background of the vainness [*Sinnlosigkeit*] of existence,' which lifts theory 'above the wretched mob [*Pöbl*] that is shortsighted enough to fight and to suffer [*Leiden*] for a betterment of social conditions.'[25] Rather, the force of the negative is productive to the extent that treating concepts and their opposites on their own, liberated from the positive moment of Hegelian reconciliation (the negation of the negation), avoids any temptation to soften (*Glätten*) determinate negation, which Adorno understood as the indissoluble expression of nonidentity in dialectical logic.[26]

The theoretical exposition turns the constant (*Ständigen*) confrontation between the concept and the thing (*Sache*) into the potency of an immanent critique committed to unveil the 'movement of the concept,' according to determinate historical situations, remaining always open to heterogeneous elements with no teleological horizon nor hierarchies grounded in progressive casual chains.[27] In this sense,

> The unifying moment survives without a negation of negation, but also without delivering itself to abstraction as a supreme principle. It survives because there is no step-by-step progression [*Fortgeschritten*] from the concepts to a more general cover concept [*Oberbegriff*]. Instead, the concepts enter into a constellation. The constellation sheds light on the specificity [*Spezifische*] of the object, that is, the element that is either a burden or indifferent to a classifying procedure.[28]

The "overarching sensibility" of the dialectical constellation points out that the effort at unifying complex social phenomena through concepts is always a tense conflict to redeem the particular and the nonidentical.[29] The moments and the

---

25 Georg Lukács, *Die Zerstörung der Vernunft: Irrationalismus zwischen den Revolutionen* (Darmstadt: Luchterhand Verlag, 1973), 218–219.
26 Adorno, *Negative Dialektik / Jargon der Eigentlichkeit*,162.
27 Adorno, *Einführung in die Dialektik*, 18–19.
28 Adorno, *Negative Dialektik / Jargon der Eigentlichkeit,* 164.
29 Max Pensky, "Adorno's Actuality," in *The Actuality of Adorno: Critical Essays on Adorno and the Postmodern*, ed. Max Pensky (Albany: State University of New York Press, 1997).

parts of the constellation are used as simultaneous categories that constantly affect each other and modify themselves. Rather than synthesis, the critical task of social theory is to deal with the contradictory process. Constellations are discontinuous, since the logic of disintegration liberates every element and sublates causal hierarchy, leaving the parts are unimpaired.[30] As a methodological tool, thus, two movements are important to the dialectical process of constructing constellations: one is conceptual-analytical (breaking apart the primeval phenomenon by isolating its elements and mediating them by means of concepts), and the other is representational, that is, the effort at bringing the elements together in an exposition of social contradictions.[31]

2 Populism and Authoritarianism

Over the last several years, the rise of far-right parties and governments, with strong populist and authoritarian trends, gained momentum in the Americas with the election of Donald Trump in 2016 (United States) and Jair Bolsonaro in 2018 (Brazil). Besides public speeches, the massive use of social media by those governments, especially Twitter and Facebook, offers lots of empirical data to analyze, and points to the political significance of information technologies and the reconfiguration of sociotechnical and communication structures that they ushered in. This is true in terms of understanding both the place of social media in "manufacturing consent" and in the ways that new masses are incorporated into populist politics.[32] Especially when looked at together, both cases – Brazil and the United States – illustrate how "authoritarian populism" comprises a constellation of elements that calls for the expansion of the mainstream definition of populism (e.g., the conflictual and moral divide between 'the people' and "the elites") in order to grasp the nuances and contradictory moments underlying the construction of 'the people' vis-à-vis the non-people, outsiders and so on.

---

30 Susan Buck-Morss, *The Origin of Negative Dialectics* (London: Macmillan, 1977), 94–95.
31 Ibid.
32 Jeremiah Morelock and Felipe Ziotti Narita, "Public Sphere and World-System: Theorizing Populism at the Margins," in *Critical Theory and Authoritarian Populism*, ed. Jeremiah Morelock (London: University of Westminster Press, 2018).

3 Typology of Populist Narratives

In authoritarian populism, the people self-articulate in contrast to the non-people, the latter comprising elites and outsiders. "The people" can only narratively exist in such contrasts and is defined as "the people" by virtue of its negative relation to the non-people. There are several overlapping dialectical relations here. We will classify three types of populist narrative: people/elite (liberation), people/outsiders (nationalism), and people/non-people. The performative rhetoric of far-right leaders can embody these experiences and motivations, appealing to and further solidifying support from 'the people,' defining reality in terms that simultaneously speak to these mentalities and promote authoritarian measures. For example, in February 2019, Trump framed the alleged need to build a wall along the U.S./Mexico border as a "National Emergency."[33]

3.1 *People/Elite*

Elites can only narratively exist if the people are articulated as non-elites, and so in this narrative, the importance of the people is in their *non-elite* status. Here, the story is that *elites* have too much power, and perhaps have recently increased their power, decreasing the people's power and recognition. The coherence and solidarity of the people grows with experience of alienation from elites, especially in light of the polarization grounded in social resentment due to a sense of growing inequalities, political exclusion, and injustice. The people want to overturn this alienated, disempowered and disrespected state, and to shrink if not erase the distance that separates them from the elite center. This can be seen across all varieties of populism – left and right, democratic and authoritarian. Concerns about power are at play here, but strategies of empowerment can be many, and so authoritarianism per se is possible but not preordained. It is essentially a revolutionary logic. Every consummated revolution requires a moment of the transfer of power that necessarily implies the forceful removal or suppression of the powerful persons or systems of the old regime. Because of this, every revolution contains at minimum what we might call an "authoritarian moment," which is also the moment that liberation is achieved, and every revolutionary movement includes the anticipation of this moment. But the size, duration, and severity of this authoritarian moment can vary widely, as can the degrees and qualities of freedom and

---

[33] Peter Baker, "Trump Declares a National Emergency, and Provokes a Constitutional Clash," *The New York Times*, February 15, 2019. https://www.nytimes.com/2019/02/15/us/politics/national-emergency-trump.html.

democracy in envisioned and enacted post-revolutionary societies. It could mark far more than just a "moment;" it could rather mark a *slip* into establishing a new authoritarian regime. And yet it also could be quite fleeting, disappearing more or less instantaneously.

3.2 People/Outsiders

Outsiders can only exist to the extent that the people are articulated as insiders, and so in this narrative, the importance of the people is in their *insider* status. Here, the story is that *outsiders* have grown in power and recognition by growing in numbers relative to the people, impoverishing the power and recognition of the people as their relative numbers shrink. The coherence and solidarity of the people grows with its experience of dis-alienation (e.g., sharing of space) from outsiders. Their experience of *difference* from outsiders makes their dis-alienation from outsiders more threatening the closer or more prominent they become; the people want to be further from the outsiders, must reject outsiders, and ultimately want to stay entirely distinct from outsiders. This one has a more implicitly authoritarian flavor, as it is prone to involve scapegoating and implies that the road to empowerment of the people is through [forceful] exclusion of outsiders. Yet without specifying a strategy of empowerment and exclusion, it is not inherently authoritarian per se. It is essentially a nationalist logic of populist mobilization. The whole affair surrounding the "immigrant caravan" approaching the U.S./Mexico border was a clear case of this narrative, using the symbol of encroaching outsiders to argue for a need to protect the people from them with increased force.

3.3 People/Non-people

This is a combination of the other two narratives and *is* specifically authoritarian. It comes in two basic variations: (a) infiltration – outsiders are or have become elites; (b) betrayal – elites are aligned with outsiders more than with the people. Also possible are (c) mixed – especially when there are multiple types of outsider groups. The people/non-people narrative is also a fertile soil for paranoia and conspiracy theory. Once again, far-right leaders will echo these various narratives in their rhetoric and public displays. One example of the mixed type is Trump's accusation of Somali American and Muslim congresswoman Ilhan Omar of supporting al-Qaeda.[34] The accusation of betrayal is clear, but infiltration is also implied, due to Omar's ethnic background,

---

34   Salvador Rizzo, "President Trump Accuses Rep. Omar of supporting al-Qaeda," *Washington Post*, July 17, 2019.

which marks her as an outsider to far-right America's articulation of "the people." Another example of the mixed type is Trump's frequent use of the issue of immigration to portray Democrats (elites) as caring more about immigrants (outsiders) than they do the rest of the country.[35] In the United States today, "outsiders" are generally immigrants or ethnic minorities. But in principle outsider status can accrue to any sub-population simply by not being narrated in the category of 'real' or "pure" people.

With the electoral victory in Brazil, 2018 of the conservative far-Right via Jair Bolsonaro, we can analyze an interesting example: due to its peripheral integration into the modern world-system, immigration is not a key concern in Brazilian populism. Brazil is far from attracting immigrants like the United States or Western Europe. In Brazil, mass migration and border crises play a minor role in public debate. In populist mobilizations of peripheral countries like Brazil, outsider status falls on successful political opponents, their parties and the established institutions of liberal democracy. In Brazil, the people/non-people narrative (variation b) is the rule. The establishment is associated with "corrupted" liberal elites (centrist and center-left groups that embrace political correctness and the progressive agenda) and the center-left Worker's Party, which ruled the country from 2003 to 2016. A cultural tension is aesthetically expressed with the intensive public use of national symbols and green and yellow colors by supporters of the far-right government and/or the supporters of anti-establishment movements.[36] Despite the strong nationalist rhetoric, populism in Brazil is an internal dispute over political cleavages within the population – in other words, "the people" is a nationalist – but not nativist – designation.

4   Dialectics of Authoritarian Populism

4.1   *Power and Liberation*

"The people," under the experienced threat of disempowerment from the "non-people," (the elites and outsiders) look toward strengthening their power. The people feel disempowered due to expanded power and presence of non-people. Empowerment is, for the people, understood as *liberation* from this disempowerment. The people/elite narrative states that the elites have power

---

35   Mark Barabak and Noam Levey, "Are Democrats Helping Trump by Promising Healthcare to Undocumented Migrants?" *Los Angeles Times*, July 9, 2019.
36   David Biller, "Brazilian Politics Stain the Famous Yellow and Green Jersey," *Bloomberg*, July 7, 2019.

over the people, and that the people should rise to liberate and reclaim their alienated *power-to*. One example is Bolsonaro's campaign for liberating the use of firepower to defend "our liberty": he states that 'the people must have the right to arms to defend themselves against those who dare to take away their freedom,' since he stands 'for individual weaponry for our people so that temptations will not pass over the heads of rulers by taking power absolutely. We have examples in Latin America. We don't want to repeat it' (his examples are leftist governments).[37] Another example is Trump's executive order concerning freedom of speech on college campuses in March 2019. The freedom of speech argument is likewise generally touted by the political Right in response to left-wing pressures for "political correctness." During the Black Lives Matter protests in the summer of 2020, right wing voices used terms like "mob rule" to refer to them. One article in *The Federalist* donned a subheading: 'BLM Isn't Interested in Free Speech, It Wants Power.'[38] At the same time, the response to the protests under Trump included tear gas, rubber bullets, the National Guard, and Trump's praise for "overwhelming force" and "domination."[39] During this same period of time, Trump responded to Twitter's fact-checking his posts by claiming it to be a violation of his first amendment rights. He threatened to shut down social media sites and signed an executive order to pull back legal protections for them – allegedly to defend free speech.[40]

It should be obvious that guns are tools for power – to force others' lives to end, to physically debilitate them, or to force their actions under the threat of death or debilitation. Yet "freedom of speech" against "political correctness" and freedom of the market against government regulation also contribute to other dominations. In the freedom of speech case, the curbing of discourse to adopt new terms for minority populations, new terms that do not carry the baggage of immediate and explicit or historical and implicit prejudice,

---

37 Twitter – Jair Bolsonaro @jairbolsonaro, June 17, 2019.
38 John Daniel Davidson, "If You Don't Support Black Lives Matter, You're Fired," *The Federalist,* June 11, 2020. https://thefederalist.com/2020/06/11/if-you-dont-support-black-lives-matter-youre-fired/.
39 Jordyn Phelps and Ben Gittleson, "Trump Praises 'Overwhelming Force' and 'Domination' in DC Morning After Peaceful Protest Broken Up for Photo Op," *ABC News,* June 3, 2020. https://abcnews.go.com/Politics/trump-praises-overwhelming-force-domination-dc-morning-peaceful/story?id=71.
40 Ryan Bort, "Trump Threatens to Shred First Amendment to Defend 'Free Speech,'" *Rolling Stone,* May 28, 2020. https://www.rollingstone.com/politics/politics-news/trump-twitter-mail-in-voting-free-speech-1005629/; Queenie Wong, "Trump vs. Twitter: Here's What You Need to Know About the Free Speech Showdown," *CNET,* June 2, 2020. https://www.cnet.com/news/trumps-social-media-executive-order-faces-lawsuit/.

is an attempt in the interests of liberating minority populations from a cultural tyranny of the majority.[41] When embodied in policy, "politically correct" movements achieve new freedoms for oppressed populations. For example, legalization of same-sex marriage can be understood as liberation for sexual minorities from subordinate legal status. Yet some argue that this is not properly liberation, because it involves the assimilation of sexual minorities to the norms of straight society, and the institutionalized regulation of queer coupledom by the state.[42]

In our era of neoliberalism, liberation discourse is also used to refer to liberation of the market from government regulation. For instance, the far-right caucus in the American government, called the "Freedom Caucas," are aligned with the *libertarian* Tea Party. In class terms, neoliberal reforms empower the capitalist class and social accumulation at the expense of workers. This might not be the case were available jobs to outnumber workers. But, as Karl Marx indicates in his theory of the reserve army of labor, with a surplus of unemployed persons, workers are pressed to accept whatever working conditions are allotted.[43] The more free-choices the capitalist class has, the more their whims exert power over the working class. As John Bellamy Foster emphasizes, in the case of "externalities" such as pollution and its impacts on the environment and human health the capitalist class has the 'freedom' to toxify the natural world, which all humans – never mind all species – live in.[44] The greater freedom of the capitalist class from environmental regulations means

---

[41] Marcuse wrestles with this dialectic extensively in his essay "Repressive Tolerance" See Robert Paul Wolff, Barrington Moore, and Herbert Marcuse, *A Critique of Pure Tolerance* (Boston: Beacon Press, 1966). Marcuse's thesis, which supports the suppression of intolerant ideologies, was criticized heavily at the time of its publication due to its direct call to limit some [hate] speech. Recently it has gained much popularity again. See Rodney Fopp, "Herbert Marcuse's 'Repressive Tolerance' and His Critics." *Borderlands* 6, no. 1 (2007): 1–10; Rodney Fopp, "'Repressive Tolerance': Herbert Marcuse's Exercise in Social Epistemology," *Social Epistemology* 24, no. 2 (2010): 105–122.

[42] Ruthann Robson, "Assimilation, Marriage, and Lesbian Liberation," *Temp. L. Rev* 75 (2002): 709; Judith Butler, *Undoing gender* (London: Routledge, 2004); Tracey Lee McCormick, "Why Same-Sex Marriage is Not the Ultimate Tool for Queer Liberation," *The Conversation,* October 14, 2018. https://theconversation.com/why-same-sex-marriage-is-not-the-ultimate-tool-for-queer-liberation-103702.

[43] Karl Marx, *Das Kapital: Kritik der politischen Ökonomie* Volume 1 (Berlin: Karl Dietz Verlag, 2008), 665–667.

[44] John Bellamy Foster, "Marx's Theory of Metabolic Rift: Classical Foundations for Environmental Sociology," *American Journal of Sociology* 105, no. 2 (1999): 366–405; John Bellamy Foster and Paul Burkett. "Value Isn't everything," *Monthly Review* 70, no. 1 (2018): 1–17.

the greater powerlessness of workers (and non-humans) against the whims of the capitalists.

4.2 Alienation, Authenticity and Agitation

When considered as a whole, the non-people have an ambivalent status for the people. As insiders, the people push against outsiders to increase distance, but as non-elites, the people push against elites to decrease distance. This is not just about controlling the establishment, although that plays in. There is also a fantasy of punching through the establishment, of dismantling and recreating it with less structure, less compromise, and more connection to the lifeworld of the people. As people are further alienated from the establishment, 'the people' emerges as a self-conscious collective subject, its members representing to themselves an authentic community antithetical to the alienated establishment. There is a rejection of the alienated apparatus of government, bureaucracy, and formal procedure – which in contemporary society are not altogether different from an alienating cultural decomposition process where the individual is pitted against a largely anonymous "system world," which the elites uphold and in which the elites are entrenched.[45] The wheels of the liberal democratic system are large, and often a disappointingly small amount of action comes out of a deeply divided congress where heels are dug in on both sides of the divide.

The mobilization of popular resentment can play a key role in this case. In April and May 2020, in popular rallies that advocated a military coup and blamed liberal democracy for the corruption and crisis, Bolsonaro expressed the authoritarian content of populist agitation.[46] Amidst popular calls to close the congress and the federal court, he attacked the established elite: 'everyone in Brazil is subjected to the will of the people. The era of rascality is over; now it is the people in power. I am here because I trust you [the people].'[47] Between 2014 and 2018, alongside deep socioeconomic deterioration, a juridical crusade against corruption scandals, a crisis of representation of traditional political

---

45 Craig Calhoun, "Populist Politics, Communications Media and Large Scale Societal Integration," *Sociological Theory* 6, no. 2 (1988): 219–241.

46 These rallies took place during the COVID-19 pandemic, which infected 121.600 and killed 8.128 Brazilians (official data from Johns Hopkins University in May 6, 2020). The populist agitation of Bolsonaro has been carried out in support of right-wing protestors against social distancing and the political elite in the congress, the Supreme Court and governors that follow the measures of the World Health Organization.

47 Portal G1. "Bolsonaro Discursa em Brasília para Manifestantes que Pediam Intervenção Militar," April 19, 2020. https://g1.globo.com/politica/noticia/2020/04/19/bolsonaro-discursa-em-manifestacao-em-brasilia-que-defendeu-intervencao-militar.ghtml.

parties (materialized in the street protests between 2013 and 2015) and an institutional crisis (with an impeachment in 2016), the election of Bolsonaro in 2018 and his promises of a "new politics" promoted a constant conflict with constitutional powers.

More than just assembling and mobilizing the people, populist rationality is grounded in polarization and the presupposition of conflict without end. It thrives on antagonism and agitation, or the stoking of social divisions through political rhetoric.[48] The people, self-consciously alien from elites, amplify this alienation through polarizing rhetoric, aided by damnations from non-people. When the leader galvanizes anti-establishment rhetoric, democracy is jeopardized twofold. To explain the first by example: when Bolsonaro supports street protests as "spontaneous manifestations of the people" against instituted powers like the congress or the supreme court,[49] he posits the people and its purity not only against the corrupt (entrenched in those institutions), but more broadly: against the checks and balances limiting Executive power.[50] Second, polarization is grounded in scapegoating leftists as enemies that represent not only degradation of the political order, but moral decay associated with political correctness, multiculturalism and cultural menaces against the conservative *Weltanschauung* grounded in Western Christianity and the bourgeois family. Democracy is only meaningful if there are differences of opinion that are held to legitimate arbitration. It requires a willingness to compromise and to cooperate with persons who hold views that you do not agree with. Polarizing rhetoric is a move directly in contrast to this. When political differences are framed as irreconcilable cleavages, refusal to cooperate with the non-people may be framed as necessary and even honorable. Explicitly, it may be framed as "resistance" to their tyranny. But implicitly, this refusal, which takes the shape of political agitation, is also a refutation of liberal democracy, and by extension an endorsement of authoritarian rule.

4.3   *Emergent Elements 1: Decisionism*

All the oppositional naming and dividing by the people seeks reconciliation with the establishment, to rebirth it. In the people's move to be closer to the establishment, the establishment comes closer to the people. Like Odysseus in

---

48   Jeremiah Morelock and Felipe Ziotti Narita, "Populism and Political Agitation in Late Capitalism: Research Notes," *3rd International Seminar on Public Policy and Social Development*, ed. Alexandre Mendes (Franca: São Paulo State University Press, 2019).
49   Twitter – Jair Bolsonaro @jairbolsonaro, May 26, 2019.
50   "Bolsonaro e o Povo." *Estadão* (May 23, 2019).

the territory of the Sirens, the people tie themselves to their Homeric mast.[51] The thirst is like this: rather than ossified processes and negotiations, the authentic will of those in command should be experienced fresh, with minimal mediation from leader's mind to people's lives. The total, voluntary submission of the people to the ruler, animated by the experience of identity with the ruler, united by the all-encompassing "will of the people," constitutes true democracy, according to Nazi political theorist Carl Schmitt.[52] The leader, the spokesperson for the authentic people's will, must be *free* of bureaucracy, to command as he sees fit, by his own decisions.

Here, Trump and Bolsonaro share a common strategy: they flood the Congress with measures, executive orders and decrees in order to show the people they are trying to carry out their promises.[53] Congressional resistance is taken up as a kind of political alibi to justify autocratic action and agitate the people against the established institutions. In this case, the threat to liberal democracy does not come from a coup d'état, nor from a violent overthrow of the regime, but rather from normative alterations that can progressively corrode liberal counterchecks via autocratic legalism.[54]

Trump's penchant for executive orders (like the 2019 stratagem for the construction of the US/Mexico border wall), and his refusal for his inner circle to comply with congressional subpoenas during his impeachment inquiry, exhibit a clearly decisionist style. The justification for withholding subpoenaed documents and keeping subpoenaed witnesses from testifying before congress was couched in the Republican Party line during the proceedings, which included the insinuation that Trump's defiance of congress was a patriotic act in the name of freedom. The Republicans echoed in a seemingly unified voice throughout the proceedings the accusation that the Democratic Party was acting in an authoritarian manner via the impeachment process. The justification for the dictatorial undermining of the separation of powers in the act of Trump's defiance of Congress was a narrative of resistance to tyranny. In a letter from Trump to Democratic Speaker of the House Nancy Pelosi, Trump described his impeachment as an "attempted coup" and an 'unprecedented

---

51   Max Horkheimer and Theodor W. Adorno, *Dialectic of Enlightenment* (Redwood City: Stanford University Press, 2002).
52   Carl Schmitt, *The Crisis of Parliamentary Democracy* (Cambridge: MIT Press, 1988).
53   Fernanda Odilla, "Dos EUA ao Brasil, Como Presidentes Tentam Governar Sem Congresso," *BBC News*, June 17, 2019; Reynaldo Turollo Jr. and Cancian, Natalia, "Supremo Blinda Congresso de Medidas de Bolsonaro que Atropelam Legislativo," *Folha de São Paulo*, January 6, 2020.
54   Kim Scheppele, "Autocratic Legalism", *The University of Chicago Law Review* 85, no. 2 (2018): 545–580.

and unconstitutional abuse of power.'⁵⁵ These quotes are especially interesting considering the charges of his impeachment: abuse of power, and obstruction of congress.

During the COVID-19 pandemic, Trump spoke in support of right-wing protestors against social distancing, who framed their resistance in terms of freedom, with signs like "give me liberty or give me death" and "social distancing = communism." An advisor to Trump even compared the protestors to African American civil rights protestor Rosa Parks, who famously refused to give up her seat on the bus to a white person in 1955.⁵⁶ And yet during this same period he boasted at a press conference that his "authority is total," when discussing the issue of states letting up on social distancing measures.⁵⁷

4.4 Emergent Elements 2: the Construction of the Charismatic Leader

Leadership is not an existent; it is constructed in the political correlation of forces. The assertive behavior and political decisionism of the authoritarian populist are predicated on their construction as a leader, which in turn is dependent on there being a base of followers who are under the spell of the leader's charismatic appeal. Charisma is not properly sympathy nor courtesy, that is, it is not the product of education nor an individual skill. Max Weber points out that charisma is a *political relation* and a form of domination (*Herrschaft*) that depends both on the personal (*Persönlichkeit*) appeal and the recognition (*Anerkennung*) of the individual as a leader (*Führer*).⁵⁸ The construction of the leader, thus, implies the agitation of the affects and the social resentments of their audience, as well as the audience's trust in the leader's personal abilities. The leader's intentions aside, the sense of "authenticity" or spontaneity of a charismatic leader, rebelling against status quo mores and political processes, is implicitly deceptive. It can only persist on condition that (a) there

---

55 Michael D. Shear, "Trump Diatribe Belittles Impeachment as 'Attempted Coup' on Eve of Votes," *The New York Times,* December 17, 2019. https://www.nytimes.com/2019/12/17/us/politics/trump-impeachment.html; Chelsea Stahl, "Trump Impeached by the House on Both Articles," *NBC News: Live Blog/Live Updates,* December 19, 2019. https://www.nbcnews.com/politics/trump-impeachment-inquiry/live-blog/live-updates-house-votes-impeachment-president-trump-n1103576/ncrd1104536#liveBlogHeader.

56 Matt Steib, "Trump Adviser Stephen Moore Compares Social-Distancing Protesters to Rosa Parks," *Intelligencer,* April 20, 2020. https://nymag.com/intelligencer/2020/04/trump-advisor-compares-coronavirus-protesters-to-rosa-parks.html.

57 Arit John, "Does Trump Have 'Total Authority' During the Coronavirus Outbreak, or Any Other Time?" *Los Angeles Times,* April 18, 2020. https://www.latimes.com/politics/story/2020-04-18/trump-governors-coronavirus-authority-reopen-states.

58 Max Weber, *Wirtschaft und Gesellschaft: Grundriss der Verstehenden Soziologie.* Volume 1 (Tübingen: Mohr Siebeck Verlag, 1976), 124.

still is still an alter political establishment to rebel against, (b) the charismatic movement or community is relatively unstructured and unpredictable, and (c) the charismatic leader is still alive. In all these cases, any power gained by the charismatic leader must be transformed to survive into some sort of formal political structure. In Weber's language, charisma must be "routinized" (*Veralltäglichung*) in directions either "traditional," "rational-legal," or both.[59] With the spectacle – that is, the political exhibition of the leaders via images, voices and social media – the routinization of charisma counts on the dematerialization of the leader itself.[60] The mirage of the leader's "direct" contact with the people (with followers, likes, etc.) and the ordinary language that says things straightly produces the effect of connecting the people with the former alienated establishment.

The long secularization of political institutions since the beginning of the Modern era has produced a new kind of devotion: the secular authority of the state does not impose only outward obedience, but also a sincere inner devotion to the personal capacities of the leader. In this sense, charisma calls for obedience to the leader not because of his useful functions, but because of his alleged superhuman gifts.[61] The only way for individuals to find full, empowered expression within a collective unit, is for the individuals to become empty, disempowered expressions of the collective unit. No "authentic" nation could function as a collective unit unless morally united under a dictator or sacrosanct or cause. Upon electoral victory, this 'freedom'-seeking people loses its position of 'resistance' and becomes a force explicitly for unfreedom. Every "liberation" from the stultifying democratic architecture increases the unchecked domination of the new leader.

4.5 *Emergent Elements 3: Mythological Uses of the Past*

This break from the past is also ostensibly a return to the past before society's fall from grace. In the absence of any seemingly viable future utopian visions, the impulse toward "retrotopia" is more prominent.[62] It is expressed in Trump's "Make America Great Again" slogan, and in Bolsonaro's echo "Make Brazil Great Again." The desire to return to paradise is a common one, possibly even deeply rooted in human experience. In the Judeo-Christian tradition, the Fall of Adam and Eve opens the saga of humanity. Other very common

---

59 Ibid., 140–141.
60 Jeremiah Morelock and Felipe Ziotti Narita, *The Society of the Selfie: Social Media and the Crisis of Liberal Democracy* (London: University of Westminster Press, 2021).
61 Franz Neumann, *Behemoth* (London: Victor Gollancz, 1943).
62 Zygmunt Bauman, *Retrotopia* (London: Premier Parallèle, 2019).

examples are the religious notions of rejoining an infinite, divine consciousness in death or nirvana. Bolsonaro's constant refrain of admiration toward the 1970s Brazilian and the Chilean military dictatorships combines visions of retrotopia with attacks against liberal democracy. This rhetoric serves to reinforce decisionism and the privileging of the Executive will over the Congress and the Judiciary, which he characterizes as entrenched with corruption. In this case, conservative values fit with authoritarian slips, as blame is placed on human rights, multiculturalism and liberal democracy for the fall of the moral order of the past.[63] A particular use of the past underlies this assertion: historical process is understood as the erosion of an idealized past that must be re-enacted and imposed via conservative cultural hegemony.

There are homologous moments to the biblical Fall in the psychic life of each person, for instance in the traumatic experience of birth[64] and in the early development of an individuated sense of self with the induction into the symbolic order.[65] What "great" refers to is of course unspecified in both cases. This masks the fact that the past that was "great" for some was still *terrible* for others. In the case of the United States, the romanticized past is in the immediate past-WWII era, when the country assumed status of global capitalist hegemon and enjoyed its greatest period of economic prosperity. Of course, this was *before* the successes of the civil rights movement, second wave feminism, and protests over the Vietnam War. In other words, it was a short and transient period, where middle class straight white men may have had it "great," but many others certainly did not. Perhaps some of the wives and mothers in the successful American Dream families had it "great," and certainly there were benefits to the children of these families during the Baby Boom era, when patriotic optimism and affluence ran high and the tumult of the 1960s had not yet hit. And yet this selective memory might seem perfectly appropriate to a large portion Trump's base, considering the prevalence of older white men among his supporters.[66]

It is perhaps more effective that the designation 'great' is left at least denotatively open in this way, since as a floating signifier its vagueness facilitates the power and universality of the impulse that is tapped – for Laclau, it is desire

---

63   Morelock and Narita, "Public Sphere and World-System."
64   Otto Rank, *The Trauma of Birth* (London: Psychology Press, 1999).
65   Jacques Lacan, *Freud's Papers on Technique, 1953–1954* (New York: WW Norton & Company, 1988); Julia Kristeva, *Powers of Horror*. New York: Columbia University Press, 1982.
66   Nicki Lisa Cole, "Meet the People Behind Donald Trump's Popularity: Survey Research Reveals Stark Trends in Voters and Values," *Thoughtco*, June 29, 2019. https://www.thoughtco.com/meet-the-people-behind-donald-trumps-popularity-4068073 (accessed December 19, 2019).

that seeks Lacan's empty and impossible *"objet petit a,"* but which can be collapsed into drive for a "partial object," something – a symbol, a slogan, a social movement, a charismatic leader – that is very real and historically specific, but which is treated as a conduit for the infinite *jouissance*.[67] The evangelical notion that Trump's presidency is an expression of God's will is a case in point. In other terms, the retrotopic slogan can be like the manifest content of dreams, operating as a source of wish-fulfillment for these deep, universal longings for completeness through returning to God or the womb. The nostalgia of the authoritarian populist is an allegiance to pretense. Whether delusion or manipulation, the "authentic" community is united under a lie, that is, under the political construction and ideological use of the past.

5   Concluding Notes

In this exposition we applied a constellation methodology to contemporary authoritarian populism as object. Consistent with Adorno's approach, we do not look at the object as a whole that subsumes its parts. On the contrary, our attempt is to articulate the nuances and the contradictory moments that organize the constellation. We dialectically unfolded the conceptual moments and suggested the possibility of a critical social theory committed to the analysis of the current sociopolitical scenario in the Americas. The rise of the populist far-Right in the 2010s produced and expressed major social, economic and political shifts by giving voice to new right-wing factions and movements, which are different from the traditional Republican Party (à la George W. Bush) in the US and the neoliberal and conservative parties of the 1990s and 2000s in Brazil. Besides the impact on liberal democracy and the correlation of political forces and parties, authoritarian populism spreads and brings together multiple resonances in the social terrain.

Our point of departure is the mainstream definition of populism as the antagonism between the people and the elite, but we argue that this must be expanded. In this sense, the dialectical constellation is useful for shedding light on the elements that participate in populism and its concept, as well as how the elements interact and generate contradiction and movement. Especially with the encounter of two political domains – populism and authoritarianism – we present this dialectical constellation as a diagnostic sketch of the historical horizon of contemporary American democracies. As an expression

---

67   Ernesto Laclau, *On Populist Reason* (New York: Verso, 2005); Jacques Lacan, *The Four Fundamental Concepts of Psychoanalysis* (London: Routledge, 2018).

of multiple crises – uneven recoveries from the 2008 crisis and deep crises of representation in traditional parties and political systems – authoritarian populism is not properly an accidental detour in an inevitable destination of post-Cold War societies toward liberal democracy. As Adorno remarked in the 1960s, authoritarian regression is intrinsic to the capitalist whirlwind of crises.

Bibliography

Adorno, Theodor. *Aspekte des neuen Rechtsradikalismus: ein Vortrag*. Frankfurt am Main: Suhrkamp Verlag, 2019.

Adorno, Theodor. *Einführung in die Dialektik*, edited by Christoph Ziermann – Nachgelassene Schriften, 2/IV. Frankfurt am Main: Suhrkamp Verlag, 2010.

Adorno, Theodor. *History and Freedom: Lectures 1964–1965*. Translated by Rodney Livingstone. London: Polity, 2006.

Adorno, Theodor. *Minima Moralia: Reflexionen aus dem beschädigten Leben*. Frankfurt am Main: Suhrkamp Verlag, 2003.

Adorno, Theodor. *Negative Dialektik / Jargon der Eigentlichkeit*. Frankfurt am Main: Suhrkamp Verlag, 2003.

Adorno, Theodor. *Três Estudos sobre Hegel*. Translated by Ulisses Vaccari. São Paulo: São Paulo State University Press, 2007.

Allen, Amy. "Recognizing domination: recognition and power in Honneth's critical theory." *Journal of Power* 3, no.1 (2010): 21–32.

Baker, Peter. "Trump Declares a National Emergency, and Provokes a Constitutional Clash." *The New York Times*, February 15, 2019. https://www.nytimes.com/2019/02/15/us/politics/national-emergency-trump.html.

Barabak, Mark and Noam Levey. "Are Democrats Helping Trump by Promising Healthcare to Undocumented Migrants?" *Los Angeles Times*, July 9, 2019.

Bauman, Zygmunt. *Retrotopia*. London: Premier Parallèle, 2019.

Biller, David. "Brazilian Politics Stain the Famous Yellow and Green Jersey." *Bloomberg*, July 7, 2019.

Bort, Ryan. "Trump Threatens to Shred First Amendment to Defend 'Free Speech.'" *Rolling Stone*, May 28, 2020. https://www.rollingstone.com/politics/politics-news/trump-twitter-mail-in-voting-free-speech-1005629/.

Buck-Morss, Susan. *The Origin of Negative Dialectics*. London: Macmillan, 1977.

Bugaric, Bojan. "The Two Faces of Populism: Between Authoritarian and Democratic Populism." *German Law Journal* 20, no. 2 (2019): 390–400.

Butler, Judith. *Undoing gender*. London: Routledge, 2004.

Calhoun, Craig. "Populist Politics, Communications Media and Large Scale Societal Integration." *Sociological Theory* 6, no. 2 (1988): 219–241.

Cole, Nicki Lisa. "Meet the People Behind Donald Trump's Popularity: Survey Research Reveals Stark Trends in Voters and Values." *Thoughtco,* June 29, 2019. At https://www.thoughtco.com/meet-the-people-behind-donald-trumps-popularity-4068073 (accessed December 19, 2019).

Davidson, John Daniel. "If You Don't Support Black Lives Matter, You're Fired." *The Federalist,* June 11, 2020. https://thefederalist.com/2020/06/11/if-you-dont-support-black-lives-matter-youre-fired/.

De Kadt, Raphael. "The End of the Liberal Democratic Era?" *Journal of the Helen Suzman Foundation* 2, no. 84 (2019): 3–10.

Editorial note: "Bolsonaro e o Povo." *Estadão* (May 23, 2019).

Fopp, Rodney. "Herbert Marcuse's 'Repressive Tolerance' and His Critics." *Borderlands* 6, no. 1 (2007): 1–10.

Fopp, Rodney. "'Repressive Tolerance': Herbert Marcuse's Exercise in Social Epistemology." *Social Epistemology* 24, no. 2 (2010): 105–122.

Foster, John Bellamy. "Marx's Theory of Metabolic Rift: Classical Foundations for Environmental Sociology." *American Journal of Sociology* 105, no. 2 (1999): 366–405.

Foster, John Bellamy, and Paul Burkett. "Value Isn't everything." *Monthly Review* 70, no. 1 (2018): 1–17.

Fraser, Nancy, and Axel Honneth. *Redistribution or Recognition?: A Political-philosophical Exchange.* New York: Verso, 2003.

Galston, William. *Anti-Pluralism: The Populist Threat to Liberal Democracy.* New Haven: Yale University Press, 2018.

Gandesha, Samir. "Understanding Right and Left Populism." *Critical Theory and Authoritarian Populism,* edited by Jeremiah Morelock. London: University of Westminster Press, 2018.

Hall, Stuart. "Popular Culture, Politics and History." *Cultural Studies* 32, no. 6 (2018): 929–952.

Honneth, Axel. *The Struggle for Recognition: The Moral Grammar of Social Conflicts.* Cambridge: MIT Press, 1996.

Horkheimer, Max and Theodor W. Adorno. *Dialectic of Enlightenment.* Redwood City: Stanford University Press, 2002.

Jameson, Fredric. *Late Marxism: Adorno, or, the Persistence of the Dialectic.* New York: Verso, 1990.

John, Arit. "Does Trump Have 'Total Authority' During the Coronavirus Outbreak, or Any Other Time?" *Los Angeles Times,* April 18, 2020. https://www.latimes.com/politics/story/2020-04-18/trump-governors-coronavirus-authority-reopen-states.

Kaufmann, David. "Correlations, Constellations and the Truth: Adorno's Ontology of Redemption." *Philosophy and Social Criticism* 26, no. 5 (2000): 62–80.

Kristeva, Julia. *Powers of Horror.* New York: Columbia University Press, 1982.

Lacan, Jacques. *Freud's Papers on Technique, 1953–1954.* New York: WW Norton & Company, 1988.

Lacan, Jacques. *The Four Fundamental Concepts of Psychoanalysis*. London: Routledge, 2018.

Laclau, Ernesto. *On Populist Reason*. New York: Verso, 2005.

Laclau, Ernesto, and Chantal Mouffe. *Hegemony and Socialist Strategy: Towards a Radical Democratic Politics*. New York: Verso, 1985.

Lukács, Georg. *Die Zerstörung der Vernunft: Irrationalismus zwischen den Revolutionen*. Darmstadt: Luchterhand Verlag, 1973.

Marx, Karl. *Das Kapital: Kritik der politischen Ökonomie* Volume 1. Berlin: Karl Dietz Verlag, 2008.

McAfee, Noëlle. *Julia Kristeva*. London: Routledge, 2004.

McCormick, Tracey Lee. "Why Same-Sex Marriage is Not the Ultimate Tool for Queer Liberation." *The Conversation*, October 14, 2018. https://theconversation.com/why-same-sex-marriage-is-not-the-ultimate-tool-for-queer-liberation-103702.

Morelock, Jeremiah. "Resuscitating Sociological Theory: Nietzsche and Adorno on Error and Speculation." *Nietzsche and Critical Social Theory: Affirmation, Animosity, and Ambiguity*, edited by Michael Roberts and Christine Payne. Leiden: Brill, 2019.

Morelock, Jeremiah and Narita, Felipe Ziotti. "Public Sphere and World-System: Theorizing Populism at the Margins." *Critical Theory and Authoritarian Populism*, edited by Jeremiah Morelock. London: University of Westminster Press, 2018.

Morelock, Jeremiah and Narita, Felipe Ziotti. *O Problema do Populismo: Teoria, Política e Mobilização*. São Paulo: Paco, São Paulo State University, 2019.

Morelock, Jeremiah and Narita, Felipe Ziotti. "Populism and Political Agitation in Late Capitalism: Research Notes." In *3rd International Seminar on Public Policy and Social Development*, edited by Alexandre Mendes. Franca: São Paulo State University Press, 2019.

Morelock, Jeremiah and Narita, Felipe Ziotti. *The Society of the Selfie: Social Media and the Crisis of Liberal Democracy*. London: University of Westminster Press, 2021.

Neumann, Franz. *Behemoth*. London: Victor Gollancz, 1943.

Norris, Pippa and Ronald Inglehart. *Cultural Backlash: Trump, Brexit and Authoritarian Populism*. Cambridge: Cambridge University Press, 2019.

Odilla, Fernanda. "Dos EUA ao Brasil, Como Presidentes Tentam Governar Sem Congresso." *BBC News*, June 17, 2019.

Pensky, Max. "Adorno's Actuality." In *The Actuality of Adorno: Critical Essays on Adorno and the Postmodern*, edited by Max Pensky. Albany: State University of New York Press, 1997.

Phelps, Jordyn and Ben Gittleson. "Trump Praises 'Overwhelming Force' and 'Domination' in DC Morning After Peaceful Protest Broken Up for Photo Op." *ABC News*, June 3, 2020. https://abcnews.go.com/Politics/trump-praises-overwhelming-force-domination-dc-morning-peaceful/story?id=71.

Portal, G1. "Bolsonaro Discursa em Brasília para Manifestantes que Pediam Intervenção Militar." April 19, 2020. https://g1.globo.com/politica/noticia/2020/04/19/bolsonaro-discursa-em-manifestacao-em-brasilia-que-defendeu-intervencao-militar.ghtml.

Rank, Otto. *The Trauma of Birth*. London: Psychology Press, 1999.

Rizzo, Salvador. "President Trump Accuses Rep. Omar of supporting al-Qaeda." *Washington Post*, July 17, 2019.

Robson, Ruthann. "Assimilation, Marriage, and Lesbian Liberation." *Temp. L. Rev* 75 (2002): 709.

Scheppele, Kim. "Autocratic Legalism." *The University of Chicago Law Review* 85, no. 2 (2018): 545–580.

Schmitt, Carl. *The Crisis of Parliamentary Democracy*. Cambridge: MIT Press, 1988.

Shear, Michael D. "Trump Diatribe Belittles Impeachment as 'Attempted Coup' on Eve of Votes." *The New York Times*, December 17, 2019. https://www.nytimes.com/2019/12/17/us/politics/trump-impeachment.html.

Sherratt, Yvonne. *Adorno's Positive Dialectic*. Cambridge University Press, 2002.

Stahl, Chelsea. "Trump Impeached by the House on Both Articles." *NBC News: Live Blog/Live Updates*, December 19, 2019. https://www.nbcnews.com/politics/trump-impeachment-inquiry/live-blog/live-updates-house-votes-impeachment-president-trump-n1103576/ncrd1104536#liveBlogHeader.

Steib, Matt. "Trump Adviser Stephen Moore Compares Social-Distancing Protesters to Rosa Parks." *Intelligencer*, April 20, 2020. https://nymag.com/intelligencer/2020/04/trump-advisor-compares-coronavirus-protesters-to-rosa-parks.html.

Stone, Alison. "Adorno, Hegel and Dialectic." *British Journal for the History of Philosophy* 22, no. 6 (2014): 1118–1141.

Taylor, Charles. "The Politics of Recognition." *New Contexts of Canadian Criticism* 98 (1997): 25–73.

Thomas, William I., and Dorothy S. Thomas. *The Child in America*. New York: Alfred P. Knopf, 1928.

Turollo Jr., Reynaldo and Cancian, Natalia. "Supremo Blinda Congresso de Medidas de Bolsonaro que Atropelam Legislativo." *Folha de São Paulo*, January 6, 2020.

Weber, Max. *Wirtschaft und Gesellschaft: Grundriss der Verstehenden Soziologie*. Volume 1. Tübingen: Mohr Siebeck Verlag, 1976.

Weiß, Volker. *Die Autoritäre Revolte: Die Neue Rechte und der Untergang des Abendlandes*. Stuttgart: Klett-Cotta, 2017.

Wolff, Robert Paul, Barrington Moore, and Herbert Marcuse. *A Critique of Pure Tolerance*. Boston: Beacon Press, 1966.

Wong, Queenie. "Trump vs. Twitter: Here's What You Need to Know About the Free Speech Showdown." *CNET*, June 2, 2020. https://www.cnet.com/news/trumps-social-media-executive-order-faces-lawsuit/.

CHAPTER 9

Authoritarianism in Brazil: Interpretations from Theodor W. Adorno

Maria Cristina Dancham Simões and Carlos Antonio Giovinazzo Júnior

1   Introduction

If history apparently repeats itself, it is not because there is a law immanent to it, but rather because the objective and subjective conditions that produced certain phenomena have not changed. Thus, the return of fascism to power and political control of states governed by democracy does not mean repetition, but instead that fascism has always been alive and the social, cultural, political, and economic conditions responsible for the rise of fascism have been reproduced continuously since the beginning of the 20th century. This is why the strategies identified in Adorno's empirical research on Martin Luther Thomas' radio broadcasts can be used as a tool for analyzing Bolsonaro's speeches, even though Thomas' broadcasts and Bolsonaro's speeches are separated by more than 80 years.[1]

In our study, we used the live in-person and official speeches of the former Brazilian President Jair Messias Bolsonaro as material for a qualitative content analysis, utilizing the framework developed by Theodor W. Adorno in his empirical research as a reference for the study. We proceeded with the organization of 202 official speeches made by Bolsonaro in 2019, during which he served his first year in office. Since then, the content of his speeches (pronouncements, interviews, live orations) has only grown in authoritarianism and cruelty. The analysis of the beginning of his mandate also fulfills the function of explaining that the atrocities observed during his term were announced a long time ago through his orations.

The criterion for selecting the pronouncements was whether the transcript was inserted in full of the speeches given by the aforementioned president on the Brazilian federal government's website. We understand that the justification for studying his performance and oration is to shed light on fascism as it

---

1 Theodor W. Adorno, "La técnica psicológica de las alocuciones radiofónicas de Martin Luther Thomas," in *Escritos Sociológicos II*, ed. Rolf Tiedemann, Gretel Adorno, Susan Buck-Morss, Klaus Schultz. Trans. Agustín González Ruiz (Madrid: Akal, 2009).

appears in Latin America and Brazil, identifying its particular forms of manifestation and also its universal content, which has been repeated for decades in social structures based on the capitalist model that feeds authoritarianism.

Bolsonaro is considered by us to be an authoritarian leader, but he was democratically elected. This puts identification between him and his voters as the central point of our analysis. We understand that fascism is structural (and not occasional) in capitalist society, and similarities to the authoritarian Nazi-fascist model of government sometimes escape, consciously or not, and that is why the studies carried out by Adorno over 70 years ago may be resumed at this historic moment.

2 Methodological Considerations

Adorno starts from the text *The Authoritarian Personality* to explain how his empirical research was elaborated.[2] The author presents his appropriation of the statistical model of American sociology, demonstrating its stress on the importance of both the quantitative understanding of the elements of authoritarianism, and the explanation of the relationship of such understanding with a qualitative perspective.

Empirical studies look at the power relationship between society and individuals, which allowed Adorno to deepen the understanding of the relationship between Sociology and Psychology, society, and the individual, which he also demonstrated in several other texts, such as "Sociology and Psychology" and is what constitutes the entire methodological basis of his work.[3] The split between these two dimensions (the social and the psychic) is at the same time true and false. It is true because the individual can only constitute himself with the awareness of the distinction between himself and the non-identical (what it is not distinguishes it from the object). It is also false because the individual is socially determined, as the sociological tradition teaches. Based on this understanding, Adorno indicates that the structural changes in society as a whole are affected by their own dynamics, independent of individuals, but also through them.

---

2 Theodor W. Adorno, "Estudios sobre la personalidad autoritaria," in *Escritos Sociológicos II*, ed. Rolf Tiedemann, Gretel Adorno, Susan Buck-Morss, Klaus Schultz. Trans. Agustín González Ruiz (Madrid: Akal, 2009).

3 Theodor W. Adorno, "Sobre la relación entre sociología y psicología," in *Escritos Sociológicos I*, ed. Rolf Tiedemann, Gretel Adorno, Susan Buck-Morss, Klaus Schultz. Trans. Agustín González Ruiz (Madrid: Akal, 2004).

Adorno also presents his perspective on the relationship between the quantitative and qualitative dimensions of his research.[4] The author argues that while the former allows us to understand the games of force and counterforce that have reached a considerable level socially, the latter allows us to approach concrete cases, consider elements that are beyond strict statistical control, and escape the portion of arbitrariness always present in the investigated and the investigator. From this perspective, Adorno finds that Statistics (although often indisputable) become irrelevant when considering the deeper interdependencies – just as the analysis of concrete cases reach such interdependencies; however, they are affected by the arbitrariness of those involved in the research.

From the relationship between the quantitative and qualitative character, it appears that the need for methodological self-critique and meta-critique becomes a constant task. It should be noted that, when paralleled with the research of "The Authoritarian Personality," which discussed aspects of the totalitarian character present in the institutions, in social relations, and in the psyche of individuals, identifying that not only prejudiced people could present certain characteristics, but also those understood as not prejudiced, Adorno found that the study itself could fall into personalization and labeling.[5] From this, the author understood that:

> people really free in the series in a way that only doesn't have any damage, and they wouldn't even be forcibly determined by a concrete political conviction. More good, the knowledge presupposes the processes that lead to the lack of freedom, as well as the strength of resistance that these processes provide romantically to the past, never adhere to them blindly.[6]

We chose this methodological path after several approaches to the content. In this regard, we understand that the framework created by Adorno allowed the observation of the similarity of the forms presented by Bolsonaro with those described in detail in "The Psychological Technique of Martin Luther Thomas' radio Addresses," which corresponds to the fascist agitator. We consider it important to say that the figure of Bolsonaro, in our analysis, represents a government policy and a project of society, therefore, a way of operating that

---

4   Theodor W. Adorno, "Culpa y represión," in *Escritos Sociológicos II*, ed. Rolf Tiedemann, Gretel Adorno, Susan Buck-Morss, Klaus Schultz. Trans. Agustín González Ruiz (Madrid: Akal, 2011).
5   Theodor W. Adorno, "Prejuicio y carácter," in *Escritos Sociológicos II*, ed. Rolf Tiedemann, Gretel Adorno, Susan Buck-Morss, Klaus Schultz. Trans. Agustín González Ruiz (Madrid: Akal, 2011), 373.
6   Ibid., 373.

is not limited to him, but involves his entire group and staff, with repercussions to his followers. Furthermore, the particularity of the election of a fascist agitator for the position of president of the republic puts a new element of complexity in the analysis, since Adorno did not refer to people in political positions, but to a man of entertainment. Even so, Bolsonaro resorts to the spectacle through virtual and media means (communication through social networks), an equally new and complex component.

3   Theoretical Resources

Regarding the characteristics of the authoritarian personality, in their research, Adorno identified some traits that can be found in different social groups; including those considered liberal or even progressive.[7] They are: (1) conventionalism as an attachment to that which exists for fear of losing what one imagines having – a poor way of recognizing the risks of living in a social order that perpetuates competition and is devastating to natural resources; (2) uncritical submission as a feeling of inferiority disguised as a "spirit of sacrifice" (for example, patriotism). Individuals do not need autonomy for the sake of a "greater good" (thus the nationalist ideology operates); (3) aggressiveness as self-defense; in the name of morality and the preservation of traditional values, violence is practiced against those who violate conventional norms. Basically, this trait expresses the need to release repressed impulses; (4) destruction and cynicism: hostility and contempt for culture and civilization, which is manifested in attacks on science and education, in addition to distrust of the knowledge produced and the empirical evidence supported by intellectuals (anti-intellectualism); (5) fixation on power and stupidity as an expression of attachment to the binomial domination and submission, which, when associated with the feeling of helplessness, the aggressor develops an identification with; (6) superstition and stereotype as a mystical belief in destiny based on preconceived schemes and fixed thought patterns as an expression of the absence of contact with objective reality; (7) anti-intraception: contempt, fear and aversion to the subjective (feelings, speculations, thinking, imagination) of yourself and others, which can result in the refusal of any form of empathy or compassion. It can also lead to sadomasochism as a psychological trait (pleasure in one's own suffering, and pleasure in inflicting suffering upon others); (8) projection: transferring inner problems (subjective) to the

---

7   Adorno, "Estudios sobre la personalidad autoritaria."

outside, attributing the defect and the responsibility for what happens to those generically identified as "powerful" or to specific groups (Jews, communists, leftists, women, etc.); and (9) sexual morality: excessive preoccupation with sexuality with a strong propensity to repress oneself and others, especially those who expose that sexuality can be experienced in numerous ways.[8]

The different studies by Adorno basically cover the two poles of the authoritarian relationship. On the one hand, he was concerned with the resources used by the agitators to unconsciously capture individuals, which led him to study some representatives of this group. Some of this research includes, "The Stars Down to Earth," "The Psychological Technique of Martin Luther Thomas' Radio Addresses," "Anti-Semitism and Fascist Propaganda," and "Freudian Theory and the Model of Fascist Propaganda," among other texts.[9]

Considering that the materials studied by the author correspond, on the one hand, to the modes and inclinations of certain psychological types, on the other hand, we can find studies with the individuals that make up this mass, who seek to verify the existence and unveil the relationships between these political points of view, prejudices and personality structure. One can mention here "The Authoritarian Personality," "Guilt and Repression," and others.[10]

Regarding agitators, Adorno makes it clear that the materials studied follow a rigid and repetitive pattern, which resemble Nazi strategies, but are not limited to them.[11] With regard to individuals who are part of the authoritarian mass and who are inclined to share hate propaganda, Adorno indicates the totalitarian character as a rigid and immutable structure that has in its essence the subjection to authority. Considering the changes in the economic structure and the resulting psychological reconfigurations, some characteristics are notorious, such as conventionalism, hierarchy, the desire for destruction,

---

8   Ibid., 467–525.
9   See the following: Theodor W. Adorno, "Bajo el signo de los astros," in *Escritos Sociológicos II*, ed. Rolf Tiedemann, Gretel Adorno, Susan Buck-Morss, Klaus Schultz. Trans. Agustín González Ruiz (Madrid: Akal, 2011); Adorno, "La técnica psicológica de las alocuciones radiofónicas de Martin Luther Thomas"; Theodor W. Adorno, "Antisemitismo y propaganda fascista," in *Escritos Sociológicos I*, ed. Rolf Tiedemann, Gretel Adorno, Susan Buck-Morss, Klaus Schultz. Trans. Agustín González Ruiz (Madrid: Akal, 2004); Theodor W. Adorno, "La Teoría Freudiana y el modelo de la propaganda fascista," in *Escritos Sociológicos I*, ed. Rolf Tiedemann, Gretel Adorno, Susan Buck-Morss, Klaus Schultz. Trans. Agustín González Ruiz (Madrid: Akal, 2004).
10 Adorno, "Estudios sobre la personalidad autoritaria"; Theodor W. Adorno, "Culpa y represión," in *Escritos Sociológicos II*, ed. Rolf Tiedemann, Gretel Adorno, Susan Buck-Morss, Klaus Schultz. Trans. Agustín González Ruiz (Madrid: Akal, 2011).
11 Ibid.

cynicism and contempt for the human being, the inability to love (as a libidinal investment) and other characteristics that make up the weakness of the ego.

In "Anti-Semitism and Fascist Propaganda," Adorno presents a study of the anti-democratic and anti-Semitic propaganda of the radio broadcasts of fascist agitators, as well as of pamphlets and weekly publications.[12] The author emphasizes that he set out to study the psychological content more than the sociological problems, which are the substrate of the former.

The material studied by the author has a clear psychological focus, delineating the proposal to convince people through the exploration of unconscious mechanisms rather than through the presentation of ideas and arguments. We consider that concrete political ideas play a lesser role than applied psychological stimuli, so the ego (or its weakness) plays a big role in fascist irrationality. This irrationality operates by attacking what was imagined almost in the form of delirium, which is then broken into parts and has no commitment to reality. It also operates by the absence of discursive logic, which allows the individual to surrender to the torrent of words, through psychic economy, without subjecting the discourse to rational examination.

Adorno identifies some characteristics of the psychological approach used in fascist propaganda.[13] First, he points to the personalization of advertising by replacing a collective ego with a paternalistic image. The fascist leader approaches his audience by presenting himself as human, as the audience member is. In this sense, we mention one of Bolsonaro's first public appearances after his inauguration: alongside other figures of Brazilian politics, and of course, linked to conservative ideology, all dressed in jackets and ties, he poses for a photo dressed in a football jersey and slippers. The message conveyed is that the new president is a man of the people and simple: anyone could be in his place.

Adorno also highlights the substitution of ends by means, since there is a glorification of something that is in progress, which erases and replaces the purpose. In addition, fascist propaganda is an end-in-itself, which allows for the shared pleasure with the targeted audience through storytelling but maintains no commitment to truth or objectivity. In this regard, we emphasize that the virtual media component of advertising was an important factor in Bolsonaro's election. First, because the approximation between the leader and the chosen demographic targeted by virtual social networks promotes a kind of identification on demand, which can lead to the promotion of a feeling of power in the

---

12   Adorno, "Antisemitismo y propaganda fascista."
13   Ibid.

follower over the established relationship with the media. Second, because the speed with which false news is created and spread contributes to the attitude of libidinal economy with a view to maintaining the individual's productive capacity.[14]

We consider that the central point of Adorno's characterization is the identification relationship between the leader and his audience, which have similar characteristics that fascist propaganda seeks to reconcile before overlapping. We draw on his empirical research by claiming that fascist propaganda is a symbolic system that seeks its structure of operation in unconscious, projective elements and based on rituals that resemble religious ones. As in a ritual, collective regression operates by the symbolic revelation of the identity that the speaker verbalizes, which the listeners feel and think, but do not express in terms of the socially imposed rules of conduct. When risking making ridicule, the leader is taken seriously, gaining followers for the gratification they obtain in demonstrating this identity, as an institutionalized redemption of the feeling of "lack" experienced by the followers.[15]

In the ritual of fascist propaganda, the pattern starts from this act of symbolic revelation, which promotes identification, followed by a temporary abandonment of responsibility. The basis of the ritual is destructiveness as a delusion of annihilation disguised as salvation that operates through the identification between leader and followers. The psychological weakness of the self-contained individual promotes the loss of self-control and the fusion of individual impulses with the ritual. It is not by chance that the pro-Bolsonaro demonstrations that took place during the electoral campaign seemed to: (1) always be driven by aggressiveness and violent attitudes; (2) carry a ritual element that is related to Brazilian religious syncretism, and (3) present the growing neo-Pentecostalism views that have been present since the 1970s. From a psychological standpoint, all of these elements point to the economy of libidinal energy and its managed form, operated by authoritarianism. In these terms, the fascist ritual of revelation and identification can be considered a substitute for sexual gratification, based on the Freudian reference.

Finally, we add an element of Bolsonaro's cynicism and impudence as an indicator of his sexual views. He invariably appeals to certain aspects of sexuality. Before interpreting this appeal only as uninformed or naïve, we must consider that he knows exactly what he's doing and look to whom he addresses

---

14   Libidinal economy refers to the submission of libido, human vital energy, to the order established by the current production method. In this case, it is about the organization of desire from capital.
15   Ibid.

his speech. He provokes his opponents and, at the same time, feeds those who follow him for his macho and homophobic postures. In this regard, he stated that he is "married" to allies who became ministers of state, suggesting that it is sexless marriage; he also made fun of the penis size of someone who greeted him, whose features indicate that he was of East Asian descent. Despite being deliberate attitudes with clear and conscious objectives, he reveals more than he intended and would like, in the sense that: (1) the authoritarian personality despises everything that is different from himself and acts to make each person around him an object for his own use (a means for certain purposes); (2) contempt for the life of those who are not part of his support group; (3) the prejudiced attitude is present in a greater number of people than we would like to admit, and (4) indifference is one of the main marks of culture, which affects both the prejudiced and non-prejudiced.

4   Bolsonaro as a Fascist Leader and Agitator: the Analyzed Material

We identified that Bolsonaro works on three complementary discourse levels that are directly related to the means of communication he used. First, we find the official pronouncements in full on our source for this research, the website of the Brazilian federal government.[16] On the second level are the interviews given to the media, usually done at the door of the presidential residence, which present elements that are not choreographed and rehearsed. Such interviews were available in full on the federal government website, but were removed, keeping only those granted in a planned manner. On the third deeper and more obscure level are the lives and tweets, made at first with less ethical and political rigor, in which Bolsonaro speaks informally and at times scandalously, similar to the President of the United States, Donald J. Trump.[17]

In this chapter, we chose to deal with discourse at its most rationalized level, as we understand that we are interested in the planned psychological strategies, according to the theoretical framework adopted. Accompanying the ambivalent movement of fascist propaganda, we seek to understand not only the rationally manipulated strategy, but also its escapes, its flaws and holes, considered here as parapraxes that reveal the authoritarian character

---

16   Please give the Brazilian Federal Government website here.
17   On the relationship of Donald Trump with social media networks, see: Panayota Gounari, "Authoritarianism, Discourse and Social Media: Trump as the 'American Agitator,'" in *Critical Theory and Authoritarian Populism*, ed. Jeremiah Morelock (London: University of Westminster Press, 2018).

of the discourse and the speaker. Even so, we emphasize that the content of the other discourse levels of the investigated fascist leader probably contains more references to what is presented here. The content analysis that we use is of a qualitative nature, but some considerations are needed in relation to quantitative characterization, which will also be made throughout the text, when appropriate.

We used as source all the official speeches made by Bolsonaro during the year 2019. Considering the material published on the federal government website, we call each of the 202 insertions that year a speech, however it is important to indicate that the transcripts also contain collections of press, meetings, toast, among other situations in which Bolsonaro was officially president. Some of the inserts also present the transcription of the speeches of his interlocutors, however we take the necessary precautions to avoid confusion in the origin of the speeches.

Initially, we selected two criteria to classify the contexts of the speeches, which could be identified as national commitments (inaugurations, visits to government officials, among others) or the international agenda (such as the UN speech or meetings with other heads of state). Throughout the analysis process, carried out through the reading and identification of the titles attributed to the speeches, we noticed that two other patterns had a significant number of insertions, the speeches for military and religious speeches. We present below a list of the main types of situations in which Bolsonaro acted officially as president of Brazil. Table 9.1 fulfills the function of showing the types of events (and their incidence) in which the president spoke, in addition to showing that Bolsonaro dedicates part of his time to speak to his political support base (military and religious).

We identify in Table 9.1 that the national agenda occupied most of the official commitments in which Bolsonaro spoke. When we analyzed the content, we noticed that none of the items on this national agenda equal in number the events of the international and military agendas, in which all speeches made directly to representatives of different international sectors or to the military in general fit. If we consider that his government team has many military personnel, then the military agenda must appear more frequently than indicated in the table. This fact is made evident when, for example, Bolsonaro appointed his military ministers (an activity considered for descriptive purposes) to belong to the national agenda, by entrance or by the appointment to a team.

In addition, the number of overtly religious activities in which Bolsonaro was involved in as president does not allow for the identification of the nature of such events. All were based on Judeo-Christian religious traditions and mostly related to neo-Pentecostal groups, such as cults, visits to churches,

TABLE 9.1   Situations in which Bolsonaro spoke (2019)

Context	Quantity
National agenda	102
Team entrances and appointments	14
Publication of decrees, provisional measures, bills	15
Activities with representatives of the Executive, Legislative and Judiciary	11
Activities related to the economic agenda	20
Official events, launches, inaugurations, commemorative dates	36
Pronouncements and statements about his government	6
Internacional agenda	45
Military agenda	41
Religious agenda	14
Total	202

pastors and famous missionaries, among other activities. Specifically, when it comes to the word "religion" and its derivatives, we identified that Bolsonaro said it 41 times in 2019, always based on the same standard: he claims to be a Christian, says he respects all religions and "even" those who do not profess any religion. He affirms that the State is secular, but that "we" should act using the Christian faith as a reference for our behaviors, religious, and traditional values – although he does not exactly identify who "we" are; that will be explored later when we deal with the relationship between the leader and its followers.

5   Psychological Strategies of Fascist Propaganda as Government Policy: the Lone Maned Wolf

We began the observation with the similarity between the literal speech of Martin Luther Thomas and speeches made by Bolsonaro during his electoral campaign, because both refer to the absence of sponsors for his endeavor.[18] Bolsonaro made ten references to this in official speeches in 2019, after he

---

18   Adorno, "La técnica psicológica de las alocuciones radiofónicas de Martin Luther Thomas."

was elected. The pattern of this speech established two complementary references: in the first, the current president states that he had no campaign money or television time (in Brazil, the electoral campaign is mandatory and is offered free of charge to parties on all radio networks and television, in addition to being partly financed by the public authorities) and despite this, managed to get elected. At other times, he claims that businessmen, not companies, offered him money during his pre-campaign. And, knowing full-well that in Brazil, receiving money from companies during a campaign is prohibited by law, Bolsonaro stated that companies who did offer money were momentarily refused by him, then asked to donate the money *after* the election. His crusade would then be to fight against the powerful and the privileged, against the "injustices," such as the privileges of artists and intellectuals who receive state-funding to produce anti-Brazil "militancy" works. He generically mentions entrepreneurs, but directly or indirectly he equates those powerful and privileged with those who supposedly use the state to impose themselves as a minority over the majority.

In this sense, the entrepreneur is not the real enemy; on the contrary, he is a victim of the system as well, since the powerful people who control the state draft laws that hinder his economic activities, namely by forcing him to participate in the payment of taxes and by not providing protection to the workers. In general, we highlight that Adorno identifies this strategy as an exaggeration of the leader's integrity and value to gain the trust of his followers.

Another tactic that we observe is an attempt to always stimulate the fear of his followers, which Bolsonaro achieves (from his campaign to today) through his grip over the internet. Within his followers is a misguided appeal to the truth and to a revelation of hidden conspiracy plans. Through defamation and manipulation, Bolsonaro obtains a means of exploiting them. The revelation of false conspiracies seems to achieve a double objective: people are kept under fear and distrust and willingly put themselves under the protection of the leader, since he presents himself as someone who will unmask all who are against what he defines as "the freedom of our people." The two references presented demonstrate the president as someone who would not be committed to the economic interests of the powerful and who appears to speak the undisclosed truth. However, adherence to his ideas is only achieved by stimulating fear and hatred toward the enemy identified as responsible for insecurity and poverty.

6 Institutionalized and Legalized Emotional Release

From the writings of Theodor W. Adorno, we understand that the more the speaker breaks through the barriers of self-control in the listeners, the more easily they are subject to the will of the leader to a greater extent than to their own will. We note that Bolsonaro uses the government apparatus to institutionalize and legalize emotional liberation, which is an important component in the authoritarian identification process. We present two examples: the attempt to regulate the possession and carrying of firearms, and the removal of mobile radar for monitoring traffic on federal roads; drivers are fined when they are caught at speeds above the permitted level.

The possession of a firearm is exclusive to Brazilian military forces with one exception: civilian citizens are permitted possession, provided they undergo rigorous and costly psychotechnical aptitude tests, in addition to regular registration and monitoring of the device's status. When Bolsonaro was a federal deputy, he defended the total liberation of the possession and carrying of weapons in a model similar to that existing in some regions of the United States. As president, one of his first actions was the presentation in the National Congress of a bill expanding the possibilities for civilian firearm possession and the carrying of a weapon for military personnel.

Even though Bolsonaro knew that his radical proposals would not have full adherence, the highlight of this action is in its middle not its end, which is characteristic of fascist propaganda. His speeches in 2019 mentioned the term "firearm" 15 times, with him resorting to psychological and projective justifications, once again appealing to fear and insecurity, feelings that are social in nature, but which concern every individual. His mentioning of survival, the right to private property, self-defense, and public security, are clear examples of the relationship between the sociological and the psychological, and how much the focus of his rhetoric is on the latter.

> The Senate and the Chamber will discuss the issue of the Arms Decree. Security in the field is a very important thing and we have extended by decree the possession of a firearm throughout the perimeter of your property. Do not let, do not let these two decrees die in the Chamber or in the Senate. Our life is very important, you know how difficult it is to produce in this country. And safety has to be above all. So, I believe in you, who are going to talk to the other colleagues, so that these two decrees do not fall. After all, we have to trust one another. I trust you and you have to

> trust whoever is on your side, when it comes to this very important issue that is our security within our property (06/18/2019).[19]

Regarding the removal of mobile radars from federal highways, we highlight the importance given to this agenda, which is a disproportionate agenda considering the important position of the president occupied by Bolsonaro. At the same time, this importance sheds light on what is argued here. The justification for insisting on the removal of these radars lies in the cost and in what he and others call the "fine industry," a system built supposedly arbitrarily to harm both the driver in his right to come and go and the worker in his salary. In one of his speeches, Bolsonaro states that it is necessary to believe in human beings, using common sense and the responsibility of citizens, as a justification for the removal of the radars (05/20/19). The current regulations, he claimed, would promote cowardly and unfair situations, as it would charge high fines for traffic violations that "did not harm anyone."[20]

> I am studying a fight to end traffic radars in Brazil. I'm in an arm wrestle with the justice that doesn't want to let me end the traffic radars. I'm sure the governor will get into this fight here in Federal District – FD. Nobody can walk in FD without being fined. This is cowardice. No more stealing from the Brazilian people. I'm sure the governor will study this case. And it will end this robbery here in Brasilia too (10/08/2019).[21]

We understand that his strategy affects the subjectivity of his followers, given the way he argues, based on feelings. It also promotes the possibility of identification with the leader who takes on the responsibility of fighting for individual freedoms, based on the right to carry a firearm and to drive at the speed he considers most appropriate with his car. Ultimately, it appeals to people's responsibility and common sense, but the measure is the individual himself, stimulated to think and act in a pragmatic and selfish way, because what matters is to satisfy the instinctual needs linked to aggression and violence. On the other hand, the individual is led to not reflect on what makes the social world what it is, because armed and free to drive at high speed, which gives him a

---

19 "Presidente da República Federativa do Brasil – Discursos," Brasil, https://www.gov.br/mre/pt-br/centrais-de-conteudo/publicacoes/discursos-artigos-e-entrevistas/presidente-da-republica/presidente-da-republica-federativa-do-brasil-discursos, accessed January 10 2020.
20 Ibid.
21 Ibid.

false sense of power, he prefers not to elaborate rationally the reasons that produce individual fear. Instead, the authoritarian personality takes refuge in what provides a false sense of security and freedom, especially the selfish "right" to carry a firearm and to drive his car as he pleases. The consequence of this whole situation is a weakened ego, with people becoming less able to meet the demands of self-control, which is consistent with the administration and authoritarian control of individuals' libidinal energy.

7 Persecuted and Stabbed Innocence

In Brazil, to be elected a candidate must have 50% +1 of the valid votes calculated from the total number of voters minus the voided votes and the blank votes. Otherwise, the top two will go to the second round of the elections. Bolsonaro was stabbed a month before the first round of voting during his election campaign, exacerbating the political polarization that had gained violently clear contours since 2014. The episode changed the direction of the election because it allowed him to reach the second round and get the most votes due to a reinforcement of the victim's image as persecuted, a status that he cultivated since the beginning of the electoral campaign, and which exempted him from participating in the debates with other candidates. There were moments in which his unpreparedness for the position of president of the republic could be evident; Bolsonaro himself declared that he did not understand economics, education, healthcare, etc., when asked about topics that require certain technical knowledge. The political use made of this episode shows the insistence on the idea of innocence, (self) immolation, and persecution.

Adorno discusses the indifference toward the aggressor's sadistic and aggressive tendencies in relation to the victim, a resource with which fascist propaganda is constituted.[22] This trend goes back to a phase of psychosexual development in which the individual has not yet established the difference between subject and object, between the ego and the outside world. In this way, the projection operated from the administered economy of the libido allows imaginary events to gain the status of reality. And it also reinforces that aggressiveness is not something that springs from the interior of individuals, or that the economic and political system, which support this belligerent climate, stimulates the continuity of the situation, but it is the fair and necessary response against the invented enemies.

---

22   Adorno, "Antisemitismo y propaganda fascista."

In any case, Bolsonaro presented himself as someone who was at the service of the nation. The word "sacrifice" was said in his speeches 29 times in 2019, sometimes referring to himself, sometimes to the military – a recurring audience of his official statements and the main group to which he belongs, since he is a retired captain of the Army. Regarding the military, he summons them to sacrifice themselves for the good of the Republic, over which the communist threat hangs. This discursive rhetoric originating from the military dictatorship (1964–1985), is evoked to justify the repression of those who are supposedly anti-patriotic and against the values that formed Brazilian society (the Christian God, the patriarchal family, and private property). Regarding self-sacrifice, we identified the use of this rhetorical resource when Bolsonaro refers to his election: "And whether you like it or not, I was unlucky or not, I am the President of the Republic" (07/11/2019).[23] Self-sacrifice is related to the idea of persecuted innocence because Bolsonaro makes clear the danger that he suffered with the attack (imagined or not) to be renewed and felt also by his followers. In this way, aggression is rationalized; it justifies the use of violence not as self-defense, since the sacrifice for the country would be worthwhile, but as a defense of the nation that is under threat by the communists.

> The Armed Forces, for decades, was mistreated, persecuted, but, due to training and character, we remained standing. And this persecution is simply for one thing, it is the search on the part of those for absolute power, and they know that we military are the last obstacle to socialism. If Brazil today is a democracy and if we have freedom, in large part, we owe those who preceded us (12/12/2019).[24]

According to Adorno, the religious element embedded in Bolsonaro's rhetoric of innocence refers to the ritualistic model of fascist propaganda to point out the existence of a conspiracy that aims to oppress and enslave workers and simple, poor, naïve, and dedicated people.[25] What they risk is a submission to values that are unconnected to Brazilian history and culture (which would be submission to privileged white men and landowners). It is about attachment to an idealized past. Thus, the strengthening of the patriarchal family is an antidote against homo-affective marital unions, and the evocation of the myth of racial democracy is an antidote against rebellion and the challenge promoted by the countless organized black collectives that stand up to denounce

---

23   "Presidente da República Federativa do Brasil – Discursos," Brasil.
24   Ibid.
25   Adorno, "Bajo el signo de los astros."

Brazilian structural racism. On the other hand, there is an appeal to the legacy of European colonization – which imposed Christianity on the indigenous population that lived in the Brazilian territory – to fight all those who, with their existence, show the richness of cultural and social diversity that characterizes Brazilian society of the 21st century.

That is exactly what Bolsonaro and his followers deny. If Diversity and the struggle for democratic and egalitarian relations prevails, it jeopardizes the influential positions that have been reached by the holders of economic and political power. The reaction to this situation has repercussions on the psychology of those who feel threatened. They become affectionate and tolerant of violence and aggression and project their resentment onto their opponents: it is the other who conspires, manipulates, lies, deceives, persecutes, etc. In the supposed defense of the innocent, the president uses a very powerful resource. Jair Bolsonaro's middle name is Messias (Messiah), which he effectively utilizes as a political tool.[26] For example, he referred to his middle name on the following occasions:

> Two years ago, I was in Israel, I visited the Jordan River. By coincidence my name is also Messiah, I was moved at that moment, I accepted the call of a pastor from our delegation, and I went down the waters of the Jordan River (04/01/19).[27]
>
> In the middle of my name there is Messiah, by coincidence, I am a believer in God, I am a Christian (04/12/2019).[28]

This reference not only implies that Bolsonaro is the savior, but also as one who is persecuted by his enemies and who must sacrifice himself, even if he's innocent. This victim stratagem creates a situation that leads to the identification of Bolsonaro's followers with himself and his cause.

8 Tirelessness as a Country Project

Adorno identifies indefatigability as a strategy to encourage followers to keep a constant watch, which makes it possible to keep them disciplined, obedient,

---

26   For Christianity, Jesus Christ is the Messiah (the savior, the restorer, the chosen one).
27   "Presidente da República Federativa do Brasil – Discursos," Brasil.
28   Ibid.

and under oppression.²⁹ Again, we understand that the libidinal economy works as a means of domination and that indefatigability is the psychological expression of totalitarianism. This is because it is necessary to keep the supporter of totalitarian regimes in a permanent state of excitement, which prevents self-reflection. In this sense, on an unconscious level the fascist follower does not recognize the conflict of interest that exists within the fascist mission in relation to himself; when he acts in an aggressive and intolerant way, he is also acting against himself, since reasoning is inconvenient. Thus, individuals must remain (self) hypnotized, and the perpetuation of indefatigability is the means to maintain this state. The dictum, 'one can never rest because the enemy never rests,' points to what has been discussed previously about the undifferentiation between aggressor and victim and about the projections resulting from this undifferentiation.

> We will not rest until all the sister countries breathe democracy and freedom. Also, sister countries, may our peoples not be persuaded, or deceived, by the ease (11/30/2019).³⁰

In the case of Bolsonaro, it is important to uncover his military origin, which encourages both discipline and selflessness, and presents such values as obligatory for the successful functioning of social institutions. This can be witnessed in the proposal to introduce the military model of organization in public schools as the basic way of resolving their numerous crises. Most references to the significance of being tireless, selfless, and lacking sleep, were addressed to the military, particularly in graduation speeches at officer training schools. As a strategy, Bolsonaro observed that Brazil's younger generations had been in the hands of "communist vagrants" for a long time, which he used to his advantage. He stressed the urgency to resume a disciplinary project that must start from the base, from the *beginning* of life, that is, through the institutionalization of the military model in schools.

There is a saying in Portuguese that states that "the letter with blood gets in." We see the effect of this saying in the militarization of public schools.³¹ There is yet another element that we highlight: the indefatigability accompanied by the need to restore traditional values, which when subverted, supposedly led

---

29   Theodor W. Adorno, "La técnica psicológica de las alocuciones radiofónicas de Martin Luther Thomas."
30   "Presidente da República Federativa do Brasil – Discursos," Brasil.
31   "The letter with blood enters" is a proverb in Portuguese, which means to say that there is a need for violence in education – only in this way would learning be fixed on individuals.

the country to a situation of extreme subservience to the interests of international communism. Such devices are used to promote a state of alert and permanent war against imaginary "enemies." If the red scare is not tackled, it is claimed, the country will soon be transformed into Cuba, Venezuela, or China.

Once again, it can be clearly seen that Bolsonaro projects onto others what is typical of him and his supporters. In general, he does not know how to identify any characteristics of the economy, culture, and society of these countries, other than authoritarianism as a government regime. In fact, his projections hide his authoritarian personality from himself.

9 The Messenger, His Father, and His Sons

Adorno's research pointed out the ambivalent relationship the figure of the leader establishes with his followers. While he is the strong man, he simultaneously appears as "just a messenger," and therefore equal to the other members of the group. Considering this strategy, Adorno presents a deep psychoanalytical understanding of the agitator's conflict with his father. The author observed Thomas' ambivalent relations with the father figure, which became a psychological complex insomuch that as a leader he no longer identified with his father, but solely with his children (his followers). While at the same time, his message took the masses to the surreptitious confirmation that the precursor (the father) was the one who announced what was to come. We identified the same structure in Bolsonaro. We observed the most explicit portion of this strategy when we saw the opposition Bolsonaro made to his father in his speeches, presenting him as an authoritarian and fickle man:

> My father quickly decided my future. As he had been approved for the Preparatory School for Army Cadets, my father decided 'you will be in the military; you will be president of the Republic' (7/24/2019).[32]

> You don't have to ask the irresponsible father this question, whether or not he wants a school with ... militarization, he has to impose, he has to change it. Because we don't want these kids to grow up and in the future be dependent until they die on government social programs (9/5/2019).[33]

---

32 Ibid.
33 Ibid.

But just as he had no choice, neither should the children of the Brazilian homeland. Ambivalence appears when repeating the importance of children overcoming their parents: (04/17) "let each boy look at his father and mother to be better than him," (and also on 05/06 and 07/25), while not wanting his own children (and other politicians) to leave his side (04/11, 07/24, 08/01, 08/06, 08/29) and have a life of their own.[34] On this, Bolsonaro has the peculiarity of having three politically-involved sons, who were elected as city councilor in Rio de Janeiro, federal deputy for the state of São Paulo, and senator for the state of Rio de Janeiro.

In the images in which they appear together, it is difficult to identify who the father is and who the children are, given the similarity not only in terms of kinship, but also in terms of posture, clothes, and facial features. We understand that this configuration also represents the undifferentiation between leader and followers, according to our understanding of the libido's managed economy, since the fascist leader obtains control of the collective by surrendering to it. The fascist leader does not correspond to the paternalistic image, but rather to the representation of all the children of the community of which he is a part. He is an equal and that is exactly what makes his leadership possible: he denies his superiority and his authority over the followers exactly to exercise authoritarian power over them. This type of dulled-down power display is related to the decline in power of both the family economic unit and the father who supported it. This power was transferred to the economic sphere, as pointed out by Horkheimer and Adorno.[35]

While he presents himself as a strong man, he is also weak and in need of redemption, that is, subject to parental authority, dependent, and in the service of something more important than him. This greater entity is not the father, but something vague and indefinite. Adorno (2009) identifies the figure of the leader in the materials surveyed as a representative of the "children."[36] In contrast to this, we understand that Bolsonaro names the indefinite element "god," which is in harmony with the fascist ritualistic strategy. This "god" appears in his "messages" based on religious and biblical references (03/08, 03/23, 04/08).[37]

---

34 "Presidente da República Federativa do Brasil – Discursos," Brasil.
35 Max Horkheimer and Theodor W. Adorno, "Família," in *Temas básicos da Sociologia*. Trans. by Álvaro Cabral. (São Paulo: Cultrix / Ed. da Universidade de São Paulo, 1973).
36 Adorno, "La técnica psicológica de las alocuciones radiofónicas de Martin Luther Thomas."
37 "Presidente da República Federativa do Brasil – Discursos," Brasil, 2019.

The message that I want to convey to you, to anyone who is a Christian, from the rib of a man came a woman, and from that moment, by the grace of God, from you, all men came. ... Thank God I have a consistent family. We must seek that only in this way we can build a great nation (08/03/2019).[38]

And I don't want to give a testimony here, but a quick passage, because there are certain things in people's lives that only God comforts us. I remember, and my mother used to tell me when I was born, in [19]55, that it was a very complicated pregnancy. At that time, they had few resources and on the eve of my birth, there was a heavy hailstorm and many of the houses from Glicério [Bolsonaro's hometown] were unroofed. And when I was born, I obviously survived, and my mother, as she was very Catholic, decided to name me Messiah. So, my name is Jair Messias Bolsonaro. Just as many of you have a biblical name, considering your fathers or mothers.

And I went on with my life. My father was a true wanderer. He was a dentist and traveled throughout the state of São Paulo. We ended up in Eldorado Paulista. When I was 15 years old, I got to know the armed struggle, when the battalion of men called Carlos Lamarca passed through the city. I approached the Army and there was love at first sight; I joined the Army. I became an aspiring officer in [19]77, I went to the border, I returned to Rio, I went to the Paratroopers Brigade, I was closer to God than many people, closer only to my minister Marcos Pontes [He is a Brazilian Air Force pilot and astronaut. He became the first South American and the first Lusophone to go into space when he docked onto the International Space Station on March 30, 2006], 40 thousand km high. And I carried on with my life (08/04/2019).[39]

We understand this strategy as an antonomastic resource, in which the understanding of a word loses its original reference and can therefore be linked to anything.[40] From the perspective of identification on demand that takes place between leader and followers, "god" can be everything and nothing, being what each one desires. This mechanism, which connects leaders and followers, is mediated by a vague idea of God. It also illustrates the indefinite pattern of the superior force that governs the chosen leader as representative of

---

38   Ibid.
39   "Presidente da República Federativa do Brasil – Discursos," Brasil, 2019.
40   Maria Cristina Dancham Simões, Formação do indivíduo, formação docente e educação especial: o lugar do sujeito e o compromisso com a adaptação (São Paulo: PUC, 2016).

the collective, thus exercising its power authoritatively. This is only possible because those led, with a weakened ego, yearn for submission.

10 The Little Big President

Regarding the leader's ambivalence, Adorno names him "little big man," because the fascist agitator sometimes shows himself as strong, by representing the power of the collective, as well as sometimes weak, as each member can identify with him, and neither is considered inferior.[41] For this identification to occur, the leader must rely on divergent unconscious dispositions, not on consistent rational beliefs, which allows for this double approach. While there is an intimate identification, there is also a flattering distance.

Again, unveiling the use of psychological strategies, Adorno identifies a link with money and therefore with the individual fear of economic forces. The author names this movement "attitude of begging," which allows the leader to put himself on an equal footing with his followers, but also ambivalently and unconsciously act in the "redemption" process when he engages in the humiliating act of begging, which everyone can be subject.[42] In doing so, the leader bears the burden and redeems his followers. With the help of the internet, this begging attitude can be catapulted. In addition to the official website, 29 pages were identified on a single crowdfunding site with the same objective: to raise funds for Bolsonaro's election campaign. We question whether this has anything to do with the transformation of means-into-ends, as is already presented as one of the characteristics of fascist propaganda.

The relationship with money, within the logic on demand, establishes a relationship of exchange in which the followers are like "bosses," and to that extent it is also configured a disproportionality pattern, because the small amount donated to the campaign turns the follower into a partner in a grandiose enterprise (saving Brazil). Recent strategies to reconfigure the work type based on the fallacy of entrepreneurship make this other kind of link between the leader and his followers possible. On the other hand, disproportionality is also seen in the discourse: there is a balance between banal matters and grandiose statements that intertwine without logical connections, and in the

---

41 Adorno, "La técnica psicológica de las alocuciones radiofónicas de Martin Luther Thomas."
42 Ibid., 29.

case of Bolsonaro, without discursive connection, because at various times he does not conclude his sentences, opening space again for the antonomastic resource, only now using incompleteness.

Adorno's analysis of Pastor Martin Luther Thomas in the 1940s allowed us to understand the survival of fascism in these first decades of the 21st century. In short, scientific and social advances, the expansion of access to education, and the consolidation of democratic institutions (all indicators of progress) were not enough to stop the psychosocial trends that produces "weak" people. As such, they are easily "captured" by authoritarian leaders and groups. Such leaders get stronger when most of the population is kept under constant threat. However, we emphasize that the threat is disseminated by the fascists and sustained by the capitalist economic system that feeds on institutionalized fear. It is this fear that drives fragile people to seek support from those who are deceptively seen as strong. Finally, we affirm that the devices used in fascist propaganda for over a century are very much alive precisely because people remain powerless in the face of the political power derived from economic realities.

11 The Specifics of the Brazilian Elite

We understand that for each psychological element there are corresponding sociological and historical elements. We have the intersection of the subjective conditions produced in Brazilian society, i.e., patriarchy accompanied by a slave-labor past, in confluence with urban and industrial development (with the objective conditions), in a current stage of late capitalism (predatory and monopolistically managed economic model), all the while occupying a position in the international division of labor. Its latifundio combined with agribusiness produced submission to international capital, controlled by conglomerates of companies based in specific countries, was central to the capitalist system. In addition, any political, economic, or psychological analysis must consider enslavement (exploitation of the labor force by the holders of economic power), the extermination of undesirable sections of the population (blacks, indigenous people, slum dwellers, peasants, poor youth, women), and structural oppression (institutionalized violence against those who resist and struggle against oppression) as determining factors in the Brazilian reality of the 21st century.

We acknowledge that, historically, the Brazilian economic elite has never had to defend its wealth. The power of this elite is guaranteed by private property and by the use of the State for its own exclusive benefit. Therefore, entrepreneurs and landowners, with very few exceptions, remain in political power without the need for a society-mobilizing project, and as there is no collective project, every attempt to propose one on behalf of other groups and social classes are immediately attacked. We understand that the Brazilian economic elite are lazy. However, they hide this this persecutory trait by projecting it onto the general population, especially the poor and the marginalized.

This elite, located geographically in large cities in the Southeast, especially São Paulo and Rio de Janeiro, continuously point out the supposed indolence of the indigenous and/or slowness of the Bahian (people from the state of Bahia, located in the Northeast of Brazil), among others. These assumed defects and "inconveniences," born of horrible prejudices, are viewed as problems to be solved in view of capitalist development (just to mention two of the most unbearable clichés present in the cultural imagination). Ultimately, such view are mere projections, as these characteristics refer to the specific conditions of the owners' enslaved black individuals and land. The elite are always exempt from partaking in hard labor, as it was enough for them to deforest the land, expand the area of agricultural production, and buy slave labor – the abolition of slavery happened only in 1888.

In addition, in rural Brazil it is the possession of land that gives political and economic power, which in turn leads to the *latifundio* (large lands, closer to the idea of *plantation*), often with the violent expulsion of small landowners, making them either rural workers or forcing them to migrate to urban areas. Finally, we emphasize that agribusiness, focused on the foreign market, introduced capitalism into the Brazilian field, but did not alter the social relations typical of slavery and the patriarchal past. Indolence, laziness, and the lack of initiative are often projections of the Brazilian elite, as those historical characteristics belong to those who have been released from intellectual and manual work. This projection makes it look as if these traits were psychological and anthropological traits of all Brazilians and not just a specific social class.[43]

We resort to this aspect of Brazil's historical trajectory to understand the present. The lack of elaboration of the past and the insistence on its idealization made, along with other factors, the rise of fascist tendencies. The groups that felt affected by the democratization of Brazilian society (after the end of the military dictatorship in 1984) attack democracy, education, culture, and science, which they believe are responsible for their social ills and for the relative loss of positions of power that the economic elite historically held.

---

43   We thank Professor Circe Maria Fernandes Bittencourt for the allusion to this explanatory thesis of the historical and social development of Brazil. For further clarification, consult: Sérgio Buarque de Hollanda, *Raízes do Brasil* [Roots of Brasil] (São Paulo: Companhia das Letras, 1995).

This elite insists that Brazil remains a servile and subservient nation and with most of its population subject to the standards that perpetuate social, ethnic-racial, regional, and gender inequality, the elite make use of devices such as the manipulation of facts, threats of violence, and repression to perpetuate that servility. One of the historical features of Brazilian society is the violence practiced against groups and individuals who oppose this social order, often simply because their very existence calls into question social standards and norms.

Viewed within this context, groups and individuals whose existence and practices are the expression of the richness of cultural and human diversity are treated as enemies to be eliminated, precisely because in the last 30 or 40 years they have achieved prominent positions despite the inequality and structural violence of the status quo. Their social and political elevation demonstrates the effectiveness of the efforts made to overcome such conditions. In an intentional (albeit timid) way, the historical situation that gave rise to fascism daily feeds racism, machismo, injustice, and social inequality.

This situation expresses the irrationality contained in the social relations that take place in Brazil. A significant number of people are victimized, assaulted, and raped daily because such people exist in a certain way that is considered subversive, thus threatening the established way of life. Those who practice violence are people who, consciously or unconsciously, do not admit to giving up the position of power they hold or are averse to human differences and diversity. What prevails in this scenario is aggressiveness as a social trend. It is a generalized aggressiveness, because, in a country where the concentration of income has reached extreme levels, those with some position or portion of power also feel attacked because they are always at a disadvantage in relation to someone more privileged.[44]

In short, many Brazilians seem to have the perception that they have been wronged, that they are at the receiving end of some type of aggression, but also

---

44 According to the Human Development Report, 2019, beyond income, beyond averages, beyond the present, inequalities in human development in the 21st century, from the United Nations Development Program (UNDP), Brazil is the second country in the world with the highest concentration of income: the richest 1% hold 28.3% of the socially produced wealth. Available at: http://hdr.undp.org/sites/default/files/hdr_2019_pt.pdf. Access: 12/22/2020. However, Technical Note no. 17/2020, of the National Association of Tax Auditors of the Federal Revenue of Brazil (UNAFISCO Nacional) points out that the situation can be even more serious: about 30% of the assets and net rights declared in the Individual Income Tax belong to only 220,220 taxpayers, which represents 0.1% of the Brazilian population. All of these taxpayers have a total monthly income of more than 80 minimum wages combined. Available at: https://unafisconacional.org.br/wp-content/uploads/2020/09/NT-17-1.pdf. Access: 12/22/2020.

that it is necessary to conform, since they feel powerless to rebel against the situation they live in and against the "powerful people," who are almost never identified. A great effort of self-renunciation and self-repression is necessary, since the understanding is that social order and the law of life have always been as such, with the strongest and most powerful violently subjugating the weak. Few develop an awareness that the situation could be different.

But what has been renounced and repressed remains and at any moment can come out in an explosive, uncontrollable, regressive, and irrational way. All of this seems to lead to the naturalization of sadomasochism as a psychological trait that defines social relationships; one endures pain, one is severe with oneself, because self-preservation depends on sacrifice, which authorizes and justifies the imposition of suffering, pain, and severity upon the other. In March 2023, those who ordered murdering councilwoman Mariele Franco were finally identified, after six years of investigations. They are directly related to Bolsonaro in the political environment. The former president has also been questioned about the secrecy of 100 years imposed on some of his actions, such as the fact that he was probably not vaccinated or supposedly forged his certificate of covid vaccination. Those are examples of the irrationality imposed as a policy and now being unraveled.

Bibliography

Adorno, Theodor W. "Sobre la relación entre sociología y psicología." In *Escritos Sociológicos I*, edited by Rolf Tiedemann, Gretel Adorno, Susan Buck-Morss, Klaus Schultz. Translated by Agustín González Ruiz. Madrid: Akal, 2004.

Adorno, Theodor W. "Antisemitismo y propaganda fascista." In *Escritos Sociológicos I*, edited by Rolf Tiedemann, Gretel Adorno, Susan Buck-Morss, Klaus Schultz. Translated by Agustín González Ruiz. Madrid: Akal, 2004.

Adorno, Theodor W. "La Teoría Freudiana y el modelo de la propaganda fascista." In *Escritos Sociológicos I*, edited by Rolf Tiedemann, Gretel Adorno, Susan Buck-Morss, Klaus Schultz. Translated by Agustín González Ruiz. Madrid: Akal, 2004.

Adorno, Theodor W. "Estudios sobre la personalidad autoritaria." In *Escritos Sociológicos II*, edited by Rolf Tiedemann, Gretel Adorno, Susan Buck-Morss, Klaus Schultz. Translated by Agustín González Ruiz. Madrid: Akal, 2009.

Adorno, Theodor W. "La técnica psicológica de las alocuciones radiofónicas de Martin Luther Thomas." In *Escritos Sociológicos II*, edited by Rolf Tiedemann, Gretel Adorno, Susan Buck-Morss, Klaus Schultz. Translated by Agustín González Ruiz. Madrid: Akal, 2009.

Adorno, Theodor W. "Culpa y represión." In *Escritos Sociológicos II*, edited by Rolf Tiedemann, Gretel Adorno, Susan Buck-Morss, Klaus Schultz. Translated by Agustín González Ruiz. Madrid: Akal, 2011.

Adorno, Theodor W. "Prejuicio y carácter." In *Escritos Sociológicos II*, edited by Rolf Tiedemann, Gretel Adorno, Susan Buck-Morss, Klaus Schultz. Translated by Agustín González Ruiz. Madrid: Akal, 2011.

Adorno, Theodor W. "Bajo el signo de los astros." In *Escritos Sociológicos II*, edited by Rolf Tiedemann, Gretel Adorno, Susan Buck-Morss, Klaus Schultz. Translated by Agustín González Ruiz. Madrid: Akal, 2011.

Gounari, Panayota. "Authoritarianism, Discourse and Social Media: Trump as the 'American Agitator.'" In *Critical Theory and Authoritarian Populism*, edited by Jeremiah Morelock. London: University of Westminster Press, 2018.

Hollanda, Sérgio Buarque de. *Raízes do Brasil*. São Paulo: Companhia das Letras, 1995.

Horkheimer, Max and Theodor W. Adorno. "Família." In *Temas básicos da Sociologia*. Translated by Álvaro Cabral. São Paulo: Cultrix / Ed. da Universidade de São Paulo, 1973.

Simões, Maria Cristina Dancham. *Formação do indivíduo, formação docente e educação especial: o lugar do sujeito e o compromisso com a adaptação*. São Paulo: PUC, 2016.

CHAPTER 10

Reimagining Saudi Arabia: Authoritarian Populism, State Power and Nationalism

Hassan Zaheer

1   Introduction

Authoritarianism and populism are integral components of the state structures in the post-colonial Arab political order. Asserting their distinctive historical experiences, these state structures thrive to cultivate an authentic appeal to the legitimacy and authority of their rule. The attempts by rulers to fuse populism with autocracy have been embodied in three different contexts: (a) personalities (Gamal Abdul Nasser and King Faisal), (b) ideas (pan-Arabism and pan-Islamism), and (c) political parties (Baath Party and the Muslim Brotherhood). With time, this delicate balance between populism and autocracy came under significant tension. In 2011, this tension was manifested in the Arab Spring as the confluence of factors such as economic distress, social conservatism, and political authoritarianism upended the political order.

Witnessing these disturbing happenings across the Arab world, the Kingdom of Saudi Arabia (KSA) sensed the exhaustion of its governing model. Concurrently, the Saudi monarchy underwent a succession with the ascent of King Salman and his son, Crown Prince Mohammed bin Salman (MBS), to the Saudi imperium, which also coincided with the revolting anger in the region. The new elite under the Salman clan intends to herald a new era for the Saudi nation.

Comprehending the limitations of the economic model and state-sponsored welfare system, MBS envisioned a new grand strategic framework for the Saudi state – *Vision 2030*.[1] The vision is not merely imagined as an economic idea to diversify the economy from oil dependence; it encompasses the society as a whole in its consideration. It is intended as a paradigm shift in the very conception of national identity, liberalization in economy and society, and model

---

1   Government of the Kingdom of Saudi Arabia, *Vision 2030*, https://www.vision2030.gov.sa/media/rcob5oy1/saudi_vision2o3.pdf.

of governance. The vision seeks to establish the Saudi state as the modern heart of the Arab world.

In what follows, this chapter intends to examine the paradigm shift envisioned in *Vision 2030* as an authoritarian-populist project – forging a new kind of social contract wherein loyalty of the public especially the younger generation is maintained through socioeconomic liberalization while the political foundations of the ruling order remain undisturbed. It is a project by MBS to reconfigure the Saudi state and society. In its essence, *Vision 2030* seeks to reimagine the core concepts such as nationalism, loyalty, socio-economic development, and practices of royal governance in the primary notions of state power, legitimacy of the rule, and political authority. In studying *Vision 2030* as an authoritarian-populist project, this chapter will apply the theories of the German political theorist Carl Schmitt whose theorization over identity, politics, and law envisages a political order based on a unique expression of the popular will.

Notwithstanding the development of Schmitt's theories in the political context of Weimar Germany, these theories offer a distinctive template for reimagining authoritarian-populist projects in other contexts. The ideas that underpin Schmitt's theories are the great starting point in highlighting the authoritarian populists who do not merely seek to arbitrarily exercise their political power but to construct a longing for themselves in the consciousness of the people. In this sense, Schmitt's theories provide a blueprint that coheres with the authoritarian-populist model underpinning *Vision 2030* and motives that guide MSB's political endeavors.

2 New Politics and New Imaginings

Amidst the perilous era of the Weimar Republic, Carl Schmitt developed a unique comprehension of the political essence concerning identity, law, and the will of the people. His influential writings enshrined these ideas, challenging the dominant liberal ideology and ultimately laying the foundation for contemporary authoritarian populism.[2] Delving deeper into his theoretical

---

2 Carl Schmitt, *The Concept of the Political: Expanded Edition* (Chicago: University of Chicago Press, 2007); Carl Schmitt, *Political Theology: Four Chapters on the Concept of Sovereignty* (Chicago: University of Chicago, 2006); Carl Schmitt, *Constitutional Theory* (Durham: Duke University Press, 2008); Carl Schmitt, *Crisis of Parliamentary Democracy* (Massachusetts: MIT Press, 1988).

contributions, three central concepts emerge: the sovereign leader, political distinction, and the people's will.

In his works, "Political Theology" and "Constitutional Theory," Schmitt delved into the essence of authority and law, offering a distinctive legalist perspective on political power. He argued that the Weimar state's shortcomings could be traced back to its liberal understanding of law and authority. The Weimar constitutional framework, rooted in this liberal approach, was primarily designed for ordinary circumstances, relying on a balance of power among institutions. However, this approach proved inadequate in accounting for exceptional situations, leading to strategic failures within the system.[3]

According to Schmitt, during a severe political crisis, the Weimar constitutional system faltered in upholding law and order due to its inherent structural flaw. In the classical Schmidtian sense, he contended that for any political-legal order to sustain itself in times of exceptional circumstances, a polity must possess a sovereign authority that operates only in times of extreme peril and exists outside the confines of codified legal structures.[4] This sovereign authority serves to protect society from the dangers of disorder, reinforce stability, and restore a sense of normality. Its role is pivotal in determining new laws, emphasizing the importance of its decision-making power rather than the adherence to the content of previous laws.[5]

The sovereign authority operates on behalf of the people and restores normalcy by wielding extra-legal powers, declaring a state of exception, or situational exceptionality. This exceptional state then establishes the framework for new laws. In any political entity, an individual, group, or institution that fulfills these two essential conditions can be deemed the sovereign authority. However, Schmitt's juristic philosophy posits that for a sovereign authority to effectively act in the name of the people, it must first ensure the existence of a political community by defining political distinctions within society. Schmitt further expounds on the political nature of identity and emphasizes the inevitability of perpetual group conflict as essential elements in his theory.

They assume central importance in his conceptions of the political community. For Schmitt, identity triumphs over representation as the society cannot come into being in a politically concrete sense by assuming equality in the rights and status of all people. It follows then that society can only exist in a political sense whenever it introduces conflict into the system. This conflict

---

3   Schmitt, *Political Theology*, 5–35.
4   Schmitt, *Constitutional Theory*, 169–196.
5   Schmitt, *Political Theology*, 33–35.

then defines new identity formations and group relations that create and sustain new forms of social relations and values.

Schmitt's theory of the Concept of the Political revolves around the notions of identity and group conflict. According to him, the foundation of a polity hinges on the establishment of a political distinction, and this distinction is built upon binary concepts of Friend and Enemy. Schmitt emphasizes that the political distinction based on Friend/Enemy represents an associational relationship that stands apart from other associational relations and their respective values in society. These other relationships pertain to economics (profit and loss), religion (virtue and sin), aesthetics (beautiful and ugly), and morality (good and bad).[6] Accordingly, the value that determines the associational relation of *Friend/Enemy* is the "intensity of the degree of animosity and separation between communities." In other words, a political distinction is formed whenever a group of people in society is ready to go to war with other groups for the preservation of their outlook on life.[7] This intensity of animosity gives value to the associational relation of *Friend/Enemy* and leads to the production of political distinction in society. This political distinction then determines concrete meaning to the communal or national existence and forms a political community that is based on notions of nationalism, ethnicity, religion or sectarianism, etc. Building upon his exploration of political distinctions, Schmitt delved further into the nature of enmity in his *Theory of the Partisan*. He posited that there are three types of enemies: conventional, real, and absolute. A conventional enemy is characterized by an antagonistic relationship that adheres to norms and rules, implying a conflict within the framework of established conventions. A real enemy arises when an external force poses a threat to a nation's territory or identity, leading to an antagonistic relation driven by the immediate concern for self-preservation. The absolute enemy represents the most perilous form of enmity as it seeks to overthrow the existing political order entirely, transcending the boundaries of conventional conflicts and posing a significant threat to the established system.

Hence, absolute enemy moreover can only be defeated by applying absolute means.[8] Schmitt emphasizes the significance of the political distinction between Friend and Enemy as a fundamental pillar in any political system. This distinction is deliberately established by the exceptional nature of sovereign authority rather than being an inherent or natural process. The sovereign

---

6 Schmitt, *The Concept of the Political,* 26–27.
7 Ibid., 35–36, 126.
8 Carl Schmitt, *Theory of the Partisan,* trans. G. L. Ulmen (New York: Telos Press Publishing, 2007), 81–95.

authority consciously shapes the character of antagonism within society, working to foster the formation of a cohesive political community. By engaging in this conscious process, the sovereign continually seeks out and identifies enemies, while also reinforcing ideas, norms, behaviors, notions, and artifacts that invigorate nationalist sentiments among the people. This approach enables the cultivation of a sense of unity and collective identity, essential for the stability and continuity of the political order.

Schmitt's emphasis on enacting the people's will become particularly relevant in his works like "Crisis of Parliamentary Democracy" and "Constitutional Theory." Understanding this aspect is crucial as it allows us to draw parallels between his theory and recent political developments among the elite in Saudi Arabia. Schmitt challenges the concept of the people's will based solely on electoral majorities, arguing that such a notion can lead to a form of dictatorship masked under the banner of popular support. According to him, this approach undermines the essence of a political community as it treats all individuals as equal in rights and status, neglecting the necessary distinctions that define a cohesive society. To advance his theory on enacting the people's will, Schmitt stresses the importance of constructing legal frameworks based on the principle of the political community. By doing so, political equality is achieved, aligning the will of the people with the concept of the political community. In Schmitt's perspective, political equality emerges from the shared understanding of the Friend/Enemy distinction within society, forming the very foundation upon which the people's will is realized. In essence, Schmitt's theory suggests that true enactment of the people's will requires acknowledging and fostering political equality through a mutual understanding of the Friend/Enemy distinctions within the community. This shared understanding then becomes the driving force behind shaping political decisions and policies that represent the collective interests of the people.[9]

In the end, to summarize important points in regard to Schmitt's work and as a useful conceptual tool to understand present developments in Saudi Arabia it is important to highlight his impact on some recent authoritarian populists and the notion of populism in general.[10] In recent decades one could see

---

9 Schmitt, *Constitutional Theory*, 255–257.
10 Xie Libin and Haig Patapan, "Schmitt Fever: The use and abuse of Carl Schmitt in contemporary China," *International Journal of Constitutional Law* 18, no. 1 (2020): 130–146; Gabor Meszaros, "Carl Schmitt in Hungary: Constitutional Crisis in the Shadow of Covid-19," *Review of Central and East European Law* 46 (2020): 69–90; Acar Kutay, "From Weimar to Ankara: Carl Schmitt, sovereignty and democracy," *Philosophy and Social Criticism* 45, no. 6 (2019): 728–752; Stefan Auer, "Carl Schmitt in the Kremlin: the Ukraine crisis and the return of geopolitics," *International Affairs* 91, no. 5 (2015): 953–968; John Pincince,

a surge of literature on the nature and definition of populism.[11] In the interest of building a coherent theoretical explanation by relating Schmitt's theorization with populism, I will be referring to the ideational approach to populism which is derived by Cas Mudde and Cristóbal Rovira Kaltwasser. While the term "populism" has been contested as vague and context-dependent, Mudde and Kaltwasser derived a definition that is context-independent and concrete:

> [Populism is a] thin-centered ideology that considers society to be ultimately separated into two homogenous and antagonistic camps, "the pure people" versus "the corrupt elite," and which argues that politics should be an expression of the *volonte generale* (general will) of the people.[12]

What is important to draw from this short excerpt is that their ideational approach identifies three core concepts: the people, the elite, and the general will. According to this definition, a contemporary populist leader thrives to cultivate antagonistic social relations in terms of "us" versus "them," similar to Schmitt's concepts of *"Friend"* and *"Enemy."* Moreover, such an understanding of populist leader directs these variables of "us" or "the people" toward "them" or "the corrupt elite." This creates the core of populist ontology as most of the recent examples of political populism center around these binaries that allow the constitution of political narratives and system of beliefs that nurture public support and sentiments. Additionally, the concept of general will also alludes to Schmitt's idea of people's will in that, as their analysis argued how general will could be identified by having a shared communal understanding of " the corrupt elite" or "the *Enemy*" that would solidify the connection between the ruler and the ruled.[13] Ultimately, while Mudde and Kaltwasser's ideational

---

"De-centering Carl Schmitt: The Colonial State of Exception and the Criminalization of the Political in British India, 1905–1920," *Politica Comun* 5 (2014): 1–18; Joel I. Colon-Rios, "Carl Schmitt and Constituent Power in Latin American Courts: The Cases of Venezuela and Colombia," *Constellations* 18, no. 3 (2011): 365–388.

11 Jan-Werner Muller, *What is Populism?* (Philadelphia: University of Pennsylvania Press, 2016); Ernesto Laclau, *On Populist Reason* (New York: Verso Books, 2007); Thorsten Wojczewski, "'Enemies of the People': Populism and the Politics of (In)security," *European Journal of International Security* 5, no. 1 (2020): 5–24; Maria Esperanza Casullo, "The Body Speaks Before It Even Talks: Deliberation, Populism and Bodily Representation," *Journal of Deliberative Democracy* 16, no. 1 (2020): 27–36; Filipe Carreira da Silva and Monica Brito Vieira, "Populism as a Logic of Political Action," *European Journal of Social Theory* 22, no. 4 (2019): 497–512; Rogers Brubaker, "Why populism," *Theory and Society* 46 (2017): 357–385.
12 Cas Mudde and Cristobal Rovira Kaltwasser, *Populism: A Very Short Introduction* (Oxford: Oxford University Press, 2017), 6.
13 Mudde and Kaltwasser, *Populism*, 9–19.

approach to populism may draw inspiration from Schmitt's theories on identity, authority, and the general will, it is essential to recognize that these theoretical underpinnings play a significant role in explaining MBS's authoritarian-populist model in the subsequent sections.

3 The New Saudi Political

In this section, I examine how MBS's endeavor to cultivate a new nationalism in Saudi Arabia through Vision 2030 involves the establishment of a fresh political distinction, which forms the core of his authoritarian-populist model. This analysis draws insights from Schmitt, Mudde, and Kaltwasser's theorizations on political identity and explores how MBS's new nationalism aligns with their concepts. Through *Vision 2030*, MBS envisions a reconfiguration of identity formations and group relations in Saudi Arabia, laying the groundwork for a novel brand of nationalism. While previous nationalist projects have been undertaken in the kingdom, MBS's commitment to this undertaking sets it apart, representing a paradigmatic departure from previous iterations of Saudi nationalism.[14] Historically, KSA ventured into constructing nationalisms in two different phases that can be termed "religious conservatism" and "pan-Islamism." However, it is important to note that MBS led-nationalism project is distinct from these past two forms of nationalism in three key elements: essence, grand strategic vision, and focused participants.

Looking back, Muhammad ibn Saud, the founder of the Saudi dynasty, embarked on the initial project of religious conservatism. This endeavor entailed a momentous alliance with Muhammad ibn Abd al-Wahhab, a relatively obscure religious preacher situated on the fringes of the Arabian Peninsula. Ibn Saud sought to reclaim the territory that now constitutes modern-day Saudi Arabia from the grasp of the Ottoman Empire. However, to wage an assault against a dominant Muslim imperial power, ibn Saud required religious legitimacy for his political ambitions. Ibn Wahhab, who propagated an exceptionally puritanical version of Islam, later known as Wahhabism, provided this much-needed legitimacy.[15]

---

14   Fatiha Dazi-Heni, "How Mbs Is Rethinking Saudi Nationalism," *Italian Institute for International Political Studies*, May 16, 2019, https://www.ispionline.it/en/pubblicazione/how-mbs-rethinking-saudi-nationalism-23083.

15   Muhammad al-Atawneh, "Is Saudi Arabia a Theocracy? Religion and Governance in Contemporary Saudi Arabia," *Middle Eastern Studies* 45, no. 5 (2009): 721–737; Yury Barmin, "Can Mohammed bin Salman break the Saudi-Wahhabi pact?," *Al Jazeera*,

Through a symbiotic alliance, ibn Saud and ibn Wahhab successfully ousted the Ottomans and laid the foundation for the present-day Saudi state. Consequently, the balance of power in the nascent Saudi nation was delicately maintained, relying on coexistence and tolerance between the Saudi monarchy and the Wahhabi religious establishment. However, this historically preserved equilibrium has not remained without frictions. The second form of nationalism emerged as a response to counter the influence of Arab nationalism during the 1960s-1970s and later, in the 1980s, amid the Iranian revolution. Fearing that the identity rooted in Wahhabism could be at risk, the Saudi state crafted an expanded nationalism, integrating nationalist elements with the earlier Wahhabi identity determinants. This new concept was grounded in pan-Islamism, aiming to export the ideology of Wahhabism to the Muslim world, countering prevailing notions of national identity based on ethnicity and sectarianism. However, MBS's current nationalism project is undermining this export of Wahhabism, signaling a shift in the trajectory of Saudi national identity and its relation to the wider Muslim world.[16]

Looking at the essence, grand strategic vision, and focused participants of these past two types of nationalisms, their longevity and impact on Saudi consciousness were ultimately restricted. In terms of essence, both nationalisms had limited relevance and utility considering the aspirations of present-day Saudis. Particularly, the younger generation no longer feels compelled to adhere to the Wahhabi interpretation of religion or participate in exporting Wahhabism. As a result, these ideologies have become anachronistic and disconnected from the contemporary Saudi mindset. In the element of grand strategic vision, both nationalisms were endowed with an absence of a continued stream of ideas prolonging them. Religious conservatism was merely concerned with crafting domestic legitimacy for both the monarchs and clerics with a pliant citizenry. Consequently, pan-Islamism was imagined as an extension of domestic religious nationalism. The aim was to harness the power of Wahhabism to cultivate a favorable international environment. In this context,

---

January 7, 2018, https://www.aljazeera.com/opinions/2018/1/7/can-mohammed-bin-salman-break-the-saudi-wahhabi-pact.

16   Krithika Varagur, *The Call: Inside the Global Saudi Religious Project* (New York: Columbia Global Reports, 2020); Kim Ghattas, *Black Wave: Saudi Arabia, Iran, and the 40-Year Rivalry that Unraveled Culture, Religion, Collective Memory in the Middle East* (New York: Henry Holt and Co., 2020); Shadi Hamid and Peter Mandaville, "Islam as statecraft: How governments use religion in foreign policy," *Brookings Institution*, November, 2018, https://www.brookings.edu/research/islam-as-statecraft-how-governments-use-religion-in-foreign-policy.

both forms of nationalisms were not interested in disturbing domestic equilibrium and order.[17]

Additionally, the third element, "the focused participants" was poorly developed in the earlier nationalisms. On one hand, religious conservatism was intended for all Saudis without discrimination of demographics. On the other hand, pan-Islamism was intended for foreign participants. The focused participants of both nationalisms were either too broad or too foreign for the public reception. However, the nationalism imagined by MBS to materialize his *Vision 2030* reshapes the contours of these three key elements in constituting new paradigms of identity, belongingness, and group relations in a way that appeals to the popular sentiments. While MBS is not formally borrowing from Schmitt's conception of political distinctions, his policies seem to heavily reflect Schmitt's approach. With approximately 60% of the population in KSA being under 30 years old, MBS's authoritarian-populist model strategically aims to capture and align with the aspirations and ambitions of the youth, effectively designating them as the "Friend" in his political distinction. In contrast, he positions the pillars of the old sociopolitical order, including religious clerics, elder family members (including royals), business and media tycoons, and any opposition to Vision 2030, as the "Enemy." By co-opting the support of the youth and identifying adversaries among the established power structures, MBS seeks to consolidate his authority and bolster his vision for the country.[18]

MBS's authoritarian-populism exhibits a notable parallel with the concepts of Schmitt, Mudde, and Kaltwasser. It aims to identify the "Friend-people" primarily within the youth demographic and considers them integral to the nation's progress, actively participating in Vision 2030. Unlike previous rulers, MBS successfully concretizes the political distinctions by pinpointing a specific constituency within the broader population – the youth – making them

---

17 Madawi Al-Rasheed, "The New Populist Nationalism in Saudi Arabia: Imagined Utopia by Royal Decree," *London School of Economics Middle East Centre Blog*, May 5, 2020, https://blogs.lse.ac.uk/mec/2020/05/05/the-new-populist-nationalism-in-saudi-arabia-imagined-utopia-by-royal-decree; Stasa Salacanin, "New nationalism on the rise in Saudi Arabia," *The New Arab*, August 20, 2019, https://english.alaraby.co.uk/english/indepth/2019/8/20/new-nationalism-on-the-rise%E2%80%8B-in-saudi-arabia.

18 Fahad Nazer, "Saudi youth at centre stage of vision 2030," *The Arab Weekly*, March 26, 2017, https://thearabweekly.com/saudi-youth-centre-stage-vision-2030; Varun Godinho, "Two-thirds of Saudi Arabia's population is under the age of 35," *Gulf Business*, August 10, 2020, https://gulfbusiness.com/two-thirds-of-saudi-arabias-population-is-under-the-age-of-35/; Furthermore, in their work on populism, Mudde and Kaltwasser identified *people* as having been socially constructed and having three meanings: as sovereign, as the common people, and as the nation, *Populism*, p. 9.

the core of his popular support group. He recognizes the need to deliver tangible results and benefits to this youth demographic as they form the backbone of his backing and the driving force behind his political vision.[19] MBS crafted an effective *essence* to his nationalism that continually generate popular support and appeal for his reforms.

> Our country is rich in its natural resources. We are not dependent solely on oil for our energy needs. Gold, phosphate, uranium, and many other valuable minerals are found beneath our lands. But our real wealth lies in the ambition of our people and the potential of our younger generation.[20]

In his grand strategic vision, MBS's new nationalism presents a transformative vision to the people, envisioning a complete reconfiguration of state-society relations. Central to this vision is the integration of youth aspirations as a core priority, aligning them with the goals of Vision 2030 to foster a conducive environment for progress and development. With this goal in mind, MBS is implementing significant political measures to disrupt the power equilibrium and consolidate authority, a departure from previous rulers' approaches. Consequently, the primary participants in this political endeavor are the Saudi youth, envisioned as active participants for whom his reforms are specifically intended. They play a central role in shaping the direction and success of his transformative initiatives.

> We commit ourselves to providing world-class government services which effectively and efficiently meet the needs of our citizens. Together we will continue building a better country, fulfilling our dream of prosperity and unlocking the talent, potential, and dedication of our young men and women.[21]

Through the establishment of new contours of his envisioned form of nationalism, MBS deliberately aims to reintroduce conflict into the Saudi social

---

19　Annalisa Pavan, ""The Sky is the Limit": Saudi Youth in a Changing Kingdom, Beyond Narratives, Interpretations and Misperceptions," *World Journal of Social Science*, 8, no. 2 (2021): 1–12; Kristin Smith Diwan, "Youth Appeal of Saudi Vision 2030," *The Arab Gulf States Institute in Washington*, May 6, 2016, https://agsiw.org/youth-appeal-of-saudi-vision-2030.

20　Government of the Kingdom of Saudi Arabia, *Vision 2030*, pg. 5, https://www.vision2030.gov.sa/media/rc0b5oy1/saudi_vision203.pdf.

21　Ibid., 6.

fabric, reshaping group relations and intensifying antagonism between them. This strategic move by MBS seeks to pave the way for a transformed Saudi political landscape, redefining power dynamics and societal interactions in pursuit of his ambitious vision. In cultivating the youth-based constituency, MBS embarked upon a fundamental revision of laws and behaviors in terms of culture, religion, and entertainment. When climbing up the ladder of monarchical hierarchy, MBS curbed the powers of the much-dreaded religious police, allowed women to drive and associated relaxation of rules, opened cinemas and other entertainment avenues, allowed mixed social gatherings, and sponsored concerts.[22] By loosening historically present socio-economic restrictions, MBS seeks to buy their loyalty through liberalization while keeping the foundations of political authoritarianism intact.

As Schmitt has theorized, a political distinction of *Friend/Enemy* does not necessitate that both should not share any kind of relationship. For instance, in this associational relation, *Friend/Enemy* could be economic competitors or have social relations but the value of the *Enemy* emanates from its nature of being a "stranger," something "foreign," which entails a possibility of intense existential conflict with it.[23] In the Saudi context, the degree of animosity between the Saudi youth and the older population does not motivate group conflict on the streets, but a possibility of an existential conflict between them is always there as the younger generation abhors the social codes of "the old guards."[24] Moreover, this "strangeness" of the political *Enemy* also extends to the historiography of the modern state. Besides the markedly visible changes to culture, MBS is also striving to cultivate a new Saudi past that also takes pride in its pre-Islamic archaeological sites. This secular identification with history started with former Kings Fahd and Abdullah but the power MBS currently exercises allows him to fuse this secular identification with the new contours of national identity and project a modern face of the kingdom.[25] This

---

22   Aseel Bashraheel, "Rise and fall of the Saudi religious police," *Arab News*, September 23, 2019, https://www.arabnews.com/node/1558176/saudi-arabia; Yaroslav Trofimov, "A Social Revolution in Saudi Arabia," *Wall Street Journal*, November 15, 2019, https://www.wsj.com/articles/a-social-revolution-in-saudi-arabia-11573833669.
23   Schmitt, *Concept of the Political*, 27.
24   Hana Al-Khamri, "Why did Saudi Arabia lift the driving ban on women only now?," *Al Jazeera*, June 24, 2018, https://www.aljazeera.com/opinions/2018/6/24/why-did-saudi-arabia-lift-the-driving-ban-on-women-only-now.
25   Rosie Bsheer, *Archive Wars: The Politics of History in Saudi Arabia* (Redwood City, CA: Stanford University Press, 2020); Noor Nugali, "Saudi Arabia rich with undiscovered archeological sites," *Arab News*, January 27, 2019, https://www.arabnews.com/node/1441401/saudi-arabia.

new identification with history also incorporates the authoritarian method of historical revisionism. It features prominently in the rewriting of the textbooks alongside presenting a moderate version of religion.[26]

> We take immense pride in the historical and cultural legacy of our Saudi, Arab, and Islamic heritage. Our land was, and continues to be, known for its ancient civilizations and trade routes at the crossroads of global trade. This heritage has given our society the cultural richness and diversity it is known for today. We recognize the importance of preserving this sophisticated heritage in order to promote national unity and consolidate true Islamic and Arab values.[27]

Moreover, as a mindful authoritarian-populist, MBS recognizes the globalizing power of media in influence operations and projection of nationalist narratives. To this end, KSA constructed the digital influence machine to browbeat criticism of the Kingdom's domestic and foreign policies, shape narratives and conversations, and craft a new image of the Kingdom in the digital world for audiences everywhere. The man behind this digital influence machine was Saud al-Qahtani. He created the virtual juggernaut to project Saudi power and narrative and unleashes a sort of digital nationalist puritanism to publicly shame and punish those state and non-state actors who are not buying into the promise of reforms.[28]

This machine also introduces a new label for dissenters in the public consciousness – traitor. This labeling itself reflects the shifting dynamics of nationalism, as dissenters were previously characterized in religious terms. Schmitt argued that to eliminate the political Enemy, a fresh "pacifist vocabulary" should be created to designate the Enemy as someone existing outside the norm and deserving condemnation. Similarly, under MBS's populism, there has been a transformation in political vocabulary, shifting from religious connotations to nationalist ones. The term "traitor" holds significant weight in

---

26   Najah Al-Otaibi, "Vision 2030: Religious Education Reform in the Kingdom of Saudi Arabia," *King Faisal Center for Research and Islamic Studies*, September, 2020, https://kfcris.com/pdf/cc53a3201f65554c400886325b5f715e5f577d35934f7.pdf; Eman Alhussein, "New Saudi Textbooks Put Nation First," *The Arab Gulf States Institute in Washington*, October 17, 2019, https://agsiw.org/new-saudi-textbooks-put-nation-first.

27   Government of the Kingdom of Saudi Arabia, *Vision 2030*, pg. 16 https://www.vision2030.gov.sa/media/rc0b50y1/saudi_vision2o3.pdf.

28   Katie Benner, Mark Mazzetti, Ben Hubbard, and Mike Isaac, "Saudis' Image Makers: A Troll Army and A Twitter Insider," *New York Times*, October 20, 2018, https://www.nytimes.com/2018/10/20/us/politics/saudi-image-campaign-twitter.html.

fostering solidarity among the people, compelling them to distance themselves from critical voices and effectively excluding dissenters from the national community. This concept is powerfully mobilizing, enforcing a sense of unity and loyalty among the people, and promoting conformity to the dominant nationalist narrative.[29]

These political actions exemplify the emergence of new symbols and identifiers in the transforming landscape of KSA under MBS's authoritarian populism. Following Mudde and Kaltwasser's concept of the meaning of the people, MBS is actively shaping and socially constructing a new nation based on a notion of nationalism that revolves around their allegiance to Vision 2030 – a unified national community driven by a grand vision for the future.

> We will endeavor to strengthen, preserve and highlight our national identity so that it can guide the lives of future generations. We will do so by keeping true to our national values and principles, as well as by encouraging social development and upholding the Arabic language. We will continue to work on the restoration of national, Arab, Islamic and ancient cultural sites and strive to have them registered internationally to make them accessible to everyone and, in the process, create cultural events and build world-class museums which will attract visitors from near and far. This will create a living witness to our ancient heritage, showcasing our prominent place in history and on the map of civilizations.[30]

These actions involving the shifting of socio-cultural codes, altering historiography, and introducing a nationalistic vocabulary to the discourses align closely with Schmitt's concept of the political Enemy – a formidable adversary in a political conflict. According to Schmitt, for intense antagonism to arise, the political Enemy must be portrayed as a "collectivity of people." Conflict only emerges when such a collectivity confronts another comparable collectivity. Consequently, the political Enemy, in this context, becomes a public enemy that fosters a shared perception of the Enemy between the ruler and

---

29   Vivian Nereim, "'Traitor' is the new 'Infidel' as Nationalism Grips Saudi Arabia," *Bloomberg*, March 3, 2019, https://www.bloomberg.com/news/articles/2019-03-03/-traitor-is-the-new-infidel-as-nationalism-grips-saudi-arabia; Martin Chulov, "Saudi crown prince signals new purge with 'treason' arrests," *The Guardian*, March 7, 2020, https://www.theguardian.com/world/2020/mar/07/saudi-crown-prince-in-new-purge-with-treason-arrests.

30   Government of the Kingdom of Saudi Arabia, *Vision 2030*, pg. 16 https://www.vision2030.gov.sa/media/rc0b5oy1/saudi_vision203.pdf.

the ruled. This shared perception forms the foundation of the political distinctions found in MBS's new nationalism.

4   Forging a New Elite Consensus

Determination of the *Sovereign Authority* is one of the paramount concerns for Schmitt. In order to establish a new normal in KSA, MBS needed to confront intra-royal opposition, clerical establishment, and embedded interest groups in bureaucracy, businesses and other elites. This section underscores how MBS confronted the preexisting state of normality in the kingdom and turned it into a state of exception to fulfill his objectives of centralized power and authority. Historically, moderation dictated the governing model of KSA. It established a high degree of certainty that was necessary for the orderly functioning of the state. Notions of consensus, seniority and balancing were the predominant features of the Saudi statecraft before the ascension of the Salman clan to the throne.[31] The delicate practice of power, authority, and decision-making enabled the state to traverse global challenges such as the Iranian revolution, the dissolution of the Soviet Union, and the war on terror with a great degree of monarchical coherence and stability.

In the Schmidtian context, the Saudi state was existing in a state of normality. By exercising governing notion of consensus-building and decentralized practice of power, monarchy in unison with clerics and other elites in business and bureaucracy negated the need to induct norms and practices that appreciated changing global environment. The ascension of the Salman clan upended this delicate understanding among the Saudi elites – and between Saudi elites and the *people* – by exercising sovereign logic in the Schmidtian sense.[32]

As Schmitt argued: whenever an individual, a group, or an institution perceives extreme peril to stability and order, they act in the people's name in pronouncing a state of exception and subsequently determine a new normal. This is where the sovereign authority lies. Schmitt captured this profound meaning of sovereign authority in his famous dictum, "Sovereign is he who decides on the state of exception."[33] Although the Saudi elites were aware of the

---

31   Christopher M. Davidson, *From Sheikhs to Sultanism: Statecraft and Authority in Saudi Arabia and UAE* (Oxford: Oxford University Press, 2021).
32   Ben Hubbard, *MBS: The Rise to Power of Mohammed bin Salman* (New York: Tim Duggan Books, 2020); Bradley Hope and Justin Scheck, *Blood and Oil: Mohammed bin Salman's Ruthless Quest for Global Power* (Paris: Hachette Books, 2020).
33   Schmitt, *Political Theology*, 5.

consequences of relying on an oil-dependent economic model, they were hesitant to disrupt the traditional power balance within the state structure. In the context of elites, Mudde and Kaltwasser proposed that populist perceptions of elites tend to be diverse, with the definition of "elites" evolving in response to changing circumstances. Populists may categorize elites based on factors such as power, economics, and culture. However, these categories are not rigidly separate, as over time, populist determinations of elites tend to encompass elements from all these categories, creating overlaps and complexities in their characterization. Acting as a Schmidtian sovereign, MBS perceived traditional power relations and balances within the state structure as detrimental to the implementation of *Vision 2030*. He pronounced a state of exception and determined that, foremost, *elites* within the royal family had to be weakened for the centralization of power in his own hands. These royal *elites* were targeted as the first ones to be weakened in MBS populist mind owing to their high potential in mounting an intra-royal opposition against him and *Vision 2030*. As MBS ascended to the position of the crown prince, he initiated the first mega purge in detaining royals on the charges of graft and abuse of power, charges which were demonstrably not unfounded.[34]

This episode shocked the foundations of the traditional balance of power and led to some commentators equating it with *"Night of the Long Knives."*[35] This detention of royal *elites* continues under the authoritarian system of the crown prince as evident in the latest round of detentions wherein state authorities detained senior members of the royal family.[36] Moreover, corruption charge is a favorite tool in the inventory of authoritarian populists in undermining their political opposition.[37] This charge has been used extravagantly by MBS in the successive purges in the power structure that included clerics, business moguls, media tycoons, military personnel, intellectuals, and activists, etc.

---

34 Madwai Al-Rasheed, *The Son King: Reform and Repression in Saudi Arabia* (Oxford: Oxford University Press, 2021); Samia Nakhoul, Angus McDowall, and Stephen Kalin, "A house divided: How Saudi Crown Prince purged royal family rivals," *Reuters*, November 10, 2017, https://www.reuters.com/article/us-saudi-arrests-crownprince-insight-idUSKB N1DA23M.

35 Pepe Escobar, "The inside story of the Saudi night of long knives," *Asia Times*, November 6, 2017, https://asiatimes.com/2017/11/inside-story-saudi-night-long-knives.

36 David D. Kirkpatrick, Ben Hubbard, and Eric Schmitt, "Roundup of Saudi Royals Expands With Detention of a 4th Prince," *New York Times*, March 7, 2020, https://www.nytimes.com/2020/03/07/world/middleeast/saudi-arabia-mohammed-bin-salman.html.

37 Alessandra Foresta, "The rise of populist parties in the aftermath of a massive corruption scandal," *Public Choice* 184 (2020): 289–306; Dalibor Rohac, Sahana Kumar, and Andreas Johansson Heino, "The wisdom of demagogues: institutions, corruption and support for authoritarian populists," *Economic Affairs* 37, no. 3 (2017): 382–396.

In his power consolidation mode, MBS followed this approach in his offense against the clergy and religious establishment. After taming intra-royal opposition, the second pillar in the power hierarchy that could hinder MBS's modernizing vision was the clerical establishment and their expansive entrenchment in the power structure. In recognition of their entrenchment, MBS did a first swift strike with a shakedown of the clergy, detaining many clerics, and announcing a reformist vision of religion that is to be followed by the kingdom in the future.[38]

> The principles of Islam will be the driving force for us to realize our Vision. The values of moderation, tolerance, excellence, discipline, equity, and transparency will be the bedrock of our success.[39]

> Our Vision is a strong, thriving, and stable Saudi Arabia that provides opportunity for all. Our Vision is a tolerant country with Islam as its constitution and moderation as its method. We will welcome qualified individuals from all over the world and will respect those who have come to join our journey and our success.[40]

Signifying his new authoritarian-populist model, MBS curbed the powers of the religious police thereby broadening his appeal in the consciousness of the youth. Subsequently, he also detained popular preachers such as Ali al-Omari, Awad al-Qarni, and Musa al-Qarni who recently died in detention allegedly from torture.[41] Additionally, the influence of the Saudi state under MBS is such that Twitter recently suspended accounts and removed verification of

---

38   Susanne Koelbl, *Behind the Kingdom's Veil: Inside the New Saudi Arabia under Crown Prince Mohammed bin Salman* (Miami: Mango Publishers, 2020); Simon Mabon, "It's a Family Affairs: Religion, Geopolitics and the Rise of Mohammed bin Salman," *Insight Turkey* 20, no. 2 (2018): 51–66; Yasmine Faroukh and Nathan J. Brown, "Saudi Arabia's Religious Reforms Are Touching Nothing but Changing Everything," *Carnegie Endowment*, 2021, https://carnegieendowment.org/research/2021/06/islamic-institutions-in-arab-states-mapping-the-dynamics-of-control-co-option-and-contention#saudi-arabias-religious-reforms-are-touching-nothing-but-changing-everything.

39   Government of the Kingdom of Saudi Arabia, *Vision 2030*, pg. 15 https://www.vision2030.gov.sa/media/rc0b50y1/saudi_vision203.pdf.

40   Ibid., pg. 6.

41   "Killing of jailed reformer Musa al-Qarni highlights use of torture in Saudi prisons," *MENA Rights Group*, October 19, 2021; http://menarights.org/en/articles/killing-jailed-reformer-musa-al-qarni-highlights-use-torture-saudi-prisons; "Who are the key Sahwa figures Saudi Arabia is cracking down on?," *Al Jazeera*, June 5, 2019, https://www.aljazeera.com/features/2019/6/5/who-are-the-key-sahwa-figures-saudi-arabia-is-cracking-down-on.

religious scholars stripping them of their outreach.[42] The crackdown on clergy resultantly was a populist endeavor akin to the crackdown on the royal family. It was, and still is with the continued crackdowns, a most palpably potent symbol in the authoritarian-populist approach to redefining the balance of power with – and between – monarchs and clergy.[43] It ensures that they would not protest or even offer the mildest criticism of *Vision 2030* and articulate their loyalty to the modernizing vision.

Accordingly, as Schmitt theorized, by subduing the two critical pillars of power and authority in KSA, MBS effectively shaped a new juristic reality and gave birth to a new normal. The pivotal authority, as Schmitt argued, cultivates a new determination of law in the nation. Empowered by the state of exception, the new sovereign authority acts as a constituent power in shaping new contours of permissibility in discourses and practices. This power is accorded to the constituent sovereign authority by his very act of *decisive action* in times of extreme peril and salvaging the nation from impending calamity.[44] Simultaneously, these crackdowns on royals and clerics were also in the context of populist determination of *elites* by MBS in terms of power and economics as both of these pillars held significant clout over state structures of law and finance.

However, MBS authoritarianism does not halt at the subduing of these two pillars. By shaking up the traditional balance of power and shaping a new juristic reality, MBS seeks ubiquitous loyalty and submission to his modernizing vision and policies from all segments of society. The focus is to embed the new juristic reality in the popular consciousness, which stretches beyond the royals and the clerics. In this view, the subject of the third wave of MBS crackdown was the women's rights activists, most of whom were demanding to uplift the ban on women driving which the state eventually did. However, the crackdown on women activists by the state was more informed by pragmatic thinking, as it does not want to highlight the impression that political action could work. The Saudi state shifted the narrative, claiming that it lifted the ban on women

---

42 "Twitter suspends accounts, removes verification of Saudi political prisoners," *Middle East Eye*, February 9, 2021, https://www.middleeasteye.net/news/saudi-arabia-twitter-jailed-scholars-verification-removed.

43 Sarah Dadouch, "Saudi Crown Prince Mohammed seeks to reduce influential clerics' power," *Washington Post*, August 3, 2021, https://www.washingtonpost.com/world/middle_east/saudi-clerics-crown-prince-mohammed/2021/08/02/9ae796a0-e3ed-11eb-88c5-4fd6382c47cb_story.html; David Ottaway, "Saudi Crown Prince Lambasts His Kingdom's Wahhabis Establishment," *Wilson Center*, May 6, 2021, https://www.wilsoncenter.org/article/saudi-crown-prince-lambasts-his-kingdoms-wahhabi-establishment.

44 Schmitt, *Political Theology*, 13–35.

driving to promote their equal participation in the economy under Vision 2030. However, despite this claim, the continued detention of women activists even after the ban was lifted seemed to serve the purpose of instilling fear and ensuring obedience to the new power structure in Riyadh.[45]

Similarly, in the fourth wave of arrests, Saudi authorities detained nearly 300 officials including civil servants and military personnel on the allegations of corruption and embezzlement. In between these four waves of crackdowns, there were intermittent attacks on intellectuals, ministers, businesses, activists, and royals on varied notions of undermining public order, graft, and bribery.[46] The pattern of crackdowns reflects MBS's approach to governance, wherein the state promises social and economic liberalization in return for the people's compliance to relinquish political freedoms and refrain from voicing criticism against the current government's policies. This trade-off positions the state as the guarantor of certain liberties while imposing restrictions on political dissent and critical expression.

It is in this reasoning that MBS's dealing with the opposition is often wrapped in the rhetoric of anti-corruption. Besides the necessity of curbing corruption for reforms, the rhetoric of anti-corruption appeals to the public consciousness as they bore the brunt of the rampant corruption in the kingdom for decades.[47] Moreover, the MBS modernization drive is intended to buy the loyalty of the *people* and harness it against the old *elites*. His introduction of the new judicial, labor, and guardianship laws opened new avenues of entertainment, leisure, and arts, as well as diversified the kingdom's investment

---

45 Deborah L. Wheeler, "Saudi Women Driving Change? Rebranding, Resistance and the Kingdom of Change," *The Journal of the Middle East and Africa* 11, no. 1 (2020): 87–109; Najamuddin Khairur Rijal and Rizka Zahrotun Khoirina, "The Roles of Civil Society to Changing of Women Driving Policy in Saudi Arabia: The Case of Women2Drive Campaign," *Islamic World and Politics* 3, no. 1 (2019): 435–447.

46 Tuqa Khalid, "Saudi Arabia arrests 32 in corruption case worth $3 billion," *Al Arabiya English*, January 27, 2021, https://english.alarabiya.net/News/gulf/2021/01/28/Saudi-Arabia-arrests-32-in-corruption-case-worth-3-billion; "Saudi king sacks two royals under defence corruption probe," *Reuters*, September 16, 2020, https://www.reuters.com/article/saudi-king-defense-int-idUSKBN25R2YA; "New Saudi anti-corruption chief to target public servants," *Reuters*, September 1, 2019, https://www.reuters.com/article/us-saudi-corruption-idUSKCN1VM10X.

47 David Gardner, "Visions of Mohammed bin Salman – the reality and the fantasy," *Financial Times*, October 12, 2020, https://www.ft.com/content/ffe2f60f-06da-4716-af4a-b06f631f391c; Kristin Smith Diwan, "The Big Gamble of Mohammed bin Salman – and Saudi Arabia," *The Arab Gulf States Institute in Washington*, March 23, 2020, https://agsiw.org/the-big-gamble-of-mohammed-bin-salman-and-saudi-arabia.

portfolio in youth-intensive industries such as sports, video games, and film studios.⁴⁸

> We will expand the variety of digital services to reduce delays and cut tedious bureaucracy. We will immediately adopt wide-ranging transparency and accountability reforms and, through the body set up to measure the performance of government agencies, hold them accountable for any shortcomings.⁴⁹

Concurrently, in the populist determination of *elites* by Mudde and Kaltwasser, these crackdowns represent the heterogeneous nature of *elites* in the populist mind of MBS. In the crackdowns on royals, power and economics were the primary determinants. However, in subsequent attacks on clerics and state officials, culture is incorporated alongside power and economics as a determinant factor in constructing an image of these *elites* as the guardians of the traditional power structure recalcitrant to reforms and embracing *Vision 2030*.

Drawing from Schmitt's theories on different types of enemies, the animosity between MBS's new order and the old guards can be categorized into two contexts: real and absolute. As mentioned earlier, any intrusive force that threatens the notions of identity or land, whether domestic or foreign, establishes an antagonistic relationship and falls under the category of the real enemy. The rest of society is then mobilized against this real enemy. On the other hand, the absolute enemy seeks a complete reordering of the established

---

48 "Only Saudis can work in malls as local hiring drive accelerates," *Arab News*, April 9, 2021, https://www.arabnews.com/node/1839156/business-economy; Hala Tashkandi, "Saudi cinema chain announces $218.6m expansion plan," *Arab News*, April 4, 2021, https://www.arabnews.com/node/1837406/business-economy; Dimah Talal Al-Sharif, "Labor Reform Initiative to help boost Saudi Arabia's private sector," *Arab News*, March 17, 2021, https://www.arabnews.com/node/1826736; Scott Mitchell, "F1's Saudi deal will run for 'a decade, if not longer,'" *The Race*, February 25, 2021, https://the-race.com/formula-1/f1s-saudi-deal-will-run-a-decade-if-not-longer/; "Saudi PIF acquires $3.3bn stake in US video-game makers," *Arab News*, February 17, 2021, https://www.arabnews.com/node/1810896/business-economy; Ismaeel Naar, "Saudi Crown Prince announces 4 new laws to reform Kingdom's judicial institutions," *Al Arabiya English*, February 8, 2021, https://english.alarabiya.net/News/gulf/2021/02/08/Saudi-Vision-2030-Saudi-Crown-Prince-announces-reforms-to-improve-legislative-environment; Reem Krimly, "Revamped guardianship laws under in a new era for Saudi women," *Al Arabiya English*, August 3, 2019, https://english.alarabiya.net/features/2019/08/03/Revamped-guardianship-laws-usher-in-a-new-era-for-Saudi-women.

49 Government of the Kingdom of Saudi Arabia, *Vision 2030*, pg. 6 https://www.vision2030.gov.sa/media/rc0b50y1/saudi_vision203.pdf.

political order or the preservation of the old order against the new one. In both contexts, MBS's authoritarian-populism perceives these challenges from elites within the royal family, business, clergy, media, military, and bureaucracy, and categorizes them accordingly to facilitate their elimination, all while empowering the sense of sovereign authority.

As Schmitt postulated in his theories, MBS's actions of bringing both the royal monarchy and clergy into submission to his Vision 2030 reflect a classic Schmidtian approach. By doing so, he establishes himself as a new sovereign authority within the power structure, redefining political distinctions and creating a new consensus among the elite. MBS's actions resonate with Schmitt's concept of a strong leader who wields significant influence and power to shape the political landscape and forge a united front among the ruling class.

5 Identifying with the Saudi Will

One of the most crucial aspects of authoritarian populists lies in their strong identification with "the people" against the perceived "corrupt elite." This identification empowers them to tap into the force of the "general will" and utilize it to bring about a new order. Embracing the people's will become a potent tool in the playbook of authoritarian populists, enabling them to reshape existing power structures often for their own gain. MBS follows a similar playbook, harnessing the power of the "general will" to realize his Vision 2030. In doing so, his approach bears the hallmarks of the ideas put forth by Schmitt, Mudde, and Kaltwasser, aligning with the framework of his authoritarian-populist model.

In a Schmidtian sense, MBS actively seeks to enact and uphold the *Saudi Will* by fostering a process of will-formation and identification through the use of symbolism and iconography. The cornerstone of MBS's populism lies in his grand myth that is encapsulated in Vision 2030. This vision imparts a sense of historical significance to the Saudi people and a renewed focus on a historical mission termed as "The Great Rejuvenation of the Saudi Nation." Given the monarchical nature of the state structure, there are no democratic elections to determine the general will leading MBS to employ an intriguing and unique practice in the pursuit of will-formation and identification. This practice is representative in nature and responsive in its actions. It is anchored in the reforms that have reshaped the political distinctions within society, as discussed earlier. Through these transformative reforms and visionary projects, MBS endeavors to forge a collective sense of identity and purpose among the Saudi people and consolidating the *Saudi Will*.

The antagonistic political distinction of Friend/Enemy serves as a crucial prerequisite for enacting the general will, as it fosters political equality. This concept aligns with Mudde and Kaltwasser's argument about the populist determination of the general will. They suggest that populism follows a unique logic that gives rise to a strong and unified identity of the "popular subject" that challenges the perceived "corrupt elite." Once the political distinction is established, the question of political equality naturally arises. According to Schmitt, political equality is established in society whenever there is a shared understanding between the sovereign authority and the people regarding the political distinction. In other words, whenever the ruler and the ruled share a common view about who belongs in the categories of *"the people"* and *"the corrupt elite,"* it establishes political equality in society. In a similar vein, the sovereign authority of MBS and the *people* have a shared sense of who belongs to the *National Self* and who is the political *Enemy*, therefore creating political equality.[50]

Having established political equality in the Saudi context, the task of generating the general will become relatively straightforward, as any measures or actions undertaken by MBS in the name of the people are representative of the enacted *Saudi Will*. MBS endeavors to align himself with the *Saudi Will* by shaping his persona, reforms, and projects around ideas and symbols that resonate with the youth. His reforms, particularly those aimed at expanding opportunities, are specifically designed to engage the nation's youth as a central reference point. This novel approach of envisioning Saudi citizens as active participants in national life is unprecedented in the history of KSA. It marks a significant shift from viewing citizens as passive subjects under a monarchy to recognizing them as an engaged and responsive citizenry within an authoritarian state. MBS's calculated approach serves two primary purposes: firstly, it seeks to generate popular appeal among the youth constituency for his persona, and secondly, it aims to harness this popular appeal to sustain and uphold the general will.

Among the most palpable expressions of this approach in identification with the *Saudi Will* is the state-led instrumentalization of entertainment festivals organized by the General Entertainment Authority (GEA). For the first time in the kingdom's history, KSA organized a music festival, MDL Beast, where the youth of the nation danced to the tunes of world-renowned artists such as David Guetta, Tiesto, and Martin Garrix amongst many others. One of the most significant features of the festival was the dedication of a music tune

---

50 Schmitt, *Constitutional Theory*, 255–257.

to the new monarchs – the Salman clan.⁵¹ More recently, GEA organized the Riyadh Season festival which has an extensive itinerary of international shows including music, games, jewelry, toys, performing arts, a WWE championship, and a car show. It is an annual festival season held over five months. In the 2021 iteration, music artist Pitbull held a sold-out concert, and three million visitors came to the festival only in the first month. Considering the enormous potential in investment, publicity, image reshaping, and entertainment with far-reaching dividends, KSA announced an investment of $64 billion in the entertainment sector.⁵² Subsequently, these festivals are not just a form of economic opportunity, rather they are crucial tool for the authoritarian populism of MBS as they develop a direct relationship between the reigning monarchs and their youthful citizens.

As a result, MBS is keenly aware of the power of imagery. In his pursuit of becoming the primary symbol in the minds of Saudi youth, MBS portrays himself as a youthful and perceptive monarch whenever he participates in global events and meetings. His deliberate actions involve ensuring extensive media coverage of his engagements with people and events that resonate with the aspirations of the youth. By carefully crafting and promoting this image, MBS aims to establish a strong connection with the younger generation and position himself as a leader who understands and represents their desires and aspirations. An example is one of the tours of MBS to the United States in which he made sure that his engagement with the technologists of the Silicon Valley was comprehensively reported in the press with a profusion of images.⁵³ Consonant to the populist conduct of image-making and attentive to the yearning of the youth, MBS attended Formula E in the Saudi city of Diriyah and the Formula

---

51 "MDL Beast announces groundbreaking debut festival Riyadh," *Arab News*, December 5, 2019, https://www.arabnews.com/node/1594391/lifestyle; Michelle Cioffoletti, "Saudi Arabia Sings a Nationalist Tune," *The Arab Gulf States Institute in Washington*, January 7, 2019, https://agsiw.org/saudi-arabia-sings-a-nationalist-tune/.

52 Lojien Ben Gassem, "Riyadh Season welcomes 3 million visitors during first month since launch," *Arab News*, November 21, 2021, https://www.arabnews.com/node/1972506/saudi-arabia; Josh Wilson, "Saudi Arabia To Invest $64 Billion In Its Entertainment Sector," *Forbes*, November 9, 2021, https://www.forbes.com/sites/joshwilson/2021/11/09/saudi-arabia-to-invest-64-billion-in-its-entertainment-sector; "250, 000 witnessed Pitbull exceptional concert in Riyadh Season 2021 opening," *Saudi Gazette*, October 21, 2021, https://saudigazette.com.sa/article/612490; Lojien Ben Gassem, "Rap star Pitbull to launch Riyadh Season with sold-out concert," *Arab News*, October 20, 2021, https://www.arabnews.com/node/1951251/saudi-arabia.

53 Shirin Ghaffary, "Photos: The Saudi Crown Prince met with tech VIPs this week in Silicon Valley, including Sergey Brin and Magic Leap's CEO," *Vox*, April 6, 2018, https://www.vox.com/2018/4/6/17206358/saudi-crown-prince-visit-tech-silicon-valley.

F1 Grand Prix finale in Abu Dhabi. Indeed, the rationale behind MBS attendance partially had to do with the usual attendance of the high-profile figures from the world of finance, entertainment, and politics in these racing events. However, it is also related to the populist image-making process of MBS as these racing events are also markers of youth aspirations.[54]

Another important aspect of MBS's populism is that it also extends to the economic sphere. When the kingdom introduced a value-added tax, there were speculations that an income tax might follow. In response, MBS swiftly addressed the public concern, reassuring citizens that the VAT is merely a temporary measure and that KSA has no intention of implementing income tax. This response exemplifies MBS's populist approach, as he prioritized addressing public worries and offering reassurance, even if it meant putting aside necessary economic reforms.[55] MBS's economic reforms are carefully tailored to resonate with the aspirations of the Saudi youth. To achieve this, he focuses on generating employment opportunities in the private sector, promoting environmentally friendly initiatives like the Green Saudi project, and empowering women to play a more prominent role in Saudi public life. These measures are unmistakably designed to align with the interests and desires of the Saudi youth and demonstrate MBS's efforts to connect with and represent their ambitions.[56]

---

54 "MBS flags off Formula E race," *Saudi Gazette*, November 22, 2019, https://saudigazette.com.sa/article/583218/SAUDI-ARABIA/MBS-flags-off-Formula-E-race; "MBS attends Abu Dhabi F1 Grand Prix finale," *Saudi Gazette*, December 1, 2019, https://saudigazette.com.sa/article/583899.

55 "No plans for income tax, VAT increase is temporary: Saudi Crown Prince Mohammed bin Salman," *Arab News*, April 28, 2021, https://www.arabnews.com/node/1850091/business-economy.

56 Liliane Tannoury, "Start of regional league ushers in new era for women's football in Saudi Arabia," *Arab News*, November 21, 2021, https://www.arabnews.com/node/1972281/sport; Reem Krimly, "Females can register for Hajj with other women without male guardian: Saudi ministry," *Al Arabiya English*, June 14, 2021, https://english.alarabiya.net/News/gulf/2021/06/14/Women-can-register-for-Hajj-with-other-women-without-male-guardian-Saudi-ministry; Deema Al-Khudair, "'An honor and duty:' Meet the female Saudi officers guarding the Prophet's Mosque in Madinah," *Arab News*, April 29, 2021, https://www.arabnews.com/node/1850621/saudi-arabia; "Over 25k Saudis get jobs through Hadaf in March," *Arab News*, April 27, 2021, https://www.arabnews.com/node/1849536/saudi-arabia; Hala Tashkandi, "Saudi female students excited over opening of admissions to KFUPM," *Arab News*, April 28, 2021, https://www.arabnews.com/node/1850036/offbeat; "Saudi crown prince announces Green Saudi Initiative, Green Middle East Initiative," *Arab News*, April 30, 2021, https://www.arabnews.com/node/1832861/saudi-arabia.

> One of our most significant assets is our lively and vibrant youth. We will guarantee their skills are developed and properly deployed. While many other countries are concerned with aging populations, more than half of the Saudi population is below the age of 25 years. We will take advantage of this demographic dividend by harnessing our youth's energy and by expanding entrepreneurship and enterprise opportunities.[57]

> Saudi women are yet another great asset. With over 50 percent of our university graduates being female, we will continue to develop their talents, invest in their productive capabilities and enable them to strengthen their future and contribute to the development of our society and economy.[58]

In line with symbolism, the MBS approach to identifying with the *Saudi Will* also involves the use of iconography. As described by Mudde and Kaltwasser, populists establish a direct connection with their constituents by strategically promoting institutions that represent the general will.[59] In the kingdom, this strategy is evident in the iconography of the new power through a particular tactic – grandiosity. As the crown prince reshaped power structures and introduced new identity markers, the element of grandiosity takes center stage in physically manifesting the new order. This authoritarian-populist approach of grandiosity shares similarities with other authoritarian leaders in countries like Egypt and India, where grandiose projects mark their space with the unmistakable imprint of their leaders. Through grandiosity, MBS seeks to create a more pronounced and awe-inspiring representation of his vision, further emphasizing his strong authority and connection with the *Saudi Will*.[60]

In the end, what is important for context of KSA, MBS also seeks to venture upon the same path through projects such as *Neom*, *Oxagon*, and *Prince Mohammed bin Salman Nonprofit City* (MBSNPC). These projects are pertinent examples to illustrate the crown prince's populism in the dimension of grandiosity. These grand projects are attempts by MBS to reshape the territorial make-up of the kingdom in a typical authoritarian-populist framework – from

---

57 Government of the Kingdom of Saudi Arabia, *Vision 2030*, pg. 36 https://www.vision2 030.gov.sa/media/rc0b50y1/saudi_vision203.pdf.
58 Ibid.
59 Mudde and Kaltwasser, *Populism*, 17.
60 Kyle J. Anderson, "How Egypt's grandiose neo-Pharaonism lends legitimacy to its strongman," *The New Arab*, November 23, 2021, https://english.alaraby.co.uk/opin ion/egypts-grandiose-neo-pharaonism-and-strongman-politics; Atul Dev, "Modi's Folly," *The New York Review*, May 10, 2021, https://www.nybooks.com/daily/2021/05/10/modis -folly.

a futuristic, artificial intelligence-driven project like *Neom* to the largest industrial floating city like *Oxagon* to the world's first non-profit city like MBSNPC.[61] These projects unmistakably demonstrate MBS's intent to integrate his symbolism with grand iconography, thereby perpetuating the expression of the *Saudi Will* through his persona, actions, and reforms. By skillfully employing controlled liberalization and embracing a populist image, the Salman clan has established a starkly different approach from previous monarchs – one that exudes bold authority while remaining highly responsive to the people's aspirations. Through this strategic blend of symbolism and grandiosity, MBS seeks to solidify his connection with the *Saudi Will*, presenting himself as a leader who is both audacious and attuned to the desires of the nation.

6 Conclusion

In his authoritarian-populist approach, MBS envisions a new kingdom with a profound historical mission, embodied in Vision 2030, aiming to revitalize the Saudi nation and elevate it to global prominence beyond its reputation as a major oil exporter. Furthermore, MBS seeks to redefine the national identity of the people, moving beyond religious and social conservatism. In pursuit of these pivotal objectives, MBS's strategy bears a distinct resemblance to Carl Schmitt's ideas, as it involves reshaping the polity and reconfiguring traditional power dynamics within society.

Ever since the introduction of Vision 2030 in 2016, MBS has relentlessly disrupted the prevailing norms, championing a modernizing vision through an authoritarian-populist model. This approach encompasses fundamental elements such as the restructuring of political distinctions and the cultivation of a new political community characterized by the Friend/Enemy polarity. MBS has also worked towards establishing a new elite consensus, uniting all under his leadership and the shared commitment to Vision 2030. Additionally, he has revitalized the monarchical identification with the *Saudi Will* by strategically employing symbolism and iconography that resonate primarily with the youth.

---

61 Ismaeel Naar, "Saudi Crown Prince announces OXAGON, largest floating industrial complex in the world," *Al Arabiya* English, November 16, 2021, https://english.alarabiya.net/News/gulf/2021/11/16/Saudi-Crown-Prince-announces-Oxagon-largest-floating-industrial-complex-in-the-world; "Saudi crown prince announces world's first non-profit city," *Arab News*, November 14, 2021, https://www.arabnews.com/node/1967761/saudi-arabia; Ellen R. Wald, "The Dream of a City," *Cairo Review*, March 5, 2019, https://www.thecairoreview.com/tahrir-forum/the-dream-of-a-city.

Notwithstanding the fear-induced absence of opposition to the modernizing vision, MBS reforms still hang on a delicate balance. While his social reforms start to manifest visible changes, his economic reforms are still uncertain. The modernizing vision of MBS could face serious challenges to its legitimacy if it fails to live up to its economic promises. While social reforms have undoubtedly played a role in reshaping identity, belonging, and group relations, the political authoritarianism exhibited by MBS may have some counterproductive consequences. By not allowing legitimate criticism over certain socio-economic reforms that warrant closer scrutiny, he risks hindering progress and potential backlash. Although MBS has captured the public's imagination and given the youth hope for a more active role as citizens rather than subjects of the Saudi state, fulfilling the promises made will require skillful statecraft. The lessons from the Arab Spring remind us that economic distress can overshadow any socio-cultural reforms, becoming a significant driver of unrest. To build upon the hope he has instilled, MBS must consistently address the economic needs and rising demands of the public while navigating through turbulent times. Striking the right balance in sustaining economic prosperity and social progress will be crucial for maintaining public support and ensuring the success of his vision for Saudi Arabia.

Bibliography

Al-Atawneh, Muhammad. "Is Saudi Arabia a Theocracy? Religion and Governance in Contemporary Saudi Arabia." *Middle Eastern Studies* 45, no. 5 (2009): 721–737.

Alhussein, Eman. "New Saudi Textbooks Put Nation First." *The Arab Gulf States Institute in Washington*, October 17, 2019. https://agsiw.org/new-saudi-textbooks-put-nation-first.

Al-Khamri, Hana. "Why did Saudi Arabia lift the driving ban on women only now?." *Al Jazeera*, June 24, 2018. https://www.aljazeera.com/opinions/2018/6/24/why-did-saudi-arabia-lift-the-driving-ban-on-women-only-now.

Al-Khudair, Deema. "'An honor and duty:' Meet the female Saudi officers guarding the Prophet's Mosque in Madinah." *Arab News*, April 29, 2021. https://www.arabnews.com/node/1850621/saudi-arabia.

Al-Otaibi, Najah. "Vision 2030: Religious Education Reform in the Kingdom of Saudi Arabia." *King Faisal Center for Research and Islamic Studies*, September, 2020. https://kfcris.com/pdf/cc53a3201f65554c400886325b5f715e5f577d35934f7.pdf.

Al-Rasheed, Madawi. *The Son King: Reform and Repression in Saudi Arabia*. Oxford: Oxford University Press, 2021.

Al-Rasheed, Madawi. "The New Populist Nationalism in Saudi Arabia: Imagined Utopia by Royal Decree." *London School of Economics Middle East Centre Blog*, May 5, 2020. https://blogs.lse.ac.uk/mec/2020/05/05/the-new-populist-nationalism-in-saudi-arabia-imagined-utopia-by-royal-decree.

Anderson, Kyle J. "How Egypt's grandiose neo-Pharaonism lends legitimacy to its strongman." *The New Arab*, November 23, 2021. https://english.alaraby.co.uk/opinion/egypts-grandiose-neo-pharaonism-and-strongman-politics.

Auer, Stefan. "Carl Schmitt in the Kremlin: the Ukraine crisis and the return of geopolitics." *International Affairs* 91, no. 5 (2015): 953–968.

Barmin, Yury. "Can Mohammed bin Salman break the Saudi-Wahhabi pact?." *Al Jazeera,* January 7, 2018. https://www.aljazeera.com/opinions/2018/1/7/can-mohammed-bin-salman-break-the-saudi-wahhabi-pact.

Bashraheel, Aseel. "Rise and fall of the Saudi religious police." *Arab News*, September 23, 2019. https://www.arabnews.com/node/1558176/saudi-arabia.

Ben Gassem, Lojien. "Riyadh Season welcomes 3 million visitors during first month since launch." *Arab News*, November 21, 2021. https://www.arabnews.com/node/1972506/saudi-arabia.

Ben Gassem, Lojien. "Rap star Pitbull to launch Riyadh Season with sold-out concert." *Arab News*, October 20, 2021. https://www.arabnews.com/node/1951251/saudi-arabia.

Benner, Katie, Mark Mazzetti, Ben Hubbard and Mike Isaac. "Saudis' Image Makers: A Troll Army and A Twitter Insider." *New York Times*, October 20, 2018. https://www.nytimes.com/2018/10/20/us/politics/saudi-image-campaign-twitter.html.

Brubaker, Rogers. "Why populism." *Theory and Society* 46, (2017): 357–385.

Bsheer, Rosie. *Archive Wars: The Politics of History in Saudi Arabia*. Redwood City, CA: Stanford University Press, 2020.

Carreira da Silva, Filipe and Monica Brito Vieira. "Populism as a logic of political action." *European Journal of Social Theory* 22, no. 4 (2019): 497–512.

Chulov, Martin. "Saudi crown prince signals new purge with 'treason' arrests." *The Guardian*, March 7, 2020. https://www.theguardian.com/world/2020/mar/07/saudi-crown-prince-in-new-purge-with-treason-arrests.

Cioffoletti, Michelle. "Saudi Arabia Sings a Nationalist Tune." *The Arab Gulf States Institute in Washington*, January 7, 2019. https://agsiw.org/saudi-arabia-sings-a-nationalist-tune/.

Colon-Rios, Joel I. "Carl Schmitt and Constituent Power in Latin American Courts: The Cases of Venezuela and Colombia." *Constellations* 18, no. 3 (2011): 365–388.

Dadouch, Sarah. "Saudi Crown Prince Mohammed seeks to reduce influential clerics' power." *Washington Post*, August 3, 2021. https://www.washingtonpost.com/world/middle_east/saudi-clerics-crown-prince-mohammed/2021/08/02/9ae796a0-e3ed-11eb-88c5-4fd6382c47cb_story.html.

Davidson, Christopher M. *From Sheikhs to Sultanism: Statecraft and Authority in Saudi Arabia and UAE*. Oxford: Oxford University Press, 2021.

Dazi-Heni, Fatiha. "How Mbs Is Rethinking Saudi Nationalism." *Italian Institute for International Political Studies*, May 16, 2019. https://www.ispionline.it/en/pubblicazione/how-mbs-rethinking-saudi-nationalism-23083.

Dev, Atul. "Modi's Folly." *The New York Review*, May 10, 2021. https://www.nybooks.com/daily/2021/05/10/modis-folly.

Escobar, Pepe. "The inside story of the Saudi night of long knives." *Asia Times*, November 6, 2017. https://asiatimes.com/2017/11/inside-story-saudi-night-long-knives.

Esperanza Casullo, Maria. "The Body Speaks Before It Even Talks: Deliberation, Populism and Bodily Representation." *Journal of Deliberative Democracy* 16, no. 1 (2020): 27–36.

Faroukh, Yasmine and Nathan J. Brown. "Saudi Arabia's Religious Reforms Are Touching Nothing but Changing Everything." *Carnegie Endowment*, 2021. https://carnegieendowment.org/research/2021/06/islamic-institutions-in-arab-states-mapping-the-dynamics-of-control-co-option-and-contention#saudi-arabias-religious-reforms-are-touching-nothing-but-changing-everything.

Foresta, Alessandra. "The rise of populist parties in the aftermath of a massive corruption scandal." *Public Choice* 184 (2020): 289–306.

Gardner, David. "Visions of Mohammed bin Salman – the reality and the fantasy." *Financial Times*, October 12, 2020. https://www.ft.com/content/ffe2f60f-06da-4716-af4a-b06f631f391c.

Ghaffary, Shirin. "Photos: The Saudi Crown Prince met with tech VIPs this week in Silicon Valley, including Sergey Brin and Magic Leap's CEO." *Vox*, April 6, 2018. https://www.vox.com/2018/4/6/17206358/saudi-crown-prince-visit-tech-silicon-valley.

Ghattas, Kim. *Black Wave: Saudi Arabia, Iran, and the 40-Year Rivalry that Unraveled Culture, Religion, Collective Memory in the Middle East*. New York, Henry Holt and Co., 2020.

Godinho, Varun. "Two-thirds of Saudi Arabia's population is under the age of 35." *Gulf Business*, August 10, 2020. https://gulfbusiness.com/two-thirds-of-saudi-arabias-population-is-under-the-age-of-35/.

Government of the Kingdom of Saudi Arabia. "Vision 2030." https://www.vision2030.gov.sa/media/rc0b50y1/saudi_vision2o3.pdf.

Hamid, Shadi and Peter Mandaville. "Islam as statecraft: How governments use religion in foreign policy." *Brookings Institution*, November, 2018. https://www.brookings.edu/research/islam-as-statecraft-how-governments-use-religion-in-foreign-policy.

Hope, Bradley and Justin Scheck. *Blood and Oil: Mohammed bin Salman's Ruthless Quest for Global Power*. Paris: Hachette Books, 2020.

Hubbard, Ben. *MBS: The Rise to Power of Mohammed bin Salman*. New York: Tim Duggan Books, 2020.

Khairur Rijal, Najamuddin and Rizka Zahrotun Khoirina. "The Roles of Civil Society to Changing of Women Driving Policy in Saudi Arabia: The Case of Women2Drive Campaign." *Islamic World and Politics* 3, no. 1 (2019): 435–447.

Khalid, Tuqa. "Saudi Arabia arrests 32 in corruption case worth $3 billion." *Al Arabiya English*, January 27, 2021. https://english.alarabiya.net/News/gulf/2021/01/28/Saudi-Arabia-arrests-32-in-corruption-case-worth-3-billion.

"Killing of jailed reformer Musa al-Qarni highlights use of torture in Saudi prisons." MENA *Rights Group*, October 19, 2021. http://menarights.org/en/articles/killing-jailed-reformer-musa-al-qarni-highlights-use-torture-saudi-prisons.

Kirkpatrick, David D., Ben Hubbard and Eric Schmitt. "Roundup of Saudi Royals Expands With Detention of a 4th Prince." *New York Times*, March 7, 2020. https://www.nytimes.com/2020/03/07/world/middleeast/saudi-arabia-mohammed-bin-salman.html.

Koelbl, Susanne. *Behind the Kingdom's Veil: Inside the New Saudi Arabia under Crown Prince Mohammed bin Salman*. Miami: Mango Publishers, 2020.

Krimly, Reem. "Females can register for Hajj with other women without male guardian: Saudi ministry." *Al Arabiya English*, June 14, 2021. https://english.alarabiya.net/News/gulf/2021/06/14/Women-can-register-for-Hajj-with-other-women-without-male-guardian-Saudi-ministry.

Krimly, Reem. "Revamped guardianship laws under in a new era for Saudi women." *Al Arabiya English*, August 3, 2019. https://english.alarabiya.net/features/2019/08/03/Revamped-guardianship-laws-usher-in-a-new-era-for-Saudi-women.

Kutay, Acar. "From Weimar to Ankara: Carl Schmitt, sovereignty and democracy." *Philosophy and Social Criticism* 45, no. 6 (2019): 728–752.

Laclau, Ernesto. *On Populist Reason*. New York: Verso Books, 2007.

Libin, Xie and Haig Patapan. "Schmitt Fever: The use and abuse of Carl Schmitt in contemporary China." *International Journal of Constitutional Law* 18, no. 1 (2020): 130–146.

Mabon, Simon. "It's a Family Affairs: Religion, Geopolitics and the Rise of Mohammed bin Salman." *Insight Turkey* 20, no. 2 (2018): 51–66.

"MBS attends Abu Dhabi F1 Grand Prix finale." *Saudi Gazette*, December 1, 2019. https://saudigazette.com.sa/article/583899.

"MBS flags off Formula E race." *Saudi Gazette*, November 22, 2019. https://saudigazette.com.sa/article/583218/SAUDI-ARABIA/MBS-flags-off-Formula-E-race.

"MDL Beast announces groundbreaking debut festival Riyadh." *Arab News*, December 5, 2019. https://www.arabnews.com/node/1594391/lifestyle.

Meszaros, Gabor. "Carl Schmitt in Hungary: Constitutional Crisis in the Shadow of COVID-19." *Review of Central and East European Law* 46, (2020): 69–90.

Mitchell, Scott. "F1's Saudi deal will run for 'a decade, if not longer.'" *The Race*, February 25, 2021. https://the-race.com/formula-1/f1s-saudi-deal-will-run-a-decade-if-not-longer/.

Mudde, Cas and Cristobal Rovira Kaltwasser. *Populism: A Very Short Introduction*. Oxford: Oxford University Press, 2017.

Muller, Jan-Werner. *What is Populism?* Philadelphia: University of Pennsylvania Press, 2016.

Naar, Ismaeel. "Saudi Crown Prince announces OXAGON, largest floating industrial complex in the world." *Al Arabiya* English, November 16, 2021. https://english.alarabiya.net/News/gulf/2021/11/16/Saudi-Crown-Prince-announces-Oxagon-largest-floating-industrial-complex-in-the-world.

Naar, Ismaeel. "Saudi Crown Prince announces 4 new laws to reform Kingdom's judicial institutions." *Al Arabiya English*, February 8, 2021. https://english.alarabiya.net/News/gulf/2021/02/08/Saudi-Vision-2030-Saudi-Crown-Prince-announces-reforms-to-improve-legislative-environment.

Nakhoul, Samia, Angus McDowall and Stephen Kalin. "A house divided: How Saudi Crown Prince purged royal family rivals." *Reuters*, November 10, 2017. https://www.reuters.com/article/us-saudi-arrests-crownprince-insight-idUSKBN1DA23M

Nazer, Fahad. "Saudi youth at centre stage of vision 2030." *The Arab Weekly*, March 26, 2017. https://thearabweekly.com/saudi-youth-centre-stage-vision-2030.

Nereim, Vivian. "'Traitor' is the new 'Infidel' as Nationalism Grips Saudi Arabia." *Bloomberg*, March 3, 2019. https://www.bloomberg.com/news/articles/2019-03-03/-traitor-is-the-new-infidel-as-nationalism-grips-saudi-arabia.

"New Saudi anti-corruption chief to target public servants." *Reuters*, September 1, 2019. https://www.reuters.com/article/us-saudi-corruption-idUSKCN1VM10X.

"No plans for income tax, VAT increase is temporary: Saudi Crown Prince Mohammed bin Salman." *Arab News*, April 28, 2021. https://www.arabnews.com/node/1850091/business-economy.

Nugali, Noor. "Saudi Arabia rich with undiscovered archeological sites." *Arab News*, January 27, 2019. https://www.arabnews.com/node/1441401/saudi-arabia.

"Only Saudis can work in malls as local hiring drive accelerates." *Arab News*, April 9, 2021. https://www.arabnews.com/node/1839156/business-economy.

Ottaway, David. "Saudi Crown Prince Lambasts His Kingdom's Wahhabis Establishment." *Wilson Center*, May 6, 2021. https://www.wilsoncenter.org/article/saudi-crown-prince-lambasts-his-kingdoms-wahhabi-establishment.

"Over 25k Saudis get jobs through Hadaf in March." *Arab News*, April 27, 2021. https://www.arabnews.com/node/1849536/saudi-arabia.

Pavan, Annalisa. "The Sky is the Limit": Saudi Youth in a Changing Kingdom, Beyond Narratives, Interpretations and Misperceptions." *World Journal of Social Science*, 8, no. 2 (2021): 1–12.

Pincince, John. "De-centering Carl Schmitt: The Colonial State of Exception and the Criminalization of the Political in British India, 1905–1920." *Politica Comun* 5, (2014): 1–18.

Rohac, Dalibor, Sahana Kumar, and Andreas Johansson Heino. "The wisdom of demagogues: institutions, corruption and support for authoritarian populists." *Economic Affairs* 37, no. 3 (2017): 382–396.

Salacanin, Stasa. "New nationalism on the rise in Saudi Arabia." *The New Arab*, August 20, 2019. https://english.alaraby.co.uk/english/indepth/2019/8/20/new-nationalism-on-the-rise%E2%80%8B-in-saudi-arabia.

"Saudi crown prince announces Green Saudi Initiative, Green Middle East Initiative." *Arab News*, April 30, 2021. https://www.arabnews.com/node/1832861/saudi-arabia.

"Saudi crown prince announces world's first non-profit city." *Arab News*, November 14, 2021. https://www.arabnews.com/node/1967761/saudi-arabia.

"Saudi king sacks two royals under defence corruption probe." *Reuters*, September 16, 2020. https://www.reuters.com/article/saudi-king-defense-int-idUSKBN25R2YA.

"Saudi PIF acquires $3.3bn stake in US video-game makers." *Arab News*, February 17, 2021. https://www.arabnews.com/node/1810896/business-economy.

Schmitt, Carl. *The Concept of the Political: Expanded Edition*. Chicago: University of Chicago Press, 2007.

Schmitt, Carl. *Political Theology: Four Chapters on the Concept of Sovereignty*. Chicago: University of Chicago, 2006.

Schmitt, Carl. *Constitutional Theory*. Durham: Duke University Press, 2008.

Schmitt, Carl. *Crisis of Parliamentary Democracy*. Massachusetts: MIT Press, 1988.

Schmitt, Carl. *Theory of the Partisan, trans. G. L. Ulmen*. New York: Telos Press Publishing, 2007.

Smith Diwan, Kristin. "The Big Gamble of Mohammed bin Salman – and Saudi Arabia." *The Arab Gulf States Institute in Washington*, March 23, 2020. https://agsiw.org/the-big-gamble-of-mohammed-bin-salman-and-saudi-arabia.

Smith Diwan, Kristin. "Youth Appeal of Saudi Vision 2030." *The Arab Gulf States Institute in Washington*. May 6, 2016. https://agsiw.org/youth-appeal-of-saudi-vision-2030.

Stiegler, Bernard. *Réenchanter le monde: la valeur esprit contre le populisme industriel*. Flammarion, 2013.

Talal Al-Sharif, Dimah. "Labor Reform Initiative to help boost Saudi Arabia's private sector." *Arab News*, March 17, 2021. https://www.arabnews.com/node/1826736.

Tannoury, Liliane. "Start of regional league ushers in new era for women's football in Saudi Arabia." *Arab News*, November 21, 2021. https://www.arabnews.com/node/1972281/sport.

Tashkandi, Hala. "Saudi female students excited over opening of admissions to KFUPM." *Arab News*, April 28, 2021. https://www.arabnews.com/node/1850036/offbeat.

Tashkandi, Hala. "Saudi cinema chain announces $218.6m expansion plan." *Arab News*, April 4, 2021. https://www.arabnews.com/node/1837406/business-economy.

Trofimov, Yaroslav. "A Social Revolution in Saudi Arabia." *Wall Street Journal*, November 15, 2019. https://www.wsj.com/articles/a-social-revolution-in-saudi-arabia-11573833669.

"Twitter suspends accounts, removes verification of Saudi political prisoners." *Middle East Eye*, February 9, 2021. https://www.middleeasteye.net/news/saudi-arabia-twitter-jailed-scholars-verification-removed.

Varagur, Krithika. *The Call: Inside the Global Saudi Religious Project*. New York: Columbia Global Reports, 2020.

Wald, Ellen R. "The Dream of a City." *Cairo Review*, March 5, 2019. https://www.thecairoreview.com/tahrir-forum/the-dream-of-a-city.

Wheeler, Deborah L. "Saudi Women Driving Change? Rebranding, Resistance and the Kingdom of Change." *The Journal of the Middle East and Africa* 11, no. 1 (2020): 87–109.

"Who are the key Sahwa figures Saudi Arabia is cracking down on?" *Al Jazeera*, June 5, 2019. https://www.aljazeera.com/features/2019/6/5/who-are-the-key-sahwa-figures-saudi-arabia-is-cracking-down-on.

Wilson, Josh. "Saudi Arabia to Invest $64 Billion In Its Entertainment Sector." *Forbes*, November 9, 2021. https://www.forbes.com/sites/joshwilson/2021/11/09/saudi-arabia-to-invest-64-billion-in-its-entertainment-sector.

"250, 000 witnessed Pitbull exceptional concert in Riyadh Season 2021 opening." *Saudi Gazette*, October 21, 2021. https://saudigazette.com.sa/article/612490.

Wojczewski, Thorsten. "'Enemies of the People': Populism and the Politics of (In)security." *European Journal of International Security* 5, no. 1 (2020): 5–24.

Index

Abdal-Wahhab, Muhammad ibn   250–251
Abu Dhabi   266
Adorno, Theodor W.   11–17, 24, 36, 37, 96, 103, 105, 107, 110, 123–129, 147, 148, 149, 193–200, 208, 213, 218–224, 227, 228, 229, 231, 232, 233, 234, 235–236, 238–239
Affordable Care Act (Obamacare)   75
Ahmed, Sara   102
Al-Omari, Ali   259
Al-Qaeda   203
Al-Qahtani, Saud   255
Al-Qarni, Awad   259
Al-Qarni, Musa   259
Alt-Right   44–53, 96, 108
Alternative for Germany (*Alternativ für Deutschland*) (AfD)   1, 115, 127
American Dharma (film)   43, 44, 48, 49, 52, 53
Analytical Psychology   62, 63, 64, 66, 67, 74, 81, 82
Arab Spring   86, 108, 244
Argentina   3, 161, 169–171, 173–178, 184, 185, 186
Australia   88
Authoritarian Populism   1, 3, 9, 12, 13, 18, 19, 47, 74, 85, 86, 87, 89, 93, 96–97, 99–101, 103, 108, 110, 117, 123–125, 136, 192–197, 201–204, 213, 244–245, 248, 250, 252, 256, 263, 265, 267

Baath Party   244
Bannon, Stephen (Steve) K.   42–58, 87, 92
Bauman, Zygmunt   57, 211
Belgium   88
Berlin Wall   27
Biden, Joseph R.   42, 76, 87, 88
Bois, W.E.B. du   87
Bolsonaro, Jair   46, 57, 106, 141, 144, 157, 159, 201, 204, 205, 207–209, 211, 218, 219, 220, 221, 223–239, 242
Bourdieu, Pierre   30
Brazil   4, 46, 97, 105, 170, 178, 192, 201, 204, 207, 211, 213, 218–241
Brennan, Jason   150, 152
Brexit   1, 3, 57, 108, 109, 123
Bródy, János   29, 30, 31, 33, 35–36

Bruni, Frank   43
Brussels   25, 44
Buchanan, Patrick   51
Burke, Edmund   95
Bush, George W.   51, 213

Camus, Renaud   87, 100
Capitalism   7, 12, 13, 15, 43, 47, 57, 89, 97, 104, 123, 143, 145, 146, 147, 148, 152, 153, 155, 156, 162, 163, 169, 174, 175, 185, 197, 239, 240
Carvalho, Olavo de   46
Catholicism   43, 44, 74, 237
Charisma   65, 74, 75, 76, 82, 88, 172, 192, 210–211, 212
Charlottesville, Virginia   53, 54
Chávez, Hugo   1
Cheney, Liz   88
Chile   110, 170, 211
China   1, 43, 45, 47, 48, 56, 235
Christianity   43, 44, 208, 233
Clinton, Hillary   54, 70, 71, 92
Cold War   118, 213
Colonization   18, 104, 145, 160, 233
Corbyn, Jeremy   86, 93, 101
Corea, Rafael   174
Coughlin, (Father) Charles   74
COVID-19   6, 22, 86, 101, 207, 210, 242
Cuba   235
Cultural Hegemony   4, 12, 16–17, 192, 212
Cultural Marxism   106
Culture Industry   11, 13, 105, 106–107, 111, 123–126

Davos   47
Demos   86, 143
DeNora, Tia   14–15, 36
Die Linke   101
Dudinsky, Igor   52
Dugin, Alexander   45–47, 52
Duhalde, Eduardo   174
Dworkin, Ronald   150
Dyer-Witheford, Nick   104

Ego Ideal   63, 66, 69
Erdoğan, Recep Tayyip   1

Esposito, Roberto 146, 147, 149
Essex School of Discourse Analysis 172
Estlund, David 150
European Central Bank (ECB) 180, 182
European Commission (EC) 180
European Union (EU) 44, 118, 119
Evola, Julius 45–46

Faisal, King (Saudi Arabia) 244
Farage, Nigel 52, 57, 109
Fascism 46, 52, 53, 90, 99, 103, 126, 143, 172, 218, 219, 239, 241
Federici, Silvia 143, 145, 146, 149
Fidesz (Hungary) 1, 12, 15, 19–22, 25, 28, 37
Finn, Ed 1
Foster, John Bellamy 206
Foucault, Michel 161
France 1, 88, 169
Francis, Samuel 51
Franco, Mariele 242
Frankfurt School 11, 13, 16, 74, 117, 123, 125, 136
Freedom Party of Austria (*FreiheitsparteiÖsterreichs*) 115
Friedman, Milton 97
Fromm, Erich 97
Front for Victory (FpV) (Argentina) 170, 174

Galanopoulos, Antonis 181
Gandesha, Samir 194
Germany 1, 13, 101, 115, 120, 127, 128, 245
Gilets jaunes 88
Giuliani, Rudolph 87
Glazer, Nathan 85
Globalization 1–4, 7, 9, 10, 57, 99, 101, 116, 118, 120, 132, 134
Goffman, Erwin 108
Goldman Sachs 43, 48, 49
Gorka, Sebastian 71
Gottfried, Paul 51
Gramsci, Antonio 17, 94, 99
Grass, Gunter 107
Great Replacement 87, 100
Green, Joshua 50
Gudavarthy, Ajay 103
Guterman, Norbert 74, 102, 109

Hall, Stuart 14, 17, 19, 99

Hayek, Friedrich 97
Hegel, G.W.F. 82, 197, 198, 199, 200
Heidegger, Martin 164
Hennion, Antoine 14, 15
Homophobia 152, 157
Honneth, Axel 147, 195
Horkheimer, Max 11, 13, 105, 107, 123–125, 147, 148, 236
Humanitarianism 10, 131, 136
Hungary 1, 4, 11–12, 15–16, 18–22, 24–25, 29, 32, 37, 120

Iglesias, Pablo 183
Individualization 66–67, 69, 81
Institutional Authoritarianism 18
International Monetary Fund (IMF) 161, 175, 176, 178, 180, 182
Iran Nuclear Agreement 56, 75
Iranian Revolution 251, 257
Islam 44, 48, 153, 255, 256, 259
Islamism 244, 250, 251–252
Islamization 127
Islamophobia 50

James, C.L.R. 147
January 6th, 2021 42, 88, 92, 93, 106, 152, 158
Jesus of Nazareth 76, 233
Jews 87, 222
Jim Crow 87
Jobbik 22, 120
Jung, Carl Gustav 61–83

Kafka, Franz 163, 164
Kaltwasser, Cristóbal Rovira 90–93, 119, 249, 250, 252, 256, 258, 262, 263, 264, 267
Kammenos, Panos 179
Kant, Immanuel 103, 105, 108
Kefala, Eleni 171
Kefala, Nicos Mouzelis 171
Kelly, John (General) 56
Kinzinger, Adam 88
Kipling, Rudyard 24
Kirchner, Cristina Fernandez de 174
Kirchner, Néstor 170, 174
Kirchnerism 173–178, 184–186
Koncz, Zsuzsa 29, 36

Lacan, Jacques 165, 212

INDEX

Laclau, Ernesto   93, 98, 139, 155, 172, 194, 195, 212
Lanier, Jaron   106
Le Pen, Marine   1
Löwenthal, Leo   74, 102, 109
Lukács, Georg   200
Lula, Luiz Inácio   174

Machiavelli, Niccolò   48, 80, 82
Macron, Emmanuel   53
Maduro, Nicolás   1
Maiguashca, Bice   16
Make America Great Again (MAGA)   61, 73, 74, 98, 211
Marcuse, Herbert   97, 105, 205
Marx, Karl   13, 43, 106, 107, 145, 155, 174, 197, 206
Matviyenko, Svitlana   104
McCain, John (Senator)   58, 70
McWilliams, Joe   74
Meadows, Mark   50
Menem, Carlos   170
Menemism   175
Metaverse   102
Mexico   160, 178, 202, 203, 209
Middleton, Richard   14, 15, 36
Miller, Stephen   51
Misogyny   91
Modi, Narendra   1, 103, 106
Moffit, Benjamin   18, 172
Mohammed bin Salman Nonprofit City (MBSNPC)   267–268
Morales, Evo   174, 184
Morris, Errol   42, 49, 51, 52, 53
Mote, Carl H.   74
Mouffe, Chantal   141, 142, 153, 155, 194
Mudde, Cas   90–93, 119, 249, 250, 252, 256, 258, 262, 263, 264, 267
Müller, Jan-Werner   90–93
Musicological Group Analysis   12, 15, 26
Musil, Robert   140, 154, 157, 163, 164
Muslim Brotherhood   244

Narcissism   50, 67, 80, 82
Nasser, Gamal Abdul   244
National Front   44, 100
National Policy Institute   46
National Rally   44

National Socialism (Nazism)   107
Nationalism   1, 3, 9, 10, 35, 45, 47, 50, 54, 56, 57, 58, 96, 117, 133, 172, 175, 202, 244, 245, 247, 250–253, 256, 257
Nélküled   21–22, 26, 32, 37
New Democratic Party (Canada)   89
New Zealand   88
Nietzsche, Friedrich   66, 79
Nigeria   161
Nixon, Richard   95
Nyerges, Attila   21, 24

Oath Keepers   87
Obama, Barack   53, 71, 73
Occupy Wall Street   86, 98, 109
Oedipus Complex   100
Omar, Ilhan   203
Orbán, Viktor   1, 12, 18, 19, 20, 27, 35, 36, 37, 52, 57
Ostiguy, Pierre   18, 23, 172, 176

Pan-Islamism   250, 251, 252
Papandreou, Andreas   173, 185
Pathological Persona   68–71
Patriotic Europeans Against the Islamization of the Occident (PEGIDA)   127–128
Peace Treaty of Trianon   20
Pelley, William Dudley   74
Pelosi, Nancy   209
Perón, Juan Domingo   3, 173
Persecuted Strongman Persona   76–77
Persona   61–84
Peru   145, 178
Philippines   4
Podemos (Spain)   2, 86, 93, 101, 183
Populist Persona   61–83
Powell, Enoch   87, 99
Prophets of Deceit   74
Proud Boys   87–88
Psychopathy   80, 82
Psychosis   76
Puer Aeternus   62, 80
Putin, Vladimir   1, 44–47, 50, 86, 96

QAnon   157, 160

Racism   24, 52, 54–55, 57, 92, 99, 152, 157, 233, 241

Rancière, Jacques   139, 142, 143, 152–157, 164
Raspail, Jean   87
Rawls, John   142, 143, 150, 152
Raz, Joseph   150
Reckwitz, Andreas   85, 86, 96
Robinson, Tommy (Stephen
   Yaxley-Lennon)   53
Romania   20, 21
Rúa, Fernando de la   170
Russia   33, 43–46, 55, 56, 75, 86, 89, 102

Sadomasochism   221, 242
Salman, (Crown Prince) Mohammed bin
   (MBS)   244–275
Salvini, Matteo   57
Sandel, Michael   54–55
Sanders, Bernie   86, 93, 99, 101
Saudi Arabia   244–275
Saudi Will   263–268
Scheiring, Gábor   18, 19
Schmitt, Carl   94, 209, 245–250, 252–258,
   260, 262–264, 268
September 11th, 2001   118
Serbia   4, 20
Sexism   57
Shadow   61, 65, 77–81
Sherman, Gabriel   56
Sims, John Marion   145, 157
Slave Morality   79–80
Slovakia
Smith, Gerald L.K.   74
Social Darwinism   145
Socialism   9, 29, 32, 54, 90, 101, 232
Soros, George   25
Soviet Union   101, 197, 257
Spencer, Richard   45
Stavrakakis, Yannis   172
Syria   48, 119
Syriza (Coalition of the Radical Left)
   (Greece)   2, 170, 173, 179–186

Táltos   31
Taylor, Mary   19, 21
Tax Cut and Jobs Act of   2017 75

Tea Party   42, 44, 45, 50, 86, 98, 206
Teitelbaum, Benjamin   46, 47
Thatcher, Margaret   19, 99, 100, 101, 110, 153
Thomas, Martin Luther   218, 220, 222,
   227, 239
Thucydides   43
Tomsic, Samo   104
Totalitarianism   13, 103, 153, 234
Transylvania   21, 24
Trinidad & Tobago   161
True Self   62–65, 67–68, 76, 81–82
Trump, Donald J.   61–84
Trump, Fredrick   72

Übermensch   66
UK Independence Party (UKIP)   44
Ukraine   20
Ultra-MAGA   61
Ultra-Persona (King Midas)   70–72,
   77, 82–83
United Kingdom   1, 44, 169
United States Supreme Court   145

Vatican   43, 45, 52
Venezuela   170, 174, 178, 235
Vision 2030   244–245, 250, 252–263, 268–269
Vörösmarty, Mihály   24
Vox (Spain)   120
Vysotsky, Vladimir   33

Wagenknecht, Sara   101
Wahhabism   250–251
Weber, Max   95, 97
White Supremacy   91
Williams, Thomas   52
Wolff, Michael   56
Woodward, Bob   54
World War II   118, 212

Xenophobia   52

Yiannopoulos, Milo   45

Žižek, Slavoj   81–82

www.ingramcontent.com/pod-product-compliance
Lightning Source LLC
Chambersburg PA
CBHW070614030426
42337CB00020B/3788